THE REPRESENTATION GAP

THE REPRESENTATION GAP

*Change and Reform in the British and
American Workplace*

BRIAN TOWERS

OXFORD UNIVERSITY PRESS
1997

Oxford University Press, Great Clarendon Street, Oxford OX2 6DP
Oxford New York
Athens Auckland Bangkok Bogota Bombay
Buenos Aires Calcutta Cape Town Dar es Salaam
Delhi Florence Hong Kong Istanbul Karachi
Kuala Lumpur Madras Madrid Melbourne
Mexico City Nairobi Paris Singapore
Taipei Tokyo Toronto Warsaw
and associated companies in
Berlin Ibadan

Oxford is a trade mark of Oxford University Press

Published in the United States by
Oxford University Press Inc., New York

British Library Cataloguing in Publication Data
Data available

Library of Congress Cataloging-in-Publication Data
Towers, Brian.
The Representation Gap : Change and Reform in the British and American
Workplace / Brian Towers.
Includes bibliographical references.
1. Industrial relations—Great Britain.   2. Industrial relations—
United States.   3. Industrial relations—Cross-cultural studies.
4. Trade-unions—Great Britain.   5. Trade-unions—United States.
6. Trade-unions—Cross-cultural studies.   I. Title.
HD8391.T69   1997   331'.0941—dc21   97–12717

ISBN 0–19–829319–4 (pbk)
ISBN 0–19–828946–4

Typeset by Graphicraft Typesetters Ltd., Hong Kong
Printed in Great Britain by
Biddles Ltd, Guildford & King's Lynn

For my parents, children, grandchildren, and, especially, for Joan

Preface and Acknowledgements

I started this book in the USA, during study leave beginning in the late summer of 1994, just before the British Trade Union Congress's annual gathering which was held, that year, in Blackpool. I returned to Scotland in August 1995 and completed the first stage of the final manuscript at the end of September 1996, just after the Congress of that year which was again in Blackpool under the customary rota. The second-stage corrected copy of the manuscript was sent to the publisher in January 1997 and the page proofs were corrected in April and May, during the period covering the British General Election campaign and the first week after the result became known. Some final, minor corrections were also made in July. Over that period, in the USA and, especially in Britain, major political changes have occurred with important implications for industrial relations. The Democrats, by the end of 1994, had lost their traditional control of Capitol Hill and seemed destined to possible, though slow, political eclipse—if not the political oblivion which appeared to await President Clinton. In the event, as the late Harold Wilson would have reminded us, a week, let alone more than two years, is a long time in politics. It can also lead to mixed outcomes. In November 1996 the President won a second term with some ease whilst the Democrats, though regaining some ground in the House, fell further behind in the Senate.

The contribution of the US trade union movement to the Democrats' campaign was substantial in terms of people, time, and, not least, money: the financial contribution was reported at $35m. Yet the final political outcome, for the unions, was no more favourable, at the beginning of 1997, than in 1994. Furthermore, after the election, the AFL-CIO's preferred Secretary of Labor to replace the resigning Robert Reich—the highly experienced and well-regarded former senator from Pennsylvania, Harris Wofford—was passed over in favour of the relatively unknown Alexis Herman, although her earlier experience as Director of the Women's Bureau at the Department of Labor under the Carter presidency gave some strength to her appointment.

At the same time the movement had clearly begun to set out on a course of reform and self-help. It had replaced its old-style, long-serving, political lobbying, low-profile leadership at the AFL-CIO with new, campaigning, verbally aggressive leaders. There was even some promise, under their guidance and a substantial increase in resources for organizing, of a revival in membership. In the USA, unions were also winning some victories in their battles with employers, most significantly in the auto industry. Their recovering popularity and political campaigning successes were also beginning to attract the closer attentions of the troubled Democratic Party. A potential political rival to the Democrats was also in the field. An emerging Labor Party offered some prospects, in the summer of 1996, for new productive alliances between radical union and political activists at the lower levels of the US industrial relations system which could yet provide the basis for a 'labour movement' on the British model. Yet whilst still unlikely there must be some challenge to the status quo unless the Democrats can begin to recover their control of Congress in 1998 and the President succeeds in delivering tangible benefits to the trade unions. The first of these conditions remains highly uncertain and the second virtually ruled out during a second presidential term with Congress in Republican hands.

Meanwhile, the prospects for British trade unions were substantially improved, though not necessarily transformed, by the Labour Party's landslide victory in May 1997 which even eclipsed, in its proportions, the historic victory of 1945. However, even before the General Election, British unions were beginning to recover their old readiness for a good fight, although with much more skilful footwork, as postal workers, railway workers, London Underground workers, firefighters, dockers, and civil servants opposed what they saw as arbitrary and unfair actions by employers who were greatly helped by the framework of industrial relations legislation installed between 1980 and 1993. The TUC was also listening to organizing lessons given by its US, Dutch, and Australian counterparts, as its principal affiliates were experimenting with new approaches to reversing the deep erosion of their membership base. Nor was the loud musing of the Labour Party's leadership, at the end of 1996, on the case for a further weakening of its traditionally close relationship with the trade unions as threatening as it sounded: it was certainly not in line with the Party's preference for EU-style social partnership when in office and its declared intention to opt into the Social Chapter, an intention which was confirmed within days of the formation of Mr Blair's Government.

Hence, although it was difficult, in 1994 for the US and British proponents of trade unions and collective bargaining to be cheerful about the future, by 1997 pessimism was less rational than qualified optimism as the political wheels began to turn, although clearly much more favourably in Britain than the USA. But even without positive political support the unions were beginning to demonstrate that some membership revival could yet lie in their own hands and could follow their new organizing priorities and strategies. False dawns and single swallow summers have, of course, been commonplace in US labour circles and a sustained return to the scale of the organizing successes of the New Deal period is required to reverse the membership losses of the past twenty years—at best an unlikely development. In Britain, much still

depends upon the Labour Government for a revival in the unions' fortunes and the recovery of collective bargaining although other forms of
employee representation, influenced by other EU countries and the EU
itself, may yet be placed on the political agenda.

If two years is a long time in politics it is also a long time in writing
a book which, by its subject matter, must be related to current developments. These developments, unfolding as I wrote, are reflected, in
the writing, mainly up to January 1997 with some later, though mostly
minor, revision covering the period to early July. Whilst keeping the text
as up-to-date as possible, I have also, in the Conclusions, tried, in outline, to project some of the alternative contexts and political scenarios.
Whilst the scenarios are speculative, the implications are less so. In
particular the revival, even survival, of the present industrial relations
systems remains, in both countries, closely linked to favourable political
outcomes. I have also drawn upon British and American historical experience in trying to assess the prospects for proposed reforms. Industrial
relations reformers, as others, must learn from history if they are not to
condemn us all to repeat it. It has also been valuable for me to record
the events and developments from the 1960s to the 1980s, which I lived
through whilst teaching shop stewards and coalminers—although I am
still far from sure who was doing the teaching! These 'ordinary' men
and women were major influences upon the way I still see the world of
work—and much else. I have also had the privilege, on many occasions
since 1984, of being closely involved with their counterparts in the US
labour movement. I thank them all for the experience as well as the
friendship freely given.

In the two years of writing this book I have accumulated many debts
although few of them are financial: Penn State generously provided a
salary, travel and conference expenses, an office, and a good library; and
Strathclyde University gave me some additional financial support as
well as allowing me to be away for twelve months. All this was much
appreciated.

At Penn State I had the benefit of stimulating, hospitable colleagues
in the Department of Labor Studies and Industrial Relations. Those
deserving special mention include Mark Wardell, Paul Clarke, and
Frieda Rozen. Dick Hindle, recently retired, provided a number of
valuable contacts in the Pennsylvania labour movement as well as offering and sharing some good times. Arlene Smith, Mitzi Dailey, and Pat
Ellenburger provided good advice and consistent friendship, and my
students on the Comparative Industrial Relations Course remained loyal
and committed despite the second semester scheduling for an 8 a.m.
class! Outside Labor Studies I learned much from regular attendance at
Dan Letwin's Labor History seminar series which on one occasion,
included a lively contribution from the distinguished labour historian

David Montgomery. I also benefited greatly from the conversations, over excellent dinners, at the home of Heinz and Bridget Henisch. In and around Pennsylvania I discussed current labour issues with trade unionists at union schools in Bradford, Hershey, Philadelphia, and Steelton. I also returned to Penn State in June 1996 as co-organizer (with Mark Wardell) of a symposium on 'Jobs and Justice' *Industrial Relations Journal* (1997) funded jointly by Penn State and Strathclyde. This invited gathering of eminent American and British academics emphasized how far good research and scholarship can help to promote justice in the workplace.

Beyond Penn State I took the opportunity for renewed discussions with Hal Stack, Steve Babson, and Doug Fraser at Wayne State University, old friends from earlier years. The University of Alberta at Edmonton and Oregon State University also provided funding for visits for which I thank Philip Raworth and Ron Miller who became friends as well as colleagues. I also saw old comrades from my Nottingham days—Laurie and Jan Clements—now major figures in labour education at the University of Iowa. Time, sadly, prevented me from what also would have been productive discussions at the University of Notre Dame with Chuck Craypo and Teresa Ghilarducci. However at the 1996 Penn State symposium, and earlier at the 1995 IIRA World Conference in Washington, I once again had the benefit of the wisdom and compassion of Bill Gould, now Chairman of the NLRB. I am also grateful to Maria Fiordellisi, the AFL-CIO's legislative representative in Washington who provided me with up-to-date briefing on the vetoed TEAM Bill, the legal challenge to President Clinton's Executive Order 12954, and an account of the successful campaign for an increase in the federal minimum wage.

Back home, I am grateful to Mike Grindley and Brian Johnson (two of the fourteen trade union members dismissed from GCHQ during 1988–9) for a helpful discussion on how trade union rights and recognition could be restored at Cheltenham. Stephen Woodland of the DTI let me have useful data on trade union density and Bryan Stevens, Director of the IPA, discussed with me, and sent detailed accounts of, the more interesting British labour–management partnership agreements. David Musson, Oxford University Press's Management and Business Editor, offered gentle encouragement through the long, much delayed, gestation of the manuscript even to the extent of sending me relevant book news and photocopies of interesting articles on US industrial relations themes! Leonie Hayler, an assistant editor at OUP, was also always helpful and supportive and the manuscript was greatly improved by the meticulous copy editing of Virginia Williams. Within the Department at Strathclyde, I must give special thanks to Pat McTaggart for her skill in converting my stapled and sellotaped output into beautiful, clean pages in a remarkably short period of time.

A special debt is also due to Ronald Filippelli of Penn State and Ram Singh of Lancaster University. Ron read the entire manuscript, subjecting it to his deep knowledge of US labour history and industrial relations. Ram did the same at the copy-editing stage, bringing to bear his knowledge of US, British, and EU labour and employment law and its impact upon industrial relations. Their advice and comments were invaluable although any errors remaining and opinions expressed remain my responsibility.

Finally, above all, Joan (with some help from Max and Carl) kept the home fires burning and the home cooking coming throughout. The writing of a book is always a major trial for those close to the inevitable silences, preoccupations, and long absences, especially for a book which took such an unconscionable time in the writing. They accepted it all with exceptional tolerance and resilience. I hope I deserved it.

Brian Towers

University of Strathclyde, Glasgow

Contents

List of Figures

List of Tables

List of Abbreviations

AA	Automobile Association
AAA	American Automobile Association
ACAS	Advisory, Conciliation and Arbitration Service
ACTSS	Association of Clerical, Technical and Supervisory Staff
ACTU	Australian Council of Trade Unions
AEEU	Amalgamated Engineering and Electrical Union
AEU	Amalgamated Engineering Union
AFL	American Federation of Labor
AFL-CIO	American Federation of Labor-Congress of Industrial Organizations
AFSCME	American Federation of State, County and Municipal Employees
AFT	American Federation of Teachers
APEX	Association of Professional, Executive, Clerical and Computer Staff
ASTMS	Association of Scientific, Technical and Managerial Staffs
BMW	Bayerische Motoren-Werke
CAB	Citizens' Advice Bureaux
CAC	Central Arbitration Committee
CAS	Conciliation and Arbitration Service (1974: ACAS in 1975)
CBI	Confederation of British Industry
CEO	Chief Executive Officer
CIO	Congress of Industrial Organizations
CIR	Commission on Industrial Relations
CO	Certification Office; Certification Officer
COHSE	Confederation of Health Service Employees
COLA	cost-of-living adjustment
COPE	Committee on Political Education
CPC	Corn Product Corporation
CWA	Communication Workers of America
CWU	Communication Workers Union

DC	District of Columbia
DE	Department of Employment
DGB	Deutscher Gewerkschaftsbund
DTI	Department of Trade and Industry
ECJ	European Court of Justice
EEC	European Employees' Council (at CPC)
EETPU	Electrical, Electronic, Telecommunication and Plumbing Union
EI	employee involvement
EIRR	*European Industrial Relations Review*
EPC	Employee Participation Committee
ESOP	Employee Stock Ownership Plan; Employee Share Ownership Plan
EU	European Union
EWC	European Works Council
FBU	Fire Brigades Union
FMCS	Federal Mediation and Conciliation Service
FNV	Federatie Nederlandse Vakbeweging (Netherlands Trade Union Confederation)
GATT	General Agreement on Tariffs and Trade
GCHQ	Government Communications Headquarters
GDP	Gross Domestic Product
GFTU	General Federation of Trade Unions
GM	General Motors
GMB	This is the name of the union. It was formed in 1989 from the merger of two unions: GMBATU and GMWU-APEX.
GMBATU	General, Municipal, Boilermakers and Allied Trades Union
GMWU	General and Municipal Workers Union
GPMU	Graphical, Paper and Media Union
HP	A British food manufacturing company. 'HP' is a famous brand of table sauce, an abbreviation for 'Houses of Parliament'.
HRM	human resource management
IAM	International Association of Machinists and Aerospace Workers

IDS	Incomes Data Services
IG Metall	Industriegewerkschaft Metall
IIRA	International Industrial Relations Association
ILO	International Labour Organization
IPA	Involvement and Participation Association
IRS	Industrial Relations Services
JNC	joint negotiating committee
LBJ	Lyndon B. Johnson
LFJ	Learning from Japan
LFS	Labour Force Survey
LMRA	Labor Management Relations Act (Taft–Hartley Act)
LPA	Labor Party Advocates
LRC	Labour Representation Committee
MSF	Manufacturing, Science and Finance Union
NAFTA	North American Free Trade Agreement
NALGO	National and Local Government Officers' Association
NCB	National Coal Board
NEA	National Education Association
NGA	National Graphical Association '82
NHS	National Health Service
NIRC	National Industrial Relations Court
NLRA	National Labor Relations Act (Wagner Act)
NLRB	National Labor Relations Board
NOP	National Opinion Polls
NUBE	National Union of Bank Employees
NUM	National Union of Mineworkers
NUMMI	New United Motor Manufacturing Inc.
NUPE	National Union of Public Employees
OECD	Organization for Economic Cooperation and Development
PAC	Political Action Committee
PATCO	Professional Air Traffic Controllers Organization
RCM	Royal College of Midwives
RCN	Royal College of Nursing

RMT	National Union of Rail, Maritime, and Transport Workers
RPI	Index of Retail Prices
SAC	Strategic Action Council
SEA	Single European Act
SEIU	Service Employees' International Union
SOGAT	Society of Graphical and Allied Trades '82
TEAM	Teamwork for Employees and Managers Bill
TGWU	Transport and General Workers Union
TQI	total quality improvement
TQM	total quality management
TUC	Trades Union Congress
UAW	United Automobile Workers: this is the abbreviated name. The union's members also include aerospace and agricultural implement workers.
UCATT	Union of Construction, Allied Trades and Technicians
UCS	Upper Clyde Shipbuilders
UCW	Union of Communication Workers
UFCW	International Union of Food and Commercial Workers
UNISON	This is the name of the union. It was formed in 1994 from the merger of three unions: NALGO, NUPE and COHSE.
USWA	United Steelworkers of America
WIRS	(British) Workplace Industrial Relations Survey

Introduction: Two Systems in Crisis

> British industry and commerce appear to be moving towards the situation in which non-managerial employees are treated as a 'factor of production'.
>
> (Millward 1994: 133)

> While there is no evidence that unions can come back and reverse their downward movement in this century, it is quite possible that unorganized workers, less well protected than their union counterparts in different economic circumstances may be storing away a resentment that will explode in coming years.
>
> (Gould 1994: 263)

It is not difficult to describe the US industrial relations system as 'in crisis', even though the crisis has been in the making over a very long period. Both unionization (i.e. 'density' or the proportion of employed wage and salary earners in unions) and collective bargaining have been falling and contracting in the USA for over forty years with the density figures now back to the levels of the early years of the Great Depression. The British 'crisis' has been more recent. For the twenty years up to 1979 unionization moved in the opposite direction to the USA as the labour movement reached a high point in its strength and influence. Then all the indicators began to fall so fast that by 1995 total membership was at 1945 levels and unionization back to the last years of the 1930s. These reminders of hard times have, in Britain, been reinforced by rates of unemployment in the 1980s and 1990s frequently matching those of the 1930s, and by the reappearance of poverty in employment, alongside growing insecurity, as union influence has waned and state protections eroded. Similar developments have been taking place in the USA. The real pay of most workers has been declining since the early 1970s, benefits have been consistently cut by employers, and welfare entitlements have been undermined. The good news for the USA is that its labour market seems better able to create jobs and get the unemployed back into work than is the case in most EU countries but even that is qualified good news given the evidence of the often poor quality, part-time nature, and limited tenure of the extra jobs.

The downward pressure on workers' living standards, employment conditions, and traditional rights is largely associated with the decline in trade union membership. This wide, and widening, 'representation gap' means that only one out of six US employees, and one out of three

British, have access to the independent representation of their individual and collective interests. There is also evidence from the USA that many more employees would like access to some form of effective representation, including trade unions, but that employers largely prevent this happening. In Britain, unionized employees do not have any legal right to trade union recognition even when they form a majority of the bargaining unit. Employers can also withdraw recognition at any level of membership and since 1979 derecognition has been slowly gaining ground as an employer practice.

The denial of legitimate representation aspirations at work has important political implications. In political systems dominated by representation rights and the rule of majorities how can the ability of British employers lawfully to deny a 'voice' to the wishes of a majority of their employees be justified? Or, in US contexts, though the law nominally guarantees the representation rights of majorities, how is it that employers are allowed to evade, even flout, the application of those laws? Furthermore, what is to be made of the freedom to strike, under the law, when in both countries strikers are severely handicapped by contrary laws, judicial decisions, and serious threats to their livelihoods? More widely, and fundamentally, how 'democratic' are societies in which representation is largely only available outside the workplace?

The democratic case for freely available access, by employees, to independent representation of their interests is the central argument of this book. It is also maintained that the democratic case is the primary one: representation at work, like democratic representation itself, does not need to be justified on economic grounds. However research, though mainly American, is now consistently revealing that 'high performance', competitive companies seem to work best in supportive industrial relations contexts, that is, where management recognizes the legitimacy of workers' organizations and the value of collective bargaining as an instrument for change and innovation in working practices.

Aside from advocacy, the book is also intended to be a contribution to comparative industrial relations, specifically a comparison of Britain and the USA. Both of these intentions need to be discussed and the second requires some justification.

Comparative industrial relations has many traps for the unwary. Schregle (1981), from an ILO perspective, advises an approach which compares institutions, such as collective bargaining, within their national contexts, ideally from a multidisciplinary perspective and 'combined with the need to adopt an attitude of genuine modesty, humility and respect for the institutions of other peoples ... the major value of comparative industrial relations' (p. 29). This advice is especially appropriate to policy-makers seeking to transplant seemingly successful institutions, laws, and practices from other countries without detailed consideration as to whether or not they would flourish outside the historical, political, and socio-economic contexts in which they originated, were implemented, and developed.[1]

Yet despite the problems and difficulties faced by policy-makers, or even perhaps because of them, the study of comparative industrial relations is attracting increasing interest as well as growing numbers into its ranks.[2] This development is somewhat paradoxical, especially in the cases of the USA and Britain, where the study of their national systems is less attractive to academics and research funders as collective bargaining continues to contract and where, in universities, the teaching of industrial relations is being replaced by human resource management. How, therefore, is the growing attraction of comparative industrial relations to be explained?

Of the factors at work, perhaps the most important is the increasing internationalization of national economies with the associated increase in international competition leading to pressure on organizations to improve their competitiveness. Global competition has been commonly advanced as the major influence explaining American employers' search for alternatives to the claimed inflexibility and high costs of collective bargaining.[3] It has also clearly concentrated attention on the management, employment, and industrial relations practices of other countries to see what might be learned, or imported. American companies are of course strongly influenced by organizational practices in other countries, including those of companies operating within the USA itself, mainly Japanese-owned or joint ventures (Kenney and Florida 1993). German companies, notably in the auto industry, have also attracted recent detailed comparative attention from US academics interested in the case for works councils in US contexts (Turner 1991). The British, too, including the Trades Union Congress (TUC 1994*b*), have developed an interest in the lessons of German works councils, although the main focus of study has been Japanese companies in Britain (Bassett 1986; Oliver and Wilkinson 1992). There is also a literature of concern over the deep-rooted problems of British competitiveness extending back to Victorian times, and this literature also includes some influential postwar studies by Americans (Caves and Associates 1968; Ulman 1968; Wiener 1981).

A more recent variation on the competitiveness theme has been the attention given to differences between countries' labour market institutions and behaviour, and the role of the state. Thus there has been considerable debate over the alleged tendency of the 'inflexible' European 'model' (especially the German) of institutionalized collective bargaining, combined with widely available and generously funded employment protection and social benefits, to generate high and uncompetitive labour costs and impede job creation (Buechtemann 1993). This debate has attracted the strong interest of policy-makers influenced by the case for greater flexibility, deregulation, and limited collective bargaining, such as the British Conservatives since 1979 and, increasingly, other EU governments as they limit their support for the social market economy. In this they have also been influenced by the experience of the 'flexible' US labour market and its greater capacity for job creation, especially in the context of the high and continuing levels of unemployment in EU countries (Towers 1994).

The liberalization of world trade, through GATT, as well as the regional liberalization of NAFTA and the EU's internal market, have also generated greater interest in comparative industrial relations and studies of employment practices. ILO studies and reports have consistently put the case for the wider application and enforcement of internationally acceptable labour standards through clauses in trade agreements (Sengenberger and Campbell 1994). A study of NAFTA has also considered how far the agreement could be extended to include a social dimension on the EU model (Adams and Turner 1994). Free trade and economic integration have also encouraged some renewal of interest in the potential for international labour solidarity (Regini 1992).

Bilateral industrial relations studies are common, such as the USA and Canada, the USA and Japan, and the USA and Germany. American and Canadian comparative research is especially abundant, most recently Troy (1992), and Kumar (1993). Lipset (1991), in the case of Canada and the USA, argues that it is the similarity of the two cultures which makes it easier to identify those factors which make them different. Comparative study of the two North American countries is also likely to be encouraged by their membership of NAFTA, as for example with the Adams and Turner (1994) collection. Bilateral comparisons of British and American industrial relations are extremely rare although the two countries invariably feature in edited, international collections.[4] This rarity may be because of the academic emphasis on American 'exceptionalism'[5] although it is not an emphasis necessarily shared by US labour historians. The 'new' labour historians, such as David Montgomery and his successors, influenced by the writings of the British labour historian E. P. Thompson, sought to undermine the established picture of the conservative and individualistic nineteenth-century US working class. They have revealed that their communities, cultural values, and ideologies were no different from those which prevailed in Europe and that the 'pure and simple' business unionism of the principal architect of the American Federation of Labor (Samuel Gompers) was a minority perspective (Forbath 1992). At the same time, business unionism has always been present in British unions as it must be if leaders are to be elected by members whose immediate concerns are bread-and-butter issues and who wish to avoid 'dangerously ambitious political solutions' (Fox 1985: 114). Even if British unions in the second half of the nineteenth century had less to fear than American unions from employers and the state, the 'aristocrats of labour' who came together in 1868 to form the Trades Union Congress (TUC) were little different, in perspective, from those who formed the American Federation of Labor (AFL) in 1886.

Both the TUC and the AFL were later to be challenged by the rise of organized, industrial workers, some of whose leaders sought to improve the lot of their members by more radical means as well as by collective bargaining. The difference was that the British craft unions did not wish to exclude the 'new unions' from the TUC and together they parented the Labour Representation Committee which, in 1906, became the Labour Party; in the USA, the AFL and the CIO went their separate, bitter ways until 1955 by which time the communists had been purged from the CIO unions as the CIO's 'social democratic tinge' had begun to fade with postwar prosperity (Lipset 1991: 18). Thus comparative labour history can help to explain why the Labour Party rose rapidly in Britain but failed to establish roots in the USA.[6] More generally, as Forbath put it:

Comparative history is said to work best when it begins with similar contexts and concurrent events in the histories of two societies and proceeds from such sameness to the exploration of revealing differences. A comparative approach seems promising here because of the profound similarities in the contexts—both institutional and cultural—of labor activity in the two countries. (1992: 202–3)

Forbath's 'profound similarities in the contexts' have not entirely disappeared and more recent ones have emerged to complement them. Seven similarities may be identified.

First, as we have already seen, both countries since 1979 have shared a common experience of decline in unionization and a related contraction of collective bargaining, at a speed which is exceptional in comparison with other industrialized countries and to levels not experienced for sixty years. This parallel decline can be explained through a similar set of factors which offer some answer as to how far both industrial relations systems are under 'transformation'.[7] Furthermore, if such an important 'sub-system' has, or is being, transformed, what are the implications for the wider society beyond the world of the collective bargainers?

Secondly, and this is a partial explanation of parallel decline, employers and governments in both countries, with differences in kind and degree, have achieved freer, less regulated labour markets by privatization, deregulation, the removal or weakening of minimum wage controls, and measures and policies to limit and roll back trade unions and collective bargaining. In the case of unions and collective bargaining, this, in the USA, has been essentially an employer-led initiative; in Britain it has largely been implemented by legislation and government-led public sector policy. In Britain, too, uninterrupted Conservative government from

1979 to 1997 has allowed for policy continuation and implementation. However in the USA, the Clinton administration's labour market policies, especially towards labour law reform, have so far failed to shift the status quo in the private sector—as Carter also failed to do in 1978. This legislative failure is largely, if not entirely, explained by the strong opposition, backed by resources and influence, of the employers. In Britain, employer anti-union ideology is much less in evidence, although growing, and it is clear that bargaining power has shifted markedly away from the unions. British membership of the European Union does, however, act as a counterpoise, via EU laws on social and employment issues, to the policies and actions of the government and employers.

Thirdly Britain, on several occasions since 1945, has found, in the USA, a model for industrial relations reforms, mainly in the belief that the appropriate reforms would assist in the long-term revival of a slowly growing and under-performing economy. The most vivid example of this borrowing, noted earlier, was the 'spectacularly unsuccessful'[8] 1971 Industrial Relations Act which was followed, from 1980, by a programme of piecemeal, 'step-by-step' legislation which was claimed to have drawn on the negative experience of 1971–4. The British trade union movement has also been influenced by the approach to organizing of its US counterparts, as both their memberships fell rapidly from the 1980s, although by the 1990s British unions were also beginning to look to EU works council experience as a possible route to the revival of their flagging fortunes. The British–US institutional borrowing process has not, however, been two way, although by 1994 Clinton's Dunlop Commission was mandated to look for improvements in productivity and economic performance through more cooperative, participative, and less adversarial industrial relations as the US economy was increasingly revealing some of the sluggishness long associated with Britain.

Fourthly, the political ideology contexts in which industrial relations takes place have been remarkably similar over long periods, not least in the 1980s when anti-union governments were in power and contributing towards the weakening of trade unions and collective bargaining. These contexts diverged after the elections of 1992 when a Democratic president took office for the first time since 1980 as the Conservatives won their fourth election in a row. Yet the complex, shifting compromises and alliances of American politics ensured that the election of President Clinton marked, in practice, a less significant change than his supporters—not least the labour unions—had hoped for. Furthermore, though Clinton's second term has now coincided, in 1997, with a British Labour government, neither is now likely to pursue active pro-labour industrial relations policies—although mostly for different reasons. Clinton is much less pro-union than his Democratic predecessors; has the handicap of a second, final, term; and is again required to deal with a Republican Congress. Labour, even with a record majority in the House of Commons, is only committed to minimal labour law reform and continues to develop a cooler, 'no favours' arm's-length approach towards the trade unions.

Fifthly, the characteristics of the two industrial relations systems are sufficiently similar to make meaningful comparisons. Collective bargaining, despite the legislative inroads of the past thirty years, remains the dominant influence upon the employment relationship—a source of strength when unions are strong, but a debilitating weakness in decline. Collective bargaining, in both countries, is also largely focused on the workplace. This has for long largely been the case in the USA and most British employers, especially since the 1980s, have also implemented policies which have shifted collective bargaining to the enterprise and the workplace. These changes in Britain have, of course, not succeeded in converting British plant bargaining to the status, form, and detailed content of that which still partly exists at local level in the USA, albeit increasingly being changed by employers as unions have been forced or persuaded to accept new bargaining arrangements alongside new working practices. Nor is British plant bargaining in any sense conditioned by the frequency and central importance accorded in the USA to legal decisions within a written constitutional framework giving exceptional power to the Supreme Court. However despite these very different legal contexts the continuing central significance of collective bargaining in the two countries, and especially at plant level, marks them out as distinctive systems which are essentially different from those prevailing in EU countries outside Britain.

Yet, and sixthly, it is at least arguable that the legal framework intended to protect and encourage collective bargaining in the USA now largely does the opposite. American labour laws, in specific cases, also bear down heavily on trade unions, most obviously in the case of the employers' ability to frustrate the certification (recognition) and contract negotiation processes and effectively limit the right to strike. In Britain, and especially since the legislation of the 1980s and 1990s, the employers' unilateral control over recognition and derecognition has been restored,[9] strike procedures have been tightly regulated, and strikers' exposure to dismissal has been increased. Broadly, it can be maintained that both countries' laws relating to trade union recognition and strikes, though the detail is different, are similarly restrictive in their outcomes and have become more so over the last two decades. It can also be maintained that in this respect, as others, the two countries are significantly different from other comparable, industrialized countries.

Seventhly, and finally, a comparative study of industrial relations in Britain and the USA is justifiable on the grounds that industrial relations remains a significant activity. In total there are about 16 million trade union members in the USA and over 7 million in Britain, representing respectively about one-seventh and one-third of those in employment. These are large numbers which may yet begin to grow again and are much beyond the concept of 'special interest'. Collective bargaining's influence also extends beyond the unionized workforce and, even in decline, it still remains an important activity. In Britain, collective bargaining agreements currently cover 37 per cent of employees and although recent (1995) data show the US figure to be much lower, at under 17 per cent, in fifteen states it is over 20 per cent and in New York it is close to 30 per cent (Hirsch and Macpherson 1996).[10]

Industrial relations is also significant in that its focus is the place of work where many of us still spend a substantial part of our lives and in which we experience degrees of fulfilment, satisfaction (even happiness!), and, sometimes, misery. Some of these outcomes are closely connected with the existence, or absence, of effective mechanisms for defending and advancing employee rights. One of these mechanisms—collective bargaining underpinned by strong trade unions and historically far and away the most important and effective mechanism—is now in clear, though not necessarily permanent, decline. The case for restoring the influence of collective bargaining, or exploring alternatives or complements to it, are matters deserving serious study, public debate, and the close attentions of policy-makers.

The scale and pace of, and explanations for, the decline of trade unions and collective bargaining are the themes of Chapter 3, followed, in Chapter 4, mainly by an assessment as to how far, and by what means, the trade unions by their own efforts can restore their fortunes. However, for a fuller assessment, it is important to place the explanations for decline, and strategies for revival, within their economic, political, legal, and public policy contexts. These important contexts, which are of course subject to change—perhaps mostly slowly and in a piecemeal way but, occasionally, transforming—are the subject matter of Chapters 1 and 2. Chapter 5 is concerned with the book's central argument, outlined earlier, that the case for employees' unimpeded access to independent representation of their interests is primarily to be made on political (that is democratic) grounds although it is also clear that there can be a positive association, at the workplace, between democracy and efficiency in contexts where there is a supportive, management-backed, industrial relations climate.

The outcome of change and reform in both countries, or failed reform in the US, has been a serious erosion of employees' access to independent representation of their interests. This widening of the 'representation gap' and the two more important approaches towards bridging the gap—works councils and labour–management partnerships—are the themes of Chapter 8. Here there is also a return to the question as to how far the unions, acting alone, can find their own salvation. This possibility is taken up again, in the Conclusions, within a wider discussion of the prospects for British and American industrial relations.

NOTES

1. The most instructive British example of misguided policy-making of this kind was the passage of the ill-fated Industrial Relations Act of 1971 which drew, unwisely, upon the National Labor Relations Act (Wagner Act) of 1935 and the 1947 Labor Management Relations Act (Taft–Hartley Act). See Ch. 6. The USA shows no evidence of having been seriously influenced by the experience of other countries' industrial relations legislation, although in the late nineteenth century its craft-based trade unions and the American Federation of Labor were very close in organization, tactics, and ideology to their British counterparts. British and American companies do of course commonly adopt some of the practices of other countries' organizations, not least the inward investors from Japan. See e.g. Kenney and Florida (1993) for the USA and Oliver and Wilkinson (1992) for Britain.
2. Two prominent, and widely adopted course texts are Bamber and Lansbury (1993) and Bean (1994). An expanded version of *Trade Unions of the World* by Martin Upham (1993), now including employers' organizations, is also available. Ferner and Hyman (1992) and Hyman and Ferner (1994) have published two substantial edited volumes on European industrial relations. Notable comparative studies recently published in the USA include Turner (1991), Thelen (1992), Freeman (1994a), Rogers and Streeck (1995), and Adams (1995). The literature on newly industrializing countries is becoming more extensive. Recent additions include Deery and Mitchell (1993) and Rodgers (1994). Regular, detailed, government-funded statistical surveys of workplace industrial relations are also now a regular feature of British research (Millward *et al.* 1992) and a single survey has been completed for Australia (Callus *et al.* 1991). These British and Australian surveys are also being developed, by researchers, on a comparative basis (Whitfield *et al.* 1994).

    The International Industrial Relations Association (IIRA) has recently expanded its publishing activity. The proceedings of its most recent world conference (in Washington in 1995) have been published in five international academic journals. The IIRA's world and regional conferences continue to attract large numbers. Its membership has also been growing strongly. National association membership grew from 23 to 33 between 1984 and 1992. Institutional membership increased from 26 to 47 and individual membership from 179 to 1,269 over the same period (IIRA 1992).

    Academic journals, specializing in comparative themes, include the Belgium-based *Bulletin of Comparative Labour Relations*. Two new journals were first published in 1995: *Transfer* from the European Trade Union Institute and the *European Industrial Relations Journal*. Of the main British journals, the *Industrial Relations Journal* regularly includes international and comparative articles as does the *British Journal of Industrial Relations*. Of the human resource management journals published in Britain, the *International Human Resource Management Journal* is of interest to comparative specialists. The *Human Resource Management Journal* is also expanding its international coverage. The two prominent US journals (*Industrial and Labor Relations Review* and *Industrial Relations*) also publish comparative articles, as does the Canadian journal, *Industrial Relations/Relations Industrielles*.

3. See e.g. Hirsch (1991). Bluestone and Bluestone (1992) argue similarly, although from a trade union perspective.

4. Phelps Brown (1986) includes an interesting Anglo-US comparison as part of a wider study. Hughes published a comparative study of US and British labour markets and unemployment in 1984. Recent journal articles are those of Freeman (1995a; 1995b). Edited collections are relatively numerous with two recently published: Bélanger *et al.* (1994) and Rogers and Streeck (1995).

5. A wide-ranging, multidisciplinary contribution to the 'exceptionalism' literature is Shafer (1991).

6. There is however now another attempt to found a Labor Party in the USA, ninety years after the foundation of the Labour Party in Britain in 1906. See Ch. 4, n. 17.

7. The much-cited study of Kochan *et al.* (1986) does not have a single, British matching equivalent although the Workplace Industrial Relations Surveys (with a further one in preparation) may yet provide the inspiration for a British study. A recent, edited British collection which includes historical and contemporary overviews is Edwards (1995).

8. Davies (1980: 267). Cited in Fox (1985: 392).

9. This is not to say that the statutory procedure available to trade unions from 1975 to 1980 was a success. The procedure is discussed in Ch. 2. See also Beaumont and Towers (1992).

10. The US public sector also has much higher collective bargaining coverage, and is comparable to the British. The US public sector, as a whole, covered over 43% of employees in 1995. This varied widely between states with South Carolina at 10.8% and Connecticut 74.2%. US public sector employment was 16.7% of all employment in 1995 (Hirsch and Macpherson 1996: 24, table 9a). For Britain the public sector employed 29.3% of all employment in 1991; by 1995 it was 20.5% (Hughes 1996: 374, table 1).

1

Economic and Employment Contexts

In the preceding discussion, an industrial relations system was developed at one moment in time. But an industrial relations system may also be thought of as moving through time, or, more rigorously, as responding to changes that affect the constitution of the system.

(Dunlop 1993: 61)

Massive and stubborn resistances are apt to be encountered by attempts to transform basic, long-standing responses of large numbers of people in their everyday behaviour; or by attempts to reverse institutional dispositions that have changed over a long period; or by attempts to repudiate expectations that have likewise been developed by persistent historical continuities.

(Fox 1985, p. xiii)

Industrial relations scholars are accustomed to thinking of change in industrial relations 'systems' as a slow process in which the forces of movement, both internal and external, are tempered by those which slow down, or even reverse, the tide of change. This is especially true in the case of industrial relations in liberal democracies where institutionalized, legitimate opposition to change is possible. Alan Fox's 'persistent historical continuities' can also be seen in sharper focus in international, comparative contexts. Forty years ago scholars wrote of the influence of advancing industrialization on industrial relations systems, suggesting an inevitable convergence (Kerr *et al.* 1960). Convergence theory is now much less persuasive. For example, despite the European Union's forty years of developing economic integration, some political integration, and the increasing influence of more standardized individual employment law across all the member states, these processes have only marginally influenced the way the individual member states regulate and conduct their collective industrial relations. Hence in the cases of Germany and Britain, for example, their systems remain characteristically different from each other and the changes in the latter over the last thirty years, and specifically since 1979, have been largely determined by developments and policies which would have exerted their influence even if Britain had remained outside the Union. And even as the internal market develops through the growth of European multinationals and foreign multinationals within Europe, these organizations could both strengthen and weaken converging tendencies (Marginson and Sisson 1994).

In North America too, despite strong economic pressures favouring convergence, the US and Canadian systems still exhibit remarkable differences, not least in the experience of their labour movements.[1] Within the USA itself, Kochan *et al.*'s (1986) transformation thesis is not without influential critics, most persistently Dunlop who argues that collective bargaining was never, even at its peak, a process covering the majority of employees and 'the developments of the 1980s . . . did not fundamentally transform the US industrial relations system' (1993: 21).

Yet if not necessarily transformed, traditional industrial relations in which collective bargaining is the defining characteristic (Clegg 1978) has been in substantial retreat in the United States for over forty years. Retreat has also been the experience of Britain, although in the British case that retreat, although remarkable in its extent and occurring in the relatively short time period since 1979, still leaves intact a collective bargaining territory much greater than is the case for the United States. But that should not minimize, for Britain, the significance of the changes in industrial relations which have taken place and are continuing to do so. Many analysts would see these changes, in both countries, as largely explained by 'structural' factors such as the growth in the service sector, the corresponding relative and perhaps even absolute decline in manufacturing, and the unemployment, employment, and occupational consequences of these developments. In this chapter we will be concerned with the structural changes themselves, leaving a discussion of their relative impact on industrial relations until Chapter 3. The structural changes have also taken place in a context of relative economic decline, although for the US relative decline remains arguable and even if conceded has only been evident for the past twenty years; for Britain the evidence for a fall from economic grace is more solidly based and more deeply rooted, with its first indications occurring towards the end of the nineteenth century. In both countries, however, economic decline has often been linked, by analysts and policy-makers, to industrial relations, not least in the role and conduct of trade unions, so that policies to limit their influence have preoccupied British governments for the past thirty years. These policies will be discussed in Chapter 2. Initially, in this chapter, we will concentrate on the general dimensions of relative economic decline, economic change, and restructuring; the nature and extent of the specific, associated changes in employment and occupational structure; and the differences in the capacity of the two economies' labour markets to maximize employment and minimize unemployment.

ECONOMIC CHANGE, DECLINE, AND RESTRUCTURING

The Decline of Manufacturing

The relative decline of manufacturing in advanced, industrial economies is a general phenomenon with important consequences for employment

TABLE 1.1. *Value added in manufacturing in advanced industrial countries, 1960–1990 (% of GDP)*

Year	USA	UK	Japan	Germany	France
1960	28.3	32.1	33.9	40.3	29.1
1971	24.9	27.4	35.2	37.0	28.5
1979	23.0	25.8	29.3	33.8	27.0
1983	20.6	20.4	29.0	31.1	22.5
1985	20.1	20.7	29.5	31.7	22.0
1987	19.3	19.8	28.5	31.4	21.4
1989	19.7	20.7	28.9	31.1	21.3
1990	19.6	19.9	28.9	30.8	21.1

Source: OECD, cited in Mayes and Soteri (1994: 379, table 1).

and occupational structure. However, it is not a uniform process. This is illustrated in Table 1.1. These features are also revealed in the employment data. The general decline in manufacturing employment and the associated increase in service sector employment does not only vary widely between countries, it is also possible to hypothesize different 'models' of development. Thus the USA, UK, and Canada form the 'service economy' model, experiencing rapid declines in manufacturing employment; Germany and Japan, with manufacturing employment falling much more slowly are the 'info-industrial' model; with a third group (France and Italy) coming between these two extremes (Castells and Aoyama 1994: 26–8). Table 1.2 shows these trends and disparities since 1970.

The essentially similar, and steep, decline in manufacturing and manufacturing employment in the USA, UK, and Canada is clearly more pronounced than in other comparable, industrialized countries, especially the former West Germany and the present Germany, followed by Japan. Furthermore, in the latter group, business services jobs, linked to manufacturing,[2] are much more important than financial services employment—given the stronger manufacturing orientation of their economies (Castells and Aoyama 1994: 26–7).

These differences are significant in revealing that, although a fall in the relative share of manufacturing activity and manufacturing employment is a standard feature of all advanced economies, and should be expected to continue, the speed with which it has occurred in the 'service economy model' is not necessarily inevitable, with obvious implications for interventionist policies—subject to cultural and institutional differences. The USA and UK may now also be vulnerable in having led the way towards the 'service economy' with the relative decline in manufacturing becoming absolute. For the UK, the loss of manufacturing capacity

TABLE 1.2. *Non-agricultural employment in industry and services in seven industrialized countries, 1970–1990 (% of total employment)*

		1970	1980	1990
USA	Industry	34.0	30.5	24.9
	Services	66.0	69.5	75.1
UK	Industry	49.4	39.4	29.6
	Services	50.6	60.6	70.4
Canada	Industry	29.8 (1971)	29.0 (1981)	23.5 (1992)
	Services	70.2 (1971)	71.0 (1981)	76.5 (1992)
West Germany	Industry	51.2	—	41.5 (1987)
	Services	48.6	—	58.5 (1987)
Japan	Industry	42.1	37.4	35.8
	Services	57.9	62.6	64.2
France	Industry	43.8 (1968)	37.4	30.6 (1989)
	Services	56.2 (1968)	62.6	69.4 (1989)
Italy	Industry	52.5 (1971)	45.0 (1981)	31.9
	Services	47.5 (1971)	55.0 (1981)	68.1

Notes: For the comparability of this data see Castells and Aoyama (1993). The figures may not total 100 because of rounding.

Source: Castells and Aoyama (1994: table 2).

and the deflationary actions of the government in the recession of 1979–81 ensured that manufacturing output did not regain its 1979 level until 1987 (Mayes and Soteri 1994: 378). The US economy's experience was similar over the same period, manufacturing output declining in real terms between 1979 and 1980 and not recovering until 1984, and for durables until 1987 (Franklin 1993: 42–3).

On the ground, the de-industrialization process has not been uniform. In the US, the contraction of manufacturing has been essentially regional in its impact given the location of auto, rubber, and steel primarily in the East, North, and Midwest states. These industries have shrunk through merger, downsizing, and closure. In steel the vast employment concentrations of 'basic steel' have been superseded by much smaller, high technology mini-plants whilst elsewhere similar sized, flexibly specialized operations have become the norm (Piore and Sabel 1984; Kenney and Florida 1993; Appelbaum and Batt 1994).

US corporations have also increased their ability to relocate as well as their taste for it. Externally, transformed electronic communication and easier movement of capital have eased the transfer of capacity in steel making, auto, garment production, and microelectronics to European, Asian, and other countries in the Americas. More recently, the new GATT round and the North American Free Trade Agreement (NAFTA) have provided further incentives for capital movement and relocation in pursuit of lower labour costs. Within the USA the long-established corporate relocation from the old 'rustbelt' to the 'sunbelt' and the anti-union 'right-to-work' states[3] has been paralleled by internal investors locating primarily in the states of the South, South West, and West. This process, according to one analyst, could ultimately confine US companies to the Midwest serving local communities (Clark 1989: 249–50).

Similar processes have been evident in Britain. The British machine tools industry was almost eliminated in the sharp contraction of manufacturing capacity in 1981–2 and by that time Japanese motor cycle manufacturers had completed their control of the British market. However, the experience of the car and truck manufacturers has been ultimately different to machine tools and motor cycles. Although experiencing similar inroads from foreign competition as well as special, seemingly intractable, industrial relations problems, the last British volume producer, Rover, began to reverse its misfortunes in the 1980s in partnership with Honda. Finally in 1994, with BMW's purchase of Rover, virtually the entire industry was owned by American and Japanese companies. The outcome was that the 'British' vehicles industry was beginning to grow again by the 1990s.

The pace of British de-industrialization has been assisted by privatization. Steel and shipbuilding were returned to the private sector in the 1980s, followed by coal in the 1990s. Steel capacity has been progressively reduced, under commercial and European Union (EU) pressures, to half of its capacity in the 1970s. Shipbuilding has all but disappeared on the larger scale sites except for the state-subsidized operation of Harland and Wolff in Belfast, the foreign-owned former Swan Hunter yard on the Tyne, Vosper Thorneycroft in Southampton, and three yards on the once world-leading Clyde of which one is owned, and run, by a multinational Norwegian company attracted by skilled labour which is relatively low cost compared to mainland European yards. Coal, a cauldron of industrial relations and political troubles in the 1980s and 1990s, was the last of the old 'heights of the economy' public sector industries to be privatized in the wake of the loss of its assured markets as the electricity industry was privatized. The outcome was the transformation of British coal from its role as the dominant source of primary energy to a minor industry of collieries and opencast operations still vulnerable to competition from alternative energy sources.[4]

As in the USA, the contraction of manufacturing in Britain has been uneven in its regional impact. The lost manufacturing jobs have been mainly confined to the traditional regions of the North, North West, and Midlands (in England) as well as Scotland, Northern Ireland, and South Wales. This regional effect has been compounded by the further growth of services in the traditionally service-dominated regions of London and the South East of England, although in recent years the unemployment disparity between the southern regions and other regions has narrowed as the service sector has gone into recession, an experience once largely confined to industry and manufacturing. The locational preferences of inward investors, notably American electronics companies and Japanese electronics and auto manufacturers, have also favoured the older industrial regions, making a contribution to narrowing regional disparities. There is also substantial research evidence to suggest that the inward investors are transforming production methods not only in their own wholly owned operations but also in jointly owned enterprises, as well as by a 'copycat' influence on other enterprises, an 'industrial osmosis' process which seems to be active on both sides of the Atlantic (Kenney and Florida 1993; Oliver and Wilkinson 1992).

Does De-industrialization Matter?

In terms of relative economic success de-industrialization may not matter if at least offset by viable, service sector activity; the loss of employment in manufacturing may also be compensated for by an expansion of service sector jobs.[5] However, British evidence suggests that about one-fifth of all services are sold to manufacturing and would therefore be partially linked to its success or failure;[6] that services may not be able to expand fast enough to compensate for a decline in manufacturing; and that the export of services contributes much less in value-added, or productivity, than the export of manufactured goods (Mayes and Soteri 1994: 383–6). For the US, the rapid growth of services is at least part of the explanation for the economy's relatively poor productivity record given that sector's generally inferior performance relative to manufacturing.[7]

World Trade and Competitiveness

Changes in the competitiveness of the British and US economies, and the impact of this upon their shares of world trade, have dominated public policy debate in recent years, although such a debate in the UK goes back much further reflecting, as we have noted, the economy's more disappointing performance over a much longer period. The ammunition of the competitiveness battle has been the published data on productivity, pay, and unit labour costs.

Bluestone and Bluestone (1992: 83–4) cite long-run data to demonstrate that US productivity growth peaked in the 1950s but by the early 1980s had fallen to less than half of the peak performance and was easily exceeded by all its major industrial competitors, including, at that time, the UK. The data is however volatile over long periods and the Bluestones concede some evidence of a productivity recovery beginning in

TABLE 1.3. *Increases in business sector pay and unit labour costs in the OECD, 1980–1995 (annual averages %)*

Country	Pay per Employee		Unit Labour Costs*	
	1980–90	1991–95	1980–90	1991–95
USA	5.0	4.3	4.1	2.8
UK	8.6	5.1	5.9	2.9
Canada	6.4	3.2	4.9	1.8
Germany**	3.6	5.0	1.8	2.4
Japan	3.9	1.9	0.9	0.7
France	7.3	2.8	4.7	1.0
Italy	11.5	5.2	9.4	3.0
OECD	6.0	4.0	4.2	2.3

Notes: * At 1991 purchasing power parities.
** West Germany up to, and including, 1991; Germany thereafter.
Source: Calculated from *Employment Outlook* (1994: 8, table 1.5).

the 1980s, although perhaps limited to the computer industry. Hirsch (1991) however suggests a more widely based recovery as American employers in the 1980s responded to intensifying foreign competition by putting downward pressure on employment and labour costs whilst maintaining output and introducing new methods. This external dimension is also frequently used to explain, or justify, the increasingly anti-union policies of employers, both in the UK and USA, an aspect to which we shall return later.

The 'downward pressure' on pay and labour costs is evident from OECD data, as Table 1.3 makes clear. For the OECD countries as a whole, competitive pressures intensified into the 1990s. Both the USA and the UK experienced sharp falls in the rate at which unit labour costs were increasing and both improved their relative positions, even though out-performed by Japan and France. However both the USA and UK almost bridged their substantial relative disadvantage with Germany. German pay and labour costs moved upwards in the 1990s as the bills for reunification began to come in, exacerbating Germany's concerns over the impact of its already high labour costs on its competitive position.

Downward pressure on employment is also reflected in the OECD data. There was a fall in employment in the OECD area as a whole from the 1980s into the 1990s. In the US, however, employment growth actually continued although at a much slower rate until in 1994 falling employment was converting to an upward path in all countries (*Employment Outlook* 1994: 5, Table 1.2).

TABLE 1.4. *Comparative levels of GDP per head in five industrialized countries, 1950–1990 (USA = 100)*

Country	1950	1960	1973	1979	1990
USA	100	100	100	100	100
UK	68	74	72	71	74
Germany	44	73	79	84	85
Japan	18	33	65	67	82
France	50	62	76	81	82

Source: Cited in Temple (1994: 33, table 1).

Are the British and US Economies in Decline?

The greatly improved performance of the US and UK economies in the 1990s is difficult to place alongside the view that both economies are in long-term, though relative, decline. This long-term decline, as measured in terms of GDP per head of population, is seen in Table 1.4. The relative relationship between the USA and UK has shifted remarkably little since 1950. There has, however, been a substantial narrowing of the gap between the USA and Germany, Japan and France, as well as all the last three now being ahead of the UK.

For the USA there are a number of major objections to this apparently clear picture. First, Table 1.4 itself reveals that German and French economic growth has clearly levelled out since 1973. Secondly, the Japanese economy has recently begun to falter, faced with internal problems of economic management and the continuing rise of strong competition from other Pacific Rim countries. Thirdly, the US economy's *levels* of productivity remain, overall, higher than other economies; and there is recent evidence, as the Bluestones (1992: 84–5) partly concede, that productivity growth is beginning to revive. Fourthly, and related to productivity improvements, the OECD data discussed earlier points to recent relative improvements in competitiveness.[8] Fifthly, and more broadly, it can be argued that US world economic domination in the thirty years after World War II was an exceptional historical phase which could not last and the loss of economic hegemony should not necessarily be used as an indicator of economic decline (Kennedy 1987; Nau 1992). Sixthly, the USA in recent years has enjoyed consistently lower levels of unemployment and a superior capacity for job creation than its European competitors, notably Germany and the EU as a whole (Towers 1994: 389–91), although the explanation in more flexible labour markets may be achieved at the price of lower pay, inequality, and poverty.

TABLE 1.5. *Hourly and weekly earnings of US workers at constant*
(1993) prices, 1973–1993

Year	Average hourly earnings ($)	Average weekly earnings ($)
1973	12.06	445.10
1979	12.03	429.42
1982	11.61	403.97
1989	11.26	389.50
1991	10.95	375.55
1993	10.83	373.64

Note: Data are for production and non-supervisory workers.
Source: Mishel and Bernstein (1994: 116, table 3.3).

Yet despite these caveats, the US economy's relative decline, especially since the 1970s, remains apparent and has primarily been felt by the 'middle class'[9] majority of the population (which normally includes trade union members) as well as the lowest paid, and the poor. For production and non-supervisory workers, that is, more than 80 per cent of all wage and salary earners, both average weekly and hourly earnings were substantially higher in 1973 than 1993 and fell consistently between the two years, as Table 1.5 reveals. Within the overall picture of declining earnings and living standards for most US workers, the greatest losses have been among those with the least education and training, although since 1987 the earnings of white collar workers and college graduates have also been falling. Furthermore, within the middle class, those in occupations with wages at the bottom of the distribution experienced the sharpest fall, pushing many into poverty and placing great additional pressure on the taxes and transfer payments safety net (Mishel and Bernstein 1994: 295–6). This increase in wage inequality associated with differences in education and training has also been the experience of Britain, albeit to a less severe extent, during the 1980s. The USA does, however, appear to be unique, among other developed economies, in experiencing *declining* real wages and on such a scale. In Britain real wages continued to rise, even for the lowest paid (Freeman 1994*a*: 30).

The outcome is that the USA is no longer the world's leader in both money and real pay and the gap between countries has narrowed. Furthermore, the relative position of the USA, on present trends, is predicted to continue to deteriorate, as shown in Table 1.6 for manufacturing workers.[10] Britain's economic problems are at least a century old, emerging at a time when British global hegemony was being seriously

TABLE 1.6. *Real hourly earnings of workers in manufacturing in seven industrialized countries, 1992 and 2000 (USA = 100)*

Country	1992	2000
USA	100	100
UK	82	98
Canada	97	96
Germany	119	135
France	85	91
Italy	100	105
Japan	66	96

Note: Data have been adjusted for differences in purchasing power.

Source: Cited in Freeman (1994*a*: 11, table 1.2).

challenged by the newly industrializing economies of Germany, the USA, and Japan (Hobsbawm 1968; Gamble 1981; Coates and Hillard 1986). Yet it did not surface as a major issue of policy until the early 1960s, although the extent and seriousness of the productivity gap between Britain and other comparable countries was evident twenty years earlier (Cairncross 1985: 17).

The emergence of serious problems in the US economy, although more recent, has, as with Britain, attracted a large volume of analysis and prescription, largely beginning with the publication of Bluestone and Harrison's 1982 study.[11] The emphasis of much of this work was primarily, as in Britain, on the productivity gap. And, again as in Britain, the search for explanations, and appropriate policies, increasingly focused on the processes and outcomes of industrial relations. This we will return to in Chapter 2.

EMPLOYMENT AND OCCUPATIONAL CHANGE

Occupational Structure

The decline of manufacturing employment and the growth in service sector employment involve corresponding shifts in occupational structure. The broad projected changes[12] for Britain and the USA into the next century are illustrated in Table 1.7. For the USA all main occupational groups are projected to grow as the labour force expands rapidly. The British labour force, in contrast, will remain virtually static up to the year 2000 with falls in the absolute and relative size of employment in manual occupations at all levels of skill as well as in agriculture. However both economies are experiencing a growth in professional, technical,

TABLE 1.7. *Projected employment growth by major occupational group in the UK and USA*

Major Occupational Group	UK					USA				
	1990		2000		Change	1992		2005		Change
	Thousands	%	Thousands	%	%	Thousands	%	Thousands	%	%
Professional and technical	4,784	18.3	5,679	21.1	18.7	20,874	17.2	28,465	19.3	36.4
Administrative and managerial	3,675	14.1	4,139	15.3	12.6	12,066	10.0	15,195	10.3	25.9
Clerical and related	4,437	17.0	4,435	16.4	0.0	22,349	18.5	25,406	17.2	13.7
Craft and skilled manual	4,048	15.5	3,789	14.0	−6.4	13,580	11.2	15,380	10.4	13.3
Production, service, and labourer	6,943	26.5	6,627	24.6	−4.6	35,707	29.5	43,722	29.6	22.4
Sales workers	2,074	7.9	2,141	7.9	3.2	12,993	10.7	15,664	10.6	20.6
Agricultural and related	196	0.7	159	0.6	−18.9	3,530	2.9	3,650	2.5	3.4
Total	26,155	100.0	26,969	100.0	0.1	121,099	100.0	147,482	100.0	21.8

Source: Employment Outlook (1994: 87, table 2.8).

managerial, and administrative occupational groups. Combined, their relative share of total employment, in 1990, will continue to grow towards the end of the decade and into the next century. Clerical occupations, again in both cases, are projected to decline, although in the US case total employment will grow.

The decline in British manual work occupational groups contrasts with the USA where their relative position will remain virtually unchanged, whilst in absolute numbers substantial growth is projected—again in a context of strong employment growth, a general feature of the US economy which we will discuss later in the chapter. The familiar skilled worker shortages of the British economy are also revealed in this comparison, emphasizing the need for effective policies to increase the numbers of skilled employees as well as improving the general levels of education, training, and skills. These shortages have strongly influenced official supply-side policy towards education, training, and employment in both countries in recent years although British Conservative governments, since 1979, have turned away from direct, job creation measures.

At the level of actual jobs, Table 1.8 shows those US occupations which are projected to be the fastest growing and declining. The projections in Table 1.8 suggest the pressures for growth on occupations which serve the needs of an ageing population. They also reveal a rapid decline in domestic household workers reflecting, perhaps, the availability of alternative work, household income constraints, and changing social attitudes. The pervasive influence of new technology is also evident, assisting the growth of higher status professional and technical occupations at the expense of the operating and repetitive typing and word processor jobs.

British research suggests similar forces at work as in the USA, not least through the influence of high skill job content and from the growth of the recreational, leisure, and health industries where the demand is mainly for employment on flexible, part-time contracts. This is shown in Figure 1.1.

Technology and Skill

Technology, and especially information technology, is, as we have observed in the case of changes in professional and clerical occupations, an important explanatory factor working alongside, and influencing, structural economic change. It has eliminated[13] many traditional occupations in favour of newer ones whilst some occupations, though surviving, have been transformed in content as, for example, in printing where a much lower skill content is required, or in port and dock work, where 'containerization' has greatly reduced the numbers employed as well as eliminating most of the traditional loading, unloading, and warehousing skills.

TABLE 1.8. *Projections of fastest growing and declining occupations in the USA, 1992–2005 (%)*

	Fastest Growing	%	Fastest Declining	%
1	Home health aides	+138	Computer operators except peripheral equipment	−39
2	Human services workers	+136	Child care workers, private household	−35
3	Personal and home care aides	+130	Cleaners and servants, private household	−32
4	Computer engineers and scientists	+112	Sewing machine operators, garment workers	−29
5	Systems analysts	+110	Packaging and filling machine operators and tenders	−22
6	Physical and corrective therapy assistants and aides	+93	Switchboard operators	−21
7	Physical therapists	+88	Farmers	−21
8	Paralegals	+86	Farm workers	−16
9	Teachers, special education	+74	Typists and word processor operators	−16
10	Medical assistants	+71	Inspectors, testers and graders, precision	−10

Source: Silvestri (1993: tables 3, 5).

In office work, recent British research does however show that new technology has not yet radically changed the organization and employment practices of the office, although secretarial jobs have often been upgraded as word processors have released workers for administrative and managerial tasks (Lane 1989: 74–8). For the USA the projections show that typists and word processor jobs are in decline (Table 1.8) as the personal computer increasingly allows professional and managerial employees to do this work themselves (*Employment Outlook* 1994: 82 and 91). Manual work in Britain, however, is not apparently on course for elimination although in the longer run technology will increasingly reduce the numbers employed and significantly change work content (Martin 1989). The survival of low skill and maintenance work has also been predicted for the USA although its extent relative to high skilled work (i.e. 'polarization' of the labour force) remains controversial.[14]

Overall, the impact of technological change on total employment, its distribution, occupational structure, and skills, although often transforming, can be variable and unpredictable in its effects; nor is there an agreed meaning as to the nature of skill. Yet it is widely accepted, not least by policy-makers, that technology has generally raised the levels of skill

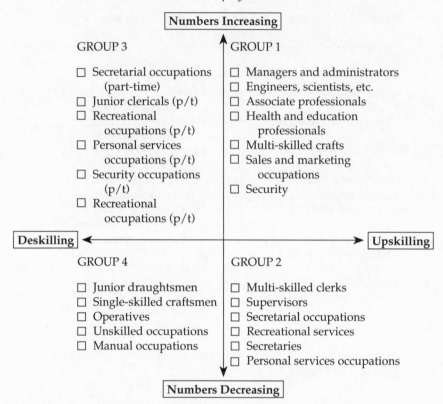

FIG. 1.1. Jobs affected by changes in numbers and skill levels in Britain
Source: Rajan (1993).

and those jobs with the highest skill content will grow much faster than those with the least (*Economic Outlook* 1994: 77). Hence raising skills and gaining qualifications through individual and/or public investment in education and training can be seen as an important contribution to reducing unemployment although complementary macroeconomic policies for job creation remain as unfashionable as they are perhaps necessary (Towers 1994).

LABOUR MARKET FLEXIBILITY

Women and the Flexible Labour Force

The growing numbers of women in the labour force is a major development in industrialized countries paralleled by a lesser role for men.

TABLE 1.9. *Women's share in part-time employment in five advanced industrial countries, 1979–1993 (%)*

	1973	1983	1993
USA	66.0	66.8	66.2
UK	90.9	89.8	85.2 (1992)
Japan	70.0	72.9	67.7
West Germany	89.0	91.9	91.0 (1992)*
France	82.3	84.4	83.7 (1992)

Note: * Data for Germany.
Source: *Employment Outlook* (1994: 198, statistical annex, table D).

For the UK, the male labour force participation rate in the twenty years to 1993 fell from 93.9 per cent to 83.3 per cent as that for females rose from 53.2 per cent to 64.3 per cent. In the USA, male participation fell much more slowly (86.2% to 84.5%) but rose faster for women: 51.1 per cent to 69.1 per cent (*Economic Outlook* 1994, statistical annex, table J). The outcome is that the total number of women in the labour force, in both countries, is projected to reach about half the labour force in the first decade after 2000 (Fullerton 1993; *Labour Market and Skill Trends* 1994/95).

Yet although women dominate labour force growth in industrialized countries, the jobs they secure are primarily part-time although economic and occupational change and the continuing high incidence of male unemployment may be beginning to weaken the link between women and part-time work. It is also clear that this link remains much stronger in Europe (including Britain) than in the USA. This is shown in Table 1.9. Part-time work in industrialized countries is generally the largest component of the flexible, atypical, or contingent labour force, with temporary workers and the self-employed making up the rest. A British study (Hakim 1987) estimated the flexible labour force at 30 per cent of all employment in 1981 rising to 35 per cent in 1986. More than half of all flexible workers were part-timers (54%), with self-employment and temporary work at 29 per cent and 17 per cent respectively. However the categories, in practice, were not discrete: it was not uncommon for workers to combine two of them, such as part-time and temporary work, with some even combining all three. A follow-up study (Watson 1994) found that by 1993 the British flexible workforce had grown to 38 per cent of which part-timers had increased their share. The continuing expansion of part-time work in fact appears to be a long-term trend largely accounted for by changing economic structure (Beatston 1995*a*).

TABLE 1.10. *The flexible labour force in the USA, 1973–1993*
(% of total employment)

	Part-time	Temporary*	Self-employed**
1973	16.6	n/a	6.7
1979	17.6	0.5 (1982)	7.1
1989	18.1	1.1	7.5
1993	18.8	1.5	7.8

Notes: * Temporary and employment agencies.
** In 1948 self-employment was 12.1%.

Source: Mishel and Bernstein (1994: tables 4.12, 4.24, 4.26).

Although women's share of part-time work seems, as we have noted earlier, to be stabilizing, with the share of men expanding (Watson 1994).

The dominance of part-time work in the flexible labour force is also a feature of the US data, as Table 1.10 shows. In the USA the growth of part-time work has undoubtedly been a function of the growth in the service sector with young people, adult women, and the retired constituting the bulk of the labour force (Mishel and Bernstein 1994: 220–2). In Britain too these groups are those normally to be found in the growing service industries, especially adult women who made up 57 per cent of all employment in the service sector in 1993 and 81 per cent of part-timers (*Employment Gazette*, October 1994).

Part-time work is however generally associated with inferior pay and conditions. Indeed, the extension of full-time pay and benefits to part-timers is the subject of a possible European Union (EU) Directive, and a 1994 legal decision in the British House of Lords extended, pro rata, unfair dismissal and redundancy rights to part-time workers on the grounds that differential rights under British statutes were discriminatory against women—the majority of part-time workers.

Yet the position remains that part-time work still pays generally much less than full-time. For example in Britain part-time female average hourly earnings in 1993 were 74 per cent of those for female full-time workers (*Labour Research*, July 1994) and in the USA the corresponding figure for 1989 was 76 per cent (Mishel and Bernstein 1994: Table 4.16).

Despite the unfavourable rewards, part-time working continues to grow reflecting employer demand and workers' preferences, although Mishel and Bernstein (1994: 219–20) argue that the growth in part-time work in the USA has little to do with worker preference. This stress on the 'involuntary' nature of part-time work has also been the position of the TUC in its claim that flexible work largely arises from high unemployment and employed workers' fears of losing their jobs (Bassett 1995).

The Flexible Organization

Whilst in the external labour market full-time permanent employment has been in decline in both Britain and the USA, and has been increasingly replaced by more flexible forms, *within* organizations more flexible ways of working have also become widespread. This so-called 'workplace transformation' has been an important development in both countries,[15] although in Britain a more flexible approach to hours and shiftwork has also been evident alongside the reorganization of jobs and work.

The Dunlop Commission's first, fact-finding report (Commission on the Future of Worker-Management Relations, May 1994) was directly concerned with the extent of work transformation in organizations and its impact upon organizational performance and productivity.[16] The Commission drew upon Osterman's (1994) workplace survey. He found 'substantial use' of flexible work practices (i.e. about 35% of private sector establishments with 50 or more employees). This evidence of 'transformed' or 'high performance' US workplaces is however a recent development and may prove as short-lived as earlier experiments. Nor are the productivity outcomes clear although the evidence is that greater economic effects accrue from introducing a systematic, comprehensive range of innovations over a sustained period. A number of studies also show that a by-product of the innovations has been more investment in education and training (Commission on the Future of Worker-Management Relations, May 1994: 45–6). Furthermore, international competitive pressures are among the variables encouraging the adoption of flexible work practices (Osterman 1994: 186).[17]

International competition also seems to have been a factor in British developments which have been termed 'new wave manufacturing strategies' (Storey 1994). The 'new wave' also seems to have been extensive. The Workplace Industrial Relations Survey (Millward *et al.* 1992) found that 36 per cent of establishments had changed their working practices, a proportion remarkably similar to Osterman's for the USA. This, scarcely concealed enthusiasm of commentators for workplace transformation is not however universally shared in actual workplaces. Academic, critical work on an international scale is also beginning to reflect this as, for example, Babson's (1995) collection and, in Britain, Adler (1994) and Garrahan and Stewart (1992).

British employers seem to have a greater preoccupation with flexibility in the form of hours of work, extending much beyond traditional shiftwork which itself has been subjected to variations in the frequency of shifts and their length, as well as variations in the actual days worked in each cycle. Shiftworking arrangements, on recent evidence, extend to more than 18 per cent of all employees although other practices, such

TABLE 1.11. *Employees'* patterns of working hours by gender in the UK, 1993*
(% of all employees)

	All Employees	Men	Women
Flexitime	11.9	10.4	13.5
Annualized hours contract**	9.0	8.5	9.5
Term-time working	5.3	2.1	8.7
Job-sharing	1.1	0.3	1.9
Nine-day fortnight	0.6	0.8	0.4
Four-and-a-half-day week	2.9	3.4	2.3
Shiftwork	18.1	21.4	14.4

Notes: * Full-time and part-time.
** Contracted annual hours can be varied throughout the year in accordance with seasonal and demand fluctuations.
Source: Watson (1994: 242, table 3).

as flexitime and 'annualization', now cover significant numbers of employees. Recent survey data on British patterns of working hours is shown in Table 1.11.

The length of the working week and patterns of hours worked have long been the subjects of major disagreement between Britain and other members of the EU given the British tendency to work longer hours, have shorter holidays, be more likely to be shiftworkers, and have less legal protection than their EU counterparts (Bridgford and Stirling 1994: 215). British employers and the Conservative government argued strongly against the proposed Directive to limit the working week to forty-eight hours and night shifts to eight hours, on the grounds that this inflexibility would add to British costs and undermine competitiveness. The Directive was eventually approved, by EU qualified majority, as a 'health and safety' issue. This interpretation, which avoided the unanimity procedure, was unsuccessfully challenged by the British government in the European Court in 1996.[18]

Unemployment and Job Creation

The dispute over the working time Directive reveals the wider British government view that maximum labour market and employment flexibility contributes to competitiveness, minimizes unemployment, and creates jobs. Its role model, for many years, has been the USA. The major international recessions of the 1970s and 1980s pushed unemployment rates to levels unprecedented since the 1930s. The increases were especially marked in the UK and West Germany, and in Europe, in the 1990s, mass, long-term unemployment was generating severe social and political

TABLE 1.12. *Standardized unemployment rates in six advanced industrial countries, 1973–1993 (monthly averages, % of total labour force)*

	1973	1983	1993
USA	4.8	9.5	6.7
UK	3.0	12.4	10.3
Canada	5.5	11.8	11.1
Japan	1.3	2.6	2.5
West Germany*	0.8	7.7	5.8
France	2.7	8.3	11.6

Note: * 1993 data are for Germany.

Source: Mishel and Bernstein (1994: table 8.20); *Employment Outlook* (1994: 203, table K).

TABLE 1.13. *Jobs created in advanced industrial countries, 1979–1992 (%)**

	1979–89	1989–92
USA	18.7	0.2
UK	5.7	–3.4
Canada	20.1	–2.0
Japan	12.0	5.2
West Germany	6.8	5.3
France	2.6	0.8

Note: * New jobs created 1979–89 and 1989–92 as a percentage of employment in 1979 and 1989.

Source: Mishel and Bernstein (1994: 354, table 8.15).

problems. Table 1.12 shows the rise in unemployment in the years after 1973. The USA was, however, performing much better: from the mid-1980s US unemployment began to fall to levels significantly below Europe as a whole: by the end of 1994 the average for the EU was 11.5 per cent, for the UK 9.2 per cent, and for the USA 5.7 per cent (*Employment Gazette*, January 1995).

The US economy's superior unemployment record is partly associated with its capacity for job creation. This was especially the case in the 1980s, although when measuring new jobs as a percentage of employment Canada had a better record and Japan, with a long-term unemployment rate much lower than the USA (Table 1.11), was not far behind in job creation. By the 1990s the US performance was not impressive—as Table 1.13 reveals. However, the cyclical employment data does seem to confirm the view that the US economy has a greater ability to recover quickly from recession, as is clear from Table 1.14. It is also now well established that

　　　　　　Economic and Employment Contexts

TABLE 1.14. *Civilian employment* in the USA, UK, Germany, and Japan,*
1992–1994 (millions)

		USA	UK	Germany	Japan
1992	Q4	118.0	25.0	28.6	64.6
1993	Q1	118.4	25.0	28.4	64.4
	Q2	119.0	25.0	28.3	64.4
	Q3	119.5	25.1	28.2	64.5
	Q4	120.3	25.1	28.1	64.7
1994	Q1	121.6	25.0	28.0	64.6
	Q2	122.6	25.0	28.0	64.6

Note: * OECD, national definitions.

Source: *Employment Gazette* (November 1994).

the US labour force is more mobile and that US management still has a relatively greater ability to hire, fire, or change working conditions than other countries; and US workers are less likely to be out of work for long periods than in Europe or Japan (Freeman 1993: 5). Yet, for a number of reasons, it is still not self-evident that the greater flexibility of the US labour force explains its better record on job creation and unemployment.

First, Europe's unemployment rates were actually lower than those of the USA in the 1950s and 1960s when European countries had already established extensive job rights and employment security provisions. Secondly, the UK government increasingly deregulated its labour market, on the US model, in the 1980s and 1990s yet, although job creation improved, the UK unemployment record has been little different from the EU average over the same period, although in recent years British unemployment has fallen below the EU average. Thirdly, high and persistent levels of unemployment in EU countries, in contrast to the USA, must be partly explained by the greater centralization of macroeconomic controls in those countries and the consistent policy emphasis, since the early 1980s, on containing inflation at the expense of employment. Fourthly, there is even some doubt that the British labour force has become significantly more flexible. It has been maintained by the TUC (Bassett 1995) that temporary work and self-employment is not growing and that, although part-time jobs are increasing, this is a well-established long-term trend only marginally related to the government's policy of encouraging greater flexibility in employment. The TUC's scepticism is also partly echoed in a Department of Employment study which was only able to maintain that 'on balance it can reasonably be concluded that the British labour market has become more flexible' (Beatston 1995*b*:

55–6). Furthermore, even if greater labour market flexibility contributes to higher employment and lower unemployment, it does so at a price. Employment insecurity in organizations is not a setting conducive to employee commitment, labour–management cooperation, and investment in a training culture. Additionally, in the case of the USA, as in Britain, job creation is closely associated with the expansion of service sector jobs which are, as we have seen, likely to be part-time, lower paid, and with minimal benefits.[19]

CONCLUSIONS

Over the past twenty years it is clear that there have been major changes in the structural context of industrial relations in both the USA and Britain.[20] Furthermore, these changes, despite some differences in direction and impact, have been remarkably similar. Of course this should not surprise us: structural changes of the kind we have described are familiar features of industrialized economies. Yet the USA and Britain may well be different from the rest in so far as economic 'change' may be a less accurate description than 'decline' and, less arguably, because their service sectors are significantly larger than those of other comparable countries.

The dominance of the service sector may, however, be more than a reflection of inevitable economic development. The two economies may constitute a separate 'service sector' model distinguished from economies where manufacturing remains of greater relative importance—notably Germany and Japan. The greater manufacturing strength of these economies, and the generally inferior productivity performance of services relative to manufacturing, can explain their superior long-term productivity performance and they are now being joined by the rising new economies of the Pacific Rim region. The Japanese have also competed with great success in once traditional Western markets and have, through direct inward investment, made great inroads in key manufacturing sectors, especially in automobiles and electronics in both countries as well as in basic industries such as steel and rubber in the USA.

British and US manufacturers have responded to global competition partly by determined attempts to improve their performance through major changes in work organization, frequently through adapting Japanese methods and innovations to their own special circumstances, or by entering into joint ventures with their former competitors within their own domestic markets. At the same time, employers have taken much stronger positions on costs, especially unit labour costs, through their policies on pay, productivity, and numbers employed. These responses have made a direct impact on US and British performance and competitiveness in manufacturing and there is some recent evidence that service sector productivity may be improving and contributing to overall economic performance, although the longer term evidence of relative decline remains intact.

The large and growing service sectors in both countries, combined with technological change, have radically disturbed traditional occupational structures especially in favour of professional, managerial, and high skill content jobs. However for both countries this does not imply the disappearance of manual work even though it will be reduced and transformed by technology. Furthermore, the continuing rise in the part-time labour force, mainly in the service sector, is providing large numbers of new jobs in occupations which are low in status, skill, and earnings. This growth in part-time work is largely associated with the increasing growth of women in the labour force, although the decline of traditional full-time, male employment is now having a positive impact, in both countries, on the number of men in the part-time, service sector labour force.

Yet despite the similarities in labour force developments there is substantial evidence, and on all indicators, that the US labour force is more flexible than the British. This arguably contributes towards lower unemployment levels in the USA, partly because of a superior record on job creation relative to Britain. However, it also implies higher lay-off as well as hiring rates, and the new jobs are largely associated with low earnings contributing to greater earnings inequality.

The implications for industrial relations of such far-reaching changes in economic and employment contexts can be very great. Trade union membership is directly influenced by rising unemployment levels, especially given its preponderance in occupations in which membership is traditionally strong—such as male, manual work. Similarly, the rise of the service sector permanently diminishes the highly unionized, goods-producing sector and growing part-time work increases recruitment and retention problems for unions, again especially where it is concentrated in low-paying, service sector occupations. The rise of services is, at the same time, associated with the growth of managerial and professional occupations. These occupational groups are normally more resistant to unionization than blue collar workers and, in the USA, they are also excluded from the law's protections for unionization and collective bargaining, an aspect to which we shall return in Chapter 2.

Changes in the contexts which weaken trade unions also provide opportunities for employers to strengthen their bargaining power. In particular they allow for a freer hand in reducing employment, reorganizing work, and containing labour costs. Additionally, employers in industries subject to international competition will be able to press for cutbacks and concessions from their employees even if organized in trade unions, and even if such sacrifices are not always fully warranted.

Of course none of these outcomes is inevitable, as the differing experiences of countries testify, and even when they do occur the weight to be attached to each of the different elements of structural change is open to dispute. We must also allow for the influence of the political process, public policy and the law, and the policies and actions of trade unions as well as employers in the drawing of conclusions. This second group of influences is the subject matter of the next chapter. We shall return to the question of explaining the relative importance of these influences in greater detail in Chapter 3.

NOTES

1. For a comprehensive, recent, comparative review of the US and Canadian experience see Kumar (1993).
2. Manufacturing and services are frequently related, overlapping activities.
3. The 'right-to-work' states are discussed in Ch. 3, n. 9.
4. The scale and speed of the contraction was at least as significant as the contraction itself. It took place over ten years from 1984–94 with the bulk of the closures after 1990. See also Ch. 2.
5. Of course this matters for trade unions with membership concentrated in the declining manufacturing sector as well as having implications for the balance of power within the trade union movement given the growing dominance of white collar union membership.
6. See also Castells and Aoyama (1994: 26–7).
7. US productivity performance was reviewed, in the early 1990s, in the context of labour–management relations by Bluestone and Bluestone (1992: 82–9).
8. See also Dean and Sherwood (1994).
9. The American concept of 'middle class', which emerged late in the 19th century, is both elusive and politically potent. In distinguishing it from the rich and the poor it does not imply a state of equilibrium but 'an all-encompassing process of escalation that will eventually include everyone' (Bellah *et al.* 1985: 119). Membership of the middle class is for 'working people' who are sometimes referred to as 'working class' but not in the European sense. Being middle class involves expectations of reasonably secure, comfortable, lifestyles which over the past twenty years have often been frustrated by economic changes affecting jobs and incomes and largely ensuring that 'developments, economic or otherwise, which did not please this broad middle stratum would not succeed' (Shafer 1991: 246). Trade union members, in 'good' blue collar jobs would see themselves as part of the middle class.
10. Whilst these figures relate only to manufacturing workers they are broadly representative of the pay of workers in the wider economy (Freeman 1994*a*: 12).
11. A recent review of this literature and commentary within an industrial relations context is to be found in Bluestone and Bluestone (1992), especially ch. 4.
12. The occupational data in Table 1.7 and subsequent tables have to be interpreted with caution. The comparability of the data is satisfactory but the

projections pose problems. The OECD statisticians warn that the projections are 'simply extrapolation of past trends ... and are therefore insensitive to different outcomes as new products and services arise and the labour market adjusts, through changes in relative pay, to imbalances in the demand for, and supply of, different occupations' (*Employment Outlook* 1994: 85).

13. This is not to suggest that technological change is an independent variable. Technological advances and innovations are subject to control. They have to be introduced into work situations by conscious decision and can be applied in different ways.

14. See *Employment Outlook* (1994: 90–92) for a review of this literature. Castells and Aoyama (1994) also discuss the 'polarization' thesis.

15. See Ch. 5. For a British overview and analysis of these changes see Storey (1994). Recent additions to the US literature include Doeringer *et al.* (1991), Appelbaum and Batt (1994), and Osterman (1994).

16. The Commission's recommendations, which are discussed in detail in Ch. 7, carefully distinguished between 'indirect participation or representation' and 'direct employee participation and work redesign' noting that the latter is currently more widespread than the former which was characteristic of 'earlier periods' (Commission on the Future of Worker-Management Relations, May 1994: 48).

17. Workforce transformation, including the Osterman survey, and its extent in the USA and Britain is discussed, in detail, in Ch. 5.

18. Examples of average annual hours worked per person per year for 1993 were: Canada 1,719, Finland 1,744, Germany 1,588, Norway 1,416, Spain 1,905, Sweden 1,507, USA 1,776. Japan recorded 1,965 in 1992, the most recently available figure (*Employment Outlook* 1994: 196, table 3). For the USA, multiple job-holding is a practice which is adding significantly to the average hours worked by employees (Mishel and Bernstein 1994: 230, table 4.21).

19. For a recent, comparative contribution to the flexibility debate see Blank (1994).

20. A readable 'official' summary of structural change in the USA is to be found in the Dunlop Commission Report (Commission on the Future of Worker-Management Relations, May 1994), 'The Changing Environment for Worker-Management Relations', ch. 2: 1–27. For Britain, the House of Commons Employment Committee Reports (Employment Committee 1994*b*; 1994*c*), contain similar material, including comparative data, but in a less concise and less accessible form.

2

Politics, Public Policy, and the Law

its primary practitioners and theoreticians in the realm of industrial
relations declared the American system near perfect, a thing of won-
der in which bargaining and decision-making could be ceded to . . .
unions and corporations unimpeded by an intrusive state or the
demands of political parties.

(Dubofsky 1994: 198)

collective *laissez-faire* . . . the governmental policy of leaving the regulation of terms and conditions of employment to the joint voluntary
machinery of collective bargaining . . . the method best adapted to the
needs of industry and to the demands of the national character . . .
involved the Ministry in the negative commitment of keeping the
law out of a coercive role in industrial relations, and the positive
one of maintaining a smooth-running triangular relationship between
the Ministry, the employers and the trade union movement.

(Freedland 1992: 276)

The satisfaction of the British and Americans with their systems of
industrial relations in the years following World War II was built upon
their favourable view of its foundations in voluntarism and corporatism
and, perhaps especially, the widespread belief in the efficacy of Keynesian
economic policies or the 'politics of productivity' (Dubofsky 1994: 198).
But the favourable political, public policy, and legal contexts within which
the two countries' industrial relations systems flourished began to shift
when it eventually became clear that national economic success and progress were not easily guaranteed and that relative economic failure was
believed to be linked, by key policy-makers and their advisers, to the
Keynesianism and voluntarist/corporatist ideology of industrial relations
and the industrial relations establishment.

Similarities can also be seen in political continuities. For example, the
old New Deal alliance between the Democrats and organized labour and
the constructive opposition, even support, of liberal Republicans, gave
a stability and continuity to American society and government right up
to the 1970s which was, in substance, little different from the long political and economic consensus between the 'one nation' Conservatives and
the Labour Party's right wing—whichever party was in government—
which lasted until Mrs Thatcher and her backers turned the Conservative Party away from the legacy of Disraeli, beginning with the removal

of Edward Heath from the party leadership in 1975. Furthermore, the remarkable political concurrence of President Reagan and Mrs Thatcher in the decade after 1979 confirmed the similarity of, as well as strengthening, the influences undermining the New Deal alliance and 'Butskellite'[1] consensus. The early 1980s also witnessed a process of mutual influence and example in both ideology and policy as both governments sought to deregulate product and labour markets. In that, of course, the British had a longer road to travel and had the US example to follow, and although Mrs Thatcher's enthusiasm for the journey could not be matched, her successor in government, John Major, maintained 'Thatcherite' policies, or, at the least, was required to genuflect to them.

But though we can find intriguing similarities and parallels in outcomes we must not pass over the major differences in political, governmental, and legal structures and processes which ensure that in British and American industrial relations, as in other areas, much remains distinctive and is likely to continue to be so. Here, four features stand out. First, the continuing existence and electability (despite four successive defeats from 1979 to 1992) of the Labour Party which now, in government with an overwhelming majority, could still provide positive outcomes for collective bargaining and the trade unions. This party-political context to industrial relations is of course not absent in the USA but remains very different in form and outcome from the UK. Secondly, membership of the now enlarged European Union (EU) is already a significant influence on British individual employment law and a potential influence on collective labour law, an influence which is likely to increase with the removal of the Conservative government. In contrast, the North American Free Trade Agreement (NAFTA) has none of the purposes, structure, or functions of the EU although the European experience may prove useful in any future attempts to translate NAFTA into an agreement with a social dimension (Adams and Turner 1994). Thirdly, and of great importance, US politics and government have always been, and still are, deeply influenced by regional, state, and local influences to a far greater extent than in Britain (even given the devolutionary plans of the Labour Government) resulting in very different constitutional and law-making processes and different industrial relations outcomes. Fourthly, US employers undoubtedly differ from their British counterparts in their attitudes towards, and actions against, trade unions and collective bargaining. In US contexts (which generally favour employers' interests) this can be the decisive factor in explaining the continuing weakness of the labour movement.

These, and other similarities and differences, underly the themes of this chapter beginning with political and public policy contexts (mainly from 1979); continuing with an analysis of frameworks and selected themes from the legal contexts to industrial relations; and, in the final part, drawing some general conclusions.

POLITICS AND PUBLIC POLICY

'Revolutionary' Politics

In 1994, the newly elected Speaker Gingrich of the US House of Representatives frequently spoke of the 'revolutionary' policies of the Republicans who for the first time for forty years had won majorities in both chambers with a mandate for change. It was perhaps a more significant victory than that of Ronald Reagan in 1980. Although Reagan's policy approach was similar, he held office with the Democrats in firm control of the House and finally regaining the Senate, which they had lost on Reagan's 'coat tails', in 1986. In that context the style and policies of the Republicans in 1994, especially those newly elected, were more akin to those of the British Conservatives at their victory in 1979 under Margaret Thatcher's leadership than they were to Reagan and his fellow Republicans when they assumed a less complete control of the reins of power.

Although the British Conservatives had only been out of office since 1974, their return to power in 1979 also brought in a period of 'revolutionary' change, which proved to be the longest period of continuous Conservative government since World War II and, even without Mrs Thatcher retained a commitment to 'Thatcherism'.[2] The critique of 'big' government, the stress on reducing the state's fiscal role and balancing the budget, the attack on the welfare state and dependency, and the admiration for 'Victorian values' were all characteristic features of Thatcherism and remarkably similar to the 'revolutionary' philosophy of the American Republicans in 1994.

Yet in one sense Mrs Thatcher's 'revolution' went further: it repudiated the 'one nation' philosophy[3] of the Conservative Party established by Disraeli in his bid for the emerging working class vote; replaced the patrician 'grandees' by the new 'self-made' men and women, and rejected the consensus politics which had dominated British politics and policy since the Churchill, wartime coalition government. A manifestation of the rejection of consensus was in industrial relations. Henceforth industrial relations policy was contingent upon economic policy,[4] and trade unions, in particular, were seen as impediments to the operation of efficient, flexible labour markets. Trade unions could also be seen as unpatriotic, such as when membership of an independent trade union was considered incompatible with intelligence surveillance work.[5] They could also be the 'enemy within' as Mrs Thatcher described the leadership and striking members of the National Union of Mineworkers (NUM) in 1984–5. Her view of industrial relations and trade unions was however paralleled by the actions of Ronald Reagan in his destruction of PATCO and in that respect the Reagan/Thatcher comparison is strong.

Striking the Enemy Within

In industrial relations terms, both Thatcher and Reagan established their credentials early by their approach to strikes. The first Thatcher election victory was won in the wake of the public sector strikes under Labour in the 'winter of discontent' of 1978–9. In another early test, the publicly owned steel industry's newly hired Scottish born American chairman, Ian MacGregor, faced out and defeated a national strike lasting three months in 1980 in which there were suspicions that the government had been covertly involved to ensure a victory for British Steel (Kessler and Bayliss 1992: 127). A year later President Reagan acted more directly in a strike, albeit an illegal one, dismissing 12,000 federally employed air traffic controllers and decertifying their union (PATCO). It is also commonplace to argue that the 1981 action of the President against federal employees was a major influence upon private sector companies in their increasing use of permanent replacements to break legal strikes (Weiler 1990: 20) and in this they would be helped by workers demoralized by such a major and visible defeat as that of PATCO (Goldfield 1987: 186). Employers were however also likely to be encouraged to replace strikers by foreign competition in manufacturing and deregulation in airlines, trucking, and rail—all industries with high levels of unionization. Whatever the explanations, there was undoubtedly a clear trend towards the use of permanent replacement of strikers, especially after 1985 (Gould 1994: 185–6). Striker dismissal was of course a tactic always available to British employers under the law but it was made even easier, specifically in the case of selective dismissal, by the 1982 Employment Act.[6]

If PATCO was a turning-point in making the strike a much less effective trade union sanction against US employers, the National Union of Mineworkers' (NUM) defeat in 1985 after almost a year on strike undoubtedly demoralized British trade union members and, especially, their leaders, fearful of the swingeing fines and sequestration of assets available to the courts. It was even possible to find close parallels between the PATCO and NUM strikes (Ghilarducci 1986).

The 1984–5 British miners' strike was against the public sector employer, the National Coal Board (NCB), chaired by the same Ian MacGregor who had been at British Steel four years earlier (MacGregor 1986). However covert, later overt, government involvement decisively tipped the balance against the NUM (Adeney and Lloyd 1986; Beynon 1985; Towers 1985) and within ten years the industry had been privatized, and its state-protected electricity generation market largely removed as

TABLE 2.1. *Labour disputes:* working days lost per 1,000 employees in six industrialized countries, all industries and services 1980–1993*

	1980–4	1984–93
USA	160	70
UK	480	240
Canada	660	350
Japan	10	—
West Germany	50	40
France	90	50

Note: * National definitions.

Source: Bird (D 1994: 434, table 1); Kessler and Bayliss (1992: 214, table 11.5).

part of a reconstruction of the energy sector. From 250 deep-mined pits in 1974 employing more than 250,000, by 1994 there were 16 employing under 10,000, with the NUM facing extinction, like PATCO in 1981, but in this case as a result of the virtual elimination by the government of the industry which sustained it (Milne 1994). The NUM's defeat in 1984–5 was then followed, only a year later, by that of the powerful printing union (SOGAT) by Rupert Murdoch's News International. However SOGAT in due course was to merge with the other major print union, the NGA, to form one union for the printing and related industries, the GPMU.

The major setbacks for British and American organized labour in the 1990s coincided with a substantial fall in working days lost through strikes, as Table 2.1 shows. Table 2.1 raises a number of interesting aspects regarding public policy. In Britain, the legislation of the 1980s undoubtedly made striking a far more difficult option for unions to take but employers only rarely took advantage of the new laws: even the legal actions against the National Union of Mineworkers during the 1984–5 strike were initiated by union members, albeit fully backed and encouraged by the employer (National Coal Board) and the government. Yet strike incidence undoubtedly fell and Mrs Thatcher regularly maintained that her main achievement, in office, was to tame the trade unions. However, a decline in strikes and days lost through strikes was an international phenomenon in the 1980s which was present in countries where trade union strength was maintained, such as Canada where total membership increased between 1980 and 1992 and density (membership as a proportion of non-agricultural employment) was 37 per cent in 1980 and 37.4 per cent in 1992 (Kumar 1993: 13 table 1). For the OECD countries as a whole, working days lost through labour disputes per 1,000 employees fell, between 1984 to 1993, from 300 to 100 and showed a small downward trend into the 1990s (Bird 1994: 434 table 1).

For Britain this general fall in strike activity suggests the impact of the economic cycle and global competition in the 1980s and into the 1990s where unions, faced with job losses and even closures, generally chose the path of non-resistance (Kessler and Bayliss 1995: 260–3). Nor was this loss in bargaining power restored as the international economy revived in the mid-1980s, given the continuing importance of global competition putting downward pressure on costs and employment levels.

Public Policy, Unions, and Employers

These pressures were of course also at work in the USA shifting the balance of bargaining power firmly against the unions where public policy, as in Britain, remained hostile throughout the 1980s even though different in form. The Reagan and Bush administrations, aside from the PATCO intervention and the making of anti-union appointments to the NLRB, generally did not intervene in industrial relations processes, leaving unions to the tender mercies of powerful employers using, to their full advantage, existing labour laws, interpreted by a generally helpful judiciary, as well as resorting to the use of some dubious quasi-legal practices. In contrast, the British government played an active anti-union role in public sector industrial relations and industrial disputes. It also enacted, in a space of thirteen years, eight major statutes regulating trade unions and diminishing the role of collective bargaining. However, this highly active role for public policy has not generally encouraged private sector employers to imitate the government or to use the new, legal sanctions against trade unions. Hence employer action interacts with public policy in contrasting ways. In the USA, it normally runs with the grain of a public policy which only rarely resists, and mostly in practice supports, employer actions against unions; in Britain, employers commonly prefer to pursue industrial relations policies which are only partly influenced by governmental, anti-union preoccupations and actions.

For US unions, however, 1992 was a promising year. The election of President Clinton alongside solid Democratic majorities in Congress promised some reward for the labour unions' part in Democratic electoral success. The early list proposed by the AFL-CIO and its affiliates included opposition to the North American Free Trade Agreement (NAFTA) in its potential impact on jobs; a bill outlawing the growing employer practice, since the early 1980s, of permanently replacing striking workers; the reform of the funding of health care to guarantee adequate provision by employers; and the raising of the minimum wage. The outcome, except for the 1996 success on the minimum wage, was a major disappointment for the unions. NAFTA became law in 1993 with minimal safeguards against job losses and despite a major and expensive lobbying effort by the AFL-CIO. The Workplace Fairness Bill banning permanent replacement of strikers fell to a Senate filibuster in the summer of 1994 followed by the final collapse of radical health care reform in October. Then, in the elections of 1994, the Republicans took control of both House and Senate for the first time in forty years.

The retention of the Republicans' hold on Congress in the 1996 elections may have confirmed long-term electoral changes undermining Democratic control. For the labour unions and collective bargaining it was also perhaps a more important outcome than President Clinton's second term victory. Even under a Democratic Congress and Presidency from 1992–4 the unions gained little and the loss of both House and Senate after 1994 revealed the major problems facing the labour movement. The first indications, early in 1995, were the proposals to repeal the Davis–Bacon Act of 1931 (which protects the pay levels of workers on federal construction projects) and a proposed bill amending the National Labor Relations Act of 1935 to permit employers to be involved in initiating, or participating in, employee organizations.[7] For its part, the Clinton administration countered with proposed legislation to raise the minimum wage and in March of 1995 President Clinton used his executive order powers to prohibit future federal contracts with companies which hired permanent replacements during strikes. The minimum wage legislation, after a high profile AFL-CIO campaign, did eventually secure majorities but the executive order, which faced strong opposition in Congress and from the employers, was eventually overturned in the courts leaving only a possible appeal to the Supreme Court.

The political changes of 1994–6 in the USA have clearly signalled a further potential tightening of public policy against trade unions and collective bargaining. In Britain, with the replacement of Mrs Thatcher in 1990, it was widely believed that there would follow a partial rapprochement with the trade unions, and public opinion, through the polls, was indicating little support for further anti-union legislation. Yet the Trade Union Reform and Employment Rights Act was passed by Parliament in 1993. This in particular further threatened trade union finances through more stringent conditions applying to the system of automatic employer deduction of union dues from pay (the 'check-off') and permitted employers to offer pay and conditions inducements to employees to abandon their trade union membership. The Advisory, Conciliation, and Arbitration Service (ACAS) was also, under the Act, no longer required to encourage collective bargaining, a *de jure* duty which dated back to its foundation in 1974 and *de facto* much earlier under the old Ministry of Labour and its successors in the machinery of government. Then in November 1996 the Conservative Government published proposals for further legislation to limit industrial action in 'essential services' (Department of Trade and Industry 1996*a*; *b*), notably public transport and the postal service which experienced a number of bitterly fought strikes throughout 1996. Although the Labour Party challenged these proposals in opposition (see the conclusions) the public sector and public sector pay remain as major problems for the Blair Government.

Social Dimensions and Social Clauses

The anti-union policies of Mrs Thatcher and Mr Major did however co-exist with countervailing pressures, primarily those arising from British membership of the European Union (EU) and the continuing pragmatism of British employers. EU influences were evident in the 1993 Act in the increased regulation of the form, and terms, of employment contracts, protection against unfair dismissal for pregnant employees, and the extension of maternity leave to a basic provision of fourteen weeks. Additional health and safety provisions were also included in the Act, forming part of the EU Commission's increasing role in standardizing health and safety regulations across the member states. Other EU legislation includes the regulation of working hours; protection for the pay and benefits of employees affected by business transfers; and the extension of protective redundancy and unfair dismissal procedures to part-time workers.[8]

The influence of the EU's social dimension has however largely been confined to extending the employment rights of individual workers. Collective industrial relations have been reserved as matters for member states. A recent exception to this approach, with potentially major implications for Britain, has been in the area of informational and consultation rights for employees. This is currently primarily through the European Works Council (EWC) Directive which many British multi-nationals implemented on a voluntary basis despite the British 'opt-out', in 1992, from the Social Chapter.[9] Less directly, the absence of works councils (on the model widespread in the EU) was beginning to cause legal difficulties for the Conservative government through directives which require companies to provide specified information and consultation to their *employees*. The most recent examples concern cases in which employees are affected by redundancy and transfer of business ownership. Prior to 1994, under British employment legislation, workers affected in these ways could only exercise their rights to information and consultation through recognized trade unions. At the same time, British employers have no *legal* compulsion, under any circumstances, to recognize trade unions and can derecognize them by unilateral decision. Hence the statutory rights were conditional upon recognition and derecognition would remove them.

In June 1994 the European Court of Justice (ECJ) ruled that the UK's legislation was in breach of the two relevant Directives on redundancies and business transfers, in that the guaranteeing of information and consultation rights for employees affected required the election of representatives to consultative bodies. The British passed regulations amending British law in October 1995 to comply with the rulings. These regulations allow employers three options. They can consult representatives of recognized trade unions, representatives elected by employees, or elected representatives of existing consultative councils or committees. However employers are able to choose which representatives to consult, which gives them the opportunity to bypass trade unions. Nor do the regulations require employers to set up permanent bodies, that is, they can be disbanded on completion of the redundancy or transfer processes. Consultation, in the case of redundancy, is also only required when twenty or more workers are affected.

The government's application of the ECJ rulings raised two wider, longer term issues concerning different approaches to representation and reform. First, the EU's emphasis on guaranteeing information and consultation rights through permanent, elected committees or councils (as, for example, the EWC) is at odds with the well-established British approach of primarily making these rights effective through trade unions on a voluntary recognition basis. Secondly, the EU's model of employee representation might offer a viable complement to declining representation via the 'single channel' of the trade unions as well as providing a platform for membership revival.[10]

In the shorter term, other than through a Labour government intervention, there is the possibility of a successful legal challenge to the Conservative government's application of the ECJ rulings.[11] It is also unlikely that British employers, in general, will take advantage of the greater opportunities to bypass the trade unions offered by the regulations. Their view of unions is still essentially pragmatic, including EU social dimension initiatives which allow for union involvement, as the example of the EWC, even under the British opt-out from the Social Chapter, illustrates.

The far more confrontational tradition of US employers, at least within the USA,[12] is strongly supportive of anti-union public policies and resistant to more supportive policies. Nor is there any equivalent of the power and influence of the European Union as a factor in moderating government policies. The North American Free Trade Agreement (NAFTA) has a minimal 'social dimension' with its side agreements on labour laws and labour standards, and under the General Agreement on Tariffs and Trade (GATT) trade unions, national and international federations, and the ILO continue to press for 'social clauses' as prior conditions for trade liberalization (*Employment Outlook* 1994: ch. 4)[13]. There have also been, as noted earlier, recent academic attempts to apply the experience and lessons of the EU case to NAFTA (Adams and Turner 1994). The social dimension of NAFTA must however be seen as no more than a political device to reduce opposition from the labour move-ments in the three countries. NAFTA is essentially a trade agreement that is greatly removed from the customs union, single market, and eco-nomic integration ambitions developed by the EU over almost forty years. Nor is it seriously addressing the 'social dumping' issue, that is, the relocation of enterprises in search of lower labour costs and labour standards.

THE ROLE OF THE LAW

Law, Immunities, and Constitutions

Collective bargaining in the USA, though primarily regulated by a series of federal laws passed over a period of fifty years between 1926 and 1976, remains strongly influenced in its form and outcomes by the pres-sures towards decentralization and localism inherent in the political system. These pressures are reinforced by an anti-federalist, states' rights ideology which extends back even beyond the formation of the USA and periodically re-emerges as a major force in American politics, most recently during and after the Congressional elections of 1994. Federal legislation can also be used to set a standard allowing for state variation. Many states, for example, have their own minimum wage laws along-side the federal minimum wage with some setting a level above the federal floor. The Taft–Hartley Act's union security provisions also allow states to go beyond the federal standard. The Act outlaws the pre-entry closed shop without exception whilst permitting individual states to enact their own laws banning the other less restrictive, forms of union security such as the union and agency shops. Even the more federalist Wagner Act has to be implemented in local contexts. The NLRB, for example, discharges its functions primarily on a local basis via its regional offices. It has also been argued that the Wagner Act, in particular the NLRB's certification procedures, favour single plant localism, reinforcing decentralizing pressures, and inhibiting the development of national, as well as cross-plant, occupational unionism (Clark 1989; Cobble 1994). The sheer size of the USA also reinforces regional and local pressures. In Britain, as Phelps Brown (1986) observes, localism was undermined in early Victorian times, by an extensive railway network which greatly assisted the growth of national trade unions. In the USA, a comparable network never developed and even modern transportation systems and electronic communication have not so far succeeded in fully diluting well-entrenched localisms, strengthened by race, ethnicity, and language.

American localism and the tension between federal power and states' rights severely limit the capacity for radical change from both the left and the right. Change is also constrained by the constitutional doctrine and political practice of separation of powers, especially when the President's party is not in control of one, or both, chambers of Congress. In Britain, in contrast, radical changes in collective and individual employment laws are made possible by a constitutional and political system which to a high degree concentrates power in the leadership of the party which forms the government through an almost guaranteed, disciplined majority in the House of Commons and, under Conservative governments, this control also extends, except on rare occasions, to the House of Lords. Parliament is also constitutionally sovereign without any potential challenge from the equivalent of the US Supreme Court. However this sovereignty is now, to a degree, qualified by the EU treaties which bind the UK. The government is required to issue regulations or pass laws putting into effect EU 'legislation' which is normally in the form of Directives. However the treaties only extend to a limited number of issues and not all decisions can be taken under the qualified majority procedure. The outcome is that the authority of Parliament, on most issues and including *collective* labour law, is not seriously limited. Further, there is no constitutional limit on the tenure of office of the Prime Minister, although there are obvious political limits. A British Prime Minister's authority is limited when faced with dissident factions within the party or when forced to rely upon other parties for majorities; but even then holds the ultimate sanction of the power to call general elections when members can lose their seats and their livelihoods. This system of constitutional and political practices makes it possible to implement major programmes of statutory social and economic reform and, normally, without effective local and regional challenges, although devolutionary, nationalist pressures are beginning to disturb the settled order.

Yet despite the extensive powers available to British governments, the traditional system of industrial relations still guarantees a large measure of freedom to employers and trade unions to conduct their bargaining relationship voluntarily, with minimal intervention from the courts. Acts of Parliament grant immunities to trade unions (although these were restricted in the 1980s) in circumstances where, in promoting their legitimate purposes, they conflict with the common law—primarily in relation to breach of commercial and employment contracts.

In the USA the framework of labour laws at federal and state level complemented by the active role of quasi-judicial agencies, such as the National Labor Relations Board (NLRB), has provided a detailed set of 'positive' rights enforceable (or challengeable) in the courts. Whilst this contrasts with traditional British voluntarism protected by 'negative' immunities for trade unions, the American system was itself voluntarist before the New Deal legislation, and the Wagner Act, according to Senator Wagner himself, was not intended to disturb the capacity of

employers and unions to make their own voluntary, collective bargaining arrangements; the Act was only intended to establish collective
bargaining where employers stood in the way of their employees' wishes
(Dubofsky 1994: 128–31). In the event voluntarism has virtually disappeared in the private sector and this must largely be explained by the
non-cooperation of employers. In the public sector anti-union employer
actions are much less in evidence (Bronfenbrenner and Juravich 1995).

The restrictions on British voluntarism over the past twenty years have
taken two forms. First, *collective* labour law statutes have tightened the
controls on the trade unions' capacity to take effective industrial action;
have intervened in their internal procedures and methods of collecting
dues; and have restricted their freedom to pursue political purposes and
activities. Secondly, through individual employment legislation, there is
now a more detailed regulation of the employment relationship although
this has been increasingly amended and enlarged by the laws of the
European Community and European Union, a process which is still
continuing.[14]

Overall, though there are real contrasts between the two systems, and
their contexts and outcomes, the contrasts should not be exaggerated. If
the US system, unlike the British, tends more towards compromise, even
stalemate, it is still capable of radical change and action in times of emergency and national crisis under a strong President, as for example under
the New Deal and during World War II. Furthermore, in Britain a major
programme of social and economic reform emerged from the 1939–45
coalition government and remained almost completely intact under the
consensus politics of the two major parties for forty years. Furthermore,
even in the specific case of changes in the laws affecting labour, the scale
of the 'transformation' in Britain from 1980 to 1993 needs some ques-
tioning; and over the same period the legal contexts affecting US labour
were far from static. However, in the USA, voluntary recognition, for
example, is rare and this must largely be explained by effective employer
resistance.

Employers and the Right to Manage

The trade union legislation of the Thatcher era was far-reaching. It placed
severe legal constraints on trade unions and exposed their funds to crip-
pling fines and penal powers of sequestration by the courts at a time
when their membership was falling rapidly—threatening their finances,
influence, and bargaining power. Yet British employers in unionized
companies in the main refrained from taking advantage of this manifest
weakness, retaining their faith in collective bargaining even though they
decentralized the level at which they bargained with trade unions, largely

abandoning multi-employer and, to a large extent, corporate arrangements. Employers, by and large, also avoided litigation:[15] voluntarism has deep roots and offers substantial advantages to employers as well as unions and, tellingly, when the government was proposing, during 1992–3, to make collective agreements legally binding, the employers' objections influenced the dropping of the proposal, echoing the experience of the 1971 Industrial Relations Act.[16] Of course throughout the 1980s trade union derecognition did increase, some employers did take advantage of their new legal powers, and 'macho' management tactics were more common[17] but without a general change in employer actions. The EU's internal market also began to offer employers transnational mobility and 'whipsawing' as bargaining tactics although, as yet, the instances have been few[18] and over much of British industry a 'management offensive' on any significant scale has not yet emerged.

US employers had and have far fewer inhibitions and still retain their historic 'propensity to compete with one another in the product market, and to combine with one another against trade unions in the labour market' (Phelps Brown 1986: 207). Employer resources, political lobbying, and a Senate filibuster were deployed to great effect to help defeat the Labor Law Reform Bill in 1978 against the wishes of the President and majorities in both chambers. The 1994 measure outlawing permanent replacements for strikers (the Workplace Fairness Bill) also failed to overturn a filibuster. In 1995, defence turned to offence with the introduction of the Teamwork for Employees and Managers (TEAM) Bill amending Section 8(a)(2) of the National Labor Relations Act, that is, the section which bans company unions. At state level the present twenty-one 'right-to-work' states which outlaw all forms of employment conditional on union membership (the 'closed shop' *per se* was banned at federal level in 1947) sought to increase their numbers in the wake of local political and business campaigns and the efforts of the National Right-to-Work Committee and other trade associations and business pressure groups.[19] At corporate level, management consulting firms specializing in anti-union work began to emerge in the early 1950s, growing rapidly thereafter, and there is much evidence that both consultants and employers used illegal as well as legal tactics to achieve their ends, and to great effect.

Industrial Relations and the Courts

The courts have also provided a consistent route for employer success against striking workers. As early as 1938, that is, only three years after the NLRA guaranteed the right to conduct an 'economic' strike, the Supreme Court held that the employer's right to maintain production extended to the hiring of permanent replacements (*NLRB* v. *Mackay*

Radio & Telegraph Co. 1938). However a curious distinction was drawn by the Court in 1967 and 1970 in that workers 'permanently replaced' were not fired, that is they were still employees and entitled to preferential re-engagement.[20] Yet the practice of permanent replacement, though within the law after 1938, was not widely used by employers until the early 1980s. Since then, in big disputes outside the auto industry, permanent replacements have become a standard employer tactic in companies such as Phelps Dodge (in copper mining), Greyhound, Hormel Meatpacking, and International Paper (Bluestone and Bluestone 1992: *passim*). However the permanent replacement tactic has been less evident in recent years although it was notable, in the protracted triple company dispute in the Illinois town of Decatur where Bridgestone/ Firestone began hiring replacements early in 1995, eight months into the strike (James B. Parks 1995).

The permanent replacement of strikers is perhaps the most important example in which judicial interpretation appears to have frustrated the intentions of the Wagner Act and, from the unions' perspective, its use has effectively nullified the strike weapon, their only reasonably effective tactic against increasingly powerful, especially multinational, companies. Another important example relates to the intention of the 1935 Act to grant the right to unionize and bargain solely to 'employees', that is, excluding management and supervisors with the purpose of assisting the separation and independence of unions from management, thus making bargaining possible. Yet a 1980 Supreme Court decision (*NLRB* v. *Yeshiva University* 1980) ruled that university professors, although 'professionals' with rights to unionize, exercised significant 'managerial' functions which placed them beyond the Act's protection. This loss of protection argument returned in 1994 in the case of nurses exercising supervisory functions (*NLRB* v. *Health Care and Retirement Corporation of America* 1994).

The wider significance of these rulings is that they may be beginning to reflect the changes in technology and occupational skills discussed in Chapter 1, which are increasingly blurring job demarcations and distinctions and spreading 'managerial' and 'supervisory' responsibilities across traditional job hierarchies. In particular, the law could imperil the growing fashion for inter-job flexibility and teamwork in key industries, such as automobile manufacturing, by its threat to union organization. There are also implications for schemes placing workers on boards or joint labour–management programmes (Gould 1994: 142–9).

Mackay and the 'Golden Formula'

The law in Britain, as in the USA, consistently favours the interests of employers in matters of interpreting and applying the common law tradition, rooted in individual rights. This views the *collective* actions of trade unions, especially strikes, with suspicion, even incomprehension, and where statutes override the common law, judges' interpretation, in cases before them, will normally follow an anti-collectivist perspective.[21] The Mackay interpretation of the Wagner Act can be seen in this light; whilst in Britain even the two statutes of 1871 and 1875 protecting trade unions involved in strikes from the common law doctrine of restraint of trade and actions for criminal conspiracy did not deter the courts from seeking 'to check and subdue a growing labour collectivism . . . threatening property, freedom of contract, economic progress and individual rights' (Fox 1985: 179): they simply switched their attention to allowing claims for civil damages against trade unions involved in strikes or other industrial action as in the famous Taff Vale judgment of the House of Lords (the final court of appeal) in 1901.

The Taff Vale threat to trade union's finances, as well as a later legal challenge to the legitimacy of their political purposes in the 1909 Osborne judgement, occurred at a time when political opinion, spurred by the rise of the Labour Party, favoured giving trade unions unequivocal statutory protection to carry out their purposes. The outcome was two significant pieces of legislation. The first, the Trade Disputes Act of 1906, sought to control the courts' application of the common law to industrial disputes. The second, the Trade Union Act of 1913, protected the political aims of trade unions by the device of separating their funds for 'political' from those for 'general' purposes.

The Trade Disputes Act codified the peculiar British approach[22] to giving reasonable freedom to trade unions to engage in strikes and other forms of industrial action. From 1906, under the so-called 'golden formula', trade unions when acting 'in contemplation or furtherance of a trade dispute' were given immunity against claims for civil damages by employers.

The 'golden formula' continues to remain the framework within which British unions have been able to conduct industrial action, of which the most important form is the strike. However, under the Employment Act of 1982 there were three significant changes. First, the 'golden formula' was narrowed by altering the definition of a trade dispute 'wholly or mainly' to terms and conditions of employment, thus severely limiting the legality of 'political' strikes as, for example, against the privatization of a government service.[23] Secondly, for the first time since 1906, trade unions could be taken to court under actions for tort and sued for damages. Thirdly, it became much easier to dismiss strikers selectively (and permanently) without the employer being liable to individual actions for unfair dismissal at industrial tribunals.

The limiting of strikes mainly to 'terms and conditions' was only the beginning. In further legislation unofficial strikes (i.e. those taking place without the union's authority) became the responsibility of the union officials who could be sued; and secondary action (i.e. sympathy) strikes were banned as were those involving inter-union disputes and disputes against victimization. For lawful strikes, detailed balloting provisions were introduced in 1984, 1988, and 1993, as well as requirements to give notice to employers on the timing of ballots and time limits on the calling of any subsequent strike.[24] Injunctions were available to employers against unions failing to keep to the rules as well as punitive financial penalties through fines, asset sequestration, and even imprisonment.[25]

In general terms, strike action has always left British workers liable to dismissal. Under the common law, a strike is a serious breach of the individual employment contract, justifying dismissal: unlike in almost all other EU countries where a strike is a suspension of the contract of employment (Wedderburn 1992: 152). However in practice British employers rarely exercised their common law rights, if only for pragmatic reasons. Furthermore, prior to 1982, selective dismissal, perhaps of the strike leaders, made employers liable to claims for unfair dismissal on discriminatory grounds at an industrial tribunal. Hence an employer could only dismiss all of the strikers and would then be obliged to rehire all of them at the conclusion of the strike—an unlikely series of actions which effectively ruled out discrimination. The 1982 Act opened up discriminatory possibilities by introducing a time limit. Employers can now rehire individual employees on a selective basis three months after the date of the return to work. Anti-strike tactics can therefore involve dismissing all of them and then rehiring selectively without incurring unfair dismissal claims. Additionally, during the strike, and after, the employer is free to hire other employees to replace those dismissed and can offer them different terms and conditions. This clearly opens up de-unionization possibilities, perhaps following a strike deliberately provoked by the employer, especially in multinationals with the ability to transfer production and workers, and where unions are handicapped by high local unemployment and union weakness.

Despite different legal contexts, the scope available to employers in both countries is both wide and similar. In practice however, as we have already observed, British employers generally remain reluctant to take advantage of the changes in the law, unlike their US counterparts. The notable, and important, recent exception was the dispute at Timex, Dundee in Scotland in 1993.[26] Yet despite the general differences in employer attitudes and behaviour in the two countries, the fact remains that the opportunities, in law, available to British employers to neutralize the use of the strike by dismissal and permanent replacement tactics are in essence no different to those available to US employers.

There is, however, a difference in context. There have been legislative attempts in the USA to reverse the Mackay decision of 1938, the most recent in 1993–4 under the Democrats' Workplace Fairness Bill which secured majorities in both houses and was only defeated on a filibuster after attempts at a constructive compromise amendment (Gould 1994: 194–8). Additionally, President Clinton's Executive Order barring future federal contracts to companies using permanent replacement tactics during strikes did succeed in surviving strong Republican challenges in Congress only to be overturned in the courts. In Britain the prospect of restoring some meaning, in law, to the right to strike, in line with most other members of the EU, has for long been off the political agenda. Nor is the present Labour Government committed to reviving such a prospect except, perhaps, through an eventual replacement of the immunities by positive rights.

Dismantling Collective Bargaining

The other important area in which trade unions, in both countries, remain at a clear disadvantage, relative to employers, is in the regulation of procedures for recognition. The two approaches are, of course, radically different. The approach of the USA is closely regulated by laws which have been in place, without change in form, although not in application, for sixty years; the approach of Britain is still greatly influenced by the tradition of voluntarism or 'collective *laissez-faire*' although on two occasions in the 1970s, under both Conservative and Labour, statutory procedures were set up only to be abandoned—the last in 1980 largely for reasons of unworkability. However, the TUC continues to develop its proposals for a workable statutory procedure, partly drawing upon US experience (TUC 1995*a*; 1995*b*).

The clearly unsatisfactory recognition procedures which apply in the USA[27] may be seen as part of the wider problem of the NLRA itself, in which the law does not effectively deter statutory violations; and the Act's intention to promote collective bargaining is not being achieved (Gould 1994: 151). It can also be argued that a preoccupation with unsatisfactory recognition procedures takes attention away from the much more important explanations for the decline of union membership and the retreat of collective bargaining in both the USA and Britain. There is substance in this view but in the US case it is an important matter if public policy and laws seeking to regulate an aspect of the employment relationship are clearly failing. In the British case the absence of any legal controls on employer power to recognize or derecognize trade unions is out of line with the practice and principles of freedom of association and collective bargaining in advanced, industrialized countries. That absence must merit attention.

From 1975 to 1980 both countries were in parallel in having both a public policy commitment to collective bargaining and a statutory recognition procedure to make it possible to advance that commitment. They also had agencies, set up by statute, to oversee the commitment and the procedure: the National Labor Relations Board (NLRB) and the Advisory, Conciliation, and Arbitration Service (ACAS), although the two agencies were not similar in their other functions and in 1980 the British statutory procedure was abolished while the agency's duty to promote collective bargaining was also removed in 1993.[28] The NLRB does of course retain its functions under the NLRA, although changes in the membership of the NLRB can influence its interpretation of those functions.[29] Yet, despite these differences and the changes in the 1980s affecting the agencies responsible for overseeing the recognition and derecognition processes, the outcomes have been much the same, that is, falling recognition and rising derecognition.

Until the 1980s trade union derecognition in Britain was virtually unknown and even as late as the mid-1980s was exceptional (ACAS 1987). Since then, although still unusual, a clear trend has emerged: derecognition has continued to grow into the 1990s but 'still represents an extreme in industrial relations; at most, some 150,000 workers have been affected since 1988' (Gall and McKay 1994: 443). At the same time, whilst derecognition has grown only modestly since 1988, recognition successes were even more modest, estimated as bringing in only 70,000 workers —less than half of those lost by derecognition. Recognition 'success rates' (combining 'full' and 'partial' recognition)[30] have also reflected the industrial relations developments of the 1980s and 1990s, falling from 57 per cent of all claims in 1981 to 38 per cent in 1993 (Gall and McKay 1994: 444–6). For the USA a broadly similar picture emerges of declining union success. Win rates in NLRB certification and decertification elections have decreased sharply since the 1950s, although with stable rates in the 1970s and 1980s. However the *number* of elections fell steeply in the 1980s and the number of newly represented employees has fallen to insignificant numbers, given the size of the US labour force. They totalled little more than 321,000 in the four years from 1985 to 1988, or 1 in 1,000 of the labour force (Gould 1994: 153, table 5.1).[31]

These similar outcomes arise from very different systems. British employers are not obliged, in law, to grant recognition in any circumstances, even if a large majority of the appropriate bargaining unit is both unionized and in favour of recognition. The employer can also withdraw recognition previously granted and, since 1993, can also legally offer superior terms and conditions of employment to non-union members, an inducement which can be used to weaken union attachment and which can be followed by a derecognition ballot.[32] Such tactics are, of course, still relatively rare and the fact that trade union membership has fallen far more than the number lost through derecognition clearly indicates other powerful forces at work. Yet British trade unions remain particularly vulnerable to the absence of constructive recognition laws, especially given their rapid decline in membership and bargaining power since 1979. Paradoxically, the statutory system from 1975 to 1980 was associated with a minimal growth in recognition agreements. A future, revised statutory scheme may need to avoid formal election procedures on the US model and US experience also illustrates the dangers of 'trigger' percentages which can invite derecognition initiatives equally with recognition (Beaumont and Towers 1992). The relatively small numbers involved in US NLRB election procedures also suggests that more significant factors are involved in the consistent decline in trade union density since the mid-1950s. But explaining trade union decline is not all that matters. As Gould, the present NLRB chair, puts it: 'The fact is that the law is not working, and it is not performing the functions envisioned for it by its framers. This in itself is cause for alarm' (1994: 152).

The 'cause for alarm' also extends, in the US case, to the power of employers to deny newly certificated unions their first contract, that is, a 'refusal to bargain in good faith' which is unlawful under the NLRA and, even if successfully appealed against by the union through the courts, progress towards a contract can take as long as four years (Gould 1994: 168). The outcome is that, overall, unions winning elections fail to secure a first contract in about 25 per cent of cases (Bronfenbrenner 1994: 88). In such cases this means that the employer has effectively succeeded in nullifying a union's successful election campaign and the wishes of a majority of employees in the bargaining unit. In contrast, a British employer's recognition of a trade union or trade unions normally implies, even in the absence of legal compulsion, a willingness to enter into an early agreement. The existence of a legal framework clearly can invite the use of the law—especially where employers are hostile to the existence of trade unions.

However, it does not follow that the regulation of recognition and first contract procedure by the law is inevitably counter-productive. The law did work reasonably effectively in the USA before the 1980s, and appropriate reforms, drawing upon the experience of other countries, notably Canada, could produce far more satisfactory, that is, more equitable, outcomes.[33]

CONCLUSIONS

Industrial relations and collective bargaining in both Britain and the USA labour under more obvious political and public policy disadvantages than in other comparable countries. Some of this at times reflects unfavourable public opinion which takes a particularly negative view of trade unions when their actions involve crisis and major inconvenience, although the size of the USA and its essentially decentralized structure of collective bargaining generally presents a lesser problem in this respect than in Britain where trade unions striking in national contexts—such as strikes by postal, railway, energy, and public service workers—can have a major impact on the economy as a whole. British trade unions probably reached their lowest point in public esteem in the public sector strikes of the 'winter of discontent' which was followed by, even if it did not completely account for, Mrs Thatcher's election victory in 1979. Two years later, in the USA, a poll showed that half of Americans had an unfavourable view of labour leaders and two-fifths 'viewed them with hostility' (Bluestone and Bluestone 1992: 20). Since then unions in both countries have recovered much of their popularity. In Britain, in 1993, eight out of ten thought that unions were necessary to protect workers' interests; and those believing them to be not powerful enough exceeded those who thought they were too powerful—the most favourable poll outcome for twenty years (Taylor 1994: 20–1). Similarly in the USA, by 1991, only just over a quarter of respondents had a negative view of labour leaders compared to two-fifths ten years earlier (Bluestone and Bluestone 1992: 21).

Some part of the explanation for the apparent revival in the public's more favourable view of trade unions may lie both in their greater weakness combined with the growing insecurity of the workplace. Management, conversely, do not, in fact, come well out of polls. A US comparison between 1983 and 1988 of large companies ('Fortune 500') found a growing 'trust gap' between companies and all grades of employee (Bluestone and Bluestone 1992: 12). In Britain, in 1993, more than half thought that bargaining power had shifted too much in favour of management (Taylor 1994: 20) and directors and senior management regularly attract media attention and popular opprobrium for inflating their salaries, not least those running large, recently privatized, monopolies, such as gas, water, and electricity.

The unpopularity of trade unions in the early 1980s clearly made it easier for both governments to follow hostile policies and (in the British case) enact anti-union laws, especially as such actions were likely to be electorally popular and did not require taxes to be raised or public expenditure to be increased. Different approaches were of course taken, reflecting different collective bargaining circumstances, and different political systems and statutory traditions, although in both countries the common law and judicial interpretation of statute law by the judiciary has almost invariably favoured employers. This also coexists with perhaps a greater respect for the 'rule of law' in US unions than in the British which can be explained by historical circumstances, such as the earlier development of universal male suffrage in the USA.[34] The different view of law taken by British unions was most clearly seen in the bitter, and successful, boycott by the TUC, and almost all of its affiliates, of the Conservative's 1971 Industrial Relations Act. This can be compared with the equally bitter reception given by US trade unions to Taft–Hartley in 1947 but without any orchestrated action against it except for a vigorous propaganda campaign to repeal what the AFL called the 'slave labor law'. This was also at a time when US labour was probably at the height of its power if not its popularity. Furthermore, in constitutional terms the potential for influencing the law-making process is also greater in the US than in Britain given the availability of effective checks and balances.[35]

In Britain, the enactment of laws, in the form in which the government of the day wishes them to be, is much easier to achieve—provided that the prime minister is fully in control of the governing party backed by an adequate and guaranteed majority. This was the case in Britain in the 1980s when Margaret Thatcher withdrew the traditional support of government for the processes of collective bargaining and, by implication, as well as directly, for trade unions. This support, although in the case of trade unions sometimes uneasy and occasionally reversed, had essentially endured since the last quarter of the nineteenth century. Its instruments were 'voluntarism' and the 'golden formula', the latter in place in the late nineteenth century but confirmed in the Trade Disputes Act of 1906. The legislation from 1980 to 1993 contributed to the weakening of one of the parties to collective bargaining, partly by radically narrowing the industrial action immunities. But in narrowing the 1906 immunities it also sought to rule out 'political' strikes and attempted to weaken the political role of the trade unions and its ability to fund the Labour Party.[36] In legislating, the government could also generally rely upon the courts to interpret the new laws in a light unfavourable to the trade unions. This attempt to weaken the trade unions, both industrially and politically, implied a corresponding strengthening of employers as the other party to collective bargaining whilst collective bargaining as an institution lost the seal of government approval with its withdrawal as the central purpose of ACAS in 1993.

The growing weakness of the unions in the 1980s also allowed British employers to change the levels at which they were willing to bargain by accelerating the decentralization of collective bargaining away from multi-employer towards single employer bargaining and the workplace. In that respect British collective bargaining has moved closer to the American model although it is a development led by employers, not the law: in the USA it is both. 'Workplace contractualism', as it has been termed, dominated US collective bargaining from the 1940s to the 1960s but has since been making painful adjustments to the new employer demands for flexibility and change.[37] But it still embodies, where it survives, a polar extreme from those British workplaces still largely regulated by voluntarism, custom and practice, and collective agreements which do not bind the parties in law. Donovan in 1968 recommended plant 'comprehensive agreements' and the British government in 1971 tried to import some US practice into the workplace with legally binding agreements and the Wagner Act's concept of the sole bargaining agent; but these went down with the boycott of the 1971 Act by the unions and the widespread non-compliance of the employers.

As US and British collective labour law has, over the years, sometimes diverged and, at other times, converged, individual employment law has, in both countries, steadily advanced its domain. This process mainly began in the 1960s. It continued into the 1970s and 1980s with legislation regulating health and safety at work and redundancies, as well as ambitious statutes seeking to reduce discrimination across the employment relationship on the grounds of gender and race and, in the USA, age. In the growth of this legislation there has undoubtedly been some mutual policy learning, especially from the USA towards Britain. In other respects there have been separate paths, as for example in British unfair dismissal protection through a tribunal system which has been in place for over twenty years. In the USA, the declining coverage of collective bargaining has reduced such protection, although the gap is partly being bridged (and employment 'at will' eroded) by the courts and by state legislation, albeit, as yet, very limited.[38] In Britain, an important influence on the development of individual employment law in Britain, and of growing importance since the 1970s, has been the European Union. Britain has of course developed its own independent laws in this area, dating back to the 1960s, but it has undoubtedly been strengthened by law-making from Brussels, most obviously in advancing women's employment rights, in health and safety at work, and in protecting the pay, conditions, and employment security of workers affected by mergers and transfers.[39]

Overall, despite these counter developments, and in the USA the partly countervailing pressures from a Democratic presidency in the 1990s, public policy has followed an essentially hostile course towards collective bargaining and trade unions in both countries since the early 1980s. In Britain, a stream of statutes has reduced and restricted the traditional rights of trade unions; and in the USA the federal authorities have taken a passive or benign neglect approach towards the power of employers and the courts to erode rights seemingly guaranteed in law sixty years earlier. Nor, in the USA, do future prospects have any silver lining, as Congress (even under Democrats) and employers continue to inhibit reform. In Britain, the scenario is different. The EU provides some protection against public policy directed at weakening collective bargaining, trade unions, and employment rights. 1997 has also witnessed the beginning of a radical shift in political contexts with the return of the Labour Party to government after an absence approaching twenty years.

NOTES

1. R. A. Butler and Hugh Gaitskell were leading and influential politicians, respectively, in the Conservative and Labour Parties, in the early postwar period. Butler became Deputy Prime Minister and Gaitskell Leader of the Labour Party.
2. For a perceptive analysis of 'Thatcherism' in industrial relations contexts see McInnes (1987).
3. An influential representative of this tradition and a deposed minister in Mrs Thatcher's early Cabinets has written of this conflict within the Conservative Party: Gilmour (1992). See also his earlier contribution to economic policy debate (Gilmour 1983).
4. Wedderburn argues that in Britain, under Thatcherism, all policy, including industrial relations policy, was subservient to economic policy (1986: 84–6).
5. In 1984 the British government banned trade unions at the Government Communications Headquarters (GCHQ), which was linked to US intelligence-gathering facilities, as incompatible with the national interest, replacing them with an internal staff association or 'company' union. Some civil servants refused to abandon their union membership or accept transfers and were dismissed. Although the ban was strongly condemned by the ILO, the European Commission on Human Rights rejected the case brought against the government by the three unions involved. The Labour Party, in opposition, committed itself to removing the ban and restoring recognition rights to the four TUC affiliates involved. However, the staff association, which is reported to have 50 per cent of the staff in membership, could seek a certificate of independence from the Certification Officer (CO) and also apply for recognition. The new Labour Government, in May 1997, restored membership rights and access to union recognition. Some of those dismissed were also considering applying for reinstatement. See Lanning and Norton-Taylor (1991) for the earlier history of the GCHQ dispute.
6. Striker dismissal in the USA and Britain is discussed later.
7. This proposed measure, the Teamwork for Employees and Managers Bill, is discussed in Ch. 7.
8. For comprehensive reviews of the EU legislation and its impact on British industrial relations and employment law, see Hall (1994) and Gill (1992). For an overview of the Social Chapter see Gold (1993). For a highly sceptical perspective see Addison and Siebert (1994).
9. The first reported British company to do so was United Biscuits with 20,000 British employees and 6,000 in other EU countries. Others increasingly followed United Biscuits' example (Taylor 1995). United Biscuits was a leading donor of funds to the Conservative Party until it ended its donations in 1995.
10. These wider issues have recently been of considerable interest to the Trades Union Congress (TUC). They will be discussed in Ch. 6 and elsewhere. For a detailed discussion of the EU directives see Hall (1996).
11. In May 1996 the High Court dismissed a legal challenge to the regulations by three trade unions. The unions took the decision to the Court of Appeal.
12. Interestingly, US multinational employers *in Europe* are behaving just as

pragmatically over the European Works Council directive. The first US multinational to set up an EWC was the food-processing corporation, CPC, in 1994. CPC has 9,000–10,000 employees within EU countries. Its brands include Knorr, Mazola, and Hellman's (EIRR 1994: 4).

13. The European Commission (of the EU) recently indicated its support for social clauses in trade treaties and the Labour Party, in opposition, also added the same support to its policy commitments (Wighton 1996). This support, in both cases, now seems to be in doubt.

14. From 1980 Conservative governments progressively weakened employment protection legislation enacted in the 1970s under Labour, as for example in relation to protection against unfair dismissal: the qualifying period for taking a claim to a tribunal was increased, in stages, from six months to two years. Where the Conservatives strengthened employment protection, such as against the dismissal of pregnant women and in the extension of maternity leave, they only did so under the application of European Union law. The exception was in health and safety where policy was generally in line with EU initiatives. The key British Health and Safety at Work statute in fact dates from 1974, long before the legislative pressures from Brussels in the late 1980s.

15. A 1991–2 survey of union negotiators found that one-quarter had received threats of legal action but only one-quarter of these had actually resulted in action being taken. The threats mostly concerned the requirement to hold strike ballots and dismissal of workers during strikes. However, the survey also found that trade unions have adapted their practices to changes in the law (Elgar and Simpson 1993). This should be compared with earlier research for the period 1984–7 which found employer action growing but still marginal (Evans 1987).

16. Under the 1971 Act all collective agreements were deemed legally binding unless the parties specifically stated, in writing, that they did not wish to be legally bound. The outcome was that nearly all agreements were drafted, by agreement, with the heading: 'This is not a legally enforceable contract'. They became known as 'TINA LEA clauses'. For an account and an assessment of the 1971 Act see Weekes *et al.* (1975: 156–61).

17. *Trade union* evidence for this was presented to the House of Commons Select Committee on the Future of Trade Unions (see Ch. 1, n. 20). This is concisely reported in Taylor (1994: 48–55).

18. Recent examples involved Hoover and Nestlé in Glasgow, Scotland. Hoover threatened to relocate to France unless their Glasgow workers accepted job and hours flexibility and lower pay. The union accepted. Nestlé closed their 'Lion Bar' facility and moved it to France on the grounds that market conditions were more favourable in Dijon.

19. According to the AFL-CIO early in 1995, nine states were either voting on the issue or campaigns were under way (AFL-CIO 1995). For an illuminating account of the growth of anti-union industry trade associations (drawing on union sources) and the tactics of consultants and employers, see Goldfield (1987: 189–205). Recent research on employer tactics is to be found in Friedman *et al.* (1994). A personal, confessional account of 'union-busting' is in Levitt with Conrow (1993). See also Pfeffer (1994: 167–9), for a discussion of the rationale and costs of union-busting.

20. For a detailed, authoritative, discussion of the Mackay judgement and subsequent cases see Gould (1994: ch. 6). One pertinent comment on the 1967 and 1970 distinction is that of Paul Weiler: 'If a company discriminated against blacks or women and said: "We didn't fire them, we just permanently replaced them", it would get laughed out of court' (cited in Bluestone and Bluestone 1992: 259).

21. This may seem, to some, solely a matter of the legal application of doctrines and precedents to specific cases. However, in Britain, especially, it also has a socio-political dimension. British judges, notably in the High Court and above, have been almost exclusively drawn from a relatively privileged, politically insulated élite with little acquaintance with working class and trade union perspectives. There has been recent political pressure to democratize the judiciary and the legal profession, interestingly through the initiatives of Lord Mackay, responsible as Lord Chancellor for the British judiciary as well as being 'speaker' of the House of Lords. But the system still remains largely intact. For a critical, well-informed discussion of the British judiciary see Griffith (1981).

22. The explanation for the emergence of 'immunities' rather than 'positive' rights probably lies in the absence in Britain of a formal, written constitutional document and the special political circumstances in Britain at the time, i.e. the last quarter of the 19th century. For a discussion see Fox (1985: 161–4). For a detailed chronicling of the political contexts see Clegg *et al.* (1964: ch. 10, 364–95).

23. e.g. the courts prohibited industrial action by a union against privatization because of its potential impact upon its members' jobs. This was construed as a 'political' strike (*Mercury Communications Ltd* v. *Scott Garner and POEU* 1984).

24. For good, expert overviews and guidance to the vast detailed literature on these and other legislative changes between 1980 and 1993 see Lewis (1986); Wedderburn (1986 and 1995). For the relationship between industrial relations, the law, and public policy see McCarthy (1992).

25. Employers, as we have observed, generally remain reluctant to seek punitive damages against unions with whom they have to maintain constructive bargaining relationships. The courts do not have this constraint. The two unions which in recent years suffered most from the judges were the NUM, which in fines and costs lost £1m. (5% of its total funds) during the 1984–5 strike, and the National Union of Seamen, which was financially ruined in 1988 with fines and costs totalling up to £3m. It was later absorbed by the railworkers' union the RMT.

26. The Timex, Dundee plant, established in 1946, was originally part of a US-based multinational but ownership ultimately passed to a Norwegian millionaire, Fred Olsen, with interests in oil, shipbuilding, and shipping. The Dundee operation successfully shifted from 'instant' camera and mechanical watch production to electronic components in the 1970s and 1980s with the full cooperation of a long-serving, unionized, mainly female labour force. However further restructuring and job losses had by 1993 led to a strike, lockout, mass dismissals, and replacements. The dispute was significant in two respects: in the unusually aggressive tactics of management against a

traditionally cooperative and moderate workforce who eventually rejected the management–union agreement as unacceptable; and the careful use of the new anti-trade union laws, notably in the tactics of mass dismissal, replacement, and the avoidance of possible discriminatory dismissal claims by strikers and non-strikers. Finally in June 1992, the company closed the plant and agreed redundancy terms with the former workforce (Miller and Woolfson 1994).

The town of Dundee was also prominent in 1989 when Ford UK eventually decided not to locate a parts plant in the town after the TGWU refused to accept an agreement outside national arrangements. The operation was relocated to Spain following a failed conciliatory visit by a TUC delegation to Detroit.

27. Although the formal election process and ballot is carefully supervised by the NLRB its outcome is strongly influenced by the employer's normally superior resources, use of legal delays, consultants, and illegal tactics such as the intimidation and dismissal of union activists. Even a pro-certification ballot can be legally challenged, via the NLRB, and a rerun ordered. Rerun victories for unions are less common than in first elections and decertification elections are also possible after one year, especially if a contract has not been agreed—a further loophole for employers to exploit. Case law also favours employers' ability to deny access to their property during elections, notably for non-employee union organizers (*Lechmere* v. *NLRB* 1992). See Gould (1994) for detailed discussion of the certification process and potential reform. Townley (1987) offers a direct comparison of the US and British recognition procedures. See also Beaumont and Towers (1992).

28. ACAS's principal activity, taking up much of its time and resources is the advisory function. It also has the duties similar to those carried out by the Federal Mediation and Conciliation Service (FMCS) and its counterparts at state level. The FCMS is ACAS's closest equivalent. ACAS also maintains the voluntaristic tradition of the Department of Employment which remained influential up to and even beyond 1979. In that sense its style is also very different to the legal style and functions of the NLRB with its regular involvement in representation litigation. When ACAS was established under the 1975 Employment Protection Act it was required to promote collective bargaining. The 1993 Trade Union Reform and Employment Rights Act amended this duty simply to the 'improvement of industrial relations'.

29. As under the Reagan-appointed chairmanship of Donald Dotson from 1983 to 1986 when the Board became distinctly pro-management in its decisions (Gould 1994: 21–2).

30. Two forms of recognition are the practice in Britain: 'partial' for the representation of trade union members in grievance and disciplinary cases; and 'full' which includes representational rights as well as recognition of trade unions for bargaining over pay, benefits, and conditions.

31. The *relative* impact of the law and NLRB elections on trade unions and their membership is discussed in Ch. 3. For a review of the literature and detailed analysis of NLRB data see Goldfield (1987) and, more recently, Pavy (1994).

32. A ballot is not required but is commonly used by employers to give legitimacy to the derecognition.

33. See also Ch. 8 and Gould (1994: 215–19).
34. Phelps Brown (1986). This contrast may also be a factor, as Phelps Brown argued, in British trade unions' preference for protection against the courts in the form of the 'immunities' but the price they pay is the lack of positive, statutory support (211–21).
35. However, in Britain *employers*, as we have seen, were also opposed to using the 1971 Industrial Relations Act. This was clearly the opposite of the situation in the USA in 1946–7. For interesting discussions see Weekes *et al.* (1975: ch. 8), and Dubofsky (1994: ch. 8).
36. Under the 1913 Trade Union Act unions could establish political funds, separate from their general funds, which they could use for political purposes. The political funds, to be set up, required majority support by ballot of those voting. Individual members could, however, 'contract out' of paying the political levy which formed the political fund. The payment or non-payment of the levy was separate from union membership and the payment of dues. Under the 1984 Trade Union Act a ballot was required every ten years. However in the first ballots under the Act, after strenuous union campaigns in workplaces, *all* trade unions with ballots retained them and several unions inaugurated political funds for the first time. The funds are required to be renewed again by ballot in 1996. For an assessment of the impact of the political funds legislation see Leopold (1988).
37. See Brody (1993) for a recent discussion of 'workplace contractualism'. The changes in the US workplace are mainly discussed in Ch. 7.
38. These developments are discussed in Gould (1994: ch. 3, 64–108).
39. The privatization process, which has been a significant public policy development in Britain, made workers more vulnerable to mergers and transfers. It was also thought that EU regulations would not apply to transfers from non-commercial owners (i.e. the state) to commercial owners. EU case law has largely ruled otherwise, undermining the capacity of new owners to reduce pay and benefits. However case law in this area remains somewhat fluid.

3

Trade Unions and Collective Bargaining in Decline

Labor gives off an almost animal sense of weakness. Concessions, decerts, shutdowns. It's like the Italian army in 1918: cars breaking down, baggage getting lost, officers getting fired on by their troops. I joined organized labor and we just started retreating.

(Geoghegan 1991: 6)

We are not witnessing the emergence of a brave new world of non-union HRM but a tired old world of unrepresented labour.

(Brown 1994: 10)

The decline and disarray of organized labour and the associated erosion of collective bargaining are not processes confined to the USA and Britain; but nor are they universal, global features of labour movements, necessarily inevitable as a consequence of irreversible changes in economic structure. Trade unions since the 1980s have, in general, struggled in much less favourable circumstances but in some countries they have continued to hold their own, or at least avoid major losses. This is true of the Nordic countries, not least Sweden which, despite its continuing economic and social problems and a clear decline in trade union cohesion and influence since the 1980s, in 1990 still maintained a trade union membership density[1] at 80 per cent of employees in employment (Kjellberg 1992). Canada, the most comparable country to the USA, had a union density of 36 per cent in 1990 (37.4% in 1992—Kumar 1993), that is, more than double, and among OECD countries only France and Spain had lower figures at 10 and 11 per cent respectively, although both of these countries, given their different legal and institutional systems, had much higher levels of collective bargaining coverage (*Employment Outlook* 1994, ch. 5: 173, chart 5). French union density has, however, as in the USA, been on a downward path for forty years (Chang and Sorrentino 1991: 48, table 1).

Britain may now also be in the process of joining France and the USA. In the case of the USA, union density has more than halved since 1955 and on present trends the British figure could have reached half of its 1979 level by the end of the century, that is, the same order of decline as in the USA but over half the length of time. Total membership is also continuing to fall in Britain; and in the USA, although it rose slightly in 1993 and 1994, after successive falls over the previous fourteen years, it fell again in 1995. For both movements there has been a significant decline in membership of young people. In Britain, between 1990 and 1993, union members under 25 years of age fell from 30 per cent to 22 per cent; in the USA in the 1970s and 1980s, unions failed to recruit young people so that less than 9 per cent of 18–24 year olds were in membership in 1990 (Taylor 1995; Blanchflower and Freeman 1990).

The remorseless rise of the non-union sector in the USA led Kochan and his colleagues (Kochan *et al.* 1986) ten years ago to describe it as a 'transformation'. Some British scholars have, similarly, termed the post-1979 changes as the emergence of a 'new' industrial relations[2] although the form of change in the two countries is very different. Hence in the USA the growth of non-unionism is closely associated with human resource management (HRM) practices, not least among Japanese companies: the United Automobile Workers (UAW), for example, has failed to gain recognition in some three hundred Japanese-owned auto companies (Gould 1994: 16).[3] In Britain, union avoidance and HRM and Japanese owner-ship are not generally synonymous: in fact, workplaces implementing characteristic HRM practices are more likely to be those in which trade unions are recognized than otherwise.[4] Indeed, the evidence is that the growth of non-unionism in Britain has not been associated with the rise of HRM (Millward 1994: 129–30). More generally, the decline of trade union membership and the contraction of collective bargaining in Britain are much less related to employer policies and tactics than in the USA, and this despite the more extensive and more effective new laws available to British employers to use against trade unions over the period 1980–93. This may be largely explained by British unions being careful to ensure that they followed the letter of the new laws, especially on strike ballots, although British employers still undoubtedly prefer, in the main, voluntarist over legal solutions to industrial relations problems.[5]

But if employer attitudes and practices in the two countries have different significance in explanations of union decline and the contraction of collective bargaining, other factors have been similar in both direction and strength. Important among these is the major structural economic shift away from manufacturing towards the service sector and the associated changes in employment. Judicial decisions are also generally far more helpful to employers than to unions in both countries, and public policy has been, in Britain, consistently hostile towards trade unions for most of the 1980s and 1990s. In the USA, over the same period, public policy has been less hostile but has denied legitimate protection for trade unions and collective bargaining. Britain, though, has the clear edge in the case of overtly anti-union public policy as well as the government's management of its own employees in the civil service and those employed in the wider public sector. Public policy has also indirectly weakened trade unions in the progressive deregulation of a labour market in which unemployment has persisted at levels much higher than in the USA.

Assessing the relative impact of these factors is an important exercise. It has implications for policy-makers drafting laws to weaken or strengthen trade unions and collective bargaining. It also has implications for trade unions seeking to devise effective strategies for slowing or reversing decline. Such assessments will be discussed in this and the next chapters. In aggregate, though, the combined impact of the explanatory factors has led to an outcome which cannot be denied: trade unions and the institution of collective bargaining have been substantially weakened in both countries, even though over different lengths of time and differing in degree. In the USA, although public sector unions retain strength and influence, only a small minority of private sector workplaces are unionized and an effective alternative form of representation is not available to employees. British unions are stronger, and in membership density are still at about the same level as the German, but even this comparison has to be seen in context: British trade union membership continues to fall and British workplaces (as the American) are without the generally effective form of employee representation available in Germany, under the law, that is, the works council. Different ways by which employee interests can be represented will be discussed in later chapters. Yet initially, an important question needs to be borne in mind: does the weakening of trade unions and the contraction of collective bargaining matter?

It can be argued, and the British government and some British employers have recently done so, that trade unions and collective bargaining are in decline because they do not meet the needs of a competitive economy and the growing, non-union preferences of employees, a preference which is said to be reciprocated by employers' individualistic policies towards employees (Taylor 1994: 1–2; Employment Committee 1994c: 700–3). Similar views are commonplace and have a much longer history in the USA.[6]

The question 'does it matter?' can therefore be approached by dividing it into two further questions. First, what effect do trade unions and collective bargaining have on economic outcomes such as productivity, profits, and competitiveness? Secondly, aside from economic outcomes, which may even be considered as of secondary importance, how important is it, in modern conditions, that employees should be adequately represented at work by organizations which *they* control, that is which are independent of employers?

These questions of 'efficiency' and 'representation' are questions to which we shall return in later chapters, especially in Chapter 5. In this chapter we are primarily concerned with charting the extent and nature of decline and contraction and attempting to explain it.

THE DIMENSIONS OF DECLINE

'Waves of Unionisation'

Historically, union membership in the USA has been heavily influenced by cyclical fluctuations in economic activity which, at least until after World War II, were more severe than in Europe. Organization and membership which were not securely established in the boom tended to be swept away, or severely weakened, by the depression which followed (Phelps Brown 1986: 207). This process was hastened by employers taking full advantage of unemployment and associated union weakness to use lockouts, blacklists, and a suitable blend of legal, and illegal, instruments to achieve their purposes. This was especially the case in the depression of 1873 to 1879, but in the boom which followed, membership growth was strengthened and made more durable by the influx of skilled immigrants from Britain and Germany into the craft unions (Galenson 1986: 41). The AFL, formed in 1886, was later strengthened by the influx of the skilled construction unions in the 'first wave of unionization' in the first decade of the twentieth century (Bluestone and Bluestone 1992: 258). These craftsmen and their leaders, notably Gompers and Strasser, also ultimately rejected the socialism and syndicalism widespread elsewhere in the labour movement for the apolitical 'pure and simple' business unionism which, whatever its longer term consequences, in the short term protected their part of the movement from a too-powerful political backlash.

Depression, unemployment, and rapidly falling membership returned again in the 1930s alongside a new, or revived, radicalism. But industrial change and the policies and legislation of the New Deal provided new countervailing forces to the unprecedented severity of the depression of the 1930s. The 'second wave of unionization' came out of the rise of the mass production industries forming the industrial unions of the Congress of Industrial Organizations (CIO) (Bluestone and Bluestone 1992: 258) and it is in the contraction of these same industries, notably auto, steel, chemicals, and rubber, that a large part of the misfortunes of contemporary American labour lie.

'Waves' of a similar kind had characterized Britain's earlier experience in the nineteenth century. The craft unions initially formed themselves into the Trades Union Congress in 1868 (only eighteen years before the AFL) to be joined, after some early competition for their membership from the General Federation of Trade Unions (GFTU), by the 'new' unions of industrial workers: the seamen and dockworkers in the ports; the rail and transport workers; and the growing army of municipal workers as the Victorian towns and boroughs grew in population, income, and functions.

In their first phase of growth, the new unions, like the CIO unions, also favoured industrial action to achieve their aims although the former did so to improve pay and reduce the working week, as in the 'Great Dock Strike' in London in 1889; in contrast the CIO unions used the illegal, but effective, sit-down strikes[7] a half century later to achieve the first, though important, stage of recognition. The new unions and those in the CIO were also perceived, sometimes conveniently if not always accurately, by their opponents, as more socialist, left, or radical than the 'responsible', conservative craft unions. In fact the craft unions in both countries had always been ready to use the strike from their early days and within the British new unions, despite widespread syndicalism in the period before the World War I, they were still closely wedded to Fabian gradualism and support for the parliamentary socialism of the Labour Party which eventually emerged in 1906 from the earlier Labour Representation Committee (LRC).

It is also arguable that the influence and militancy of the communists and former 'wobblies' in the CIO unions in the 1930s and 1940s (Dubofsky 1994: 123–4) arose from an ideology further left than that of the socialists in the British new unions from 1900 to 1913. Indeed, it has been maintained that the British new unions were not especially less skilled, more militant, or more socialist than those of the crafts, and their only distinguishing feature was their 'newness' in organizing workers in industries previously resistant to unionization (Martin 1980: 66–7; Clegg *et al.* 1964: 92–5). In the end, of course, the craft and new unions came together in the TUC. This was in contrast to the AFL and CIO who remained bitter rivals after World War II and even without any significant ideological explanation after the communists had been finally purged from the CIO in 1949–50. Nor did the coming together of the two rival federations in 1955 coincide with another wave of unionization, a significant case study in the limitations of the merger as a platform for membership growth.

The Bluestones' 'third wave' came from a somewhat unexpected quarter: the public sector following President Kennedy's executive order 10988, permitting very limited collective bargaining for federal employees, that is, not for pay and without the right to strike—a limitation later used by President Reagan in his confrontation with PATCO. However union membership in the federal and wider public sector, for a long period, has provided an important counterweight to the long decline in private sector membership; and even though public sector unionization lost its growth momentum in the 1970s, unions of public sector employees (AFSCME) and teachers (AFT and NEA) remain large, powerful, and influential unions in their own sectors. Yet the far-reaching decline of private sector unionization poses major problems for the US labour movement; although some, like the Bluestones, see 'fourth wave' possibilities among

TABLE 3.1. *Trade union membership density in the USA and UK,* 1979–1994 (%)*

	USA	UK*
1979	24.1	53
1980	23.0	52
1981	21.4	51
1982	n/a	49
1983	20.1	48
1984	18.8	47
1985	18.0	45
1986	17.5	43
1987	17.0	42
1988	16.8	40
1989	16.4	39
1990	16.1	38
1991	16.1	37
1992	15.8	35
1993	15.9	35
1994	15.5	33

Note: * Great Britain from 1989.

Source: Hirsch and Macpherson (1996: table 1); Beatston and Butcher (1993: fig. 1); Bird and Corcoran (1994: table 6); Corcoran (1995: table 1).

professional and 'knowledge workers' or the lower skill and low paid end of the labour market among women, minorities, and immigrants (Bluestone and Bluestone 1992: 258–9).

British trade union growth in the postwar period was less 'wave-like' except perhaps for the growth in white collar unionization in the 1960s following the virtually static membership and density of the 1950s (Bain and Price 1983: table 1.1). Overall growth was, however, strong throughout the 1970s until the abrupt downturn beginning in 1979. That year may have marked Britain's 'historic peak' at 13.5 million members with a density of 53 per cent. The USA reached its own 'historic peak' many years earlier, in 1953, with 16.3 million in membership and a density of 32.5 per cent (Troy 1986: table 2).

Membership Losses since 1979

The continuing misfortunes of the two trade union movements from 1979 to 1993 are illustrated in Table 3.1. In Britain since 1979, total membership has been falling as well as density and both have been falling rapidly. In the USA, although density has remained on its downward path since 1953, total membership only began to decline in 1975 (Troy

TABLE 3.2. *Trade union membership density in the USA and Great Britain in the private and public sectors*, 1979–1993 (%)*

	USA			Great Britain		
	Private	Public	All	Private	Public	All
1979	21.2	37.0	24.1	n/a	n/a	53
1981	18.7	34.4	23.0	n/a	n/a	51
1984	15.3	35.7	18.8	42	80	47
1987	13.2	35.9	17.0	38	81	42
1990	11.9	36.5	16.1	35	72	38
1993	11.1	37.7	15.8	23	63	35

Note: * This table reflects the absence of separate long-run series for private and public sector densities in the British literature, data which are available in the USA. However the British Labour Force Survey (LFS), which began asking trade union membership questions in 1989, from 1993 distinguished between the public and private sectors. For an account of the LFS and other surveys of union data see Corcoran and Wareing (1994). For a recent, comprehensive discussion of trade union density in Britain and its relationship to job and personal characteristics see Beatston and Butcher (1993).

Source: As for Table 3.1; also Millward *et al.* (1992: 60–8; IDS (1987), cited in Beaumont (1992).

1986: 80–2) and membership increases in 1993 and 1994, though small, provided some comfort for US unions; in contrast, British total membership continues to fall and at alarmingly high annual rates averaging 3 per cent in the 1990s, although in 1996 the decline was under 1 per cent.

The US trade unions' better news is still coming from the public sector. From 1983 to 1993 public sector unions gained 1.3 million as the private sector lost 2.4 million (Hirsch and Macpherson 1994: table 1). Public sector density has also been growing, although slowly, over the same period (see Table 3.2) as the private sector begins to approach single figures. What is readily apparent from the clear trends revealed in Table 3.2 is that, should they continue, public sector workers will soon be the majority force in US trade unions: in 1993 they were 44.2 per cent of all members compared to 32.4 per cent ten years earlier (Hirsch and Macpherson 1994: table 1).

The significance of public sector unionization and industrial relations also goes beyond the numbers in membership. American presidents have executive powers to influence directly the extent and conduct of collective bargaining for federal employees. President Kennedy used these powers to encourage collective bargaining. The opposite cases of President Reagan, and to a lesser extent President Bush, may be seen as exceptional even under Republican presidents: the normal role of presidents since Roosevelt has been to extend the scope of collective bargaining where they could directly do so (that is, for federal employees) and, under Democrats, to seek to contain excessive employer power in the private sector. The latest example of such an attempt through the executive power, was President Clinton's 1995 executive order (12954) disallowing future contracts to private sector companies using permanent replacement workers during strikes.[8]

This policy of successive presidents is similar to, though much less comprehensive than, the 'good employer' model followed by British governments from all parties for their own civil servants under the Whitley Councils established during postwar reconstruction after 1919. 'Whitleyism' extended its influence through the entire public sector including local government and the nationalized industries, after they were taken into public ownership. Government encouragement of collective bargaining for its own and other public sector employees, and for the private sector, was maintained as public policy, albeit with occasional hesitations, until the reversal of traditional policies by the Conservatives after 1979. This reversal was further strengthened by the major programme of privatization leaving these industries free to follow industrial relations policies of their own choosing. The consequence (as Table 3.2 shows) has been a steady decline in the presence of trade union membership in the public sector. Recent figures also reveal continuing, serious losses, with public sector density at 61 per cent in 1995 (private sector 21%) and 32 per cent for all employees (Cully and Woodland 1996: 220, table 4). The public sector, although it retains its importance as a stronghold of British trade unionism, is a stronghold under persistent attack whilst around it private sector membership continues, as in the USA, to retreat.

Regional and Industrial Variations

US national figures do, however, conceal wide variations at state and local levels, although no state has experienced an increase in its density over a long period. The Eastern and Midwestern states generally retain much higher densities than those of the old South and the other 'right-to-work' states.[9] At metropolitan area level the highest levels of unionization are in the traditional areas of union strength in the auto and steel industries at Lansing/East Lansing, Flint in Michigan, and Youngstown in Ohio. All these areas had densities near or above 30 per cent in 1995 whilst Greenville-Spartanburg in South Carolina had a density of 0.4 per cent (Hirsch and Macpherson 1996: table 11a), and on Curme *et al.*'s (1990) estimates for 1988, Fort Worth in Texas had a density of zero. Some variations, by state since 1983, are shown in Table 3.3. Regional variation is also a feature of British union membership (Table 3.4) with Scotland, Northern England, and Wales having higher densities than East

TABLE 3.3. *Trade union membership density by selected states in the USA (%)*

	1983	1993
New York	32.5	28.8
New Jersey	26.9	22.2
Pennsylvania	27.5	19.0
Ohio	25.1	20.7
Michigan	30.4	24.5
Illinois	24.2	21.1
Indiana	24.9	18.6
Hawaii	29.2	28.1
Arizona	11.4	7.7
Florida	10.2	7.8
Mississippi	9.9	7.4
Texas	9.7	7.5
North Carolina	7.6	5.6
South Carolina	5.9	4.2
USA	20.1	15.8

Source: Hirsch and Macpherson (1994: tables 8a, 8c).

TABLE 3.4. *Trade union membership density by region in Great Britain (%)*

	1984	1994
South East*	45	27
East Anglia	40	27
South West	55	28
West Midlands	65	36
East Midlands	61	32
Yorkshire and Humberside	67	36
North West	71	40
North	72	43
Wales	71	46
Scotland	63	39
Great Britain	58	33

Note: * Includes Greater London.

Source: Millward and Stevens (1988: table 3); Corcoran (1995: table 3).

Anglia and the South East of England, reflecting to a large extent the different characteristics of employment and attachment to unionization in these regions. Regional disparities, if pronounced, weaken unionization, associating it with a few areas of strength and influence and a limited, insignificant presence elsewhere. Freeman (1989) has characterized this as 'ghetto unionism' with the USA as the emerging 'model'. The geographical size of the non-union areas, even within the most unionized states, is potentially attractive to American union-avoidance corporations as well as to the large-scale, inward investors. The lesser regional disparity of British trade union membership provides fewer non-union locations although, perhaps paradoxically, inward investors in Britain, at least for large companies, have tended to locate in the more traditionally unionized regions such as Scotland, North Eastern England and Wales. Japanese companies have been especially active in Wales although there, as elsewhere, national and local official agencies have provided substantial financial inducements to encourage investment in areas of high local unemployment.[10]

The high levels of union membership in large-scale, strategic industries were a source of strength when those industries employed large numbers; but correspondingly a source of weakness as they contracted and the expanding sectors proved more difficult to organize. This weakness has also been exaggerated by the heavy regional concentration of the high membership industries. In addition to the contracting industry effect on union membership, there has also been a general fall in the attachment of those still employed in these industries to their unions, that is, a fall in density. This is illustrated in Table 3.5. In both countries manufacturing density has fallen sharply since the early and mid-1980s, although in transport, unionization retains a strong hold, perhaps most notably among British Rail workers who were involved in a major and successful strike in 1989. However they have been subjected to greater managerial pressure in the 1990s: the check-off was unilaterally withdrawn by management in 1993; continuing friction led to a second, and protracted, strike of signalmen in 1994; and privatization from 1996 posed new threats to the railway unions. Union membership is also under pressure in British wholesale and retail distribution, an industry dominated by major companies and with a large part-time, mainly female labour force. This is especially the case in retail distribution. In 1993 the retailing labour force was 62 per cent female, who were mostly part time in an industry which employs large numbers of part-timers (46% of all employees). Retail distribution is also a significant part of the economy employing almost 11 per cent of all employees (*Employment Gazette*, July 1994: table 1.4). American retail distribution (the 'retail trade') has similar characteristics (also for 1993) although females were a smaller proportion than in Britain at 52 per cent and part-timers were 38 per cent of all employees.[11] In the USA retailing, as an employer, is, however, even more significant than in Britain totalling 17 per cent of all employment in 1993: almost the same in employment terms as manufacturing (Hirsch and Macpherson 1994: table 12a).

The postal services remain highly unionized in both countries. The British unions were comforted by the government's decision, in 1994, to

TABLE 3.5. *Trade union membership density by industry in the USA and Great Britain (%)*

	USA		Great Britain	
	1983	1993	1984	1991
Coalmining	61.5	39.0	n/a	89
Construction	28.0	21.6	36	19
Manufacturing:				
Durable goods	25.9	17.2	} 58	} 36
Non-durable goods	29.2	20.7		
Transport:				
Rail	82.9	77.5	} 85	92
Trucking/other	37.7	22.4		40
Wholesale distribution	9.3	6.9	32	13
Retail distribution	8.6	6.2	34	15
Postal and telecommunication:				
Postal	74.2	71.6	} 95	82
Telecommunication	55.4	41.2		72
Education	34.7	36.3	69	59*
Medical services:				
Hospitals	17.6	14.7	} 67	65
Other	9.7	7.1		37
Banking, insurance, finance:				
Banking and finance	} 3.4	} 2.7	} 43	48
Insurance				37
Public administration:				
National	} 30.0	} 32.5	} 78	61
Local				64

Note: * Schools only.

Source: Hirsch and Macpherson (1994: tables 12a and 12c); Millward and Stevens (1988: tables 1 and 2); Beatston and Butcher (1993: table 4).

abandon its intention to privatize the industry, although by 1996 this intention was much less firm with the onset of industrial relations problems, including a series of one day strikes, and the approach of a general election. For telecommunications, there was less equivocation. In both countries they were transformed in the 1980s by privatization and deregulation, posing substantial problems for the unions.[12]

The growing strength of the unions in US education contrasts with the weakening of their British counterparts. The British government was involved in several confrontations with the teachers' unions in the 1980s

TABLE 3.6. *Trade union membership density by selected occupations in the USA and Great Britain (%)*

	USA		Great Britain
	1983	1993	1993
Managers and administrators	8.1	6.2	24
Professional	24.0	22.3	52
Associate professional and technical	13.3	11.4	50
Clerical and secretarial	15.0	13.8	30
Craft and related	32.9	25.6	41
Protective services	39.0	40.1	30
Sales	6.7	4.7	12
Plant and machine operatives	36.9	25.0	46

Note: Data for Great Britain only available for 1993.

Source: Hirsch and Macpherson (1994: tables 13a and 13c); Bird and Corcoran (1994: table 7).

and 1990s as it forced through a radical restructuring at all levels of education and withdrew teachers' collective bargaining rights in 1987. Similar confrontations have been a feature of the British National Health Service (NHS). These arose from the Conservative government's introduction of 'internal market' reforms, and pressure to abolish national pay bargaining in favour of decentralized negotiations in the hospitals which had already been given semi-autonomous status under the reforms. Unionization is however still well-entrenched in the NHS as well as in public administration but the unions are still facing the gradual erosion of the long-standing traditions of Whitleyism. In contrast, US public administration unions continue to make unspectacular but steady progress as Republican administrations at federal, state, and local levels generally maintain a gap between their rhetoric and actions.

Occupation and Gender

The comparative occupational data (shown in Table 3.6) reveal a similar picture of falling densities. The British densities remain in almost every case substantially above those for the USA, although had data for 1983 been available it would undoubtedly have recorded a general decline, by 1993, across all occupations. It is also apparent that falling densities in clerical, secretarial, and craft jobs are far from being compensated for in the occupations in which total numbers are increasing, that is, managerial, administrative, professional, and technical occupations. In Britain,

TABLE 3.7. *Trade union membership and density by gender in the USA*

	Membership (000s)		Density (%)		Women as % of all members
	Men	Women	Men	Women	
1983	11,809	5,908	24.7	14.6	33.3
1993	10,083	6,515	18.4	13.0	39.3

Source: Hirsch and Macpherson (1994: tables 7a, 7c).

TABLE 3.8. *Trade union membership and density by gender in Great Britain*

	Membership (000s)		Density (%)		Women as % of all members
	Men	Women	Men	Women	
1979	9,544	3,902	71.1	40.1	29.0
1992	5,472	3,577	40.5	31.1	39.5

Source: *Employment Gazette* (January 1983: table 1.1 and 'Membership of Trade Unions in 1981', 26–8; *Employment Gazette* (November 1994: table 1.1); Bird and Corcoran (1994: table 4).

additionally, senior management are increasingly pressing middle managers and supervisors to accept personal contracts to set their pay rather than having it set through collective bargaining, as well as pressing them to give up their union membership.[13] In the USA, whilst statutory protection for union membership and collective bargaining is only available for 'employees', even this right is itself being eroded by occupational change and legal interpretation, as we saw in Chapter 2.

The entry of large numbers of women into employment in the 1980s and 1990s has increased the proportion of women in trade unions in both the USA and Britain, and in the former the actual numbers of women in trade unions also increased (Tables 3.7 and 3.8). This suggests further potential opportunities for US unions recruiting in industries in which women are numerous, such as clerical and service occupations. Here the growth record of the Service Employees' International Union (SEIU) has been impressive, almost doubling its membership between 1975 and 1993 (Gifford 1994: 68, appendix A). British unions have not had similar successes in recruiting women in clerical and service occupations, although in nursing, the non-TUC union, the Royal College of Nursing (RCN), has shown strong growth[14] in an occupation under pressure

TABLE 3.9. *Collective bargaining coverage in the USA and*
Great Britain, 1984–1993 (%)

	USA			Great Britain		
	All	Private	Public	All	Private	Public
1984	21.6	17.0	43.9	71	52	95
1990	18.3	13.2	43.3	54	41	78
1993	17.7	12.1	43.8	49*	34*	84*

Note: * The 1993 data for Great Britain from the LFS for the first time recorded the proportion of workplaces where trade unions are recognized for collective bargaining purposes.
However, even if recognized trade unions are in a workplace, some groups of employees
(e.g. managers, supervisors) may fall outside collective bargaining arrangements. Hence
the 1993 data will overstate collective bargaining coverage. See also Millward *et al.* (1992:
90–1).

Source: Hirsch and Macpherson (1994: table 1); Corcoran and Wareing (1994: table 3);
Millward *et al.* (1992: table 3.16; 93–4).

from hospital management and the government's NHS policies. Across
the British public sector as a whole, female densities for full-time employees are almost the same as men and exceed them for part-timers
(Cully and Woodland 1996: 220, fig. 4).

Collective Bargaining Coverage

Finally, we return to aggregate data with changes in the coverage of
collective bargaining from 1984 to 1993 (Table 3.9). The figures in
Table 3.9 complement those for density in Table 3.2. In both countries
private sector collective bargaining continues to follow density sharply
downwards. Britain in particular has, in less than a decade, declined
from private sector collective bargaining covering more than half of all
employees to a coverage of just over a third. In the public sector, British
coverage remains much higher than in the USA, although since the early
1980s this has been under strong pressure arising from the government's privatization of large parts of the public sector and its continuing
opposition to the trade unions' preference for national, Whitley-style collective bargaining. Public sector collective bargaining in the USA is much
more stable. With the spectacular exception of PATCO, the unions have
generally experienced much less hostility from federal, state, and local
public sector employers than their British counterparts or than US private sector employers. Nor is privatization such a threat, given a US
public sector of smaller scale than the British, although the difference,
in employment terms, has been substantially narrowed since the early

1980s, as the British public sector has been subjected to the government's privatization programme. However, the US federal sector, and its unions, are now beginning to experience similar problems. For example, the US postal service was converted to an agency in 1970 and constant popular and political pressure to reduce federal spending and taxes is increasing the extent of subcontracted and agency activity. Grants for the delivery of former federal programmes, recently including welfare, are also being progressively applied, by Congress, to the states. This increasing pressure on the states of welfare, and other spending, may yet force them, and municipal governments, into further privatization of programmes and services.

EXPLAINING DECLINE

International Comparisons

Trade union membership decline is not, as we have seen, confined to the USA and Britain. At the same time it is not a uniform, universal, worldwide phenomenon responding to some equally worldwide forces. Furthermore, although the USA and Britain are not alone in their experience, the scale of their trade unions' problems, among industrialized countries, is close to being unique and merits special attention.

Until the early 1980s, British academics were interested in explaining trade union growth rather than decline. Their American counterparts were confronted with a different experience requiring explanation. But even in the US case, decline only became seen as a more enduring aspect of the labour movement when the stability of the 1970s was followed by the losses of the 1980s; and even then there were still highly experienced and perceptive analysts who were not ruling out the possibility of a revival in the fortunes of the labour movement.[15]

Much of the discussion concerning trade union decline has taken place in comparative contexts. Multinational comparisons can be illuminating, although generalization is difficult since different factors, or sets of factors, can be more or less important at different times and inevitably vary in accordance with different national cultures and circumstances. A more modest, but potentially fruitful approach, is to pair countries which are sufficiently alike in their industrial relations systems but differ in those aspects which are being studied. Here the best and most popular example is the USA and Canada. Another interesting pairing is that of Britain and Ireland (Freeman and Pelletier 1990), although in the significant dimension of collective bargaining levels these two countries have diverged substantially over the last twenty years. Yet major similarities remain despite this and despite the fact that, in trade union membership decline,

1   The structure of employment
2   Macroeconomic changes
3   Public policy and legislation
4   Employer attitudes and actions
5   Union organizing
6   Public opinion and attitudes
7   Political institutions and practices
8   Major events and changes in industrial relations contexts

FIG. 3.1. The determinants of trade union growth and decline
Source: Chaison and Rose (1991: 12–45; slightly adapted).

Ireland and Britain have not followed the same path and nor have Canada and the USA.[16] Britain and Australia have also for a long time attracted comparative attention and such research has recently been made easier by the comprehensive workplace survey data, amenable to computer analysis, which is now available for both countries.[17]

For Britain and the USA a common feature of their experience in the years since 1979 has been significant trade union membership decline, an experience which has replaced strong diverging tendencies prior to 1979. Explanations of this diverging and converging experience are of course to be found among those factors, and changes in those factors, which impact upon trade unions and their members. The factors, or determinants, are not difficult to identify and useful conclusions are possible through examining the association between individual determinants (or apparently closely related pairs or groups of determinants, such as public policy and legislation) and trade union membership. The relative influence, or ranking, of the determinants is the next, but more difficult, stage. Allowance has also to be made for changes in the relative weight of the determinants, especially if it is believed that industrial relations systems, over time, are prone to transformation into quite different systems.

The Determinants of Decline

Bain and Price (1983), in their influential work on British trade union *growth*, listed six determinants, drawing upon earlier work. Metcalf (1989) identified five 'ingredients', although a recent, comprehensive study is that of Chaison and Rose (1991) who offer eight 'determinants' within a wide-ranging, comparative context. These eight determinants are illustrated in Figure 3.1 and will be used to structure the discussion. Shifts in the structure of employment in the USA and Britain have been well researched and have been summarized in Chapter 1, in terms of changing sectoral employment, occupational change, changing skills' levels, female employment growth, and employment flexibility both within organizations and in external labour markets. These are dramatic and significant developments which, although far from recent phenomena, have accelerated in the last twenty years with important and long-term consequences for the nature of employment and its availability in forms which people have traditionally required. If it is assumed that male, manual occupations in the older, declining, industries are natural trade union territory, then their replacement by the growing service sector mainly offering white collar employment and increasingly dominated by females (who are, it is often asserted, harder to organize[18]) is likely to give trade unions serious problems.

The difficulty with the supposed link between these 'compositional' changes in employment and the decline in trade union density is that the link does not always seem to exist or else its supposed impact is greatly exaggerated. All industrialized countries, with differences in degree, have experienced compositional changes in employment. Yet not all of them have experienced a decline in trade union density whilst a few have recorded increases. This may of course be because other more powerful factors have reduced, or cancelled out, the impact of compositional change, factors which vary in their incidence and strength between countries. For Britain, too, the link is far from straightforward. The compositional effects were not absent in the 1970s, yet trade union density grew strongly up to the end of the decade and then went into steep decline. What happened, of course, in 1979 was the election of a Conservative government with a mandate to reduce trade union power and which continued in office for a period long enough to deliver a significant legislative and policy programme towards this objective. Some research (interestingly by Americans) is in fact categoric that between 1980 and 1986 the British government's industrial relations legislation was responsible for the *entire* decline in UK density (Freeman and Pelletier 1990). In contrast, other research (by a British academic) suggests that the industrial relations legislation has had no 'direct effect' and that macroeconomic factors (i.e. changes in unemployment, wages, and prices) explain the rise in density in the 1970s followed by its fall in the 1980s (Disney 1990). Disney also dismisses changing employment composition as an important explanation of British density decline in the 1980s but allows for its greater importance in the long run.[19] He also, interestingly, points out that periods of legislation are 'closely intertwined' with periods of macroeconomic change, such as rapid inflation (ibid. 173).

Separating the effects of macroeconomic and public policy factors on trade union density clearly poses major problems. Nor should public policy be too narrowly identified with legislation. President Reagan's executive action against the PATCO strikers and his changes in the membership of the NLRB (and by intention the policies) reflected highly

significant shifts in public policy in the 1980s without legislative intervention. In the British case it is also arguable that the Conservative government's policies, as the executive, towards public sector trade unions
in the 1980s (civil servants, teachers, health workers, coalminers, railway
workers, and steel workers) were at least as influential in weakening
trade unions as legislation. Public sector densities fell throughout the
1980s in a climate of official disapproval and determined attempts to
break up national bargaining arrangements which dated back, in some
cases, to the origins of the Whitley system after World War I. Nor, with
legislation, is it easy to separate cause and effect (Disney 1990: 173): in
other words, does growing trade union weakness (as reflected in density data which may not tell the whole story) make it easier for governments to legislate rather than diminishing trade union strength being
the effect of legislation? Powerful union movements can even frustrate
legislation. The British Industrial Relations Act of 1971 was rendered
largely ineffective by trade union opposition (and significant employer
collusion with the unions) and it was eventually repealed in 1974.

There is also a wider dimension to public policy, associated with a prevailing ideology which can often transcend political parties and changes
in government. For example, the election of social democratic and socialist governments in Western European countries has undoubtedly provided a public policy context favourable to trade unions[20] and collective
bargaining. But this favourable context has not been seriously challenged
as Christian Democrat and other 'conservative' parties have taken their
turn in office. Hence the trade unions have become institutionalized as
one of the 'social partners', a process extended and deepened by EU institutions including the establishment of a 'social dialogue' at EU, sectoral,
and enterprise levels.

The major diverging country, from 1979, has been Britain. But before
that both parties, at least up to 1971–4, were broadly agreed on the need
for, and structure of, industrial relations reform. This prevailing ideology
was rejected by the Thatcherite Conservatives, whose own ideology
informed both legislation and executive action. This new ideology was
also seen in the progressive dismantling of the apparatus of corporatism, that is the tripartite, policy advisory bodies on which the trade unions
and TUC were represented. Union representation was also excluded
from the proliferation of trusts, agencies, and councils set up by the
Conservatives as a consequence of their policies of privatization and
deregulation. This exclusion of the unions contrasts sharply with the
inclusive ideology of the Labour government under the 'social contract'
from 1974 to 1979 as well as those of previous Conservative governments,
even including Edward Heath's after its first two years.[21]

The public policy and employment contexts in which US trade unions
declined in the 1980s and 1990s have been broadly similar in direction,

if not in form, to those of Britain. The differences in form are especially clear in public policy. New legislation, as we have noted, has played a lesser role than in Britain but this was because the main legislative framework had essentially been established in 1935 and 1947, and for more than thirty years, public policy underpinned the labour–management 'accord' which was similar to the continuity of British industrial relations policy and practice up to 1979. However, some commentators maintain that the New Deal labour laws, which ostensibly support unionization and collective bargaining, have in fact inhibited their development by effectively confining their influence to a bargaining structure which is decentralized, even fragmented. This view has been well argued by Clark (1989) who argues that from 'representation elections to the ratification and notification of contracts, the presumption of federal labor legislation is that . . . labor-management relations belong at local level' (ibid. 241). Clark even cites Representative Gildea, a Democrat, who warned against this as the Wagner Act was proceeding through Congress in 1935 (ibid. 242). Goldfield (1987), in contrast, sees the legislation as less important in the rise of unionism and its decline than employer power and 'class forces', whilst Layne Kirkland, the recently retired President of the AFL-CIO, has also openly mused, on several occasions, that the repeal of the NLRA and a return to 'collective *laissez-faire*' might be better for the labour movement (Gould 1994: 153–7).

The New Deal legislation did of course not preclude multi-employer bargaining or national level single employer bargaining or, indeed, almost anything employers and unions could agree upon. Heckscher (1988) argues, in fact, that the purpose of the Wagner Act was to encourage voluntary collective bargaining without the intervention of the state and its agencies. Yet what developed was a high level of NLRB and judicial activism alongside a system of elaborate, legally binding, workplace contracts and an institutionalized proliferation of grievance arbitration. This 'workplace contractualism', as Brody calls it (also termed 'job control unionism'), may have pre-dated the New Deal, or even unionism itself, as a system of work organization, but it was clearly a 'basic principle' of the industrial relations system which emerged after 1935 (Kochan et al. 1986: 29). After the 1960s, workplace contractualism itself was in retreat as the mass-production industries began to shrink and newer, more flexible forms of work organization were being introduced by employers to challenge the older workplace forms (Brody 1993). Later, in the 1980s, employers began to dismantle pattern bargaining[22] and to move away from company-wide agreements to local bargaining which made it easier to whipsaw local unions into accepting major changes in traditional work rules and to implement workplace involvement, participation, and teamwork. Such processes, similar in form and motive, were occurring at the same time in Great Britain and, in both countries, were made possible by weakening unions and the assertion of employer power (Katz 1993: 10–12; Towers 1992).

Employer opposition increased in importance as an explanation of trade union decline in Britain in the 1980s under the encouragement of Conservative governments, as, for example, in the well-documented case of the miners' strike of 1984–5 (MacGregor 1986; Milne 1994; Towers 1985). But, despite the evidence of convergence (within contexts where both trade union movements have been increasingly unable to resist employer power), the difference between US and British employers' attitudes and actions remains wide. The current strength of US employer opposition has deep historical roots, dating back to the earliest days of industrialization when US employers, in very different market contexts to the British, combined not to bargain with emerging unions but to destroy them (Phelps Brown 1986: 207–11). Even under the New Deal's instrumental rationale for promoting collective bargaining as an element in the revival of the economy as well as insurance against revolutionary tendencies, employer opposition to the Wagner Act (and Roosevelt himself) was as intense and as strong as it had ever been to earlier pro-labour legislation. As Dubofsky so aptly puts it: 'When Roosevelt signed the Wagner Act, the employers did not withdraw from the field of battle' (1994: 130).

Their battle tactics did, of course, vary. Opposition frequently took radical or violent forms as in the General Motors sit-down strike of 1937[23] and the confrontation between the Ford workers and the company police in Detroit in 1941. The more sophisticated, and more successful, anti-union option took the form of 'employee representation plans'. These proliferated until the passage of the Wagner Act which prohibited them. The unions, like Wagner, saw the plans as company unions designed to subvert the growth of collective bargaining between employers and independent trade unions. Although not all of these plans were dubious, and a small number even survived the NLRA ban, it was clear that most employers used them as a union avoidance tactic (Jacoby 1983; 1985). Furthermore, this historical experience still strongly influences the current attitudes of trade union leaders and membership towards any attempt to remove, or amend, Section 8(a)(2) of the Wagner Act, prohibiting 'company unions'.[24]

Some part of the explanation of union membership decline, in both countries, clearly lies with deficiencies in union organizing. In periods of rapid membership growth—as in the USA during the rise of the CIO in the 1930s and in Britain under the Labour administrations of the 1960s and 1970s—organizing amounted to little more than receiving workers into membership. After the 1970s, both labour movements became especially reliant on their own efforts to recruit new members, and the evidence from the membership figures is that they did not spend enough money or put in sufficient effort to resist influences countering membership retention and growth. Goldfield (1987: 205–17) argues that US unions have not devoted money to organizing proportionate to the scale of the problem and that this has been generally combined with passive, non-combative approaches which achieve much less than competitive aggression. British unions have also been charged with inadequate funding and disproportionate expenditure of effort in organizing. Additionally, British employers, until the 1980s, by and large did not resist new recognition attempts or else agreed to union recognition by the extension of existing agreements to new sites within the same organization. This favourable background to recruitment influenced unions, until recently, to give higher priority and rewards in career opportunities to negotiating rather than organizing skills (Beaumont and Harris 1990; 1995a; Mason and Bain 1993; IRS 1996: 605). Financial constraints, as membership has fallen, have also allowed fewer resources for recruitment campaigns. Nor, from US evidence, is it clear that actually devoting more resources and people to organizing would have a sufficiently significant impact upon membership to justify diverting scarce resources (Voos 1983; Goldfield 1987).

Organizing success, or failure, is also closely related to employer attitudes and behaviour. In both countries employers are significant, even critical influences on union organizing efforts. British unions have been traditionally assisted by the relative permissiveness of employers, responding pragmatically to rising union membership, especially up to 1979. American unions, in contrast, have faced aggressive, anti-union employers deploying substantial resources. After 1979 British unions were increasingly exposed to negative employer pressure, but this was still much less than that experienced by their US counterparts.

There is limited evidence that shifts in public opinion and attitudes can influence the growth and decline of unionization. As we saw in Chapter 2, in both Britain and the USA polls have tended to show increasing popular support for unions as density has fallen. This may, perhaps not surprisingly, suggest that unions become more popular as their power diminishes: notably through their reduced capacity to impose inconvenience upon the public through industrial action. Furthermore, the decision to join a union seems to be at least partly influenced by its ability to meet its traditional objectives (Sapper 1991) which may require the use of unpopular industrial action. Certainly British unions' popular image was negative in the 1960s and 1970s as densities rose to peak levels. The Canadian case is also interesting, where declining public approval has coexisted with at least stable density rates (Chaison and Rose 1991). Additionally, public opinion and public attitudes can only impact indirectly through the political process. For example, it is widely believed that the prolonged and highly disruptive British public sector strikes in 1978–9 were the principal reason for the election of the Thatcher government and provided the opportunity and rationale for its anti-union policies and legislation from 1980 to 1993.[25] However, even if this is accepted, it is still necessary to demonstrate that there is then a clear connection between the government's policies and legislation and trade union decline.

Much less debatable is the influence of major changes in the contexts of industrial relations. The two world wars, in particular, shifted the balance of bargaining power towards trade unions as acute shortages of goods and labour developed.[26] Governments were anxious to contain the associated price and wage inflation and needed the cooperation of trade union leaders. They also looked to them to inspire maximum shop-floor effort. In return, governments passed laws to encourage employers to recognize trade unions, as union leaders were brought into national administration and policy-making. These favourable contexts to union growth and influence were, in the US case, early casualties of the peace. The employers resumed their anti-union campaigns in the 1920s and both employers and Congress, in the 1940s, acted in unison to push back trade union power. In Britain, favourable government attitudes to trade unions survived World War I as Whitleyism became increasingly dominant, even though the economic conditions for union growth did not fully return till the economy began to move onto a war footing in the late 1930s. World War II and Whitleyism together provided a secure ride for the trade unions until strong inflationary pressures began to build before and during the Korean War (Roberts 1958). By the 1960s the honeymoon between government and unions had turned into a fractious marriage followed by painful divorce after 1979.

Wartime apart, periods of widespread economic distress, transformation, and change are also often associated with rapid growth, or decline, in trade union membership. The obvious example in the USA is the rise of the industrial unions and the CIO in the 1930s. The later decline of trade unions (including the industrial unions) can also be seen in the context of a 'transformation' of the industrial relations system, albeit a lengthy one, lasting by now for over forty years (Kochan *et al.* 1986). Certainly non-unionism is the current norm in the great majority of US workplaces although, even at their peak, unions never had more than a third of the workforce in membership. Britain too, can claim its transformation, again a slow one, following the reforms of 1919 which eventually spread, in their influence, to the private as well as the public sector, and with the Ministry of Labour, and its successors, playing a pivotal role. It was, in fact, as late as 1993 before ACAS's duty to support collective bargaining was removed, followed by the abolition of a separate ministry for labour affairs: the Department of Employment (in direct line to the old Ministry of Labour)[27] was merged with the Department for Education in 1995.

These changes, combined with the legislative and policy shifts between 1980 and 1995, could therefore be seen as a period during which British industrial relations was transformed—specifically if it is assumed that the levels of membership, power, and influence of the trade unions have been permanently reduced. Yet it may still require much lengthier hindsight (Chaison and Rose 1991: 34) to decide whether or not Thatcherism, after 1979, was a period of permanent transformation. Trade union densities are still high by US standards and old-style industrial relations continues to be tenacious in the still numerous 'older workplaces'.[28]

Assessing the Determinants

Despite the difficulty of recognizing transformations as we live through them, they have undoubtedly occurred and will do so again. A recent contribution to the transformation literature distinguishes between 'periods of institutional development' and 'periods of institutional consolidation' (Price and Bain 1989). The former are the transformations or 'paradigm shifts' which are followed by the latter, during which new laws, patterns, and practices spread and are consolidated until the next transformation begins to unfold. Furthermore, it is in the period of consolidation and relative stability that the economic and socio-political determinants hold sway in explaining trade union growth and decline.

In identifying periods of transformation in Britain and the USA, the prime candidates are Britain after 1919 and the USA following the New Deal legislation of the 1930s. In the USA, union membership and density grew strongly in the twenty years after 1935 and although British union growth was more volatile in the 1920s and 1930s, reaching a low point in 1933, it then grew more or less consistently (with a plateau in the 1950s) until 1979 (Bain and Price 1983: table 1.1). The transforming periods are also here associated with shifts in public policy, although Goldfield (1987) is sceptical. He argues that public policy favourable, or unfavourable, to union growth (e.g. Wagner and Taft–Hartley) may merely reflect 'changes in the relative strength of the working class and the employing class at the state and national level' (Goldfield 1987: 189). Certainly US employers were politically and economically weakened in the 1930s and strong labour unrest was evident before the passage of the Wagner Act. Employer political strength revived during and, particularly after, World War II despite (or even because of) a major strike offensive by the unions, leading to the restrictions of Taft–Hartley. It has also been argued by Clark, as noted earlier, that even public policy designed to favour unions (as the Wagner Act) in the long run stifled their growth and inhibited the development of a national role.

In the case of Britain, another instructive period was the decade before World War I. Public policy towards unions began to move towards a more favourable stance in the second half of the nineteenth century but this also occurred at the same time as union strength and parliamentary lobbying became more effective. Additionally, at the turn of the century the prevailing ideology was changing. Industrial unionism was extending union influence into the newer industries and local government as the emerging Labour Party was challenging the Liberal Party. The favourable and durable legislation of the 1906 Trade Disputes Act and the 1913 Trade Union Act[29] can therefore be seen as acts of public policy which interacted with the rising power of labour in its economic and political dimensions. The rise of British labour was also significantly assisted by the relative lack of aggression and accommodating tactics of the employers, here again in major contrast to the USA.

If therefore we identify periods of transformation in industrial relations, they are associated, in the British and US cases, with the interaction between, on the one hand, the relative strength of trade unions and employers and, on the other, the response and ideological nature of public policy. Hence British trade unions grew and prospered for the greater part of the twentieth century because they were able to successfully deploy their inherent strength and, in the main, were faced by employers ready to negotiate rather than resist. At the same time, by the end of the nineteenth century, British trade unions were also successfully operating within a political dimension which, after 1906, was through a party which represented the interests of labour in Parliament. By 1924 the Labour Party had formed a minority administration and from 1945 was equal with the Conservatives as the 'party of government' until 1979.[30] When in power, the Labour Party sees itself as representing the country as a whole but at significant times has enacted laws and followed policies sought by the trade unions.[31]

In the USA the experience has been very different, and the difference lies mainly in the attitudes and behaviour of employers and the normal absence of even neutral political contexts. At every stage in their often turbulent history, unions have sought to organize with determination and tenacity but have generally and consistently been faced by powerful, and normally successful, employer opposition. Furthermore, in this struggle, unions have, in the main, been regionalized and localized and unable to exert significant national industrial and political influence—unlike employers. Some part of this can be explained by the still important decentralizing tendencies in a large country. There is also the absence of a clear, influential, national political identity for trade unions. Their involvement in the coalition of interests which has maintained the Democrats' power over long periods has, overall, borne little fruit other than the New Deal legislation; and under the Carter and Clinton administrations, even when Congress has been under Democratic control, pro-labour bills have consistently failed to pass. Of course some of this is

explained by the design of the US Constitution which offers disproportionate blocking power to political minorities—very different from the
centralized powers available to British governments. Yet the decision by
Samuel Gompers and his associates to follow a predominantly business
union strategy and, in particular, not to promote a labour party representing union interests, whilst explicable in the circumstances of the first
quarter of the twentieth century,[32] has in the event helped to minimize
US labour's political influence and, in effect, reduce it to a 'special interest'.

However, the primacy given here to explaining trade union growth
or decline, especially during periods of transformation, to the influence
of public policy playing upon the interaction between trade unions and
employers, requires two caveats.

First, it does not exclude the additional influence of explanations rooted
in economic and sociological change, that is the macroeconomic and
compositional factors. Price and Bain (1989), as we have seen, suggest
that both sets of factors are important outside transformation periods
and during those of institutional consolidation. Chaison and Rose (1991),
in their comparative review of the determinants, conclude that macroeconomic variables vary in strength and direction between countries and
over long periods, although Disney (1990) explains the rise and fall of
British density in the 1970s and 1980s almost wholly through changes
in unemployment, wages, and prices.

Yet it is clear, despite some inevitable conflicts in research findings,
that macroeconomic factors (perhaps especially unemployment) can have
significant influences on trade union membership. But this influence
does not preclude the compositional factors, as some analysts argue.
The Chaison and Rose (1991) review of the research reports that international evidence suggests that compositional factors can account, in several
cases (including the USA and Britain), for about one-quarter to one-third
of the decline in union density. These are substantial proportions and translate into large numbers.[33] Additionally, the compositional effect includes
more than the impact of the assumed lower propensity to unionize of
workers in white collar and service sector occupations (Chaison and Rose
1991: 14–16). It also allows for the growth in the numbers employed in
temporary, part-time, and peripheral work and the decline in the number
of workplaces employing large numbers of people.[34]

Secondly, in explaining the differences between US and British experience, special consideration should be given to the traditional role and
practices of employers within current public policy contexts. British public policy only became wholly unfavourable to trade unions after 1979,
and even in 1980 it was not clear that there would be any anti-union
legislation beyond the Employment Act. The old ways of seeking an
accommodation with the TUC could have been resumed if Mrs Thatcher
had not strongly opposed such a policy (Taylor 1993: 286–7). It is also

possible, even perhaps probable, that there will be some return to the old ways before the end of the decade. At the same time, employers in Britain have only recently shown signs of stronger opposition to a trade union presence, but this is far from consistent and recourse to the use of the law is still rare. In the USA, both of these influences nearly always, and simultaneously, run against labour's interests. The traditional hostility of employers towards unions usually finds itself operating in supportive, or at worst neutralized, political contexts. It is this combination which primarily explains why US trade unions have always operated on the fringes of power and influence, except for brief, exceptional periods.[35] In Britain, they were only excluded from a central, on occasion pivotal, role in the years after 1979, and at least some of this role may yet be restored as the political tide turns. On their past record it is unlikely that employers will seriously oppose such an outcome.

CONCLUSIONS

Trade unions in Britain and the USA are clearly in acute crisis given the scale of the decline in their membership and the associated contraction of collective bargaining. The British case has been remarkable in that for the trade unions a long period of membership growth was transformed, in 1979, into a steep and sustained decline which is still continuing at an average rate of 3 per cent per annum. American unions have continued to experience a slower, but very much longer decline, which is perhaps more serious in its outcome given that density in the 'peak' year, in 1955, was about the same as the present low point in British membership.

Both movements are also subject, given the extent of decline, to regional marginalization or 'ghetto unionism'. This phenomenon is well advanced in the USA where many metropolitan districts and a large number of states are, for all practical purposes, virtually union-free. In Britain, too, the older regional strongholds of trade unionism retain some of their traditions, but without the industrial base to sustain them, as the rest of the country is increasingly dominated by private sector services in which trade unions find it more difficult to recruit members and secure or retain recognition. In both countries, in these contexts, trade unions struggle to retain a national identity and are likely to be seen, from outside, as simply representing special, even regional, interests. Nor are unions, in both Britain and the USA, currently attractive to the young. This is a problem of major significance as labour markets are heavily populated with young people who are without general access to long-term, stable employment and those who are employed are in sectors where unions do not have a significant presence.

In attempting to explain the decline of trade unions and the contraction of collective bargaining it is difficult to minimize the changing structure of both economies, especially over the past twenty years. In the case of Britain the 'collapse' of manufacturing in the recession of 1980–1 and its failure to recover, in employment terms, coincided with a rapid, post-1979, decline in union membership. Yet although up to 1979 both economies had been 'de-industrializing' at much the same rate, US unions were losing members and collective bargaining was contracting whilst the opposite was taking place in Britain. Furthermore, in other countries experiencing similar changes in their economies (a widespread phenomenon), where trade union membership has declined, the decline has generally been much less severe than in Britain and the USA and, in some cases, membership has not declined at all.

The continued survival, reasonably intact, of trade unions and their membership levels in many industrialized countries is likely to be largely explained, despite de-industrialization, by generally favourable political, industrial relations and labour law contexts. These contexts are well entrenched in EU countries and also exist at supranational levels through the EU's treaties and institutions. Britain has of course been an active member of the EU and its predecessors since 1973 and, up to 1979, though the British industrial relations system and traditions differed from those prevailing elsewhere in the EU, both favoured trade union membership growth, the extension of collective bargaining, and the enlargement of individual employment rights. These favourable contexts were transformed after 1979 when the political, industrial relations, and legislative contexts became progressively unfavourable under successive Conservative administrations without sufficient compensating redress from Brussels.

The contrast with the USA, especially before 1979, is clear. The political contexts, at best, were barely neutral towards trade unions. Employers, both individually and through their collective organizations, remained strongly opposed to any legislative attempt to revive union strength whilst some saw de-unionization as a corporate and national economic prize to be vigorously pursued by any means available. The earlier honeymoon between employers and labour during World War II scarcely outlasted hostilities and was followed by Taft–Hartley's partial reversal of the union gains of 1935. Nor did US labour ever reach the bargaining power and political influence of the British which, perhaps, reached its peak during the early years of Harold Wilson's 'social contract' from 1974 to 1976 (when employers were virtually excluded from Government–TUC bargaining)[36] and James Callaghan's succeeding administration. Here the year 1978 is instructive. Under a Democratic President and both houses of Congress controlled by the ostensibly pro-labour Democratic Party, the mild Labor Law Reform Bill failed to pass a filibustering Senate under the influence of the powerful employer lobbies. In the same year, in Britain, a Labour government was in power and had, since 1974, enacted a comprehensive programme of enhanced protection for individual employees, part of which brought Britain in line with the law-making initiatives of the European Commission and Council of Ministers in Brussels.

Generally, the presence of friendly Labour governments in Britain before 1979 (or reasonably benevolent Conservatives), within a favourable political culture and given employer behaviour which was normally pragmatic, cooperative, and accepting, provided the essential conditions for trade union growth. After 1979 the favourable political contexts were suddenly withdrawn and employer behaviour gradually became less supportive. The problems of the unions were then compounded by the unfavourable shift in labour market conditions and the legislation aimed at their vitals. Interestingly, the unions saw the 1971 Industrial Relations Act as a similar challenge to that of the legislation of the 1980s but in the 1970s the conditions for neutralizing the new law were present— even without a Labour government in office. After the 1974 General Election, Labour quickly moved to restoring most, if not all, of the pre-1971 voluntarism. The importance of favourable political contexts and cooperative employers was apparent after their loss after 1979 and the subsequent changes in British trade unions' prospects; the virtually continuous absence of both conditions in the USA must largely explain US unions' long-term problems.

This conclusion also suggests a contrast in prospects. The decline of US trade unions and collective bargaining may be seen as an inevitable, secular process given the highly unfavourable conditions which have endured over a long period and are probably getting stronger. Alternatively, given these adverse conditions, the revival of US trade unions is possible but the conditions for that revival, if they exist, lie in their own hands: they can expect little from government and nothing from employers. For British unions the presently unfavourable conditions can be reversed and such a shift will then directly benefit the unions' own strategies for revival of their membership base. It is also possible to see British unions' problems since 1979 as 'cyclical'[37] in contrast to the long secular decline of their US counterparts. The British and US cases may also fit a general explanation for union growth (and decline) which downgrades the influence of macroeconomic and compositional changes and emphasizes public policy and employer opposition 'as leading explanations of the divergence in union growth rates among industrialized countries' (Chaison and Rose 1991: 36).

Hence British unions have more reason to be optimistic than the American about their prospects given the presence of employers who are much less aggressive and the possibility of favourable change in political contexts. But it is a qualified optimism: without a Labour government and the likelihood of continuing hostility from a re-elected Conservative administration, the case for optimism evaporates. At the same time, despite the many problems facing the US labour movement, recent organizational successes may yet point a way forward. It may also be that British unions are much less capable, on their own, of restoring their fortunes. These prospects are discussed in Chapter 4 and the Conclusions.

NOTES

1. The important statistic of 'density' can be measured in a number of different ways with different numerators and denominators. Different measures of density serve different purposes. As an indicator of the *extent* of trade unionism at the place of work, trade union membership related to the number of employed wage and salary workers (US) and civilian employees in employment (Great Britain) is used throughout this chapter and elsewhere. However, most of the later British data (1989–93) are from the Labour Force Survey (LFS) which includes staff association membership with that of trade unions. The data from the Certification Officer are for 'independent' trade unions only which exclude some staff associations and are published annually. Here the data up to 1990 are from this source. The coverage of most of the British tables is for Great Britain (i.e. excluding Northern Ireland), especially those using LFS data. UK coverage is indicated where appropriate.

   Chaison and Rose (1991) have made a strong claim for collective bargaining 'coverage' as a measure of the *influence* of collective bargaining. Coverage is available from US sources but less so from the British although the Workplace Industrial Relations Surveys (see Millward *et al.* 1992) as well as recent additional LFS questions (see Table 3.9) have improved the position. Where available, comparative data on collective bargaining coverage have been included and complement the density data.

   Overall, given the problems of definition, coverage, and consistency over time inherent in the data, especially the British, the comparative union membership data in this chapter should only be treated as indicative of *general* or *broad* trends and developments.
2. The term is widely thought to have first emerged in Philip Bassett's (1986) study of the emergence of single union agreements in Japanese-owned companies in Britain.
3. In contrast to the USA, Japanese auto companies locating in Britain have recognized unions, albeit normally *one* per plant and of the company's choosing. The recent, important exception is Honda at its new factory in Swindon, Wiltshire, which refuses to consider recognition on the grounds that its employees do not want it.
4. Non-union HRM organizations frequently cited in academic studies (arising from their rarity) are also US owned, as for example IBM, Hewlett-Packard, and Gillette.
5. The European Works Council (EWC) again provides a good example. British Euro-companies, despite the previous Conservative government's opt-out from the Social Chapter and their own general opposition to the EWC, commonly

implemented the voluntary route (then available as an alternative to the imposition of the directive) and with some enthusiasm.

6. For an interesting discussion of the significance of union decline see Goldfield (1987: ch. 4).

7. Whilst the sit-downs were widespread, the most famous was that at General Motors in 1937. See n. 23.

8. The Order survived a Congressional intention to withdraw federal funds to implement it as part of its budget-cutting bill (*Labor Trends* 1995). It was, however, ultimately overturned in the courts with only the possibility of an appeal to the Supreme Court.

9. Under Section 14(b) of the Labor Management Relations Act (Taft–Hartley) of 1947 the 'pre-entry' closed shop was outlawed. Additionally, individual states were permitted to outlaw all other forms of 'union security'. The most important forms are the union shop (i.e. 'post-entry' closed shop) and the agency shop. The former requires new employees to join the contract union after an agreed time (minimum thirty days) or lose their jobs. The latter requires non-union members of the bargaining unit to pay a fee to the union for representation services. This provision is a response to the 'free rider' problem. States which prohibit forms of union security are known as 'right-to-work' states. Currently there are twenty-one although, since the Republican election victories of 1994, there has been political and employer pressure in a number of other states to pass right-to-work laws. The twenty-one, in 1996, with 1995 densities (Hirsch and Macpherson 1996: table 8a) were: Alabama (13.6), Arizona (8.0), Arkansas (7.8), Florida (7.3), Georgia (6.8), Idaho (8.1), Iowa (12.1), Kansas (10.2), Louisiana (7.0), Mississippi (5.2), Nebraska (9.1), Nevada (20.2), North Carolina (4.2), North Dakota (10.0), South Carolina (3.3), South Dakota (7.7), Tennessee (9.5), Texas (6.5), Utah (9.0), Virginia (6.7), Wyoming (11.2). Of these states only Nevada's density was above the 1995 national average.

10. For a comparative treatment of Japanese inward investors in Britain and the USA see Wilkinson and Oliver (1996).

11. The US and British official definitions of part-time do, however, differ: the US is *less than* thirty-five hours worked per week, the British *not more than* thirty.

12. For a comprehensive US assessment of the first decade of deregulation see Keefe and Boroff (1994); for Britain see Beaumont (1992: 84–6); Kessler and Bayliss (1995: ch. 7); and Barrett and Heery (1995).

13. Since the Trade Union Reform and Employment Rights Act (1993) employers can legally discriminate in this way.

14. The RCN, founded in 1916, grew from 162,000 members in 1979 to 282,000 in 1988 and 300,000 in 1994. Since it was founded, the union's rules have not allowed for industrial action, although this has not inhibited militant postures in recent years. However at its 1995 conference, in the context of major pay and bargaining structure pressures from government and management in the NHS, the RCN voted overwhelmingly to change its constitution to allow for 'limited legal industrial action', subject to ratification by a ballot of the membership (Kessler and Bayliss 1995: 136; Wood 1995). A much smaller nursing union—the Royal College of Midwives (RCM) with 33,000 members—has followed a similar path to the RCN. A membership ballot in 1988 rejected a change in the rules to permit industrial action although this

did not inhibit the union from organizing 'days of action' in subsequent disputes. Furthermore, in 1995, a second ballot, by a very large majority, changed the rules to allow industrial action—although short of a strike.

Other nurses, including some midwives, are members of the largest TUC union (UNISON) which was formed through a triple merger in 1993 with membership at 1.3 million. UNISON's rules permit all forms of industrial action.

15. For example, Donald Cullen (1987) with his speculations on the case for a 'rerun' and Kochan *et al.* who saw no likelihood that unions and collective bargaining would 'wither away or disappear completely' and that new organizing strategies for growing occupations and industries might, given a fair socio-political wind 'reverse the downward trend in worker representation' (1986: 250–3). These prospects are discussed in later chapters.

16. See Kumar (1993). Troy (1992) does, however, take issue with the divergence thesis, predicting similar prospects for Canadian labour as for the USA. See also the vigorous debate on Troy's dissent in the *British Journal of Industrial Relations* (1993, Special Edition).

17. See Whitfield *et al.* (1994) for the first fruits of Anglo-Australian research using survey data. See also the discussion in the Introduction.

18. Research is now invariably showing that this assertion is no more than that. For example, recent private and public sector data from the British LFS shows that 'there is no real difference between men and women in their propensity to join unions' (Cully and Woodland 1996: 220). For the USA, research suggests no relationship 'between gender and propensity to vote for union formation' (Wheeler and McClendon 1991: 64).

19. The employment composition effect has been estimated as explaining only 30% of density losses (Green 1992: 456). This may be reasonably good news for unions since it suggests substantial control over their own destiny although it still represents about 2 million members since 1979.

20. In European countries there are strong statistical correlations between average union density and control by left-wing parties (Visser 1988).

21. All Conservative governments for a century have sought some degree of rapprochement with the trade unions. This was especially the case for more than three decades after World War II. Even the Heath government's Industrial Relations Act of 1971 sought reforms which would have been far more agreeable to the trade unions than the legislation of 1980 to 1993. For a review of the relationship between British trade unions and government since 1945 see Kessler and Bayliss (1995), Marsh (1992), and Taylor (1993).

22. Pattern bargaining is a particular form of multi-employer bargaining perhaps best suited to an industry dominated by a few, oligopolistic, firms. The principal union in the industry targets one of the firms at the expiry of the contract. The eventual settlement, usually agreed after a strike, then becomes the 'pattern' for the remaining firms. Pattern bargaining is still intact between the UAW and the 'big three' in the auto industry but is under threat from the employers. In the steel industry, conventional multi-employer bargaining was ended by the employers in 1985 (Fossum 1995: 202).

23. This historic struggle has of course been analysed and celebrated in a vast literature as well as in film, documentary, and local historical initiatives. The

factory building in Flint, Michigan which was the scene of the sit-down ('Fisher 2') was demolished in 1994. The sit-down, which was illegal, had many of the features of the famous Upper Clyde Shipbuilders (UCS) sit-in of 1972, including its illegality. The Flint action was a struggle for recognition barely two years after the passing of the Wagner Act supporting collective bargaining: the UCS sit-in was against closure of the shipyard. In the literature, the best start is Fine (1969) and for UCS, Foster and Woolfson (1986).

24. This was perhaps the most significant of the problems facing the Dunlop Commission in 1993–5. It is discussed in more detail in Chapter 7.

25. For a recent, detailed account of the 'winter of discontent' and its political and economic contexts see Kessler and Bayliss (1995).

26. This literature is reviewed in Stepina and Fiorito (1986) and Chaison and Rose (1991).

27. For a concise, interesting history of the Ministry of Labour and its successors see Freedland (1992).

28. Millward (1994: 2–3). However Millward also observes 'widespread agreement that the last decade saw a major transformation in British industrial relations' (ibid. 1).

29. These statutes remained essentially intact until the scope of the 1906 Act was narrowed, and the 1913 Act amended, by the Conservative government in the 1980s (see Ch. 2).

30. From 1945 to 1979 the Labour and Conservative Parties had each exactly the same number of years in office, i.e. seventeen (see Appendix 1). After 1979 the Conservatives' election victories decisively shifted this equality, although, given the size of Labour's 1997 majority, two terms in office is, at the least, a strong possibility.

31. Particularly from 1945 to 1951 in public sector industrial relations and from 1974 to 1979 under the 'Social Contract' when individual employee protection was greatly extended and collective bargaining, under the 1975 Employment Protection Act, became a function of ACAS.

32. For an overview of the influence of Samuel Gompers see Salvatore (1984).

33. e.g. in the British case, if compositional factors explained one-quarter of the fall in density between 1979 and 1993, i.e. 4.5%, this represents almost 1.5 million members with total membership exceeding 10 million in 1993 instead of less than 9 million.

34. The British Workplace Industrial Relations Surveys (Millward *et al.* 1992) found that a large part of the fall in trade union membership and representation between 1980 and 1984 arose from 'the fall in the numbers of large, highly unionized, manufacturing plants' (p. 356).

35. V. O. Key commented on this many years ago: 'He who would understand politics in the large may ponder well the status of labor: a numerically great force in a society adhering to the doctrine of the rule of numbers, yet without proportionate durable power as a class', cited in Rogers (1992).

36. A discussion of the Social Contract of 1974 to 1979 is to be found in Ch. 6. A recent account of the period is in Kessler and Bayliss (1995).

37. This is the argument of McIlroy in his recently revised book on British trade unions (McIlroy 1995: 391–400).

4

Is Decline Inevitable?

Economic, political and industrial trends continue to militate against
trade unionism. New approaches are important if a descent to US
levels of unionisation and consequent remoulding of industrial relations are to be avoided.

(McIlroy 1995: 417)

Labor's obituary has been written at least once in every one of the
105 years of our existence . . . some of our better-known labor economists and academics have earned tenure by publishing predictions that unions would perish. It seems that we must be forever
perishing so that others may be forever publishing.

(Kirkland 1986: 393)

In reviewing and assessing the explanations for trade union decline
and the contraction of collective bargaining it is easy to conclude that
unions, by their own actions, can have only a minimal impact on the
process of decline, given the formidable array of powerful, socio-political,
and economic factors involved; and as unions weaken, their growing
incapacity to influence the process itself accelerates their decline. For
example, employers operating in public policy contexts which favour the
non-recognition and derecognition of trade unions are able to reduce
overall density, making union exclusion easier to achieve and pushing
density even further downwards. This process has been described, in
the British case, as a 'vicious circle' and it has even been maintained
that trade union leaders are powerless to arrest it (Bain and Price 1983:
33). For the USA, there is also research which concludes that organizing campaigns can only replace lost members and are unable to keep
pace with the expansion of the labour force (Chaison and Rose 1991:
27–30). The contrary view is that dynamic and skilful trade union leaders,
with appropriate policies, can have a significant influence upon membership levels (Undy *et al*. 1981). It can also be argued that the failure of
organizing drives is often simply found in the way they are implemented
and the inadequacy of allocated resources.

Yet even a well-planned, sustained, and generously resourced organizing campaign must clearly have limited outcomes if faced with powerful
contextual influences moving in the opposite direction—especially when
acting together. In Britain in the early 1980s, for example, structural
changes in the economy and employment were taking place at the same
time as unemployment was rising to record levels, with both aggravated

by deflationary, monetarist policy. Additionally, by 1982, two anti-union statutes had been passed and employers were being encouraged by legislation and government exhortation to roll back trade union power and influence. The outcome was substantial membership and density losses, which could scarcely have been influenced by even major recruitment campaigns, which in any case were not mounted until well into the 1980s and then with only very limited, and unsustained, success.

The experience of US unions was not the same in that the mix and relative impact of adverse influences were different. The structural factors were similar in their incidence and effect, although the Reagan administration's macroeconomic policies were much less consistent and subject to modification or reversal by a Democratic Congress. Nor was there anything to compare with the strength of the Thatcherite combination of policy and legislation. Reagan's actions against PATCO were, however, much more draconian than the measures taken against, for example, the GCHQ unions, whilst US employers continued to tighten their already deep anti-union screws, in contrast to the more pragmatic voluntarism of their British counterparts. Despite the differences, the climate for US unions was, however, on balance just as unfavourable as that with which British unions had to contend and with density continuing to fall, although with less severe consequences for total membership than in Britain.

But the recent combination of adverse circumstances need not be permanent. The unfavourable macroeconomic, political, and employment contexts which have made organizing new members difficult could yet change to benefit unions. Structural economic change, for example, may stabilize. Some successful economies' manufacturing sectors are, as we have seen, proportionately larger than in the USA and Britain and government policies can also influence the process of de-industrialization.[1] It is also possible that the preoccupation of governments, since the mid-1970s, with counter-inflation policy at the expense of maximizing employment may yet be reversed given the serious social and welfare-funding implications of sustained mass unemployment. Politically, too, the climate can shift to favour union revival strategies, especially in Britain, given the possibility of Labour governments which the unions can also then seek to influence, when in office, towards policies and legislation which favour reversing membership decline.

The development of effective organizing strategies is not, of course, the only option available to US and British trade unions seeking a revival in their membership and fortunes. Mergers, for example, have taken place since the early days of trade unions but from the 1980s have been pursued more vigorously in both countries in response to serious membership losses. Serious membership losses can also have direct financial implications for trade unions given their usually heavy dependence on

membership dues. However both union movements through appropriate policies, especially dues increases, have so far avoided serious
financial crises. There has also been a retreat from traditional adversarial
strategies towards much greater cooperation with management, unions
seeking to make themselves indispensable partners in the commercial
success of organizations. This much less confrontational stance in the
workplace has also been reflected, especially in Britain, in a rethinking
of the purposes and methods of trade unions in the wider society, taking
them closer to traditional US business unionism. However the workplace
may remain the principal arena in which revival must begin: an issue
to which we shall return in the conclusions to this chapter.

ORGANIZING NEW MEMBERS

Some US analysts see the seemingly waning capacity of the unions to
organize new members (as well as their former success) as the primary
explanation for declining union density with union failure related to the
low priority and inadequate spending given to organizing.[2] In Britain,
the need to spend time and resources on the recruitment of new members can conflict with the responsibility to service existing members
(Kelly and Heery 1989; 1994) and the costs incurred in recruitment may
not be justified if new members are only retained for a short period.
Since the mid-1980s most British unions have launched recruitment
campaigns but these have been criticized as high on rhetoric, low on
resources, and without a strategic approach (Mason and Bain 1993;
McIlroy 1995). But these failings have not been universal and, whilst in
terms of recruiting new members such campaigns have generally been
unsuccessful, they can contribute to other goals, such as the long-term
development of the unions involved (Snape 1994).

The TUC, which led two campaigns in the 1980s, was influenced by
the example of the AFL-CIO. This took two forms: experimental recruitment drives in specific areas[3] and an emphasis upon the services which
unions can offer such as credit cards, and legal and financial advice. The
TUC itself now has its own bank which although small is viable and
provides all the normal services. The TUC's recent discussion of the case
for institutions to represent *employees* at the place of work (see Chapter
6) might also indicate a similar approach to the 1985 recommendation
by the AFL-CIO for unions to concentrate more on offering services to
non-union members and even developing new 'affiliate' or 'associate'
categories of membership (AFL-CIO 1985). More recently, a TUC delegation to Washington has been reported as being 'impressed' by the AFL-
CIO's Organising Institute, set up in 1989 to support affiliates' campaigns,

especially its use of teams of young, university-educated, professionals (Taylor 1995).

The emphasis on services in recruitment campaigns has been criticized as a misunderstanding of the reasons which attract people to unions. British research suggests that pay, ideological commitment, and the expectation of protection are more important than an attractive range of services (Sapper 1991; IRS 1996: 605). In the USA the Service Employees' International Union (SEIU), one of the few growing unions, gained 360,000 members in the 1980s to pass the million mark. Its organizing strategy, especially in the case of its 'Justice for Janitors' campaigns beginning in 1987, energetically pressed demands for recognition and improved wages and benefits in the workplace as a right. The demands for recognition were on the basis of card counts, not NLRB certification procedures, supported by direct action through corporate campaigns, organized protests, and, where appropriate, tactical guerrilla strikes (Johnston 1994: 164–6). Other recent successful SEIU campaigns, on the Justice for Janitors model, have been among home health care, and nursing home workers. These groups are both low paid and work in expanding occupations (*Economic Notes* 1994: 8) offering, perhaps, wider recruitment lessons.

The examples of successful organizing campaigns in US conditions suggest a place for countering employer hostility by a tough, militant approach. The Justice for Janitors campaigns also emphasize the often counter-productive effect of NLRB certification procedures and that employers can be compelled to recognize unions without NLRB involvement. But these tactics may have limited scope. For example, excessive hostility in campaigns may provoke an employer reaction. Recent survey evidence suggests that the disapproval of unions, by employers, is an important negative influence on employees' decisions to join unions (Freeman and Rogers 1994).

In British contexts, the cooperation, or forced acquiescence, of employers is essential given the absence of any legal procedure for recognition or legal constraints on derecognition, regardless of the proportion unionized in bargaining units. However British employers, as we have seen, have, though only since the 1980s, begun to resist union pressure for recognition, as well as seek derecognition.

In both countries, as elsewhere, the attitudes and behaviour of employers greatly influence the recruitment and recognition processes and the development of collective bargaining. Carefully planned, adequately resourced, and energetically implemented recruitment and recognition campaigns can achieve success, as in the Justice for Janitors campaign, although such successes remain rare. The capacity of US employers to use the NLRB procedures to their maximum advantage, complemented by illegal or quasi-legal methods and the inability of the political system to deliver even the most moderate of reforms to control employer abuses, continue to act as a severe handicap to trade union recovery. Here, as we noted earlier, the recent survey of Freeman and Rogers (1994) reveals the significant negative impact of employer opposition upon the decision to join a union. It also reveals employees' reluctance, in the context of such opposition, to support the union in a certification election. Employees' fears are also real ones, that is, employers will freely use their wide powers to hire and fire to discourage or break trade unions.

British employers, despite the growth of anti-union attitudes and tactics from the 1980s, remain, in general, much less oppositional, and this is despite the continuing absence of any legal controls. British unions, even with the severe losses since 1979, have not yet reached a critical low point in their power and influence and the traditional accommodating ways of employers are still in evidence, many of whom still see positive gains from a trade union presence, not least in the implementation of changes in working practices (Storey 1994). Additionally, British membership of the European Union can encourage US-style 'whipsawing' but it can also promote the spread of transnational employment protection legislation and voluntary implementation of industrial relations institutions, as is evident in the now widespread incidence and continuing growth of European Works Councils. In Britain itself, employers, as history suggests, tend to respond pragmatically to the governing party and would normally cooperate with the legislation and policies of a Labour government favouring a return to positive employer cooperation with trade unions.

MULTI-UNIONISM, MERGERS, AND MEMBERSHIP

British union mergers in the 1950s and 1960s were often a response to the problems of demarcation and union competition for members in multi-union conditions. Employers welcomed mergers which eliminated demarcation disputes, notably in the ports and later in the key car sector where the number of unions fell progressively, through merger and absorption, from twenty-two in the 1960s to four in the 1980s. For Britain as a whole, by the late 1980s, of those workplaces with union members, just over half were represented by a single union, a process which has been positively encouraged by some employers through new approaches to bargaining such as single union agreements and single table bargaining, discussed later in this chapter. Overall, the decline in multi-unionism in Britain is closely associated with the decline in density (Millward 1994: 43) and an increase in employer bargaining power. For their part, British unions have commonly responded to declining membership by reducing the number of unions still further through merger. A fall in the number of unions, for this reason, has also been the US experience. For example, since the formation of the AFL-CIO in 1955, the number of affiliates has fallen from 135 to 96, primarily through merger (Williamson 1995). Correspondingly, in Britain, the number of TUC affiliates declined by 300 between 1945 and 1979, again mainly through merger (Buchanan 1992) and since 1979 the number has fallen from 109 to 69.

In both countries, mergers have generally taken the form of absorption, that is, a large union absorbing a much smaller one (Williamson 1995: 19; Willman *et al.* 1993: 95). In such cases, though the smaller union loses its independence, it gains the resources and protection of the larger and may even retain some of its identity as a department, section, or trade group. In the USA, merger activity through absorption has been dominated by four unions: the service workers (SEIU); machinists (IAM); the food and commercial workers (UFCW); and the communication workers (CWA) (Williamson 1994). British merger through absorption has also been mainly through big general unions such as the Transport and General Workers (TGWU) and the General and Municipal Workers (GMB).

In Britain, in the 1980s, the merger process began to take a different route as membership and influence rapidly declined. Unions which were already large sought mergers with other large unions to form 'super-unions'. In 1987 Manufacturing, Science, and Finance (MSF) was formed from two unions with memberships among managers, supervisors, white collar employees, and technicians. This was followed in 1991 by the final bringing together of printing workers into one union, the Graphical, Paper, and Media Union (GPMU) and in 1992 the Amalgamated Engineering and Electrical Union (AEEU) combining engineers, electricians, and plumbers was formed with over 1 million members. Then in 1993 a new union (UNISON) emerged in the public sector combining three unions with a total membership of 1.4 million. Finally, low key, desultory merger talks have been proceeding towards a possible merger between the TGWU and GMB which would create a union of over 1.8 million, the third largest in Europe after Germany's IG Metall with 3.6 million (*Labour Research*, September 1993).

These mergers, in the main, have industrial logic yet, overall, the British unions' experience of merger does not seem to be unequivocally positive (Waddington 1995a). Whilst larger unions, through merger, will have increased their capacity to survive in the context of membership decline, unions cannot be simply seen as analogous to businesses with unreaped economies of scale, and with potential savings from staff reductions, especially where the merger is organized on a semi-autonomous, sectional basis. However, mergers can provide the opportunity for changes in organizational structure as well as introducing more effective financial controls (Willman *et al.* 1993; Snape 1994).

Proposed 'super-union' mergers in the USA have been commonplace in recent years, not least that between the two teachers' unions, the National Education Association (NEA) and the American Federation of Teachers (AFT). The talks broke down in late 1994, despite the apparent logic, partly because the NEA is not affiliated to the AFL-CIO, but also reflecting possible diseconomies of scale, that is, doubts about whether such a large union could effectively represent all its members (Williamson 1995: 24).

The most recent merger announcement between US unions has raised most of these issues. The merger of the autoworkers (UAW), steelworkers (USWA), and machinists (IAM) would create a large union for the metalworking industry (almost 2 million), nearly analogous, it is claimed, to its much-admired, German counterpart, IG Metall. The German union is the model for both British and US large-scale mergers with its capacity to mount effective challenges to powerful German employers, including Volkswagen. The power of IG Metall is not however simply a function of its size and resources. The statutory works councils in the German metal-goods industry, as elsewhere, are controlled by trade union members (Jacobi *et al.* 1992) and both trade unions and collective bargaining of wages and conditions are institutionalized, stable features of German industrial relations. The absence of these highly favourable contexts, especially in the USA, limits the potential gains from large-scale mergers. The US metalworkers' merger arises from weakness, that is, falling membership, and is intended to be achieved over five years, casting some doubt on its eventual outcome. It may also attract concerted action from US employers who historically, unlike the British, do not stand passively by as unions are increasing their industrial strength. Furthermore the combined strike fund of the new union, estimated as $1 bn., is still dwarfed by employer resources and their capacity to negate the effectiveness of the strike weapon by the legally supported tactic, or threat, of permanent replacement of economic strikers.

For Britain, the experience of merger has generally fallen short of its potential, notably in the case of the creation of the MSF in 1987 and the GPMU in 1992. Neither has provided a platform for membership growth and the GPMU remains vulnerable to the withdrawal of the printing employers from national level bargaining. In contrast, the general union, GMB, the product of a number of mergers through its history—a policy which it still maintains—now seems to be beginning to contain membership decline, is vigorously seeking new members through expending its 'service' image, and is successfully controlling its costs (Willman *et al.* 1993: 140–53). Yet any success achieved by the GMB in expanding its membership is likely to remain in the context of inter-union competition and decline of union membership as a whole, that is, its survival is achieved at the expense of other unions. The British evidence also suggests that the initiative for mergers comes, not from the membership, but from the leadership, even though ballots are required to endorse their decisions (Willman *et al.* 1993: 94–100). The role of union leaders in mergers is also evident in the USA, most recently in the case of the UAW, IAM, and USWA merger which remained a closely guarded secret until the decision was announced. In that respect, union leaders are adopting the behaviour of their big business counterparts. Interestingly, recent British research on union members, which may also have lessons for US unions, concludes that mergers offer few representative or administrative advantages and that 'joint ventures' without merger are likely to be more viable alternatives. However neither merger nor collaboration can, by themselves, halt, much less reverse, membership decline (Willman and Cave 1994: 409–10). Even so, unions are organizations which should be run to minimize their costs and maximize their economic effectiveness and in so doing also contribute to their representative and democratic roles.

MEMBERSHIP AND FINANCE

In international terms, US unions remain among the wealthiest. Yet the US movement's wealth is still small relative to the corporate sector or even to a single, large corporation. Nor is the movement what it was. Even in better times, in 1969, the combined assets of US unions only ranked eighteenth among the list of the top 500 corporations; and by 1976 this ranking had slipped to thirty-third (Sheflin and Troy 1983). Recent British data also reveals seemingly large net union wealth (funds plus assets less liabilities) of £1.4 bn. (Certification Officer 1996), although this only equates to the annual gross *profits* of a large, successful company and at £170 per member (on a 1994 figure of 8.24 million members) provides a slender margin to meet a sustained crisis. Indeed, overall, British unions' *real* wealth has declined since 1950 (Willman *et al.* 1993: ch. 2).

The distribution of internal union assets differs between the two countries. In the USA, locals and national/international headquarters broadly control equal shares of total assets at about 45 per cent each (Sheflin and Troy 1983), reflecting and reinforcing the strong localism and decentralization of US industrial relations. British unions' assets are conventionally held and controlled at the centre, a situation unaffected by the decentralization of British collective bargaining over the past twenty years. A major, traditional exception is the National Union of Mineworkers (NUM) arising from its federal structure (Aston *et al.* 1990; Willman *et al.* 1993: ch. 8).

Both union movements remain heavily dependent upon membership income. For US unions this grew from 75 per cent of income to 81 per

Table 4.1. *Income from membership of private sector unions in the USA, 1960–1987*

	Membership (millions)	Nominal Receipts ($ billion)	Real* Receipts ($ billion)	Per Capita Receipts	
				Nominal ($)	Real ($)
1960	14.61	0.923	3.118	63	213
1970	16.98	2.363	5.937	139	350
1976	16.17	3.284	5.741	203	355
1987	10.86	5.479	4.823	504	444

Note: * Nominal receipts adjusted for the consumer price index.

Source: Bennett (1991: 4, table 2).

cent between 1962 and 1976 (Sheflin and Troy 1983). British unions' dependency on membership income was as high as 89 per cent in 1950 but was still 82 per cent in 1989 (Willman *et al*. 1993) and the most recent figure is 83 per cent (Certification Officer 1995). These figures indicate a relatively low level of investment activity, although unions, for operational reasons, need to retain a large proportion of their assets in relatively liquid form.

Yet despite the vulnerable combination of high dependence on membership income and major membership losses, overall, British and US unions have, from the 1970s, successfully maintained financial viability by increasing membership dues, although in the US case there is also access to substantial external income from federal grants, contracts, and state programmes (Bennett 1991: 5). Data for US private sector unions from 1960 to 1987 are shown in Table 4.1.

British unions' average dues over the earlier years of membership decline (1979–85) more than doubled to 64p per week and then rose to 85p in 1989 (Certification Officer 1981; 1991). The outcome, as for the USA, was the avoidance of a general financial crisis although many unions and the TUC have been forced into radical economies and staff reductions. Raising dues may also have contributed to membership losses, even though the revenue outcome justified the increases. British unions also had substantial scope for increases with traditionally low dues' levels compared to other countries. For example, even after the large increases of the 1980s, British subscription levels currently average only 0.5 to 0.6 per cent of members' gross incomes and the highest are no more than 0.8 per cent. In other European countries they commonly exceed 1.0 per cent (*Labour Research*, July 1996a: 19–21), whilst in the USA limited evidence indicates an even higher proportion.[4]

Not surprisingly, British unions remain poorer than their European or US counterparts and this has for long been largely explained by the low level of subscriptions. During the 1970s, for example, despite rapid membership growth, financial problems became acute and did not ease until declining membership in the 1980s prompted the unions to review their subscription levels (Willman *et al.* 1993: ch. 2). Membership revival growth is not therefore a financial benefit to unions unless accompanied by a growth in membership income above the costs of servicing the new members—as the experience of British unions in the 1970s demonstrates.

A similar problem also faces US unions in the federal sector. Under the Federal Service Labor-Management Relations Statute of the Civil Service Reform Act of 1978, employee representation is protected but bargaining excludes 'economic' issues and strikes are prohibited. More significantly for the federal unions' finances, while they are compelled to represent all employees, whether members of the union or not (as in the private sector), these non-union employees are not required to pay union dues under the 1978 Statute's ban on all forms of union security for federal employees.

Hence these 'free rider' employees can enjoy the benefits of membership whilst avoiding the costs, that is, union dues. Unions with high proportions of free riders are therefore liable to experience financial instability. There is in fact evidence of substantial free riding in the federal sector despite much higher rates of union membership relative to the USA as a whole (Masters and Atkin 1993). Free riding can also be a problem in the private sector where union security agreements are not concluded or in the 'right-to-work' states where, as in the federal sector, they are prohibited. However, research evidence reveals that right-to-work laws do not have a significant negative effect on union membership levels[5] although this does not imply that union security clauses are not of substantial benefit to trade unions' bargaining power or their financial stability. Certainly unions fight hard to retain such clauses in contracts.

In the USA, labour contracts incorporating union security agreements also normally include a check-off arrangement in which employers deduct union membership dues from pay. This practice has obvious benefits for unions' cash flow although the check-off is not necessarily an unmixed blessing.[6] British check-off arrangements have also been closely associated with closed shop agreements. They did, however, tend to persist despite the decline of closed shops as statutory protection was progressively removed in the 1980s.[7] The check-off was also subjected to restrictions under the 1993 Trade Union Reform and Employment Rights Act which, by August 1994, required prior written employee consent and, thereafter, renewal of consent every three years. Additionally, any increase in dues has to be notified to members at least a month in advance along with a reminder that withdrawal from the check-off is always available.

The 1993 Act was clearly intended to have a negative effect on union membership by providing regular opportunities for resignation. It also potentially constrains the ability of unions to increase dues—the means by which they have maintained their financial viability as membership has declined since 1979. In the event, the effect on membership has not been as severe as predicted and some unions have reported increases in membership through their check-off campaigns. Employers have also generally cooperated in the new check-off arrangements and, although some major employers have withdrawn from their agreements, the majority have maintained them for reasons of hard-headed advantage, such as avoiding the disruption from stewards collecting contributions as well as the wider benefits of orderly, well-established collective bargaining in securing change (Kessler and Bayliss 1995: 163–4). The provisions of the 1993 Act do, however, still pose serious problems for British unions. Some have been relatively successful in persuading their members to pay their dues through 'direct debits' via bank accounts. But these exercises in persuasion are costly as are the three-yearly campaigns to maintain membership subscription income. The Labour Government is, however, promising to repeal the restrictions on the check-off.

The decline in British union membership and continuing financial pressures on unions have had a major financial impact upon the TUC, which remains heavily dependent upon affiliation fees despite measures to secure revenue from other sources, and despite organizational economies and staff reductions. Savings through staff reductions in 1992 largely converted a deficit into a surplus of £656,000 on an income of £11.6 m. (Certification Officer 1994: appendix 4) but the main, continuing, emphasis has been upon increasing and maintaining affiliation fees at viable levels. In 1993 (and for the next two years) the old flat rate fee for each member of an affiliated union was converted to a figure linked to the weighted average level of unions' weekly dues.[8] This approach has the merit of allowing for automatic increases in revenue linked to the membership and subscription increases of affiliates. But it does not preclude affiliating at lower levels of membership[9] and tightens further the financial pressures on the unions. Some of the larger 'super-union' affiliates have also found a diminishing need for the central services of the TUC. These they can provide for themselves as, for example, can the non-affiliates to the AFL-CIO such as the National Education Association.

The British unions' financial ability to sustain the TUC is also much less than the capacity of US unions to underwrite the AFL-CIO. Nor is the TUC able to fund major organizing efforts on the scale of the AFL-CIO's 'Union Summer' of 1996, with an organizing budget set at 30 per cent of available resources (McClure 1995) which includes spending $20 m.

on training full-time organizers. The TUC's role is currently restricted to 'advice and encouragement' although it is drawing upon the organizing experience of other union movements (notably those in the USA and Australia) and is preparing proposals for 'central funding' (IRS 1996: 611, p. 4). Indeed for all labour movements it remains clear that their fortunes, in all senses, are closely linked to their membership levels, policies on members' dues, and sound financial management.

LABOUR–MANAGEMENT COOPERATION

Whilst the interests of labour and management may be seen as inherently in conflict (but not always conflictual), British and US unions have always deployed an appropriate blend of adversarial and cooperative approaches towards management. However, especially since the early 1980s, greater cooperation by trade unions in management bargaining initiatives has mainly reflected the growing weakness of trade unions. Indeed, cooperation, especially in the USA, has often been the only option available to unions faced with management who would prefer to exclude them from the workplace. Many companies have of course sought to improve productivity and quality without trade unions, notably Japanese auto manufacturers such as Nissan which easily defeated the UAW's major organizing drive at its Smyrna, Tennessee plant in 1989, as well as electronics companies such as Sanyo and Sony which have often either resisted unions or sought their decertification (Kenney and Florida 1993: 284–5). However, the exclusion strategy is not universal even in auto assembly. A famous example which has attracted much academic and media attention is the joint venture between General Motors (GM) and Toyota at their New United Motor Manufacturing Inc. (NUMMI) plant at Fremont in California as well as several partnerships between GM alone and the UAW. Of the latter, the Saturn plant is significant for its scale and innovations as well as its location in the virtually non-union state of Tennessee where Nissan, as we noted earlier, succeeded in excluding the UAW.

Heckscher (1988: 116–37) distinguishes between three major forms of labour–management cooperation: false cooperation, cooperation in the formulation of corporate strategy, and worker participation at workplace level. The false variety—in which the rhetoric of cooperation to meet serious financial problems and/or powerful competition cloaks the reality of exacting concessions from unions—need not detain us here although recent research suggests that it is well established (Perline and Sexton 1994).

The corporate strategy form is well exemplified by the Saturn case although the joint decision-making culture extends from the boardroom, through all levels of the organization, to the shop-floor (Bluestone and Bluestone 1992: 191–201). In contrast, NUMMI confines extensive coop- erative practices to the shopfloor with an emphasis on teamwork and the selection of team leaders by joint union–management committees and, unlike Saturn, is less concerned with a change in the total decision- making culture than substantial productivity gains (Levine 1995: 10–35; Kochan and Osterman 1994; Turner 1991: 53–62). Apart from auto assembly, Japanese companies in steel, rubber, and tyres have com- monly worked with unions to achieve higher workplace performance and concessions although a familiar strategy has been to use the threat of decertification to ensure cooperation (Kenney and Florida 1993: 285).

In Britain, the Japanese approach to trade unions, though much dif- ferent and more consistent, has largely been made possible, as in the USA, by the unions' growing weakness throughout the 1980s. The prin- cipal approach has been the single union agreement which for Japanese inward investors has, among its other advantages, avoided traditional British multi-unionism and allowed the employer, on greenfield sites, to select the union it was prepared to recognize. The first of these agree- ments was pioneered by Toshiba in 1981. Such agreements commonly include five principal ingredients in addition to the recognition of a single union: wide-ranging flexible work arrangements; institutionalized information disclosure and participation; a strong commitment to training and retraining; single status (i.e. common) conditions and benefits for blue and white collar employees; and a joint commitment to use arbitra- tion to settle disputes.[10]

The terms of these agreements, including the recognition of a single union, were far from unknown in Britain before 1981. The innovation was to introduce them as a single package and although they remain relatively rare, even among Japanese companies, their significance and influence has been far-reaching. Non-Japanese companies, including inward investors such as the German automotive parts company, Bosch, in South Wales, imitated the agreements (Oliver and Wilkinson 1992). Indeed, whilst initially closely associated with Japanese companies on 'greenfield' sites (Bassett 1986), recent survey evidence reveals that single union agreements are now at least as common among British-owned companies (Millward 1994: 57–8). A greenfield site gives management the option of offering representation rights to a single union of its own choice, often after competing with other unions for those rights.[11] On existing, that is, 'brown-field' sites, where a number of unions are recog- nized, single union agreements are only possible through the employer derecognizing all but one union—a process which in the late 1980s led to acute inter-union friction.[12]

The problems of securing a single union agreement on brown-field sites has led some employers, wishing to limit multi-union bargaining but to avoid derecognition, to establish 'single table bargaining'. This bargaining innovation requires the replacement of separate union–management bargaining by negotiations between management and a single, integrated negotiating body which can include blue and white collar workers. Single table bargaining does, however, have some benefits for trade unions in minimizing possible inter-union conflict and limiting management's opportunity for exploiting dissension and rivalry (Clark and Winchester 1994: 714–19) and has been encouraged by the TUC. Interestingly, the vast majority of managements have not been receptive, perhaps because their enhanced bargaining power in the 1980s was sufficient to achieve their objectives without any change in bargaining arrangements (Kessler and Bayliss 1995: 199).

British unions' acquiescence in single union agreements and single table bargaining from the 1980s was the product of a more cooperative, less adversarial, strategy. But it arose from weakness rather than strength, even though trade union leaders and their members are frequently positive, even proactive, about innovations in bargaining—especially where the benefits are undoubtedly substantial and tangible. For example, the British car company Rover—the source of many highly confrontational and protracted labour disputes in the 1960s and 1970s—in 1992 signed the 'New Deal' agreement with its five unions, providing guarantees against compulsory lay-offs and single status for blue and white collar employees. In return the unions agreed to cooperation in introducing major changes in working practices, a new grading structure, an extensive training and retraining programme, and a commitment to continuous improvement through teamwork (Taylor 1994: 122–6).

Rover's New Deal had many of the features of workplace agreements in the US auto industry as, for example, that at NUMMI, a plant which also has had a long history of industrial relations conflict.[13] In both cases, though, the unions were less complete partners than under the Saturn agreement, where there was board representation for senior union officers. This blurring of the distinction between management and unions can still attract strong opposition from within unions, especially from the rank and file. In Britain, the single union agreement on a greenfield site even involves *management* selecting the union it wishes to recognize and bargain with, a practice which is unequivocally unlawful under US legislation and normally only accepted out of necessity by British union leaders faced with rapidly declining membership and influence. The single union agreement also makes it easier for management to derecognize, a step which in any case is at the discretion of British management without any legal constraint. Furthermore, though Japanese car companies in Britain pioneered the single union agreement, Honda, at its new plant in Swindon in the West of England, has steadfastly refused to deal with any union, a refusal emphasizing the precarious nature of existing single union agreements. Much depends, in Britain, on the traditional pragmatism of management. If management can achieve radical workplace reform with union cooperation then they are unlikely to seek to exclude unions. The Honda case does however indicate that Japanese-owned car companies, even in Britain, may prefer to establish and run high performance workplaces without independent unions. This is of course now commonplace in the US auto industry, including Japanese companies supplying parts to the assemblers (Turner 1991: 83).

POLITICS AND PURPOSES

The absence in the USA of a political party founded by the trade unions to represent their interests in Congress (and its presence in Britain) is of itself a distinguishing feature which can largely explain the contrasting fortunes of the two labour movements up to 1979. Of course Labour *governments* have never seen themselves as solely representing trade union interests, and under the present leadership of the Labour Party there have been attempts to distance it from an over-strong union connection perceived as damaging to the Party's electoral prospects.[14] Yet it is also clear that British trade union decline, since 1979, is at least partly explained, in political terms, by the presence of anti-union Conservative governments and the absence of a Labour Party which, even though had it been in government, would not necessarily have maintained the relationship with the trade unions that it had in 1974–9. In effect, British unions, in the 1980s, found themselves in a wholly adverse political climate not dissimilar in its impact from that experienced by their US counterparts. The difference is that in Britain the Labour Party, though less supportive, remains electable and this is a substantial, even critical, factor in assessing the trade unions' prospects.

But the explanations for the existence of a British but not an American Labour Party are less clear. The historical exclusion of a labour party from US politics, and its presence in the British, may have had more to do with constitutional differences asserting their influence at a critical historical point rather than explanations arising from 'sociological exceptionalism'.[15] American unions did in fact come close to forming their own political party to represent their interests in the years before World War I[16] and the prospects for establishing an independent party have far from entirely disappeared.[17]

Yet the long absence of a labour party, on the British model, is not evidence of apolitical unionism. The AFL's alliance with the Democrats emerged as early as 1908 (Dubofsky 1994: 51), although since the 1940s the unions' ability to persuade their own members to vote Democrat in presidential and congressional elections has declined (Delaney and

Masters 1991: 332, table 5).[18] Political involvement by unions is also comprehensive and costly. Involvement takes place through four main channels: the political action committees (PACs) of the individual unions providing financial support for candidates favouring labour positions; political endorsements for congressional candidates through the AFL-CIO's Committee on Political Education (COPE); AFL-CIO lobbying on important issues affecting employment; and the volunteer work of union members in political campaigns (Delaney and Masters 1991; Fossum 1995: 128–34). As for costs, in 1982, for example, the UAW spent almost $1.7 m. on its PACs, with four other unions easily exceeding $1 m. (Delaney and Masters 1991: 323, table 2). In addition, PAC expenditure excludes the AFL-CIO's vastly expensive lobbying campaigns against NAFTA and in favour of the Workplace Fairness Bill, although, overall, research shows that labour's political activities—with major variations between and within states—do have some impact upon public policy (Delaney and Masters 1991: 325–33). Given, too, that action and resources are far from exclusively concentrated on supporting Democratic candidates in congressional and state and local elections, the impact can, to an extent, be sustained even when Republicans are in office. This contrasts with the 'all-or-nothing' political contexts of British unions. Conservative governments before 1979 were rarely strongly opposed to unions in contrast to the unremitting ideological, policy, and legislative hostility ushered in by the Thatcher administration. Investing scarce resources towards the election of a Labour Party has not paid any dividends for the trade unions since 1979 and the TUC was even quietly considering its political options should Labour again have failed to be re-elected in 1997.

The cold climate under Thatcher and Major also compelled the TUC's affiliates to look more carefully at their purposes, shifting the relative emphasis away from the political towards the bread-and-butter issues which normally preoccupy their memberships and which, indeed, became more significant as job security and pay came under increasing pressure in the 1980s and 1990s. Another influence was the widely held view that the revival of membership was linked to the provision of better services and not to political involvement and action. It was also frequently emphasized, not least in Conservative Party circles, that the proportion of votes in general elections cast by trade unionists for the Labour Party had been in decline for many years, although it rose slightly in 1992.[19] The Conservative government also took legislative action against the unions' freedom to pursue political objectives and to campaign against government policy.[20] The unions' political objectives were more seriously limited by the continuing defeats of the Labour Party and, given the government's hostile attitudes and actions, had little choice but to pursue a clearer business union orientation—especially since many of their leaders believed that that is what their members wanted.

In the 1980s, the unions most closely identified with the emphasis on business unionism were the electricians (EETPU) and engineers (AEU), later to merge after the crisis over the electricians' expulsion had been resolved. The EETPU, in particular, saw its first single union agreement, with the Japanese company Toshiba in 1981, solely in these terms and as a blueprint for eliminating industrial conflict (Bassett 1986: 122). However even those unions most wedded to socialist aims and political involvement could not avoid a strong professional approach in the day-to-day processes of collective bargaining. There was also the example of political defeat. The government, in the 1980s, was, directly or indirectly, a major player in three highly critical disputes: that involving the printing union SOGAT in its confrontation with Rupert Murdoch's News International; the defeat and virtual destruction of the National Union of Mineworkers (NUM) after the strike of 1984–5 and the rapid phasing out of the coal industry in the 1990s; and the government's 1989 abolition of the National Dock Labour Scheme (which decasualized port labour in 1947) despite the determined opposition, in a strike, by the dock workers supported by their union, the TGWU. 1989 was also, symbolically, the centenary of the dock workers' historic strike: a hundred years later their capacity to win great victories had been seriously weakened by technological change, determined employers, and restrictive labour laws.[21]

But although British unions, from their earliest days, have been required to adopt business union purposes and methods, and have increasingly done so since 1979,[22] they have not fully travelled down the road to apolitical business unionism and are some way behind the USA in this respect.[23] One factor explaining this is that socialism still retains some ideological power in the trade unions and Labour Party.[24] The unions also have the Labour Party as a political stage on which to press for economic and political reform, even when out of office, and, when in power, with some expectations that union influence will be translated into meaningful gains. A third factor is British membership of the European Union (EU). This provides the possibility of British labour, in alliance with other European labour movements, finding some collective correction to the power of multinational employers moving freely across the internal market. The EU also provides supranational political institutions, of substance, which trade unions can seek to influence towards legislation favouring the individual and collective interests of their members and other employees.[25]

The overtly political contexts within which British trade unions operate remain an important route to their revival as long as the Labour Party retains its position as a viable political party capable of winning power and sees continuing advantages in its links with the trade unions. In the USA, unions, though deeply involved in political activity, have a much looser relationship with the Democratic Party and, more significantly, do not have any historical or current claim on the Party to represent their interests in Congress or the presidency, other than through the normal repaying of electoral debts; and even these debts are commonly not politically honoured, not least because of the checks and balances built into the US constitution—unlike the 'elected dictatorship' powers available to a British prime minister in Parliament. More generally, the structures, processes, and ideologies of US politics, even with a British-style Labour Party as the political wing of a labour movement, would still constrain the political influence of the labour unions. But it remains difficult to avoid the conclusion that, in a comparative context, the 'pure and simple' route taken by Gompers and his associates, with hindsight, was a mistake, although an understandable one and perhaps almost unavoidable, in the contexts of the time.

CONCLUSIONS

In a recent symposium on the future of US labour, Salvatore argued that 'labor's central problem has to do with the fact that whichever way it turns it faces bleak alternatives' (1992: 88). He saw labour's weakness as a political force in the decline of the Democrats' long-established capacity to build coalitions of 'majorities out of minorities'. This incapacity was eventually translated into the historic capture of Congress by the Republicans in 1994, and continuing control in 1996, amidst the longer term significance of growing Republican domination of former Democratic strongholds, especially in the Southern states. The Republicans' long-term prospects of becoming the 'natural party of government', like the Conservatives in Britain, are now much brighter than at any time since the New Deal even allowing for some inevitable, short-term, future reverses; and, given the labour unions' presence in the fragmenting old New Deal coalition, their political route to salvation is indeed 'bleak'.

The shifting of the political ground under the feet of American labour has not been paralleled in Britain, although after the 1979 General Election persuasive and authoritative analyses were being written charting the seminal decline of the British labour movement's political and industrial wings as the old British class structure weakened (Hobsbawm 1981). The response of the British Labour Party has been in any case to weaken its overt attachment to the declining working class in a 'one nation' direction, a strategy which was successfully tested in the 1997 General Election. Hence 'Waiting for Labour' still remains as a viable option for British trade unions. But it is risky, even when Labour wins. The Party's belief in the case for its attachment to the trade unions is becoming less secure as is the totality of the TUC's and affiliated unions' commitment to the Labour Party: both sides have strongly overlapping but occasionally different routes to salvation.

In British as in US unions there does, however, remain a strong emphasis on self-help. In the USA, traditional adversarialism still has its attractions although Salvatore (1992) sees little future for the old ways as simply inviting employer retaliation. British unions, in practice, have for long behaved more cooperatively than their ideology or reputation suggests. This approach has had a good deal to do with employer behaviour which is still only exceptionally hostile to trade unions in the workplace and, in some cases, employers have positively assisted the maintenance of trade union membership (Kessler and Bayliss 1995: 289–91). Despite some change in the behaviour of British management from the 1980s, the overall gap between their approach to trade union representation, and that of American management, remains wide. It is also highly significant. Faced with the power and hostility of US employers, there has been a growing, perhaps inevitable, fashion for rejecting the old adversarialism in favour of cooperation. High profile, actual experiments in companies in traditionally adversarial sectors such as auto and steel have also been set within a wider advocacy of labour–management cooperation in the workplace.[26]

The older objections to the dilution of adversarialism still remain influential in the radical wing of the US labour movement.[27] The focus on cooperation in the workplace can also be both a strength and weakness; it accords with the reality of decentralized collective bargaining but reinforces the isolation of union organization in individual enterprises. It also has clear limits. It has a limited future in unionized workplaces where employers see no reason to cooperate; and none at all in non-unionized settings—the vast majority. Indeed, as Brody reminds us: 'no amount of union enthusiasm for cooperative relations and employee involvement is likely to persuade employers that collective bargaining is preferable to a union-free environment . . . The labor movement will not prevail by trying to persuade non union employers. It is their employees who have to be persuaded . . . what will persuade them [is] the identification of their union with industrial justice' (1992: 39; 41).

Brody's emphasis on 'industrial justice' is echoed in Britain in the reasons why people join trade unions. Research is increasingly suggesting that unions' involvement in defending rights at work—through grievance and disciplinary procedures—is perceived by members as at least as important as their role in collective bargaining. The provision of sophisticated credit and financial services is a much less attractive role and 'associate' membership, providing no more than services, would seem to have little to offer as the route to the revival of membership in both Britain and the USA.

History does offer some lessons. The CIO unions in the USA emerged and grew rapidly in a time of major economic crisis and minimal rights for people at work. The wave of sit-down strikes in 1937 were illegal actions by workers in defence of the very existence of their unions. They were also widespread, involving white collar as well as blue collar workers. This concern for industrial justice coincided with the emergence and growth of new workers, in new industries, struggling for recognition against determined employers.

This 'dynamic core' of growing numbers of industrial workers in the 1930s may have modern counterparts in the white collar workers in consumer, financial, and health services as well as the middle managers and semi-professionals in both countries. American unions seem potentially to be promising more success with the new 'dynamic core' than the British. The AFL-CIO's Organizing Institute, mobilizing and training teams of enthusiastic young organizers, could capitalize on the growing employment insecurity and downward pressure on pay and benefits. The Institute has, as yet, no counterpart in Britain where the unions need to revive their identity and influence among young people. It is also possible to organize new members using tough, militant tactics with a strong emphasis on industrial justice, as in the case of the Justice for Janitors campaigns.

In the emergence of a new dynamic core, Brody finds 'eerie parallels' with 1929 when the obstacles to union growth were at least as powerful as today. Salvatore (1992) does not, however, share this assessment, seeing little prospect of the new, rising occupational groups lifting the unions out of decline. He argues for unions building coalitions of wider community interests as the basis for campaigning but rejects adversarialism as counter-productive. This strategy is also endorsed by Kessler-Harris and Silverman (1992) who see class consciousness as a poor basis for organizing success and maintain that most workers, even those unemployed, have middle class aspirations. They propose breaking down the barriers between the public and the worker under a new, wider issues agenda including education, housing, poverty, and crime.

In US contexts the weakness of the unions, their extreme decentralization, and their minimal political influence strongly indicate the case for building local alliances of overlapping interests. The general strictures against class-conscious, adversarial unionism may also be well founded (Adams 1995: 174–80), although in the specific case of the auto industry it has been persuasively argued that in teamwork and lean production *employers* have abandoned neither Fordism nor Taylorism for non-adversarialism (Parker 1993). If true, it would indeed be a paradox if unions are increasingly advocating cooperation and partnership with employers whilst the latter dress up the practice in the clothes of rhetoric.

In Britain, the TUC's and some unions' search for 'social partnership' with employers, though following the model widespread in other EU countries, broadly parallels US developments. Interestingly, too, according to some academics, there is little evidence of British employers entering into genuine social partnerships in the workplace but rather they seek to diminish the role of unions and increase work intensification—policies which are causing resentment and entrenching adversarialism. Hence as decentralization proceeds, workplaces in some unions have become isolated from their national union's structures and, from their own experience, out of line with the social partnership advocacy of their presidents and general secretaries (Waddington 1995b).

The tendency for national unions to become distanced from their workplace organizations is a well-observed and researched phenomenon. It may even be unavoidable. However it severely handicaps policies to revive the membership base of British and American trade unions, especially when it is associated with the national leadership strategies to expand services to members, advance labour–management cooperation, and negotiate suitable mergers. None of these strategies fits easily with the evidence of why people join unions, their experience of management at work or of the limited value to them of large-scale, more remote, trade union organization. The analyses of both Parker (1993) for the USA, and Waddington (1995b) for Britain, come together in this emphasis on the workplace as the arena for membership revival and on which national union organization should focus. There is also evidence that the leadership of British and US unions is beginning to understand this (IRS 1996: 611).

NOTES

1. Green (1992: 456) argues that de-industrialization (the 'compositional effect') is susceptible to government policy, so that changes in macroeconomic policy can affect compositional change which can in turn influence trade union density. However, Green still estimates that the compositional effect, alone, on falling density can be as high as 30%. See also Towers (1989: 179).
2. This literature is reviewed in Chaison and Rose (1991: 26–30).
3. The TUC campaigns (in Manchester and London Docklands) used the same slogan as the AFL-CIO, i.e. 'Union Yes', and the thirteen unions involved, coordinated by the TUC, followed US union campaigning practices such as involving local communities (Snape 1994). The outcome in terms of new members was, however, disappointing and did not justify the resources deployed (IRS 1992: 519).
4. The initiation fee is up to $40 with dues, despite wide diversity, averaging about two hours pay per month (Fossum 1995: 108). Current UAW dues on a two hours pay per month basis, represent 1.15% of regular monthly income (UAW 1994).
5. This research is usefully summarized in Fossum 1995: 256–7.

6. British union activists commonly argue that the regular collection of dues directly from members strengthens member–activist links at the critical level with benefits beyond the simply financial.
7. Recent research also indicates that 'informal' closed shops, with employer cooperation, have partly replaced the old, 'formal' union membership agreements (Kessler and Bayliss 1995: 281).
8. The 'weighted' average is based upon each union's 'main contribution rate'. The affiliation fee is then set at a level up to 95% of the average by the TUC General Council. For the three years 1993 to 1995 it set the fee at less than 95%. The outcome was:

	Weighted Average (pence)	Affiliation Fee (pence)
1993	144	133
1994	149	140
1995	156	145

Additionally, 10% of the fee from 1994 (10p in 1993) is to be retained in the Development Fund to finance 'new work and initiatives'. In 1994 and 1995 the Fund was used to subsidize the TUC's educational programme (TUC 1995c: 179–81).

A recent comparison with the German DGB reveals that the German organization takes 12% of total membership contributions. The TUC takes less than 2% yet the DGB is also facing financial pressures (*Labour Research*, February 1994: 17–19).

9. Unions can affiliate at, above, or below their actual membership. This determines the number of delegates, and therefore votes, at the annual congress.
10. The seminal study, beginning with the Toshiba agreement, is that of Bassett (1986). A recent and wider perspective on the influence of Japanese companies in Britain is Oliver and Wilkinson (1992). Nissan's plant in North East England has been celebrated in an account by its former personnel director (Wickens 1987) but treated critically by Garrahan and Stewart (1992). Studies of working practices in Japanese companies in Britain should now perhaps more appropriately be seen as part of the global perspective 'lean production' literature. See e.g. Babson (1995).
11. In the 1980s employers would commonly invite unions to give 'presentations' (unions called them 'beauty contests') as part of the process of deciding which union should be granted recognition. This process would be unlawful in the USA as an employer unfair labour practice. See also pp. 107–8.
12. The electricians' union (EETPU), an enthusiastic pioneer of single union agreements (see Bassett 1986), was expelled from the TUC in 1988 for its refusal to comply with two decisions of the TUC's Disputes Committee involving its role in securing its own recognition at the expense of already recognized unions. In 1993, following its 1992 merger with the engineering union AEU to form the AEEU, it was readmitted to the TUC but with much bitterness and acrimony.
13. The NUMMI and Rover cases are discussed in detail in Ch. 5.

14. Recent pressure from the Party leadership towards 'one member, one vote' has led to a reduction in the unions' 'block voting' powers and influence at the annual conference (individual unions can affiliate to the Party) and in the selection of parliamentary candidates. In the formulation of Labour Party policy there has recently been some shift away from trade union formal and informal involvement. However, the role of the trade unions and the TUC is still important in policy formulation especially on matters seen as within their legitimate spheres of interest such as proposals towards establishing a national minimum wage and legally backed measures to encourage union recognition and employee representation. The trade unions, until recently, also contributed about 80% of the Labour Party's income (Fatchett 1987) and the larger part of its campaign chest in general elections (Marsh 1992). This financial contribution remains a significant, and binding, feature of the relationship between the unions and the Party. However the Party has substantially increased its membership in recent years to more than 300,000. This, as well as increasing income from donations, will help to limit its dependence upon trade union funding, which is currently now about 50%. See also the discussion of recent developments in the trade unions–Labour Party relationship in the Conclusions.

15. In the USA socialist trade union members were of course numerous at the turn of the century and important in certain 'core' unions. Labour leaders and activists were also aware of, and influenced by, what was happening in Britain and there was substantial pressure from within the labour movement to form an American Labor Party on the British model. More practically, in 1906, the labour leaders established a Labor Representation Committee 'to seek the election of trade unionists and union sympathizers to Congress'. The British influence was obvious (Dubofsky 1994: 48–51).

16. Forbath (1992) argues that Samuel Gomper's and Adolf Strasser's 'pure and simple' view of trade union purposes was in the minority against the more radical (in both thought and action) perspectives of the labour party advocates but that the power of the courts and the state, not the attitudes and ideology of trade union members, pre-empted the formation of a viable party.

17. In June 1996, 1,400 delegates to the Cleveland Convention of the 5-year-old Labor Party Advocates (LPA) voted to form the Labor Party. The new organization had support across forty states and from nine unions representing 1 million workers. Two major unions, SEIU and AFSCME, also sent delegates. The Labor Party's platform includes free higher education, a national health service, a constitutional right to a job and living wage, statutory limits on the working week, and guaranteed, minimum paid holidays. However the Party, against strong opposition from many delegates, is not yet planning to field its own candidates in elections. Hence it would not interfere with the links between the labour movement and the Democrats which the AFL-CIO continues to endorse and support (Labor Party Advocates 1995; Reed 1996; Slaughter 1996).

18. Even if the proportion of union members voting Democrat had not fallen, the decline in union membership is reflected in the total vote the unions can deliver to Democratic candidates and, therefore, in their political influence (Fossum 1995: 134).

19. 46% of trade unionists voted for Labour in the 1992 General Election compared to 31% for the Conservatives and 19% for the Social Democratic Party. In the 1964 General Election 73% voted Labour, 22% Conservative, and 5% for the Liberal Party (McIlroy 1995: 287, table 7.7).

20. The 1984 Trade Union Act amended the 1913 Act (which allowed for separate funds for political purposes) to require endorsement, by union memberships, in ballots every ten years. The 1982 Employment Act also narrowed trade union immunities by excluding 'political' as opposed to industrial action: e.g. industrial action by a union against privatization because of its negative effect on its members' jobs was prohibited in the courts.

21. See Saundry and Turnbull (1996) for a comprehensive analysis of the most recent, long-running Liverpool docks dispute. The dockers secured major international support, including that of US longshoremen, for their campaign for reinstatement.

22. For perceptive recent analyses of the changes in British unions since 1979, see Edwards P. K. (1995).

23. A recent historical and comparative analysis of this aspect of American exceptionalism is in Adams (1995: 34–62, ch. 3).

24. Since its second consecutive defeat in 1983, the Labour Party has progressively moved, under three leaders, towards the ideological centre, even removing its constitutional commitment to public ownership. In the autumn of 1995 a left-wing, breakaway Socialist Labour Party was formed under the leadership of Arthur Scargill, the President of the NUM.

25. The most recent example of this is the European Works Council as well as, more generally, the EU's Social Chapter. For recent analysis and discussion see Hall *et al.* (1995).

26. The Dunlop Commission's 'mission statement' or terms of reference assumed the case for labour–management cooperation. Recent influential texts include Bluestone and Bluestone (1992); Kochan and Osterman (1994); and Levine (1995).

27. Most prominently through the labour magazine *Labor Notes* and its annual conference of activists in Detroit and the influence of academic activists such as Mike Parker and Jane Slaughter (Parker 1993; Parker and Slaughter 1995).

5

Democracy and Efficiency in the Workplace

If unions wish to stem the tide of decreasing recognition by employers, they will need to demonstrate their worth to them.

(Department of Employment evidence
to the Employment Committee 1994c: 702)

The labor movement believes that the long run objectives of employee participation should be to enhance both economic performance and industrial democracy.

(Commission on the Future of Worker-
Management Relations May 1994: 33)

Industrial democracy can be regarded as an extension of political democracy. If citizens have a fundamental right to be included in the making of decisions which affect their interests then they have an equally fundamental right to be a part of the rule-making processes which regulate their working lives.[1] In Britain in the 1960s and 1970s this logic was widely accepted within the trade union movement, provoking work-ins and inspiring worker-cooperatives, although these were often only in response to closures and redundancies.[2] Public sector experiments in industrial democracy involved having workers on boards of directors in the public sector industries of British Steel and the Post Office; and in 1975 the Labour government, which had returned to office the year before, under strong union pressure set up the Bullock Committee to enquire into the extension of worker-directors in the private sector.[3] Bullock himself linked political and industrial democracy, but although worker-directors were too radical for some in the trade union movement others saw the proposed institution as not radical enough, preferring trade union pressure through collective bargaining as the means of extending workers' power even towards ultimate control.[4]

Collective bargaining may be a route towards greater industrial democracy which would also (arguably) include institutional innovations such as worker-directors and German-style works councils with co-determination rights. It would however exclude participative, informational, and employee involvement institutions and practices which, though they may offer benefits to employees and represent potential means for unions to extend their membership and influence, primarily serve the interests of management and, in some circumstances, may provide fertile ground for anti-union activity.[5]

The workers' control perspective of collective bargaining has, however, never approached becoming the prevailing British orthodoxy. The late Hugh Clegg, for example (Clegg 1960), saw trade unions as the 'loyal opposition', within collective bargaining, to management's government but without any route for the unions to become the government themselves. This is a similar perspective to that of the 'social partners' in European Union countries' industrial relations and the institutions of the EU itself. The New Deal labour laws, in the USA, also sought to promote collective bargaining by offering it as a free choice to employees, with statutory protection and encouragement. In the event, given the amendments to the Wagner Act and the renewed, postwar hostility of US employers, the free choice was, over time, seriously undermined as employees, realistically, feared negative consequences should they press their rights to unionization and collective bargaining. This has allowed some observers to maintain that US employees have voluntarily rejected unionization and collective bargaining although recent survey evidence indicates a wide gap between those employees' who wish to be unionized and the prevailing levels of US union membership. This is explained by their actual experience of employer opposition[6] and its implications for both the possibility of certification and their own employment security. Faced with employer power, the limitations of US labour legislation and the powers of the not always well-intentioned NLRB (e.g. under the Reagan presidency) are apparent (Gould 1994: ch. 5).

In Britain, ACAS's role in supporting collective bargaining was removed in the 1993 Trade Union Reform and Employment Rights Act. Earlier, in 1980, the statutory recognition procedure was abolished by the Employment Act. It was therefore only in the 1970s, including under the Commission on Industrial Relations (CIR) procedure from 1971 to 1974, that British employers could be compelled, in law, to recognize trade unions. Since the abolition of the statutory recognition procedure, they now have the unrestricted unilateral right to recognize trade unions, or remove recognition, as they think appropriate—subject only to the realities of the collective power and influence of their employees which has generally fallen sharply since the end of the 1970s.

The political significance of trade unions was recognized by the Commission on the Future of Worker-Management Relations (December 1994) which stressed the role of trade unions in contributing 'to the health of the nation by providing a legitimate and consistent voice to working people in the broader society' as well as citing the view of the former Secretary of State, George Schultz, that 'free societies and free trade unions go together' (ibid. 15).

These wider, democratic, considerations did not however figure in Dunlop's terms of reference or recommendations. The Commission's role was largely confined to the economic goals of labour–management cooperation and employee participation and, specifically, how these favoured

institutions could enhance productivity. There was even a recommendation for legislation to strengthen the growth of employee participation,
which could have adverse consequences for collective bargaining, even
though the Commission argued that this could be guarded against in
the same legislation.

The relative economic performance of enterprises is, of course, an
important issue affecting employment and economic welfare. Thus economists consider it proper to investigate how far the presence of trade
unions and collective bargaining influences productivity, profitability,
and competitiveness. Evaluating their impact is a matter of empirical
research interest which has for long been well established in the USA
and, in recent years, it has attracted some growing interest in Britain.

In recent years, too, workplaces have been subjected to major, even
transforming, changes in work and working practices, changes which
have also often been introduced alongside innovations in employee
participation and involvement. These practices have also sometimes
been introduced in the presence of trade unions and, usually, with their
cooperation—although the presence of unions has of course been much
less a feature in the USA than in Britain. American researchers have
also been more ready to compare the economic outcomes of change and
innovation in unionized and non-unionized workplaces.

This chapter will therefore first assess the extent, and outcomes, of
workplace change and innovation in the USA and Britain. Secondly, it
will compare the responses, through case studies, of the trade unions to
change and innovation. Thirdly, it will review the research on the impact
of trade unions on the economic performance of firms. Fourthly, it will
discuss how far human resource management, the claimed alternative
to collective bargaining, has advanced democracy and efficiency in the
workplace. Finally, in the conclusions, we will return to the wider question, that is, should there be a conflict between economic efficiency and
industrial democracy, how should that conflict be resolved?

WORKPLACE TRANSFORMATION

Evidence of the extent of 'workplace transformation' or, more limited
and more prosaically, 'flexibility' was briefly discussed in Chapter 1.
The surveys available for the USA are rich in detail, especially that by
Osterman (1994), but they are less comprehensive in coverage than the
most recent British Workplace Industrial Relations Survey (WIRS)
(Millward *et al.* 1992). Yet, although the US and British surveys have
their limitations,[7] they do provide a remarkable coincidence as to the
broad extent of change, that is, in both countries around one-third of
workplaces have initiated substantial changes in working practices.

TABLE 5.1. *Extent of changes in working practices in selected industries and services in Great Britain, 1987–1990 (% of establishments)*

All Manufacturing	39
Rubber, plastics, and other manufacturing	56*
Chemicals and manufactured fibres	52*
Leather, footwear, and clothing	51*
Textiles	43*
Vehicles and transport equipment	20
All Services	36
Banking, finance, insurance	58
Posts and telecommunications	57
Higher education	52*
Energy and water	46
Local government	46
Construction	15
All Industries	36

Note: * Percentages subject to small base of 20–50 establishments.

Source: Adapted from Millward *et al.* (1992: 346, table 9B).

This comparison does, however, pose problems. The WIRS survey, though offering a measure of workplace change across the economy[8] does not indicate the *depth* of change, as Table 5.1 illustrates. The Osterman survey, although statistically representative of all US establishments with more than fifty employees, remains concerned solely with innovation in workplace practices, rather than, as with WIRS, the entire process of workplace industrial relations change over time. This 'limitation' did, however, allow the US study to tackle its specific theme in some depth. This required a definition of 'flexible work organization'. Here, Osterman takes an eclectic approach listing the presence of one or more of four practices as evidence of some workplace innovation: teamworking, job rotation, total quality management (TQM), and quality circles. The distribution of each practice was then related to two levels of 'penetration', that is, whether it is used at all; and, if it is, what percentage of 'core employees'[9] are involved, with 50 per cent or more indicating the higher level of penetration. The outcome is shown in Table 5.2. The Osterman survey also tests how far the four practices tend to be introduced as groups or clusters, that is, as a 'new system'.[10] This is illustrated in Table 5.3. Table 5.3, for the USA, suggests that about one-third of all workplaces could reasonably be described as 'high performance', that is, those which have introduced two or more forms of innovative work practice involving more than half of their core employees. Osterman's survey also reports, somewhat unexpectedly, that smaller firms (50–499

TABLE 5.2. *Extent of use of innovative work practices in the private sector in the USA in 1992 (% of establishments)*

Type of Practice	Lower level of penetration		Higher level of penetration	
	Manufacturing	All sample	Manufacturing	All sample
Teams	50.1	54.5	32.3	40.5
Rotation	55.6	43.4	37.4	26.6
TQM	44.9	33.5	32.1	24.5
Quality circles	45.6	40.8	29.7	27.4
None	16.0	21.8	33.2	36.0

Source: Osterman (1994: 177, table 2).

TABLE 5.3. *Clustering of work practices in the USA at the higher level of penetration (% of establishments)*

Type of Practice	Manufacturing/blue collar	All sample
None	33.2	36.0
Teams only	5.5	14.4
Rotation only	11.7	7.0
Quality circles only	2.4	3.1
TQM only	4.5	2.6
Two combined	24.8	22.6
Three combined	12.1	4.9
All four combined	5.0	4.8

Source: Osterman (1994: 177, table 3).

employees) are more likely to be transformed than larger ones (Appelbaum and Batt 1994: 61) and for all firms 20–25 per cent of workers have been involved in changes in workplace practices.

Other, less representative surveys do, however, find a much lower involvement of the workforce. For example, one survey found that although change in work practices was widespread (one-quarter of US firms), it only extended to 20 per cent of all workers in large firms; and another estimate suggests transformation in only 13 per cent of firms, involving only 2 per cent of US workers.[11]

Despite the caveats and inconsistencies it is, however, reasonable to conclude that at least one-quarter, and up to about one-third, of US workplaces have instituted working practices and introduced quality programmes which can be described as significant. However, although these changes are fairly widespread, they do not yet reveal a common pattern, even with teamwork, although the evidence is that, despite their diversity, changes in work practices are not only growing, but accelerating (Appelbaum and Batt 1994: 68). Furthermore, the preoccupation with a limited definition of change—restricting it to the introduction of a few, closely related, working practices—may underestimate the depth of transformation in a handful of, usually large, firms. For example, firms introducing radical change in the organization of work will also find it necessary to invest in major training and retraining programmes and to maximize employment security. Indeed, the development of a viable training culture within the organization is a necessary consequence of workplace reorganization but, to a high degree, both are conditional on employment security.[12] High performance may also be strongly associated with participation in decision-making at all levels of the enterprise, from the performance of jobs, or tasks, to the sharing of power and may perhaps be most effectively achieved through trade union representation.[13]

The British 1990 WIRS survey, like the US surveys, also suggests that changes in workplace practices are widespread, although, as yet, this source does not allow for measurement of the depth of transformation. What is known is that between 1987 and 1990, 36 per cent of all workplaces in the WIRS sample reported changes in working practices (Millward *et al.* 1992: 334, table 9B). This economy-wide data is complemented by national sample surveys of the extent of employee communication, involvement, and consultation initiatives, innovations closely associated with the introduction of new working practices, TQM, and an expansion of training provision. Additionally, specific industry studies of the impact of Japanese companies and 'Japanese' working practices on British industry are available to give colour to the WIRS and other data.

There is substantial British evidence that the use of involvement and communication practices by employers to introduce workplace changes is both commonplace and encompasses a wide range of practices.[14] A recent National Opinion Poll (NOP) survey found that 75 per cent of employees had been affected by at least one change in working practices or changes in employment levels in the past eighteen months (most commonly in foreign-owned or mixed ownership companies) and that in introducing change a majority of companies communicated with, and/or consulted, their employees. However, where trade unions were present, employers favoured them slightly less than other mechanisms for passing information to employees or receiving it from them (Tillsley 1994).

As for the depth of the changes in working practices, the British research largely concentrates on the transforming impact of 'Japanese' working practices in actual Japanese companies operating in Britain as well as on British (or other foreign companies, operating in Britain) copying Japanese practices ('copycats'). The impact of these working practices is however described only as an aspect of 'Japanization'. This is defined as incorporating production processes, personnel and industrial relations systems, and environmental factors such as supplier relations and a supportive economic and political context—as well as the usual, characteristic bundle of working practices.[15] This definition of 'Japanization' allies it closely to that of 'lean production' and both Oliver and Wilkinson and recent British surveys of automotive components use the terms interchangeably (IRS 1995: 583; 1995: 584).

The Oliver and Wilkinson surveys reveal much evidence of the Japanization process in individual companies, especially in the 1987 survey where, for example, teamworking was in use in 85 per cent of the sampled companies; flexible working in 80 per cent; and quality circles in 68 per cent. Just-in-time production was in use in 34 per cent of the companies and a further 30 per cent were planning to introduce it or were actually doing so. Yet by the 1991 survey there was evidence that the pace of introduction was slowing and the incidence of some practices had even declined (Oliver and Wilkinson 1992: 135, 138, and 317). However a 1995 survey for one industry—automotive products—found that throughout the 1980s there had been a rapid increase in the introduction of Japanese working practices and that the pace had accelerated since 1990. Furthermore, part of the explanation is that vehicle manufacturers (dominated by the Japanese companies Nissan, Honda, and Toyota) are putting increasing demands on their suppliers (IRS 1995: 583, 9).[16] This growth in pressure on suppliers reflects the vulnerability of Japanese 'lean' production methods, especially just-in-time production, to any break in the supply chain.[17] Teamworking is also highly dependent on good attendance records which explains the practice, among leading producers, of disclosing sickness absence levels and accident/injury rates to the workforce (IRS 1995: 584, 16). Strict, even draconian, attendance rules are of course widespread among Japanese transplants in the USA, including discipline up to, and including, dismissal. Even in unionized companies, such as NUMMI, four absences over one year can lead to dismissal; and in non-unionized firms—such as Toyota's operation in Georgetown, Kentucky—the absence policy does not allow for 'sick days' and three consecutive days' absence without contacting the company are treated as resignation (Kenney and Florida 1993: 278–9).

Vulnerability may also be increased through the limited application of associated Japanese personnel practices, such as employee involvement. The 1995 British survey of automotive component suppliers found that, although the adoption of lean production practices was accelerating, employee involvement practices were lagging behind.[18] These included 'single status' terms and conditions for all blue collar and white collar employees; individualized performance payment systems; and the provision of information—with the exception (noted above) of sickness and absenteeism records (IRS 1995: 584, 16). Osterman also notes the relationship between 'a set of HRM practices . . . innovative pay schemes, extensive training and efforts to induce greater commitment on the part of the labor force' and the successful adoption of changes in working practices (1994: 186).

The potential constraints on the wider diffusion of 'Japanese' working practices may, however, be 'culturally embedded'. Oliver and Wilkinson suggest that, in Britain, the experience of managerial innovations in working practice reveals 'a gap between rhetoric and reality' (1992: 317). The capacity of British management to embrace and then reject innovations is a common observation as, for example, with quality circles, although this example may reveal that the introduction of new working practices is unlikely to be successful in the absence of much wider organizational change (Hill 1991). The short life of innovations would also seem to be the experience of US organizations. The Dunlop Commission (Commission on the Future of Worker-Management Relations, May 1994) drew on Osterman's survey to report that only about one-third of employee involvement programmes last beyond five years. The Commission also referred to the record of quality circles: over half, begun in the early 1980s, had failed to survive (Lawler and Mohrman 1987; Drago 1988). The surveys themselves may also be less than wholly reliable in their initial reporting of the extent of change (as we saw earlier) in that respondent managers may be prone to exaggeration. There may also be some exaggerated effects arising from the high incidence of 'leading-edge', well-publicized companies in the samples (Osterman 1994: 186).[19]

Kenney and Florida see wider diffusion threatened by actual opposition from domestic capital in the USA and Europe as well as from labour movements (1993: 345)—an interesting pairing. But they note that not all US Japanese transplants are non-union or even anti-union: a number have implemented major changes in working practices in unionized companies as, for example, at the NUMMI transplant in California. Osterman also found (emphasized in the Dunlop Commission's findings) that the frequency of workplace transformation practices was not related to the presence or absence of unions (1994: 186). In Britain (although generally in conditions of greater union strength), Japanese companies have normally opted for union recognition, although in the less challenging single union form, avoiding multi-unionism. But in areas of Britain where union avoidance is possible, Japanese companies have set up non-union operations, notably in the Scottish electronics industry and at Honda's new 'flagship' plant in Swindon, Wiltshire.

If pragmatism towards unions is a feature of Japanese companies overseas,[20] either as independent operations or in joint ventures, it is also a feature of transnationals from other countries including American companies in European markets.[21] British and US unions are also no strangers to pragmatism, often responding to workplace transformation, by management, with some transformations of their own making.

TRADE UNION RESPONSES TO CHANGE: TWO CASE STUDIES

Kenney and Florida note, as we have seen, that not all Japanese transplants in the USA are opposed to trade unions, and these are fairly numerous in auto assembly, steel, rubber, and tyre manufacture. These companies have adopted a number of strategies towards unions. The positive strategy is to involve the union in the change and restructuring programme. Other strategies, more typical of US employers in seeking control rather than cooperation, include the decertification threat, blaming the union for problems, and working with moderate, supportive factions of the union against more oppositional or 'radical' groups (1993: 285–7).

The involvement strategy and the response of the trade unions has received much attention and approval in both countries. In the USA, the Clinton administration strongly endorsed labour–management cooperation in the terms of reference of the Dunlop Commission and this was echoed in its recommendations. The House of Commons Employment Select Committee was equally enthusiastic and in very similar terms.[22] The Committee also gave a good deal of time and attention, through oral witnesses and a detailed written submission, to the case of Rover, the volume vehicle manufacturer. Rover, and its predecessor companies in the British Midlands, was, until the late 1980s, notable, even notorious, for its adversarial and conflictual industrial relations. It also had substantial production, quality, and commercial problems which were attributed, by many, to its poor industrial relations record. Rover entered into a production partnership in 1979 which developed, by 1989, into Honda buying 20 per cent of Rover's shares. However in 1995, Rover became a wholly owned subsidiary of the German company BMW.

An interesting US comparison with Rover is New United Motor Manufacturing Incorporated (NUMMI) at Fremont in California, which was cited in the Dunlop Commission report. A former General Motors plant, the Fremont operation became a joint venture, with Toyota, in 1985. As at Rover, the Californian operation's poor industrial relations record was substantially improved, under new policies, following the involvement of the Japanese company. There was also a major improvement, in performance, in both cases, under the new agreements and new management styles. At NUMMI, commercial viability was also achieved, although at the cost of many jobs. Rover's viability was less assured, even under its new BMW owners.

Rover and the 'New Deal'

The Rover–Honda deal, agreed in 1979, reflected the fashionable, corporate partnership response to global recession in the industry. Both companies were of similar (medium) size and Honda's reputation for quality and productivity could be allied to Rover's move into robotic technology and, most importantly, its position within the large Western European market. The partnership developed into Honda's 20 per cent share of Rover in 1989 with Rover, in the same year, taking a parallel share in Honda's new plant at Swindon in Wiltshire.[23]

The Rover–Honda venture produced three jointly manufactured vehicles and was generally considered mutually beneficial, although it was not without its problems.[24] However in 1991, the Rover management, who were responsible for industrial relations policy, initiated negotiations on the aptly named 'New Deal', which was implemented in April 1992. The agreement was the culmination of Rover management's long-running attempts both to transform industrial relations in its plants away from well-established, deep adversarial traditions and to replace mass production, Fordist working practices by lean production.

The company's New Deal proposals had a lengthy gestation beginning with its commitment to improve the quality and reliability of Rover cars, long the subject of widespread adverse criticism. Between 1987 and 1989, a total quality improvement (TQI) programme was launched beginning with the training of the Board and Executive Committee in its principles, followed by training for all employees in four-day, off-the-job, courses. Teamworking was also introduced in this period but progressively modified to remove demarcation of jobs and with team leaders working alongside other team members (IRS 1992: 514, 12).

The New Deal covered a 35,000 workforce and was signed by six unions.[25] It was put to a ballot and was only narrowly approved by those voting—11,961 to 11,793—reflecting the continuing presence of adversarialism, some shop steward opposition, and employee mistrust of management intentions. The agreement, across the six main plants of the company, included the usual changes in working practices associated with lean production: teamworking, job flexibility, training, and an emphasis upon quality and continuous improvement, the last of which had been prepared for in the extensive, prior training in TQI. The new vogue of 'empowerment' was also a feature of the agreement's implementation, that is, giving the teams control over such things as job rotation, work allocation, product quality, process improvements, informal training, and routine maintenance. Management also involved the teams, through consultation, in work planning and changes in production schedules.

Guarantees of employment security and the introduction of single status conditions and benefits for blue and white collar employees were seen, by management, as the major gains for employees under the New Deal. Single status[26] benefits and conditions for blue collar employees included the gradual elimination of time clocks (replaced by an attendance-related bonus scheme), common catering facilities, standardized sickness rules and benefits, and regular health checks. The company also intended to replace the eleven grades in the job structure (five blue collar and six white collar) by a single grade, with salary increments linked to skill acquisition. In the event, the scheme actually negotiated achieved much, but not all, of this intention: skill acquisition was introduced but with a reduced number of occupational classifications (IRS 1992: 514, 14).

Security of employment fell short of the lifetime guarantees of the big Japanese enterprises despite the agreement's statement that 'Employees who want to work with Rover will be able to stay with Rover'. However, the detailed provisions were an improvement on traditional practices. Lay-offs from normal work arising from the interruption of production, other than through industrial action, were to be replaced by other useful work within the Company. Where workforce reductions were unavoidable, they would be met through voluntary redundancy, early retirement, and 'natural wastage'. Such provisions are, of course, commonplace among large companies. Less usual was a commitment to redundant employees to provide them with useful 'out-placement' skills and advice in the search for new jobs and careers, a practice well established in the USA, but much less so in Britain.

In the event, Rover's recent employment record has been fairly good. Total output in 1989 was 500,000 vehicles with employment at 45,000. Employment fell after 1989 during the recession, reaching 35,000 at the time of the New Deal and 33,000 in 1994. However by early 1996, under BMW ownership and recovery from recession, output had returned to its 1989 level and employment had passed 40,000 (Employment Committee, 1994c: 249; Griffiths 1996: 9).

Collective bargaining, like working practices, was also significantly changed under the new agreement. In the 1980s the six unions bargained with senior management through two joint negotiating committees (JNCs) for blue and white collar employees. The JNCs were incorporated into one under a 'single table' bargaining[27] arrangement. Joint consultation agendas were also widened to include company performance, future plans, plant layout, safety, pensions and other benefits, and employee facilities. Consultation also included biannual reviews of the Company and its performance between senior management, national officials of the union, and JNC representatives. The revised procedural agreement provided for final stage, binding arbitration through a single or three person panel under Advisory, Conciliation, and Arbitration

Service (ACAS) arrangements incorporating prior joint agreement to accept any decisions as binding.[28] Through the 1990s, serious industrial action did not take place at Rover, although this may only be partly explained by the binding arbitration provision since industrial disputes reached exceptionally low levels in Britain as a whole throughout this period, as well as in other countries.[29]

The negotiations over the New Deal were, according to management, substantially assisted by a two-year pay agreement which, in its second year in 1992, saw grade rates rise by 7.5 per cent as inflation was falling to less than 5 per cent (IRS 1992: 514, 12). The agreement was nevertheless approved by the narrowest of majorities—50.4 per cent of those voting—and despite the endorsement of national union officials. The Transport and General Workers' Union, representing three-quarters of production workers at Rover and in association with management, has since been active in organizing seminars and training for its shop stewards at Rover on lean production methods and the 1992 agreement. The TGWU has also argued that at Rover the New Deal reconciles the interests of the company and the union, supporting 'the company's genuine need to become fully competitive' whilst at the same time retaining 'the independent trade union structure, albeit within a new joint trade union bargaining forum' (IRS 1993: 534, 7).[30]

NUMMI and the UAW

Rover, before the New Deal, could lay claim to 'the worst industrial relations [history] of any in Britain, and some might even say the world'. Similarly 'highly adversarial industrial relations that at the most peaceful could be termed armed truce' described the organizational culture of General Motor's (GM) plant at Fremont, California from 1962 to 1982.[31]

The old Fremont plant produced standardized cars for domestic, stable markets. The management was classic 'Taylorist' with a clear division of labour between managers and managed, planners and workers. Strong work discipline offered workers little discretion, militated against quality, and the mutual distrust between management and the workforce was replicated in relations between management and the union. When the plant closed in 1982, a list of 800 labour grievances remained outstanding and it was also common practice, at contract renewal, for management and unions to dismiss all outstanding grievances leaving the underlying problems and injustices unresolved. There were also problems related to drugs and alcohol abuse, with absenteeism averaging above 20 per cent and sometimes so high that on certain days the assembly line could not be started.[32] More conventionally, the union controlled jobs through detailed classifications (more than 100) and seniority. The local union had a difficult relationship with the national union, as well as the management, and within the local union, there were four rival caucuses, when the plant closed in 1982.[33]

The plant's industrial relations problems were clearly an important part of the explanation of low productivity and quality which were well below the GM average, just as GM, and the other US auto manufacturers, were being outperformed by their Japanese competitors. However, Fremont's 1982 closure, along with three other West Coast plants, was finally precipitated by the biggest auto sales recession in postwar history (Turner 1991: 54).

At its peak, the Fremont plant employed 7,000 and even at closure 6,000 jobs remained. There was little alternative local employment available with GM having only one remaining plant west of the Rocky Mountains: Van Nuys in Los Angeles. At the same time the Reagan administration had cut back federal retraining and placement programmes, and it was not until 1988 that Congress legislated the sixty-day-notice requirement for plant closures involving a hundred or more workers: the Fremont workers were given three weeks. The impact on the local economy, through supplier–customer relationships, was also inevitably far-reaching. It is also argued that the speed, numbers involved, and wider repercussions of the Fremont closure provoked a 'transformation of world views'[34] by the time of the opening of the NUMMI plant in 1984. There were also strong rumours, at the closure in 1982, that GM–Toyota were planning a joint venture. In the event, although 2,500 workers found jobs away from California, these largely left their families behind, encouraged by the rumours (Turner 1991: 55).

General Motors and Toyota signed a letter of intent in 1983 dividing ownership and the $200 m. investment. Under its terms, GM provided the plant, sharing the marketing and selling, but with Toyota, significantly, being responsible for the management of the factory. Toyota was, however, reluctant to work with the UAW but eventually agreed. The threat of permanent closure and the promise of the joint venture had softened the older militancy and the influence of local activists. The national union also worked cooperatively with GM–Toyota towards re-opening and, through its regional office, formed alliances with supportive local union leaders. Cooperation did not, however, preclude major concessions won by the UAW. Although it lost traditional control over job classifications and seniority, it gained an important undertaking by GM to rehire former employees, and won employment security guarantees and full-time union representation in the plant (Turner 1991: 55–6).

On the plant's reopening, nearly all of the assembly line workers and three-quarters of the skilled trades' workers were former GM employees and UAW members, although total employment fell to 2,500 from the 6,000 at closure. The plant was also little modified and could be described, in 1984, as a 'mid-technology factory' (Levine 1995: 13). The new, dominant, 'consensual' approach of the local union leadership both inside and outside the plant also came not from moderate factions but mainly from former shopfloor militants from the old GM regime, now employed at NUMMI (Turner 1991: 56–7). Turner also argues that the workforce, initially sceptical, was won over by union recognition, steady wages, and employment security. They also eventually accepted the new working practices and participative style—including teamworking.

Teamworking was the central innovation when the NUMMI plant opened. The first two hundred workers hired were team leaders, carefully selected to play a key role in reintegrating the old workforce into the new production methods. They were also intensively trained, both in Japan—for three weeks at a Toyota plant—and in Fremont, in all aspects of the Toyota philosophy and methods, from company policies and human relations to the detail of just-in-time, team organization, high work standards, and constant improvement in quality ('kaizen'). The team leader has major monitoring and problem-solving responsibilities within each job-rotating team which normally has four other members, either production or skilled workers. The teams have substantial scope in organizing work with a strong emphasis at team meetings (attended by management and union representatives) on consultation, discussion, and consensus.

Team leaders are also often union representatives who can therefore claim to have some influence, through consensus-building, on the management prerogative. However, management retains ultimate control of work standards. Grievances are few, and disciplinary cases (including absenteeism) are handled through discussion and consensus prior to action. The union is therefore inevitably drawn into the company's cooperative, non-adversarial stance. The dangers, for union independence, are reflected in the two rival caucuses (formerly four under GM) active in the union at Fremont: the Administrative Caucus and the People's Caucus. The latter's critique of the NUMMI system emphasizes four main issues: the speed of the line and increasing work intensity; favouritism in the allocation of the easier jobs; an over-friendly relationship between union and management; and autocratic, non-accountable union officials (Turner 1991: 60). This pattern of resistance has not seriously influenced the NUMMI model at Fremont but it has inhibited GM's attempts to extend teamwork to its other plants, especially its operations at Van Nuys, California and Hamtramck, Detroit. A modification of the NUMMI model, which retains seniority rights and independent union strength, has however been in operation at GM's plant in Lansing, Michigan.[35] For the industry as a whole, there have of course been a number of experiments in work organization and union involvement, although the big Japanese transplants have normally been aggressively anti-union, notably Nissan's plant in Smyrna, Tennessee where the UAW lost the certification election by the spectacular margin of 70–30.

Aside from the potential threat to the union's independence and exist-ence, there is also the contentious issue of work intensity and its impact upon employees. The People's Caucus at NUMMI, in its critique, partly reflects the traditional struggle of the UAW and other US unions against managerial control of the line and its speed. Under teamwork, the debate about work intensity has taken a different form. At NUMMI, under the union's contract with management, workers are allowed to stop the line, by pulling the 'andon cord', when they fall behind or identify a defect, although the cord is rarely used despite its availability. This has been claimed, by Japanese management, as symbolizing 'the relationship of trust between management and labor' (Levine 1995: 15). Interviews with workers at NUMMI also suggest that they prefer the new work organization to the old, 'Fordist' practices at Fremont under GM and elsewhere.[36]

More perceptive discussion of work intensity and managerial control of the line concentrates on the nature of the teams, the processes of peer group pressure, and what has been called 'management by stress'.[37] Teams under Japanese lean production are not autonomous, self-managing groups (Womack *et al*: 113–15); a better translation from the Japanese may even be 'platoon' rather than team. Worker participation, in practice, also seems to be closer to seeking consent and offering guidance, whilst the title of foreman or supervisor might have been abolished, but not the function; and in at least one Toyota plant in the USA the team leader *is* the foreman (Berggren 1992: 47–9).[38] Peer group pressure on indi-viduals in teams, controlling attendance, and 'stressing' the system, are also seen, by a number of writers, as the central features of teamwork and the price paid for the ability of workers to stop the line.[39]

Assessing the Case Studies

Workplace transformation, in commercial terms, can clearly contribute towards success. In the particular case of NUMMI it has been a factor in converting a manifestly failing operation into a productive, profitable enterprise. At Rover there have been major productivity gains but these are not necessarily explained by the changes in working practices. Nor are positive commercial outcomes assured.[40] However, the examples of Rover and NUMMI have not been isolated cases and have given rise to some imitation. In Britain, examples of the spread of 'progressive deals' include Ford at its engine plant in South Wales in 1986; and in Scotland on the Clyde, following the Norwegian Kvaerner Company's takeover of the Govan shipyard in 1989. Others include major food manufacturing companies (HP Foods and the Swiss Multinational Nestlé following its purchase of Rowntree) and the pharmaceutical company, Boots.[41] In the USA, the NUMMI example has attracted a good deal of attention but in its Fremont form has not travelled, even within GM's operations. However, the US auto and automotive products industries do, in fact, reveal a wide variety of successful approaches to transformation, with or without trade union involvement.[42] Japanese companies and their methods, both in Japan itself and in their operations overseas, have also been generally successful in commercial terms, perhaps most obviously in Britain and the USA. In both countries, for example, the electronics industry is dominated by Japanese companies. In Britain, the revived 'British' car industry is largely controlled by Japanese (and US) inward investors and in the USA the influence of Japanese transplants could be claimed as responsible for a strong, positive influence on the competitiveness and viability of the indigenous US auto manufacturers.

For the workers involved, the commercial success of these operations has provided jobs which are reasonably secure and well paid. But the jobs have been fewer in number. Lean production implies lower employment levels than old-style mass production, although this takes no account of any growth in markets and output. Rover, for example, has now returned to its 1989 employment levels, although NUMMI only employs about a third of its peak level in the GM period. Overall, for the USA, the employment effects of the Japanese transplants have attracted different estimates based upon different assumptions, although the estimates agree that job creation is exceeded by job displacement resulting from plant closures. However, the revival of manufacturing productivity in the USA may be largely explained by the transplants with benefits for competitiveness though not, at least in the short run, for jobs (Kenney and Florida 1993: 203–5).

The unions, in both countries, sometimes with enthusiasm, especially among the leadership, have supported, or even been directly involved in, negotiating and implementing the changes in working practices. The evidence also suggests that employees, including union members, have accepted and acquiesced in the changes.[43] Union support has however been more guarded among shop stewards and local union representatives and, in the USA, there has been some workplace resistance to the implications of union–management cooperation, participation, and involvement for traditional adversarialism and trade union independence. But this resistance has been limited: the decline in the strength and influence of trade unions and the pragmatic defence of even falling job levels has undoubtedly explained much of this development, although it is difficult to assess how far events have 'transformed world views' in the cases of both NUMMI and Rover.

As for those directly involved in workplace transformation, when asked, they tend to give a positive view of the work situation although, as for example at NUMMI, this is in direct comparison with earlier experience under GM. The latter had seemingly little to be said in its favour except in so far as it offered employment and even that was taken away in 1982. Following the trauma and dislocation of closure, NUMMI restored jobs, although far from all of them. Rover shed jobs, but without closure, and by 1995 employment levels had been restored along with some employment guarantees and the prospect that BMW was seriously interested in developing its British subsidiary. Lean production methods, for Rover workers, could be seen by them as a reasonable concession for such clear benefits which also included single status and a substantial pay increase. In both cases, too, union organization survived intact and in the case of NUMMI, there were concessions on the number of full-time representatives. At shop-floor level it can also be argued that the managerial prerogative, through the participative and consultative arrangements, had been eroded—though this is arguable given the nature of teamworking. However, at Rover, senior union officials have won some involvement, on a regular basis, in strategic decision-making and the acceptance of single table bargaining, on management's insistence, does not necessarily imply a union concession: a common front has traditionally been seen as strengthening, rather than weakening, union bargaining power.[44] Yet the final vote favouring the New Deal agreement was secured with the narrowest of margins whilst at NUMMI the People's Caucus remained as a focus for dissent and adversarialism alongside the positive views of change held by some employees.

In the face of reasonably satisfactory outcomes for the workers at NUMMI and Rover—and the approval of the agreements by most national union officials and a majority of local officials—the question remains as to why the new working practices received much less than complete endorsement. There were, of course, differences. Japanese managers were heavily involved in the workplace changes at NUMMI, whilst at Rover Honda's involvement was in design and technical matters. Hence teamworking at NUMMI took a more radical, far-reaching form than at Rover where the grade structure was changed, but not transformed. The People's Caucus at NUMMI also raised work intensity and the speed of the line (historic causes of labour–management conflict in the USA) as major issues of contention. GM, at its other wholly owned plants, was later required to modify its stance on these issues to secure acceptance of change. Rover's New Deal, though it included teamworking innovations and an emphasis upon quality, was a much broader industrial relations package seeking better management–workforce and management–union relationships. At NUMMI, the focus was essentially upon workplace transformation leading to a major improvement in productivity and competitiveness.

But if the reservations of Rover workers, as expressed in the narrow vote in favour of the New Deal, did not primarily arise from teamworking, this is not to suggest that Rover, or other British workers, favour its introduction. For example, a recent project by ACAS and the Tavistock Institute (IRS 1994: 556) to develop teamworking found 'negative industrial relations attitudes, which . . . can lead to scepticism and distrust' (ibid. 14). Indeed, the working practices involved in workplace transformation clearly justify a serious critique.[45] This is especially the case where unions are not present or, where they are, have minimal involvement in the implementation of change. The marginalization of unions is of course well advanced in the USA, including in the auto industry. In 1990, 39 per cent of total employment was non-union and outside the 'Big Three' (General Motors, Ford, and Chrysler) it was 76 per cent (Babson 1995: p. 13). In Britain, the industry remains largely unionized with the major, and perhaps ominous, exception of Honda's new plant in Swindon.

The presence, or absence, of trade unions is of course another term in the efficiency equation. If it is assumed that the introduction, by management, of new and transforming working practices will improve enterprise performance[46] we can then ask how far trade union presence can, and does, contribute to such an outcome.

TRADE UNIONS AND ENTERPRISE PERFORMANCE

The relatively poor performance of the economy has been an important issue in US politics for more than twenty years and, in Britain, for much longer. It has also been commonplace for governments, employers, and public opinion—in both countries—to place a large part of the blame for poor performance at the doors of the trade unions through their supposed capacity to raise wages above free market levels as well as depress productivity and profitability. Interestingly, US employers, despite their traditional hostility towards trade unions, for a time took a more positive view of their presence. In the early years after World War II, when Keynesian ideas were not seriously challenged, influential employers commonly welcomed the unions' upwards pressure on labour costs which encouraged productivity—enhancing capital investment—and contributed to wage-led growth (Bluestone and Bluestone 1992: 57–8). In Britain, in contrast, unions from the late 1940s onwards were seen, under the full employment policies of successive governments, as the engines of inflationary pay settlements, that is, unmatched by productivity growth. Few British academic studies have sought to exonerate unions from being

TABLE 5.4. *Union wage premia in selected countries*

Country	Year	Union (over Non-Union) Premium** (%)
South Africa*	1985	10–24
Mexico	1989	10
Malaysia	1988	15–20
Ghana	1992–3	31
USA	1985–7	20
UK	1985–7	10
Germany	1985–7	5

Note: * Black unions only.
** Estimate.

Source: World Bank (1995: 81); Blanchflower and Freeman (1990); Moll (1993); Panagides and Patrinos (1994); Standing (1992); Teal (1994).

blamed for inflation and poor productivity performance[47] and, until the early 1980s, US economists were mostly interested in the size of the wage mark-up or premium, of unionized over non-unionized employees (Freeman and Medoff 1984: 3). More recently, a union presence when it is cooperative has been praised but when adversarial has been said to be 'not in the economic interests of any society' (Adams 1995: 174–5). These are strong words, but the distinction between adversarial and cooperative outcomes, and how to secure the latter, is important in both analysis and practice and will be returned to later.

The proposition that trade unions do succeed in raising wages for their members higher than for non-members in similar occupations is generally agreed and supported by empirical research. Indeed, trade unions would be in some difficulty with their members if they failed in this respect. However the size of the wage premium varies widely between countries and over time within countries. Inter-country variation is illustrated in Table 5.4.

The much smaller size of the UK and German wage premia, relative to the US, is not confirmed in longer term studies before the 1980s. One estimate (Pfeffer 1994) reports an average premium for the USA of 10.3 per cent from 1967 to 1979. It also seems to be highly volatile, ranging from a low of 2 per cent in the late 1940s to 46 per cent in the early 1930s (Johnson 1981). In Britain, data has been much less complete although 1984 research reveals wide variations in the wage premium between different market contexts, especially significant being the presence or non-presence of the closed shop (Metcalf 1993: table 2). Given the rapid decline of the closed shop and union bargaining power throughout the 1980s and into the 1990s, we should expect a reduction in the British wage premium.[48] The weakening of US unions should also be putting downward pressure on the premium as well as through the specific influence of the decline of cost-of-living clauses (COLAs) in labour contracts. Research also indicates, over time, that union wage gains are dispersed among non-union workers as well as narrowing wage differentials within unions (Metcalf 1993: 263; World Bank 1995: 81).

However, although a union wage premium clearly exists, it should not simply be seen as a 'negative' effect. Nor should that effect be exaggerated at macroeconomic level. Freeman and Medoff, for example, estimate that for the USA between 1975 and 1981 the union wage premium was responsible for only 3 per cent of the inflationary increase in GNP (1984: 52–4). Additionally, for the workers involved, a wage premium is not a 'negative' effect and the larger part of it will be spent on the output of firms.

Estimating the impact of union presence on profitability is partly handicapped by differences in measuring profits.[49] Yet, however measured, the bulk of the research suggests a negative effect, although again this effect may be reflected in the positive benefits of higher wages and may be justified on 'distributive justice' arguments (Brody 1992). The negative effect on profitability, as well as the wage premium, may also be offset by superior productivity performance in unionized companies;[50] and a lengthening list of evidence is now beginning to indicate that trade unions, in the workplace, can make a significant contribution to raising organizational productivity.

Substantial, recent empirical research in the USA suggests that the unionized sector leads the way in an array of 'workplace innovations' (i.e. such as employee participation and involvement, teamworking, profit sharing, and ESOPs). Non-union firms are most likely only to have profit sharing which is generally less productive than the other innovations (Eaton and Voos 1992). Even the inevitably more sceptical neoclassical approach[51] concedes the 'important point that unionism need not have a deleterious effect on productivity' (Addison and Barnet 1982: 159); and Benson's (1994) Japanese research, which did find a negative relationship between enterprise union presence and productivity, also revealed management–union cooperation in introducing labour-saving technology to compensate for lower productivity.

The value of management–union cooperation is a central feature of other research findings. The association of union presence and productivity gains seems to be strengthened by a supportive industrial relations climate (Freeman and Medoff 1984) which includes a constructive relationship between management and unions (Eaton 1994). For Britain, in the case of Rover, there has been an improvement in productivity in the 1980s and this can be attributed, at least in part, to the more positive relationship between management and unions under the 'New Deal'.

In US conditions, especially, such a relationship is primarily determined by management (Pfeffer 1994) although, as Adams (1995) argues, management, and not just in the USA, is normally reluctant to relinquish any control even though in its long-term interests.

It is also becoming clear, from US research, that fashionable employee involvement programmes are more likely to be successful in unionized than non-unionized settings: that is, efficiency gains can be achieved through securing employee participation but in return for security of employment, best achieved by union representation (Kelley and Harrison 1992). British survey research in this area also suggests a strong association between employee involvement and productivity performance, although this relationship does not seem to require cooperative industrial relations (Metcalf 1995).

The relationship between trade union presence and economic performance is an important one but it remains difficult to assess. But it does seem that the unions' impact on wages, profitability, and profits should not be seen, overall, as negative and there is accumulating evidence that proactive management offering employment security and seeking union cooperation can provide a climate conducive to improved economic performance.

HUMAN RESOURCE MANAGEMENT

Human resource management has been viewed in the USA as an alternative to collective bargaining (Kochan *et al.* 1986), although given the limited extent of collective bargaining, even as early as the 1950s, firms had little difficulty in pursuing HRM policies without serious challenge. However HRM does claim to achieve significantly superior economic outcomes than collective bargaining. Furthermore, in its influential Harvard Business School variant, its ambitions extend beyond enhancing corporate performance by making employees more satisfied, even happier, at work and by so doing contributing to 'societal well-being' (Poole 1990: 3).

An initial problem in assessing HRM's contribution to efficiency and human happiness is defining what it is.[52] There is still much disagreement on an acceptable definition among academics and a gap between their attempts at 'surface neatness', for purposes of study and exposition, and the actual, messy, realities of organizational life (Blyton and Turnbull 1992: 2–5). One of these realities may be the existence of trade unions.

The TUC sees HRM as 'a slippery concept that means different things to different people' and considers that 'rhetoric has often been used to conceal a deliberate anti-union policy' (TUC 1994a: 5). Even within the same union the responses have been mixed as, for example, in the reaction of TGWU officials to the 'apparently painless introduction of HRM at Rover.' The strong support of some national officials for the New Deal was countered by others who saw HRM as, at bottom, a threat (Fisher 1995: 21).

The TUC's publication of wide-ranging advice to its affiliates in 1994[53] has not been matched by the AFL-CIO despite US evidence that 'HRM practices' are now more widespread in the unionized than the non-union sector and union presence assists the introduction of these practices (Beaumont 1995; Mishel and Voos 1992). However, some individual unions have been becoming more proactive at national level, such as the steel and communications workers. At local level, suspicions remain even if outright opposition is not widespread. This ambivalence may be explained by the incidence of two very different approaches to the introduction of HRM practices in unionized firms: imposition where the union is relatively weak, though adversarial; or a labour–management partnership where union membership is high and industrial relations are more harmonious (Beaumont 1995: 86–8). British unions' suspicions may also be aggravated by contrasting approaches, although the introduction of HRM practices through partnership is much less common in Britain than in the USA, casting doubt on the view that British managers value unions as partners in change more than their US counterparts (Beaumont 1995: 98–101), and some may even see collective bargaining as incompatible with the change process (Beaumont and Harris 1995b).

These two identified approaches to HRM reinforce the credibility of the 'hard' and 'soft' dichotomy commonly used by several of the British analysts (Storey 1989; Legge 1989). 'Hard' HRM sees employees as resources within an overall business strategy; 'soft' HRM gives primacy to its 'people' in making and implementing policy. Yet even this distinction may be more apparent than real when the 'soft' HRM organization seeks to justify reductions in its labour force or when hard and soft coexist in an organization maintaining a secure, well-treated, or 'core' labour force working alongside less secure, 'peripheral' workers with inferior pay and benefits (Blyton and Morris 1992).

The participative and quality-of-working-life aspects of HRM do seem, however, to have positive outcomes for employee satisfaction and organizational effectiveness. Yet even here there is a problem of management inconsistency. Schemes commonly have short lives when faced with production problems and crises (Gershenfeld 1987) widening the rhetoric–reality gap. More seriously, the empirical association of HRM with fewer grievances and lower absenteeism than collective bargaining may be because of its suppression of dissent ('worker voice') rather than a softening of conflictual attitudes (Appelbaum and Batt 1994: 20). Furthermore, even if management has genuine democratic intentions, HRM professionals must focus their attention on the firm as a business unit with strategic choices which may not serve the interests of employees. Nor does such a firm in its employment policies—aside from unavoidable legal obligations—operate as part of a wider 'system' of democratic rights and defences of which trade unions form a part (Piore 1993). HRM also weakens trade unions, even where it recognizes, negotiates, and cooperates with them. Thus it may offer tangible benefits to employees but in rejecting adversarialism weakens union independence. At the same time, HRM's focus on the individual organization draws the union away from the wider union movement undermining its capacity to resist or, in the final analysis, even to exist.

But if HRM's humanistic and democratic credentials are, at best, limited, what of its claims to raise economic efficiency? There are *some* studies, in both Britain and the USA, which point to a positive association between a strategic HRM approach and the performance of the firm (Beaumont 1995: 51–2). In both countries, though, companies with a clear commitment to the HRM model which have achieved substantial improvements in performance have usually done so on greenfield sites. In Britain, these companies have often been American or, more commonly in recent years, Japanese. In all cases they have invested heavily in new plant, equipment, and technology as well as introducing a comprehensive package of HRM policies and practices. It is obviously difficult to separate the impact of new technology on performance from that of the HRM innovations. Even if HRM does contribute towards better performance on greenfield sites, its potential is clearly much reduced at locations where the employment relationship is differently structured, well established, and difficult to change. Overall, present research knowledge, at least for the USA, suggests that 'the performance effects of the HRM model are modest at best and have not provided a basis for significant or accelerated improvement in firm performance' (Appelbaum and Batt 1994: 21).

CONCLUSIONS

A process of transformation is undoubtedly taking place in both British and American workplaces despite some doubts as to its extent, depth, and durability. It is, however, most clearly evident in a handful of large-scale organizations where it is strongly associated with extensive training and retraining of employees, some guarantee of employment security, and, not uncommonly, a strong and cooperative union presence. The changes in working practices, which are often accompanied by changes in management and personnel practices, have been closely associated with Japanese companies operating in both countries, although the success of these practices has attracted widespread imitation among indigenous companies and other inward investors. There have also been several major, joint ventures with Japanese companies in both countries, but especially in the USA.

The evidence suggests that the new working practices are unlikely to achieve success if introduced piecemeal and enhanced performance may tail off over time.[54] Nor should the working practices associated with lean production be seen as the only route to improved performance. The Swedish car industry for twenty years demonstrated that 'humanized workplaces', given certain conditions, could be compatible with high levels of productivity efficiency, quality, and commercial success;[55] and successful alternative models of work reorganization may be emerging which fit more easily into an industrial relations culture. Hence NUMMI, in particular, may be a special case given the special conditions arising from the traumatic closure in 1982.[56]

Japanese companies tend to be pragmatic in their approach to trade unions. Even in the USA not all are opposed to unions and their main strategy, where they exist, is to involve them in change and restructuring. The unions and their members are attracted by the employment flowing from commercial success, even though lean producers are likely to employ fewer people than their mass production competitors. The national officials of unions, as for example at NUMMI and Rover, commonly negotiate and endorse the changes, although their enthusiasm is much less evident among the shop stewards and on the shop-floor, where the realities are more evident. However, shop-floor resistance has been limited, perhaps here because of the decline of union membership and influence and the growing scarcity of well-paid, permanent jobs. Yet there is accumulating evidence that a union presence, alongside a cooperative management wedded to participative methods, is conducive to far-reaching and acceptable change. Unionized firms are also associated with 'workplace innovations', again introduced in cooperation with management and in participative contexts. And although unions do raise wages and reduce profitability, their inflationary impact is small and the positive impact of higher productivity may offset the negative effect on profitability, aside from wider consideration of the meaning of 'negative': wage rises, to wage earners, are always positive!

Labour–management cooperation can, therefore, reasonably claim to offer a viable route to management seeking greater enterprise efficiency. Yet the reasonably good odds of achieving success in following such a route do not essentially represent the case for trade unions, useful to them though they undoubtedly are. The involvement of unions in seeking to maximize efficiency also requires them to represent the values, interests, and rights of their members. This representation is an extension for workers of their political representation as citizens. The democratic functions of trade unions justify their existence without requiring them to deliver on enterprise efficiency even though their members would consider themselves ill served if their economic and employment needs were neglected.

Labour–management cooperation can also pose dangers for workers' representation. Fundamental conflicts of interest between labour and management have not been removed by cooperation. New pressures are also in place arising from increased job insecurity, new working practices, and greater intensification of work. The legal defences of employees have also been weakened. In Britain, as we have seen, the Conservative government sought to limit individual employment rights and weaken the trade unions' ability to protect them. In the USA, employment 'at will' remains the prevailing doctrine governing the employment relationship.[57] Trade unions and their members can gain much from cooperation with management but they must also guard against undue blurring of their separate identities and purposes. Union leaders often, of course, pursue both strategies.[58]

NOTES

1. For an interesting review and discussion see Adams (1995: 64–7).
2. A concise discussion of British cooperatives and their antecedents is to be found in McIlroy (1995: 378–82). For a comprehensive, radical account of the work-in at Upper Clyde Shipbuilders in 1971–2, see Foster and Woolfson (1986).
3. The Bullock Committee, and its significance, is discussed in Ch. 6 and in McIlroy (1995: 361–7). For research on voluntary, private sector, worker-director experiments see Towers *et al.* (1981).
4. The Institute of Workers' Control in Nottingham, Great Britain, was a leading influence in the workers' control debates in the 1970s. See Coates and Topham (1970).
5. This is the argument of US trade unions in their resistance to any encouragement of participation by legislation as a threat to collective bargaining. British trade unions and the TUC have until recently insisted on 'single channel' representation, i.e. through unions and their members. This is discussed especially in Ch. 8.
6. The Freeman and Rogers (1994) survey found that 40% would wish to be represented by a union if offered the opportunity, that is about two-and-a-half times the present rate of unionization.
7. e.g. Osterman concedes (in the absence of direct observation) the need to be cautious of the potential exaggeration, by respondents, of change in working practices (1994: 176). He is also sceptical of the value of interviewing HRM staff, experience suggesting that, even when operating at workplace level, they are not likely to have contact with changes in work organization. Hence he prefers, and uses, the most senior production, plant, or operating managers (ibid. 174). This contrasts with the WIRS surveys in which the 'primary

management respondent' is the senior industrial relations, employee relations, or personnel manager. For the 1984 survey, an additional management respondent was the production manager for new technology questions. This respondent was replaced by the financial manager in the 1990 survey (Millward *et al.* 1992: 3–4).

8. The 1990 WIRS survey was the third, following surveys in 1980 and 1984. The number of establishments, on each occasion, exceeded 2,000 with a response rate, in 1990, of 83% (Millward *et al.* 1992: 2–3). The coverage of the surveys included management organization of industrial relations; industrial relations structure; trade union organization; consultation and communication; procedures for resolving disputes; pay determination; industrial action; and employment and working practices. A fourth survey is now in preparation.

9. 'Core employees' were defined as 'the largest group of non-supervisory, non-managerial workers at this location who are directly involved in making the product or providing the service at your location' (Osterman 1994: 175).

10. For an application of the relationship between clusters of practices or 'bundles' and the economic performance of firms in the world car industry, see MacDuffie (1995).

11. The value of these surveys, and Osterman's, is assessed in Appelbaum and Batt (1994: 60–2). The Kenney and Florida (1993) survey covered Japanese transplants and Japanese–US joint ventures in the auto assembly automotive parts, steel, rubber and tyre, and electronics industries. A British study (Oliver and Wilkinson 1992) included all of these four key industries as well as chemicals, consumer goods, capital goods, textiles, food, and miscellaneous engineering and manufacturing.

    Kenney and Florida (like Oliver and Wilkinson) adopt a wide definition of the Japanese model, which the former term 'innovation-mediated production', although they ascribe less importance to the cultural context of Japanese society in achieving successful transplants (1993: 306–7). The British research reflects a much more sceptical view of the benefits of the Japanese model. Its contribution to the debates and controversies surrounding Japanese work innovations are here more closely aligned to those in the lean production literature (Berggren 1992; Babson 1995).

12. In conditions of high employment security employees are more likely to welcome training, retraining, and new technology to enhance their firm-specific skills. This will then further increase their attachment to the enterprise which will also benefit from their high skill levels and flexibility. The price for these benefits may of course be paid by workers in the peripheral and external labour markets employed in contingent, high mobility, low skill, and low paid jobs. This analysis of Japanese internal/external labour markets is developed in Hashimoto (1990). For a more extended discussion, including the German case, see Buechtemann and Soloff (1994). The case for greater employment security in US contexts is argued by Osterman (1988).

13. This is the rationale behind GM's Saturn subsidiary, discussed later and in Ch. 8. For a wide-ranging discussion of labour–management practices in successful enterprises, including the role of trade unions in workplace reform, see Pfeffer (1994).

14. These are distinguished from participation in decision-making. Involvement practices are directed at individual employees; participation focuses on the collective interests of employees exercised through representative institutions such as collective bargaining and joint consultation. See Marchington *et al.* (1992) for a discussion of this distinction. A concise review of the development of employee involvement in Britain in the 1980s is to be found in Ramsay (1991).

15. The term 'Japanization', and its difficulties, are discussed in Oliver and Wilkinson (1992: 12–19). This British study surveyed sixty-six companies in 1991 which it was able to compare with an earlier, 1987 survey. The broadly comparable US study is that of Kenney and Florida (1993) which was conducted between 1987 and 1991 by a survey, fifty site visits, and 200 interviews. Kenney and Florida, who though critical of Womack *et al.*'s (1990) concept of lean production, are close to that study in their celebration of what they judge to be a transforming new model: 'A revolutionary new system of harnessing value, generating profit and creating economic wealth is now upon us' (Kenney and Florida 1993: 324). See also the discussion of alternative production models in Appelbaum and Batt (1994).

16. Another contributory explanation is government intervention. In February 1994 the Department of Trade and Industry launched the two year 'Learning from Japan' (LFJ) programme to help the automotive component industry become 'world class'. The programme included the funding of a twelve-company visit of team leaders and lower level managers to Japan to gain practical experience of Japanese suppliers' production methods as well as working with Honda, Nissan, and Toyota in Japan and the UK to understand the requirements of lean production (IRS 1995: 583, 8).

17. For a detailed discussion of this vulnerability see Oliver and Wilkinson (1992: ch. 3). It has also been spectacularly demonstrated in the UAW's strike at GM's two parts plants in Dayton, Ohio in 1995. See Conclusions.

18. However, the NOP survey discussed earlier (Tillsley 1994) suggests a widespread, if not necessarily growing, incidence of involvement and communication practices.

19. This was also the weakness of British research in the 1980s which exaggerated the incidence and influence of the 'flexible firm'. See Pollert (1991) for a trenchant critique of this research and its implications.

20. However, in both Britain and the USA, non-unionism is clearly preferred, when available. Turner e.g. observes that the plant location and hiring policies of Japanese transplants have been linked to the scope for avoiding unions (1991: 182–90). This scope is, as we have seen, very wide.

21. This of course must be the case given differences in the relative strength of national labour movements and variations in legislative regulation of, and support for, collective bargaining and consultation machinery. The example of the US multinational, CPC, is instructive in this respect (see Ch. 2: n. 12). CPC's European Employees' Council (EEC) was established voluntarily well in advance of the EU Commission's directive. Its new EEC first met in Brussels on 1 July 1994 with representatives from all member states, including Britain and despite the British opt-out from the Social Chapter of the Maastricht Treaty.

22. The Dunlop Commission (Commission on The Future of Worker-Management Relations, December 1994) concluded that 'The evidence presented to the Commission is overwhelming that employee participation and labor-management partnerships are good for workers, firms, and the national economy. All parties want to encourage expansion and growth of these developments' (p. xvii).

    The Select Committee on Employment (Employment Committee 1994*a*) approved 'of the new initiatives involving partnership between employers and unions and regard this partnership as being crucial for the future of unions and indeed of industry . . . The Committee believes that co-operation and partnership are of vital importance for positive industrial relations in Britain and welcomes the trade union movement's positive approach to them noted during the enquiry' (p. xxxii).

23. Which, as we have seen, in sharp contrast to the arrangements under the Rover–Honda partnership, remains resolutely non-union.

24. For a concise history and assessment of Rover and its predecessors and the partnership with Honda up to the 'New Deal' see Oliver and Wilkinson (1992: 99–105).

25. These were the TGWU/ACTSS, UCATT, MSF, GMB/APEX, AEU, EETPU. The British auto industry now has five unions (at one time twenty-two) following the merger of the AEU and EETPU to form the AEEU in 1992. The overall British average, in 1990, was 2.5 unions per establishment (Millward *et al.* 1992: 77–85).

26. Single status has been an important, but not exclusive, feature of the HRM approach in Britain as a means of emphasizing the common interests of all employees and securing their commitment. However, changes in the structure of the economy, the composition of employment, and government and management attitudes from the 1980s have slowed down and limited the incidence of single status (Price and Price 1994).

27. Single table bargaining has been increasing in Britain under employer pressure, often in conjunction with the implementation of single status benefits and conditions. It has been stimulated by trade union amalgamation but there is some evidence of unions themselves taking the initiative as well as employers (Price and Price 1994: 544–5). See also IRS (1995: 577).

28. ACAS arbitration awards are of course not legally binding but are often described as 'morally binding'. However, according to senior ACAS officials, there is no known instance of an ACAS arbitration award being rejected by management or union, i.e. since it was statutorily established in 1975, under the Employment Protection Act. Arbitration in this form does, of course, predate ACAS by about a hundred years.

29. For a recent discussion of British and international strike trends see Kessler and Bayliss (1995: ch. 11).

30. This somewhat guarded approval by the TGWU contrasts sharply with the enthusiasm of the then President (Bill Jordan) of another signatory union, the engineers (AEEU) who saw the New Deal as 'a giant step forward for British industry'. John Edmonds, General Secretary of the GMB, whose union was also party to the agreement, saw the 'breakthrough' in Rover's offer of employment security which removed the potentially threatening nature, for

employees, of flexible working practices (Employment Committee 1994*b*: 62–3).

31. According to the President of the AEEU (Bill Jordan) in his evidence to the House of Commons (Employment Committee 1994*b*: 62) and Turner (1991: 54) in his discussion of NUMMI.

32. This account of the GM plant and its GM–Toyota NUMMI successor draws upon Babson (1995); Berggren (1992); Kenney and Florida (1993); Levine (1995); Mishel and Voos (1992); Parker (1993); Turner (1991); and Womack *et al.* (1990).

33. These were: conservative, moderate, militant, and sectarian left (Turner 1991: 57).

34. According to Turner (1991: 54), drawing upon Sabel (1981; 1982).

35. Lansing, as well as Van Nuys and Hamtramck are discussed in detail in Turner (1991: 62–90).

36. There is also evidence that workers' attitudes to the new methods contrast with those of the old-style, American managers in the industry who still harbour a preference for the traditional white collar, blue collar distinctions (Kenney and Florida 1993: 117–18; Turner 1991: 69–70).

37. e.g. Berggren (1992), Parker (1993), and Babson (1995).

38. At Nissan's British car plant a study of workers' attitudes also found that supervisors controlled the teams. See Garrahan and Stewart (1992) and Berggren (1992). For a senior manager's view of Nissan see Wickens (1987).

39. The andon cords at NUMMI control three coloured lights: red, with chiming bells, which stops the line, unless pulled again within a set period of time; yellow when the operator is not keeping up and needs help; and green when there are no problems. Parker, in his graphic description, argues that when all lights are green the system is not working efficiently, i.e. it is running with surplus stocks and workers—is less than 'lean'. Removing these buffers and/or speeding up the line results in the appearance of yellow and some red lights. Management can then concentrate on improving the individual performance of the line-stopping workers. When the line is restarted, the ideal, from management's perspective, is when the system is running with the lights oscillating between green and yellow. This allows for continuous readjustments towards greater efficiency at the expense of greater stress levels for workers. Workers will also be reluctant to stop the line and draw attention to themselves (Parker 1993: 262–70), an alternative explanation against that of trust between management and workers. The system of lights also allows workers to be visually and immediately aware of who is responsible for production problems. See also Schonberger's (1982) study of a Japanese motorcycle engine factory in the USA and its use of the andon system, cited in Berggren (1992: 46–7).

40. Recent research at Rover suggests that the increases in labour productivity between 1991 and 1994 could be attributed to changes in technology rather than workplace transformation—as management claims (Scarbrough and Terry 1996). Recent reports are also indicating product range and production economics problems arising from 'years of underinvestment and ownership changes'. It was also expected that BMW's losses on its Rover subsidiary

would continue until the end of the decade (Barrie 1996). Additionally, in 1996, Rover's British chief executive resigned to be replaced by a German.

41. These companies gave evidence to the House of Commons Select Committee on Employment. This evidence is discussed in Taylor (1994: 127–40). In all these cases, the trade unions were involved as partners in the change and transformation process.

42. The major example here is GM's Saturn venture in its unique involvement of the trade unions at all levels, and at all stages. Saturn is distinctive in recruiting most of its employees on a greenfield site drawn from other GM plants—unlike both Rover and NUMMI. NUMMI is also a joint venture with a Japanese company as (though to a lesser degree) was Rover with Honda at the time of the New Deal. Saturn has, of course, attracted an extensive literature, largely concerned with innovations in its approach to industrial relations (rather than the transformation of working practices), i.e. as a variant of 'enterprise unionism'. For appraisals of Saturn, as a joint labour–management partnership see Ch. 8 and Bluestone and Bluestone (1992) and Kochan and Osterman (1994).

43. British evidence also indicates strong support, by workers, for new technology even though it tends to be introduced unilaterally and commonly leads to loss of jobs among the less skilled (Daniel 1987).

44. For a survey confirming this possibility see IRS (1995: 577).

45. As e.g. in the contributors to the recent, comprehensive, conference volume edited by Babson (1995) which, in some cases, is informed by actual shop-floor experience.

46. It can be argued that lean production increases management control over individual workers, although the absence of 'buffers' in the system makes it more vulnerable to disruption (Parker and Slaughter 1995; Oliver and Wilkinson 1992: 76–81).

47. Two interesting exceptions are Jackson *et al.* (1972) and Nicholls (1986).

48. Metcalf (1993) also maintains, more generally, that though in the past strong British unions had a negative impact upon economic performance, that is no longer the case given their decline and the contraction of collective bargaining. Hence explanations for continuing economic problems need to be sought elsewhere than the unions.

49. Freeman and Medoff (1984) used the rate of return on capital and the size of the price margin over costs as measures of profitability. More recently, Addison *et al.* (1993) in their research on the impact of German works councils on economic performance also used the rate of return as did Benson in his 1994 study of the impact of unionism in Japanese manufacturing. Profitability and its relationship to unionization have also been researched on an industry-wide basis using price–cost margins incorporating sales revenue, payroll, and material costs. For a recent US review of measures of profitability in unionization studies see Belman (1992).

50. US writers reviewing the literature do not contest the negative effect (Belman, 1992) although Pfeffer concludes that the 'net effect' on profitability (i.e. taking negative wage and positive productivity effects into account) remains unclear (1994: 166–7). See also Martin (1992: 132–9). The World Bank

(1995) study, in addition to its review of the international wage premium, also cites Standing's research on the positive effects of unionization on 'productivity enhancing initiatives' in Malaysian firms (1992: 80).

51. The two 'schools' involved in this research are, first, the 'Harvard School', represented by Freeman and Medoff (1984) and Mishel and Voos (1992), using the 'collective voice' or 'exit' theory of union behaviour. The second is the 'Monopoly Model' of neoclassical economics which assumes that unions act as a constraint on the effective working of labour and product markets. For a concise overview see Addison *et al.* (1993). For a perceptive critique of the 'collective voice' and 'exit' school, suggesting that many workers have neither voice nor exit in the context of internal labour market segmentation and high levels of unemployment, see Ghilarducci (1985).

52. An influential, early contribution to the British literature is Guest (1987). A more recent addition is Sisson (1994).

53. The union-sponsored Labour Research Department has also produced a widely circulated publication written for trade union members (LRD 1995).

54. For the USA, see e.g. Parks (1995) who, in an historical and theoretical review of attempts to improve workplace performance, emphasizes the dangers of piecemeal applications and the inability to learn from the failure of earlier experiments. A survey of seventeen detailed US case studies, in the same issue of *Monthly Labor Review*, also reveals the widespread incidence of piecemeal initiatives and the case for the introduction of comprehensive systems (Kling 1995). See also Osterman (1994) earlier in this chapter. For Britain, Oliver and Wilkinson report lower success rates for Japanese working practices in the 1990s after the 'evangelism' of the mid-1980s had subsided (1992: 317). Another study (a survey) also found that the introduction of the new practices had no measurable impact on profitability between 1986 and 1992 (Oliver and Hunter 1994).

55. Berggren (1992) provides a thorough, recent, appraisal of both lean production and Swedish methods and suggests the possibility of a new, 'post-lean production' synthesis. See also Sandberg (1993) and Cressey (1993*b*) for commentary on the implications of Volvo's closure of its Kalmar and Uddevalla factories.

56. Turner, as we noted earlier, cites the example of GM's plant at Lansing, Michigan. This 'alternative to NUMMI' retains seniority rights in job allocation, weakens job rotation, and is more participative. Another example of following a different route to NUMMI is GM's Lordstown plant, the site of the famous 'wars' of the 1970s (Turner 1991: 75–82; Aronowitz 1973).

57. See the Conclusions: n. 7. For a comparative discussion, see Gould (1994: ch. 3).

58. As Lynn Williams, former President of the US steelworkers, once put it: 'When it comes to dividing up the pie, we'll be adversaries. But now we have to grow the pie and that means working together' (quoted in Dickson and Tait 1993). Adams, however, argues strongly against adversarialism in any society, but especially the American, on both economic *and* democratic grounds (1995: 174–5).

6
Change and Reform in the British Workplace

The coming of age of our democracy is a process that inevitably affects the whole of people's lives: it cannot be excluded from the workplace.
(Committee of Inquiry on Industrial Democracy 1977: 22)

The Government's reforms have led to major and important changes of attitude. The atmosphere of industrial relations today is very different from what it was in the 1970s. Management has regained the freedom to manage and the incentive and will to do so.
(Department of Employment 1988: 16)

Despite the brave words of the Bullock Committee of Inquiry on Industrial Democracy there was little support, in the 1970s, for extending democracy into the workplace through putting workers on the boards of private sector enterprises. The report drew the early fire of employers and their organizations, and the TUC and the government offered only limited backing for the Bullock recommendations. Most unions were opposed; many were suspicious of the rationale for incorporating workers on the board and still strongly attached to extending industrial democracy through collective bargaining. Collective bargaining remained the only option after the defeat of the Labour government in 1979; but it was a well-tried and clearly still viable route given the strength and dominance of collective bargaining in most sectors of the economy and the prospect, then, of a return of Labour to power sometime in the 1980s. There was also the vivid, recent memory of the power of the TUC and the unions to overturn ambitious industrial relations legislation (the 1971 Industrial Relations Act) as well as the capacity of strong unions, such as coalminers and public sector manual workers, to have some influence, even a decisive influence, on the timing and outcomes of general elections. Yet within ten years the Conservative government had won its third, successive, election victory; had presided over the defeat, in major and violently fought strikes, of the printers and coalminers; and had enacted four major pieces of industrial relations legislation (with more to come) which sought, unequivocally, to weaken trade unions and collective bargaining and undoubtedly contributed towards those objectives. In contrast, the earlier Conservative government's 1971 Act failed in its much less radical, though comprehensive, intentions, although the lessons of that failure are claimed as having influenced the 'step-by-step' approach of the 1980–93 legislation.[1]

The contraction of collective bargaining in Britain after 1979, as in the USA, but in that country over a much larger period, has had an important impact on the regulation of the employment relationship. Increasingly, collective agreements have become less significant in the degree to which they influence the individual contract of employment. Fewer and fewer employees are also covered, directly or indirectly, by collective bargaining. Employers have also taken advantage of trade union weakness to decentralize collective bargaining which is now largely a workplace activity, as in the USA and with the same, generally negative, consequences for unions. Recognition agreements are also not infrequently limited to grievance and discipline and, since 1993, under the Trade Union Reform and Employment Rights Act, employers have been lawfully able to offer financial and job advantages to employees agreeing to withdraw from collective bargaining and union membership in favour of individual contracts.[2]

The growth of collective bargaining up to 1979 as the dominant instrument of regulation of the employment relationship coincided with the increasing regulation of the individual contract of employment through the law, extending rights and protections to employees which collective bargaining did not reach or could not protect. The extension of these rights and protections had been subject to a virtual cross-party consensus but after 1979 the government sought to limit, and in some cases remove, what it regarded as excessive individual employment rights, and which it also claimed impeded enterprise efficiency. However, in a growing number of cases European Union (EU) legislation and European Court (ECJ) decisions advanced employment protection or prevented the British government from restricting it.[3]

Yet the much reduced influence of collective bargaining has only been partly replaced by legal regulation through EU directives and ECJ decisions. The outcome is that increasing numbers of British employees are working without effective employment protection through collective bargaining, the law, or a satisfactory combination of both. This of course was the intention of Conservative administrations from 1979, overturning the long-established protections afforded by collective bargaining, and a policy supported by all governments, dating back to the last quarter of the nineteenth century, especially in the twenty years from 1945 to 1965. Even the Donovan Commission, highly critical of the consequences of the separation of the 'two systems' of national and plant bargaining, saw every reason to support the institution of voluntary collective bargaining; and the growing problems of British industrial relations, which attracted the attentions of politicians in the 1960s and 1970s, were addressed, not by proposals to weaken, but to strengthen collective bargaining through 'responsible' trade unionism. This support was shared by the British employers' organizations and their members whose attitudes and actions were very different from the implacable, enduring hostility of most of their American counterparts.

These different British contexts also led to a different reform agenda from that of the USA. In the latter, the decline of collective bargaining over a long period has highlighted the need (from those who saw it in that light) to restore collective bargaining, or combine it with other appropriate forms of regulating the employment relationship. In Britain, public policy, over a long period, was not primarily concerned with regulating the employment relationship—it was already regulated to its general satisfaction—but in dealing with what it saw as the defects or excesses of the wider industrial relations system, in particular its capacity to generate damaging strikes together with the view that trade unions were primarily responsible for Britain's unsatisfactory economic performance. This supposed link has been the common thread influencing the industrial relations policies of all British governments since the Full Employment White Paper of 1944, aside from the interest in democratizing the workplace which flourished briefly in the late 1970s, although even industrial democracy had an 'efficiency' agenda.[4] After 1979, the official view of trade unions shifted significantly. They were seen as the grit impeding the perfect functioning of the neoclassical economy. Henceforth policy sought, not to take them into partnership or mitigate their behaviour, but to permanently reduce their power and influence and the collective bargaining habitat in which they flourished.

At the same time as public policy towards trade unions and collective bargaining was becoming distinctly hostile, collective bargaining itself was undergoing a major transformation. Until the 1980s, the structure of collective bargaining was a fairly stable mix of multi-employer, national agreements—providing frameworks for company and local plant agreements—and single employer agreements at national and local levels. Hence although workplace bargaining, controlled by shop stewards, was often outside the influence of national union officials and was frequently condemned by governments as the source of most British industrial relations and economic problems, the perpetuation of multi-employer agreements in most private sector industries and national agreements in the public corporations reflected, and strengthened, the national significance of the trade unions. However, from the early 1980s, British bargaining structure has largely become a system without a multi-employer framework, dominated by corporate bargaining at national and, more commonly, plant level. Employers have taken the driving seat in this transformation. As they opted out of the disciplines of multi-employer agreements they also found it easier, at local level, to introduce technological change, new working and payment systems, and a more flexible use of labour. They were also more able to control their wage costs through disaggregated plant settlements. Trade unions always protested at these changes and local bargainers had to learn new skills, but resistance was limited as trade unionism weakened in the 1980s (Towers 1992; Purcell and Ahlstrand 1994). Similar processes were also taking place at the same time in the USA (Katz 1993; Voos 1994), although these were much less significant: multi-employer agreements were never extensive or long-lasting in a system where bargaining is, and was, essentially a plant-based activity and encouraged by the 'structural-legislative imperatives' of the New Deal labour laws (Clark 1989: 241–8) which worked best with a tidy, plant-based structure.

The outcome has been that, until comparatively recently, US and British collective bargaining had different loci and focused on different issues. American bargainers, in the main, reached comprehensive, tightly drafted, local contracts covering every bargaining issue from pay, hours, and extensive benefits to detailed procedures for resolving disputes over seniority, discipline, and grievances. The contracts were also legally binding. British local bargaining was generally much more informal, with limited detail in the agreements and a good deal left to custom and practice; nor did the parties wish their agreements to have any legal standing. These local agreements were, however, an important element in the system and involved thousands of shop stewards with local power bases and significant influence. But the local system was within a corporate, or multi-employer framework in which the unions' national officials played a significant role. Beyond that, the unions' general secretaries and the TUC were heavily involved, sometimes through more than consultation, in the formulation of government policy, especially economic. But as union power waned under Thatcher and Major, the locus of collective bargaining, as in the USA, shifted decisively downwards. In the workplace, local bargainers became more preoccupied with responding to employer pressure for far-reaching change, job losses, and, increasingly, derecognition.

But if the content, location, and influence of British collective bargaining have been transformed, these remain recent developments. Up to the late 1970s British trade unions could be described as the 'fifth estate' of the realm (Taylor 1993), a position which they had occupied during, and for more than thirty years after, World War II. Yet from the early 1960s and into the 1980s and 1990s, all governments sought to reform collective bargaining, pressure the unions to change themselves, control industrial conflict and, in the 1980s, to reduce their power. These important developments are traced in this chapter, from World War II, through the Industrial Relations Act, the Donovan and Bullock Commissions, and the problems of the Labour government defeated in 1979. These important preparatory influences helped to shape the nature and extent of Thatcherite industrial relations reform.

THE ECONOMY AND THE UNIONS

British trade unions had a good war. Between 1938 and 1945 membership increased from 6.1 to 7.9 million as density grew from 30.5 to 38.6 per cent (Bain and Price 1983: 5). The growth in membership was of course to be expected as the wartime economy moved to full employment with employers also under strong, official pressure to recognize the collective organizations of their partners in the war effort. Labour's prestige was also greatly strengthened by the appointment of Ernest Bevin, the Transport and General Workers' Union (TGWU) General Secretary to the crucial cabinet post of Minister of Labour. Bevin was instrumental in securing the cooperation of the Trades Union Congress (TUC) in putting the civilian population on a war production footing. The TUC accepted the provisions outlawing unofficial strikes and picketing as well as those permitting the compulsory direction of labour. However the powers were scarcely used and Bevin maintained collective bargaining intact throughout the war despite the advice of his civil servants to suspend or abolish it. The *de facto* maintenance of the voluntarist principle (albeit with reserve powers) may indeed have been an important factor in the successful mobilization of the civilian labour force.[5]

As usual, of course, there was some distance between fact and rhetoric. Conflict and class did not disappear during the war years. Unofficial strikes were commonplace and began to increase as the war started to draw to its close. There were, however, few prosecutions given Bevin's reluctance to use coercion[6] and both the trade unions and the voluntarist principle came out of the war enjoying high prestige. However, sectionalism, inter-union competition, and the strength of shop-floor organization were already evident as potential threats to trade union unity and contributors to industrial disharmony. British working practices were also beginning to be seen as limits on improved productivity performance.[7] The high hopes of the peace also brought problems. Inflationary pressures were strong in the full employment, high earning economy of the war.[8] These were to be carried over into the peace under the commitment to full employment as Beveridge and the architects of the 1944 White Paper (*Employment Policy* 1944) were well aware in their explanation of what later came to be known as 'cost-push' inflation: 'The beginning of the "vicious spiral" of inflation is found in increased prices: these force a demand for increased wages which is generally followed by a further increase in prices and so on indefinitely' (p. 2).

The government's answer to the inflationary consequences of full employment was, by 1948, a voluntary agreement on pay restraint with the TUC.[9] The government also laid down four guidelines, one of which declared it wrong for it to interfere directly in collective bargaining, although a second put 'free' collective bargaining under threat unless the terms of collective agreements were honoured[10] (*Statement on Personal Incomes, Costs and Prices* 1948). This somewhat contradictory statement had, by 1956, developed into the government's preferred model of industrial relations: 'The healthy functioning of the economy and the progressive growth of its output depend also on cooperation within industry in maintaining an efficient and enlightened form of industrial relations' (*The Economic Implications of Full Employment* 1956).

The postwar doubts of British governments concerning the compatibility of economic success and the industrial relations system, particularly its voluntarism, were later to grow into specific measures to control the institutions of industrial relations, notably trade unions and shop stewards, and to curtail industrial action. However voluntarism remained entrenched in trade unions and the TUC, with significant support among employers, politicians, and civil servants—not to mention eminent academics such as Otto Kahn Freund, Allan Flanders, and Hugh Clegg—and was later to be endorsed, but in a particular form, by the Donovan Commission.[11] Yet although voluntarism was not to be seriously challenged until the 1970s, and still essentially informs much of the *practice* of collective bargaining in Britain, its principal adherents, the trade unions, have been subjected to increasingly systematic attempts, by government, to draw them into productive partnership until after 1979, when this approach was to be replaced by an equally systematic attempt at marginalization.[12]

The consistent explanation for British governments' interest in the trade unions lies in the performance of the economy.[13] The British economy's inability to achieve full employment and a satisfactory rate of economic growth without an unacceptable rate of inflation and a serious external payments problem has tested all governments since the early 1960s. The blame for this can be attributed to the incompatibility of the objectives and/or the limitations of policy measures.[14] It would also be attributed to the trade unions who were commonly accused of damaging growth and competitiveness, causing inflation, and, in the 1980s, of adding unemployment to the problems of their members and other employees.[15] More specifically, and particularly in the 1960s and 1970s, the critique was targeted at shop steward organization and its supposed links with British 'strike proneness'.

The historical record is that British strike activity did increase continuously from the 1940s to the 1970s but it also became less concentrated in the four traditionally most strike-prone sectors of coal, docks, cars, and shipbuilding (Durcan *et al.* 1983). However these four industries (and, within them, high incidence plants) still remained significant foci of strike activity into the late 1970s (Smith *et al.* 1978) and, in some limited respects, beyond. There is also no question that over the same period shop steward organization grew in extent and importance. For example, between 1961 and 1968 the estimated number of shop stewards (including white collar staff representatives) grew from 90,000 to 175,000 and by 1978 there were 250,000. In earlier years shop stewards were also mainly a feature of the engineering and car sectors: by 1978 they had spread well beyond those industries. They were commonplace in manufacturing as a whole and were well established in food, drink, and tobacco, leisure, footwear, services, and the public sector (Terry 1983: 67–8). Steward organization also undoubtedly grew in importance although its strength, influence, and militancy were commonly exaggerated, sometimes grossly.

The view that militant shop steward activity was closely linked to the growth in strike activity was, however, widely held throughout the period, but especially in the 1950s and 1960s when strikes were often of short duration, unofficial (i.e. not sanctioned by the union's national executive), and unconstitutional (i.e. not having been taken through procedure) (Whittingham and Towers 1972). These features were closely connected to the fragmented, sectional nature of bargaining by shop stewards with local management. Furthermore, the growth of shop steward organization could then be used to explain the spread of the 'micro' strike via the 'contagion' effect (Durcan *et al.* 1983: 411). This explanation of the large number of small strikes does not, however, demonstrate that militant stewards were both widespread and influential. Of course some were clearly important and influential for short periods.[16] More important than militant ideology was full employment. In the 1960s it strengthened the bargaining power of all stewards and enhanced the aspirations of union members at a time when inflation was significantly eroding the purchasing power of their take-home pay. Strike incidence also fell in the 1970s and 1980s, despite some protracted large-scale disputes, as unemployment rose to high levels and inflation was gradually brought under policy control (Edwards 1983: 214–18). It was also clear that many personnel and industrial relations managers found plant level industrial relations—conducted through shop stewards who could speak directly to, and on behalf of, their members—as satisfactory ways of doing business (Goodman and Whittingham 1973; Batstone *et al.* 1977; Terry 1983: 71–91).

Shop stewards were clearly not all the same and their role, in the main, was to preserve order not threaten it. Strikes, too, posed problems since they were far from being all the same thing. Durcan *et al.* (1983), from 1946 to 1973, distinguished between four periods of strike activity with different kinds of strike: the micro, macro, hybrid, and political. The macro strike, for example, virtually disappeared during the 1960s when the micro strike was the dominant form, but returned in the 1970s with major strikes by power workers, miners, and engineers. There was also the argument that strikes were not sufficiently significant to warrant the attention given to them by the media, academics, and policy-makers. The total days lost in Britain were far from exceptional in international comparisons. In an average year, between 1966 and 1973, 98 per cent of establishments in manufacturing did not experience a strike (Smith *et al.* 1978: 88). The impact on the economy was also relatively negligible. An estimate, for 1970, of the total loss of output attributable to strikes was 0.2 per cent (Whittingham and Towers 1972: 352); and lost working time from 1946 to 1973 ranged between 0.07 per cent and 0.2 per cent compared to that for unemployment at 6.0 per cent (Durcan *et al.* 1983: 403–4).

Yet despite the facts, the image of Britain as strike-ridden was a powerful one and reinforced the popular view, and that of policy-makers, that the British industrial relations system (especially in terms of the role of the trade unions) was an important factor in explaining the country's continuing economic problems. International bodies, like the OECD, also began in the 1960s to publish critical studies of the negative impact of industrial relations on British economic performance. These studies were reinforced by swingeing attacks on the trade unions by influential British journalists. Even American academics began to look closely at the British industrial relations (and social) system in their explanations of Britain's relative economic decline.[17]

These trenchant and wide-ranging critiques of the economic effects of the industrial relations system could not be separated from doubts concerning the voluntarist principle itself. This had not been seriously challenged since the 1906 Trade Disputes Act, although, in practice, the Conservative government in the early 1960s had already begun the now inexorable process of legislative intervention in employment and industrial relations with the Contracts of Employment Act (1963) and the Trade Union Amalgamations Act of 1964. The Industrial Training Act of 1964 was also implemented, with some enthusiasm, by the incoming Labour government, maintaining the still bipartisan approach to employment, industrial relations, and trade union reform. A more comprehensive strategy was the 1961 Conservative proposal to set up an inquiry into the trade unions as the basis for legislative reform. But voluntarism still had powerful defenders even outside the TUC and its affiliates. The Conservative government, for ideological and practical reasons, remained reluctant to initiate substantial legislation on industrial relations. This had to await a Royal Commission and a preparatory period in opposition.

DONOVAN AND THE INDUSTRIAL RELATIONS ACT

The Donovan Commission

Although the Conservative government prior to the general election of 1964 remained committed to voluntarism, and was careful to avoid an anti-union stance, its own right wing was advocating a legal frame-work aimed primarily at regulating the trade unions.[18] However by the election, general opinion in the Party and the government was moving towards legislation, in part stimulated by an historic judgement in the House of Lords which threw the settlement of 1906 into confusion: after almost sixty years trade union officials were once again potentially liable for damages for 'inducing' their members to breach their contracts of employment, that is, calling them out on strike.[19]

Under TUC pressure, the Conservative government reluctantly agreed to set up an inquiry to address the unsatisfactory (i.e. uncertain) nature of the law. The Labour Party promised, if it won the election, to restore trade union immunities to the 1906 position. In the event, the new Labour administration in the 1965 Trade Disputes Act legislated to meet the TUC's wishes, but only on condition that it agreed to a comprehensive review of industrial relations and labour law: the Royal Commission was appointed under Lord Donovan (a law lord) in 1965 and reported in 1968.[20]

The Commission was required to address four 'defects' (McCarthy 1992) in the British system of industrial relations: first, the increase in strikes since 1955, not least the unofficial and unconstitutional form, which comprised over 95 per cent of all strikes. This increase, from the Commission's research, was associated with shop steward involvement in pay bargaining at plant level. Secondly, inefficient labour utilization and 'restrictive practices' were claimed to limit productivity and output relative to other countries, especially in industries where powerful, local union organization was active, such as the docks, printing, engineering, and shipbuilding. Thirdly, earnings drift (the tendency for local earnings to outstrip national wage rates) was claimed to be an important explanation of cost-push inflation. Fourthly, internal trade union government was thought to need regulation to minimize undemocratic practices and the influence of 'militant shop stewards' (McCarthy 1992: 14–15).

As we have seen, the charges against shop stewards were only partly substantiated by research, including that of the Commission itself. In particular, the charges of undemocratic practices were probably far from widespread (McCarthy 1992: 15). The Commission was also widely criticized for basing the central feature of its analysis too closely on manufacturing industry, especially engineering, where academic research was well developed. This was the much-cited 'two systems' thesis:

Britain has two systems of industrial relations. One is the formal system embodied in the official institutions. The other is the informal system created by the actual behaviour of trade unions and employers' associations, of managers, shop stewards and workers . . . The informal system is often at odds with the formal system. (Royal Commission on Trade Unions and Employers' Associations 1968: 261)

Outside private sector manufacturing and industries such as chemicals, workplace bargaining did not challenge but complemented formal, national-level bargaining. There was also a well-regulated system in the public sector, which was outside the Commission's remit. Yet, despite its limitations, the two systems analysis did reflect, with some accuracy, the situation in those industries where disruptive strikes were a regular feature, that is those where shop steward organization was well entrenched. The Commission accepted this reality by recommending the development of comprehensive, formal collective agreements at plant and enterprise levels. The agreements would also include grievance, disciplinary, and redundancy procedures. It also recommended the extension of job evaluation, and the linking of pay to performance, changes in working practices, and hours worked. The shop steward's role and authority within the union would also need to be clarified and training and facilities would need to be expanded to increase knowledge, expertise, and effectiveness at plant level. Interestingly, the emphasis on the steward's importance to comprehensive agreements at plant and enterprise level implied that his or her influence needed to be strengthened rather than diminished, a view at odds with those who saw shop stewards as the architects of disorder.[21]

The Commission's solutions to the problems of British industrial relations focused therefore on bargaining reform but within an extended system of collective bargaining (an entire chapter of the report) with its voluntarist practices maintained largely intact. The support for voluntarism was not, however, unanimous[22] and even the majority recommended some legislation to strengthen the system, notably the registration of collective agreements with the Department of Employment and Productivity; the creation of a statutory Industrial Relations Commission; and the establishment of machinery protecting workers against unfair dismissal.[23] The Commission did of course support what might be seen as the centrepiece of the voluntarist system, that is, the non-legally binding nature of collective agreements. The majority also recommended some weakening of the strike immunities provided by the 1906 Trade Disputes Act. These would only be available to trade unions[24] and those *acting on their behalf*, that is, excluding shop stewards calling unofficial strikes. These two issues were to re-emerge in the early 1970s and 1980s. The Industrial Relations Act of 1971 did, however, incorporate the presumption of legally binding collective agreements but also retained the immunities for shop stewards leading unofficial strikes. The immunities for stewards were eventually removed under the Conservatives' 1990 Employment Act.

The Commission was of course preoccupied with reform of the industrial relations system. In that sense it could be said to have sidestepped the relationship between the industrial relations system, especially the trade unions, and economic performance. It did address manpower utilization issues and problems, including productivity bargaining, as well as the problem of strikes, but said little about incomes policy and nothing about inflation. The economy was, however, all-important to politicians including Barbara Castle at the Department of Employment and Productivity, significantly now having transformed itself from the Ministry of Labour.[25] The Commission could also be said to have mounted the last defence of voluntarism and collective *laissez-faire* against the strong case for its abandonment (McCarthy 1992: 18). But the report was also a long, cool, expert look at the merits and demerits of the industrial relations system *per se* and a long way removed from the view that it should serve the needs of individual enterprises and the economy as a whole—the rationale of the Thatcherite era. The Commission also provided some pickings for employers seeking the reform of industrial relations in the absence of legislation. Certainly since Donovan, employers have shifted the locus of industrial relations decisively away from national to enter-prise and plant level bargaining and made it possible to extend job evaluation, introduce performance-related pay, and change working practices—as the Commission recommended in its comprehensive plant agreements. But all this has been made possible through a substantial retreat of collective bargaining and a shift in bargaining power towards employers, both partly brought about through the legislative assault on voluntarism from 1980 to 1993. This is not what the majority on the Commission would have foreseen, or wished.[26]

The Industrial Relations Act

The Labour government's response to the Donovan Commission's recom-mendations was a White Paper, *In Place of Strife* (Department of Employ-ment and Productivity 1969). This accepted the proposed Commission on Industrial Relations (CIR)[27] which would promote collective bargain-ing and industrial relations reform. The CIR would use voluntary means, in line with the Donovan Commission's approach to industrial relations, although, significantly, it would have power to settle recognition disputes via legally binding references from the Secretary of State. It was also clear that the government preferred compulsion and the law to the Donovan Commission's voluntarism, especially in its approach to the 'strike pro-blem' which it saw as in need of urgent attention, rejecting the longer term, reformist, solutions of Donovan. The White Paper, in particular, pro-posed giving the government the power to impose strike ballots as well as 'conciliation pauses' in the case of unofficial strikes. But there was also an underlying hardening of attitude from the government towards the unions and the TUC and what it considered their negative impact on the economy. Their opposition to what were described as the 'penal clauses' did, however, eventually prevent the government from achieving legislative reform and this contributed to its electoral defeat in 1970.[28]

Interventionism was also a strong current in the Conservative Party, even before the 1964 general election. By the late 1960s it had become a flood with the publication of 'Fair Deal at Work' (Conservative Political Centre 1968) when the Conservatives were in opposition. This document established the principles guiding the legislation when they returned to power although it was also influenced, in its approach to the trade unions, by *A Giant's Strength* (Inns of Court 1958), written ten years earlier by Conservative lawyers. However, in some of 'Fair Deal at Work's' provisions there was a debt to Barbara Castle's frustrated legislation. Furthermore, the Donovan Commission's proposals to encourage comprehensive plant agreements and effective procedures were much in evidence, albeit with the availability of new legal enforcement procedures. Hence the CIR was retained and strengthened to promote bargaining reform at plant and company levels by negotiation between employers and trade unions, but with either party having the power to seek a legally binding order from the new National Industrial Relations Court (NIRC). Additionally, all existing collective agreements, including procedure agreements, were assumed to be legally enforceable unless the parties included a disclaimer clause (McCarthy 1992: 19–20).

Although voluntarism was far from abandoned under the Conservatives' reforms, and indeed the government claimed to be strongly influenced by Donovan's recommendations, the enforcement provisions of 1971 marked a major departure from the 1906 Trade Disputes Act which was concerned to set the rules within which trade unions could lawfully pursue their purposes. By 1971, the government's view was that trade unions, especially through the power of shop stewards, were an important explanation of disruptive industrial relations, primarily because they were too ready to use the strike weapon and in that they disregarded their members' more moderate views in doing so.[29]

The Act's[30] central provision (although not new and dating back to the 1871 Trade Union Act) was that of registration for trade unions. Trade unions and employers' associations had access to voluntary registration with the new Chief Registrar of Trade Unions and Employers' Associations if they were to secure the benefits provided by the Act. For trade unions this was the only way of preserving their legal position and, especially, their immunities, since unregistered organizations were open to employers taking them to court for inducing breaches of any kind of contract and there was no limit as to the damages which could be awarded. Members of unregistered trade unions were also without rights within the union since these required the authorization and supervision of the Registrar. Registered unions also had the important right to seek recognition. If a voluntary agreement could not be achieved, the union could apply for an enforcement order through the CIR and NIRC machinery. The criteria for recognition were that the bargaining agent (or agents in a multi-union bargaining unit) should be independent of management, adequately resourced, and be supported by a 'substantial proportion' of the relevant employees (Thomson and Engleman 1975: 22). The CIR could also recommend, on the request of an employer, a sole bargaining agency for a single union in a specified bargaining unit. This could involve the derecognition of all unions but one. The employer could also ask for derecognition where the union was no longer representative of the employees concerned (McCarthy 1992: 20).

The government's strong objections to the closed shop were approached by giving employees the right to belong, or not to belong, to a registered or unregistered trade union. This marked a partial move away from the British practice of 'negative' towards 'positive' rights, as is commonplace in other countries. However, for registered unions, the agency shop was available and, in certain limited circumstances, the CIR could seek an order for an 'approved closed shop'.[31]

The influence of US legislation on the 1971 Act was evident in the union security provisions. It was also evident in the introduction of unfair industrial practices and the power given to the government to take action against major strikes. Unfair industrial practices included unofficial strikes and secondary boycotts by trade unions as well as employers unlawfully denying union recognition. They were also applicable, in certain cases, to individuals. Here the most notable was unfair dismissal, by which employees could take a complaint to an industrial tribunal and claim compensation. On major strikes, the Secretary of State for Employment had emergency powers to seek a court order for a 'cooling-off' period, or a ballot of the relevant union members, where impending industrial action endangered the national economy, national security, public order, or exposed substantial numbers of people to disease or injury. The Act remained on the statute book until its repeal by the incoming Labour government in 1974, although by 1972 its provisions and remedies were being largely ignored by employers and the National Industrial Relations Court (NIRC) had lost much of its zeal. However the main reason for the Act's failure lay in the TUC's successful boycott.

The opposition of the TUC and the unions was strengthened, at an early stage, by the government's refusal to enter into meaningful consultations with the TUC over the principles and details of the Bill which passed quickly through Parliament without substantial amendment. When the Act became law, the TUC advised, and later instructed, its affiliates to refuse to register. This eventually became deregistration to counter the government's tactic of transferring unions already registered to the new register.[32] Despite the tax disadvantages, loss of immunities, and, in some cases, breach of their own rules involved in deregistration, the great majority of trade unions maintained the boycott. Thirty unions, mostly small except for the printers (NGA) and bank employees (NUBE), refused to deregister and were expelled from the TUC, although readmitted when the Act was repealed in 1974. The employers, too, proved to be less than enthusiastic in using the new powers available to them. In only a few, highly publicized, cases did employers bring actions against unions and in one of these the fine imposed on the union was paid into the NIRC by a group of anonymous businessmen.[33]

This virtual 'alliance' between the TUC, its affiliates, and the reluctance of the great majority of employers to boycott the Act's provisions demonstrated the continuing importance of voluntarist ways. But it also showed that industrial relations reform, in the circumstances of the early 1970s, could not be achieved without the consent, or at least reluctant acquiescence, of the parties. This was especially required from the trade unions who were, arguably, collectively at their strongest since 1945 and had recently demonstrated this in their successful opposition to *In Place of Strife*. The TUC had also demonstrated, on both occasions, its capacity to mobilize the trade unions' collective strength with only minimal opposition. The government, too, had misjudged the unions' general willingness to expose themselves to the penalties of deregistration, calculating that few would, in the event, actually take such a risk. The economic contexts as well as economic policy also shifted decisively after 1972. The free market ambitions of the Heath government from 1970 to 1972 were fundamentally reversed in the interventionist incomes policy phase after 1972, decisively influenced by a major challenge to government policy from the powerful National Union of Mineworkers (NUM), who provoked the government into imposing a national three-day working week to conserve energy supplies. The government's hard line on industrial relations reform could not coexist with policies seeking the support of trade unions and employers for detailed, statutory, measures to control inflationary pay claims and create a platform for economic growth and full employment. The government also had to deal again with the NUM. The union conducted a second strike which continued during the 1974 General Election campaign. By then the employers were also calling for the repeal of the Act as a measure which had 'sullied every relationship at national level between unions and employers'.[34] The government itself also showed little faith in its own legislation, using its 'cooling-off' powers only once (in a rail dispute) and refraining from doing so during the clear national emergency of the miners' strike of 1974 (Kessler and Bayliss 1995: 26).

It was also apparent that the Act had serious design faults. It sought to strengthen the authority of 'responsible' trade union leaders by weakening the influence of shop stewards in the workplace. At the same time

its action against the collectivism of the closed shop, and the strengthening of individual employees' rights against their unions on individual
libertarian grounds, was a route to undermining trade union authority.
In any case, a line of control running from strong trade union executives
supported by a disciplined rank and file could have posed even greater
problems for a government concerned about trade union power (Taylor
1993: 84–5)—as the Conservative government actually found with the
NUM in 1972 and 1974 and, later, under Mrs. Thatcher in 1984–5. An
explanation for these inner contradictions can be found in the lack of
experience and understanding of those who backed the legislation. None
had had significant managerial experience and they were opposed, in
the main, by former shop stewards in Parliament with a profound knowledge of the workplace. More fundamentally, there was a mutual clash
of incomprehension between individualistic, middle class values and the
collective values of the labour and working class movements.[35]

There was also some simplistic borrowing from the US legislative
framework: the attack on the closed shop through the right not to belong
to a trade union; the introduction of the agency shop with the possibility of an exclusive bargaining agent; the insertion of unfair industrial
(relations) practices; and the giving of emergency powers to the government. These devices and procedures were borrowed from a system
which had almost four decades' experience of using them. The US legal
framework influenced a collective bargaining system which, though essentially decentralized, was stable, predictable, and within which business
union ideology flourished. These characteristics attracted Conservative
lawyers and politicians but it was difficult to see how these could be
assimilated within an industrial relations system which was less tidy,
had been a century in the making, was still largely voluntarist, and with
unions which were more politicized and had sufficient power to influence
the nature and reform of the system within which they operated.[36]

Yet the Industrial Relations Act—though it undoubtedly failed in its
major purpose of providing a legal framework within which orderly
industrial relations could be conducted by employers and 'responsible'
trade unions—was broadly within the line of development of British
industrial relations. It shared the Donovan Commission's 'two systems'
analysis, although proposing legal rather than reformist solutions, and
in this it was at one with Barbara Castle's attempt to place legal restrictions on the trade unions. Furthermore, legal intervention was never
absent from British industrial relations. It grew rapidly in the 1960s,
mainly in the form of individual employment rights, and was to feature
strongly in the Labour Party's 'Social Contract' with the trade unions
after it was returned to government in 1974. One aspect of this contract
was a legal framework, though a 'friendly' one, under which the government passed thirteen bills in the five years up to 1979 (McCarthy

1992: 26–30). After 1979, the Conservative government's legal framework, though much less friendly to the trade unions, was still in the line of development from *In Place of Strife*.

The Act, and the contexts which influenced it and were influenced by it, also perhaps provided the Conservatives with a number of lessons. The Party remained convinced that the free market offered a solution to the economy's seemingly chronic economic problems and that such a solution was substantially impeded by trade union power. This was in fact the heart of the Heath government's economic policy in the years 1970–2 and the Industrial Relations Act formed a part of it. Heath abandoned this policy after 1972 for the earlier policy formulae of incomes policy, cooperation with the unions, and economic growth; but the policy was restored again, with a vengeance, after 1979. The difference, it can be argued, was that the complexities and contradictions of a single piece of legislation were rejected in favour of a phased introduction of a collection of simpler statutes to tame the unions 'step by step'.[37]

This argument has much to commend it in that up to 1993 a sequence of employment Acts and one trade union Act have consistently returned to a number of themes which have cumulatively sought, and partly succeeded, in weakening trade unions and collective bargaining. However the contexts of the 1980s and 1990s were and are very different from those of 1970–4. Trade unions have become much weaker for reasons extending beyond the legislation and have been unable to mount the concerted resistance so effective in the earlier period. Indeed, it is probable that a trade union movement enjoying the 1970–4 levels of power and influence would have found it easier to defeat the 1980–93 legislation. It is also perhaps more likely that the government was more opportunistic than strategic in its series of legislative steps against the unions as their power and influence continued to decline, somewhat surprisingly, throughout the 1980s.[38] The successful industrial action contexts in which the Industrial Relations Act was brought down, and their absence in the 1980s, is more instructive. The manner in which the Heath government approached industrial confrontation in the period 1970–4, especially in relation to the successful strikes of the miners, seemed to have influenced the Thatcher government's very different tactics in 1984–5. But again the wider union movement was weaker and the NUM did not have the support which it enjoyed in 1972 and 1974.

Finally, as Dunn (1993) argues, from the trade unions' perspective, given the developments since 1979, the failure of the Industrial Relations Act was a misfortune and might have enabled the unions to avoid 'their present semi-outlaw status: conspiracies whose licence is up for further curtailment and regulation every two years' (1993: 182). Hindsight can of course make wise men and women of us all.

THE SOCIAL CONTRACT

The failure of the Heath government's attempt to solve British industrial relations and economic problems by detailed statutory intervention was an important influence on the origins of the Social Contract between the trade unions and the Labour Party, later the Labour government. It was also widely believed that the open and bitter quarrels between the Labour government and unions over *In Place of Strife* had handed victory to the Conservatives in 1970. Quiet agreement between the unions and the Labour Party was the adopted tactic during the election and even the striking miners cooperated with exceptional restraint on the picket lines. The Social Contract was therefore, in its origins, part of 'an exercise in reassurance' (Pimlott 1992: 610). In its details it firmly rejected the unfortunate experience of legal sanctions from 1970 to 1974 although its 'contractual' nature and terms were never clear—it was even initially called a 'social compact'. Two of its intentions were undoubtedly radical, that is, to introduce industrial democracy into the boardroom and to redistribute income and wealth. Both, in the event, went no further, respectively, than a committee of inquiry (followed by a white paper) and a royal commission. This outcome was what the government wished, given its other urgent preoccupations with inflation and the economy. It was also what most of the trade union movement wanted. Over time, too, the nature of the Social Contract changed. At the outset it may have been 'a broad agreement between the TUC and the party on economic and social priorities' (McCarthy 1992: 26)[39] but in its post-1976 Callaghan phase it became no more than an exercise in pay restraint (or control) which the government demanded, unsuccessfully, from its friends.

However it is the industrial relations side of the Social Contract which concerns us here, rather than the success or failure, or even good sense, of the pay restraint aspects of the policy.[40] The industrial relations package, which the government was required to deliver, had three main components: the repeal of the Industrial Relations Act; the extending of certain collective and individual employee rights; and progress towards the extension of industrial democracy (Kessler and Bayliss 1995: 29).

The Repeal of the Industrial Relations Act

Simple repeal of the Act was not, in itself, sufficient.[41] It would not have restored all the pre-1971 trade union immunities, especially those deriving from the important 1906 Trade Disputes Act. Nor would it have retained the 1971 Act's unfair dismissal provisions which were widely supported within the TUC, the unions, and the Labour Party. There was also the political complication that the government, formed in early 1974, required the support of the Liberal Party until it subsequently secured an absolute majority in the second election of 1974. Hence the repeal of the 1971 Act and the enactment of replacement provisions was achieved in two stages in the Trade Union and Labour Relations Act of 1974 and the Trade Union and Labour Relations (Amendment) Act of 1976.

The 1974 Act rejected the presumption of legally binding collective agreements and earlier levels of unfair dismissal protection;[42] and both it and the 1976 legislation essentially restored the 1906 immunities, that is, covering actions in 'trade disputes' and extending it to breaches of both employment and commercial contracts. Additionally, judicial rulings, which since the 1950s had narrowed the definition of trade dispute, were overridden and restrictions placed on the judges' freedom to award injunctions against trade unions.

The legislation of 1974 and 1976 was intended to take British industrial relations back to its voluntarist traditions. Somewhat paradoxically, the instrument for doing so was more intervention, by the state, through the passing of laws. This had of course always been the case since, especially, the 1906 Act. This could claim to have provided the necessary legislative foundations without which voluntarism could not have prospered, not least the freedom of trade unions to engage in industrial action without unreasonable restrictions. The 1971 Act had significantly limited union autonomy alongside an earlier series of judicial decisions which had narrowed, or created uncertainty over, the immunities which were thought to have been definitively established in 1906 (McCarthy 1992: 26–30). Certainly the TUC and its affiliates were broadly satisfied that by 1976 the Labour government had done its statutory duty in restoring the unions' traditional freedoms.

Extending Collective and Individual Rights

The second component of the Social Contract's industrial relations commitments was mainly effected through the Employment Protection Act, 1975. This Act has collective and individual provisions. The collective provisions sought to encourage trade union recognition and collective bargaining. These intentions were to be partly achieved through three new agencies, albeit with progenitors: the Certification Office (CO); the Advisory Conciliation, and Arbitration Service (ACAS); and the Central Arbitration Committee (CAC).

The Certification Office, under the direction of the Certification Officer who replaced the Registrar of the 1971 Act and took on the functions of the Registrar of Friendly Societies, had a wide range of reporting, supervisory, and regulatory functions extending to employers' associations as well as trade unions. Perhaps the most important of these was, and still is, that relating to determining whether or not trade unions are independent of employers. The resulting certificate of independence is necessary for a trade union to benefit from the rights and immunities available to it in law.

ACAS began work as the Conciliation and Arbitration Service (CAS) in 1974. Its advisory function was added in 1975 when the agency was established on a statutory basis. Its general purpose was to promote the improvement of industrial relations, primarily through encouraging collective bargaining and the development of effective industrial relations procedures. But, unlike the Commission on Industrial Relations in the late 1960s, it was not required to favour company and plant level collective bargaining reform and nor was it given the CIR's regulatory and quasi-legal powers—an approach in line with the restoration of voluntarism and a rejection of the juridification of industrial relations under the Industrial Relations Act. However, as the CIR, although it preferred to encourage the voluntary recognition of trade unions by employers, it could initiate a statutory procedure as a fall-back. Hence if ACAS recommended recognition in a particular case, and the employer refused to comply, it could seek a compulsory arbitration award[43] from the Central Arbitration Committee (CAC). The statutory procedure, however, did little for advancing recognition and it was abolished in 1980 by the incoming Conservative government with the support of ACAS itself.[44]

Both ACAS and the CAC were 'tripartite' institutions: ACAS was governed by a council of employers, trade unions, and independents; and the CAC in its hearings had employer and trade union members under an independent chair. Hence they were intended to carry out their functions as essentially informal, non-legalistic industrial relations agencies. The voluntarist ACAS did not, of course, have any enforcement powers and even the CAC's compulsory arbitration awards did not have the sanctions of a fine or an injunction. The intention was clearly to maintain the primacy of collective bargaining, wherever possible, using the agencies as 'props' (Wedderburn 1976: 174; Lewis 1983: 375–6). The CAC's 'indirect sanctions' were however widely applied under the 1975 Act, and went much beyond supporting the recognition procedure. The indirect sanctions also covered the new duty of employers to disclose collective bargaining information to trade unions as well as cases it could bring under the Equal Pay Act. The CAC also had important pay determination functions. These involved applying the Fair Wages resolutions[45] of the House of Commons and the provision in the 1975 Employment Protection Act (Schedule 11) which allowed unions (or employers' associations) to seek arbitrated pay awards in cases where an employer was not meeting the prevailing levels in a trade or industry. These awards could be made outside incomes policy norms and guidelines leading inevitably to a substantial increase in references to the CAC in the late 1970s.

The individual rights provided for in the Employment Protection Act included paid maternity leave and paid time off for trade union training and industrial relations duties. Other rights, established in earlier statutes dating back to the 1960s, such as those relating to contracts of employment and redundancy, were brought together in the Employment Protection (Consolidation) Act of 1978.

The Employment Protection Acts were not however the only contribution towards the building of a 'floor' of individual employment rights which had been in progress, under both governments, for over twenty years. For example, Labour's Equal Pay Act of 1970 was amended by the Conservatives (although unwillingly) in 1983 and 1986 under the Equal Value Regulations and the Sex Discrimination Act to comply with European Community laws. Other statutes were the Race Relations Act of 1976[46] and the highly significant 1974 Health and Safety at Work Act which not only gave legal protection to 8 million workers but also provided major opportunities for trade unions to increase their influence in an important area.[47]

Extending Industrial Democracy

The individual rights provided for employees under the Social Contract legislation were undoubtedly more easily implemented in the presence of the restored collective rights of the trade unions. Even under the 1971 Industrial Relations Act their power was amply demonstrated through their capacity to invalidate the application of the legislation, win significant industrial disputes, and to have some influence on the outcome of the 1974 General Election. This power and influence had an important political dimension via the Labour Party and Labour governments but it was still essentially rooted in collective bargaining. The TUC and the unions pressed for, and welcomed, the extension of individual employee rights after 1974 but legislation remained complementary to the defence and advance of rights won at the bargaining table for their members (and by extension to other employees). Hence their preferred, and well-tried, route towards industrial democracy was the 'single channel' of collective bargaining. This implied a suspicion of potentially competitive alternatives to collective bargaining, such as joint consultation, works councils, and, in 1977, workers on the board.

This was the trade union context in which the Labour Government committed itself, as part of the Social Contract, to legislate on industrial democracy in the form of trade union representation on the boards of private sector companies. The Committee of Inquiry on Industrial

Democracy was the outcome, with Lord Bullock as Chair.[48] The Committee took less than one year to deliberate and report in January 1977. The report reflected deep disagreement among its membership. The main report was signed by Lord Bullock and six members; a minority report was signed by three; and one member (N. S. Wilson, a solicitor) put in 'a note of dissent on certain specific points in the main report' (Committee of Inquiry on Industrial Democracy 1977, p. vi).

The main (majority) report supported representation on unitary boards of public companies, with 2,000 or more employees in the UK, on the basis of the famous $2x + y$ formula, that is, equal numbers of employee and shareholder representatives ($2x$) plus a smaller number of directors (y) co-opted by a majority of each of the other two groups. The co-opted directors would form less than one-third of the total board and were thought likely to be drawn from people outside the business including those with company and senior managerial experience; those with specialized knowledge, such as senior professionals; and local and national trade union officials not eligible as employees of the company. The Chair would be likely to be chosen from the shareholder representatives. The employee representatives would normally be shop stewards elected by trade union members on the 'single channel' principle. However, the minority report, signed by the corporate members, rejected the single channel principle, recommending representation rights to all employees, not just union members, and including management. Employee representation would be on a supervisory board (within a two-tier system) and always with less than one-half of the membership. There would also be provision for an employee council below board level. Nor was the single channel approach at ease with variants of industrial democracy such as workers on the board. N. S. Wilson's 'note of dissent' took exception to the main report's $2x + y$ formula in favour of shareholder and employee representation only, but with the latter in a minority. He also opposed the minority report's advocacy of a two-tier board.

The serious divisions of opinion on the Committee were reflected outside it. The CBI, like the signatories to the minority report, strongly opposed control passing out of the hands of shareholders. The big unions were either firmly opposed or had major reservations mainly on the grounds of their unequivocal support for collective bargaining as the route to industrial democracy and fearing that board level involvement would compromise their independence (Taylor 1993: 241; McIlroy 1995: 364–5). There was also evidence that the few existing private sector schemes actually operating were initiated and controlled by management, with worker-directors having little influence on boards and being largely unable to represent employee interests (Towers *et al.* 1981).[49] The TUC had argued for fifty/fifty representation of employees and shareholders but its overall support, given the objections of its principal affiliates, was half-hearted. The influential Jack Jones, General Secretary of the TGWU, and a member of the Bullock Committee,[50] seemed to be the only important trade union advocate of the majority report. In the end, the government, which produced a white paper closer to the minority recommendations of the employers, was overtaken by the more pressing problems of controlling high rates of inflation, facing major strikes, and preparing for the approaching general election. Finally, the prospect of any legislative proposals on industrial democracy disappeared entirely with Mrs Thatcher's election in 1979 and the re-election of the Conservatives in 1983, 1987, and 1992.

The failure to implement what was the most radical aspect of the Social Contract (aside from the 'radical' redistribution of income and wealth) should not, however, detract from the remarkable legislative achievements of the 1974–9 period. Thirteen substantial labour law bills were passed in five years at a time of major economic and financial crisis involving unprecedented levels of inflation and unemployment and with crisis-level fiscal imbalances requiring IMF assistance. The legislation also created three principal new agencies, two of which still remain, and although its collectivist aspects were severely curtailed between 1980 and 1993, much of the legal framework of individual employment rights and protections remains intact and is even quietly prospering under EU influence.

THE UNIONS AND THE WORKPLACE SINCE 1979

The political tide turned sharply against British trade unions after 1979. Some part of the explanation for the political developments lay in the protracted and highly publicized industrial disputes of 1978–9; the associated growing disapproval of trade union actions even among their own members; and the unions still close links to the Labour Party, which from being an electoral strength in the early years of the Social Contract had become a liability in the election campaign of 1979. The incoming Conservative government had therefore, as in 1970, what it saw as a mandate to 'do something' about the trade unions. The Thatcher administration was also driven by a free market ideology not dissimilar from that of the Heath government nine years earlier. The difference was that the Heath government abandoned ideological certainties for pragmatic, detailed interventionism: Mrs Thatcher resolutely retained her allegiance to market solutions, although she was helped by the good fortune of a weakening trade union movement (for which she could legitimately claim some responsibility) and a Labour Party offering a limited electoral challenge. The Industrial Relations Act's 'one shot' approach to trade union reform was also very different from the 'step by step' legislation of 1980 to 1993. The latter was also far more effective although it again had the advantage of a trade union movement quite unable to mount the concerted challenge of the early 1970s. There were of course serious industrial disputes which severely tested the government's resolve, notably that of the miners in 1984–5. But that dispute contrasted with the successful miners' strikes of 1972 and 1974 which took place within the context of the TUC's boycott of the Industrial Relations Act and with firm, effective support from other unions. In 1984–5 the miners had financial support from other unions but without substantial sympathetic strike action; the TUC and Labour Party shifted between cautious neutrality and opposition; and the NUM was itself split from the outset of the strike.[51]

The economic and employment contexts, as we saw in Chapter 2, were also becoming increasingly unfavourable to the prospects for the revival of trade union membership as it began its remorseless decline. Additionally, up to 1979, the industrial and political strength of the trade unions, at national level, was complemented by their seemingly entrenched position in the workplace, with high levels of membership providing the power base for large, and growing, numbers of influential shop stewards. By the late 1970s shop stewards were to be found in 73 per cent of manufacturing workplaces with similar numbers in the public sector and among white collar as well as manual workers (Terry 1995: 205). They were also broadly accepted by management who commonly preferred to deal with locally based representatives rather than the more remote, full-time officials. The Donovan Commission, too, favoured stewards seeing them more as peacemakers than militants and sought to enhance their influence and authority through comprehensive plant agreements.

By the early 1990s, much of this had gone into reverse. Between 1984 and 1990 survey evidence showed that the presence of a steward in workplaces had declined from 54 per cent to 38 per cent (Millward *et al.* 1992: 110, cited in Terry 1995: 213). This, according to Terry, did not yet amount to a collapse although it was clear that 'the 1970s expansion of trade union organization, and of shop stewards as part of that, has been stopped dead in its tracks'. There is also evidence of a decline in managerial support, especially in the case of shop steward training (Terry 1995: 214), a major 'growth industry' of the 1960s and 1970s. This decline in managerial support largely explains the decreasing relevance and influence of workplace organization and shop stewards. Management was clearly taking some advantage of favourable political developments, changes in the law, and declining union membership to win back some of the workplace authority it is said to have lost in the years after 1945. Furthermore, the absence of any legal or official agency support for trade union recognition or against derecognition became much more important as trade unions lost members and their capacity to defend themselves. Yet there has not been a rush to derecognition, perhaps because British management still, pragmatically, sees advantages for itself in trade union organization. At the same time, recognition has been difficult for trade unions to obtain, and where it has been granted, this has often been on a 'greenfield site' within an agreement recognizing a single union and offering significant benefits to management. These benefits have commonly included the major changes in working practices described in earlier chapters, including teamworking which can enhance managerial control and bypass local union organization.

Nor have these changes necessarily proved more difficult to implement where local multi-union organization has remained relatively intact on 'brown-field sites'. The example of the Rover Company, discussed in Chapter 5, illustrates the degree to which local union organization has been drawn into acquiescence in major changes in working practices and relinquished some part of its traditional influence. Paradoxically, agreements such as Rover's 'New Deal' are much like the comprehensive plant agreements which the Donovan Commission favoured as the vehicle for bringing shop stewards in from the cold and giving them responsibility to match their power. The difference is that power and responsibility have moved towards management. Enhanced managerial authority has also been used to decentralize collective bargaining away from multi-employer bargaining to the single company but, more significantly, down to the workplace. This has not been of benefit to local trade union organization and, indeed, has been motivated by its weakness and management's search for both organizational flexibility and, again, substantial changes in working practices.

Finally, as was discussed in Chapter 5, workplace change in Britain has commonly taken place under the spreading banners of human resource management. The incidence of HRM may indicate that the unions have lost influence in the workplace; although it does not often seem to indicate their absence. Surveys reveal that workplaces which have introduced practices associated with HRM are also more likely to be those in which trade unions are recognized rather than those in which they are not (Millward 1994: 128).

CONCLUSIONS

In the period between 1964 and 1979 when Labour governments were in power for all but four years, the TUC and its affiliates enjoyed unprecedented power and influence, if not popularity. By 1996 the power and influence was much reduced whilst much of their popularity had returned.

In the 1960s, although a broad consensus of policy-makers and analysts, across party lines, saw the trade unions as at least a constraint upon economic performance, requiring early reform of the laws regulating their behaviour, the approach to reform attracted less agreement: it covered a spectrum from reducing their power, increasing it to give them a stake in the system, or sharing power through partnership. Both parties, when in government, in a context of detailed, official inquiries, introduced (or tried to introduce) a succession of measures and reforms which followed a largely consistent line of development. The inquiries, measures, and reforms included a Royal Commission (one of five since 1903); a major Act of Parliament in 1971 which failed primarily because of trade union efforts; and a series of statutes which, after 1974, formally restored trade union influence and extended individual employees' rights and benefits. The consistency lay in the attempt to bring trade unions, both in 1971 and 1974, into systems which sought to channel their influence, first by legal means and then by self-regulation and partnership.

By 1979 the official view of trade unions had moved decisively away from regulation and partnership towards a determined attempt, through legislation and supportive policies, to reduce their power. In the 1980s, the government saw the unions' power and influence as standing in the way of an urgent need to revive a seriously non-competitive economy. In a series of statutes, the government sought to confirm and accelerate other influences undermining the unions' strength. By the 1990s, trade unions were no longer being seen as an 'estate of the realm' attracting a Royal Commission. Instead, a House of Commons select committee undertook to inquire into what might be their future role in the British economy and welcomed 'the recognition among the major trade unions that the interests of their members are closely linked to the performance of the enterprise and the resultant cooperation with employers' human resource initiatives to increase flexibility, productivity and profit' (Employment Committee, 1994a, p. xxxiv).

The unions' relegation to the workplace was not of their choosing although, paradoxically, the workplace provided the foundation for their national influence a generation earlier and was to attract the persistent attention of governments to reduce it. The source of workplace power, at that time, was membership. Its erosion undermined the strength of workplace union organization and increasingly left employees without any form of representation in defence of their interests. In some measure this growing vacuum has been invaded by European Union directives and decisions of the European Court of Justice. But this remains limited, has attracted strong political resistance, and is mainly restricted to individual and not collective rights.

Workplace representation is, however, not yet simply a matter of retrenchment and survival. Trade union organization has not yet collapsed and, in some sectors, remains virtually intact. British unions also have little alternative to their reliance on the still widespread shop steward system. Employers, too, in their decentralized, flexible workplaces, may have won the battle for control but can still find change easier to achieve through cooperating with trade unions rather than derecognizing them. Some positive collective influences are also beginning to feed through the system from the EU. The European Works Council (EWC) is not likely to inspire an early development of transnational bargaining but there are clearly *some* benefits for unions in the establishing of institutions with rights to information and consultation on a European-wide basis. Furthermore, the Labour Government promises 'fairness without favours' for unions and its ending of the opt-out from the Social Chapter should further encourage the transnational bargaining potential of the EWC. In the longer term, Bullock's argument could also yet return. It is, in principle, difficult to resist the idea that democracy, in its fuller meaning, needs to be allowed to enter the workplace.

NOTES

1. It has also been maintained, arguably, that the successes of the striking miners in 1972 and 1974 provided lessons which influenced the different outcome of the 1984–5 strike. This is discussed later.
2. British employers, as we have seen, can also withdraw recognition for collective bargaining and individual representational purposes which it had previously granted.
3. e.g. the Conservative government was especially concerned to reduce the number of claims for unfair dismissal (70% of all cases) going to industrial tribunals. Since 1979 the qualifying conditions have been progressively increased, notably the continuous employment condition, raised in stages from six months to two years for full-time employees. In 1995 the House of Lords, interpreting EU law, ruled that the qualifying employment period for part-time employees (five years) was discriminatory against women in employment since women constitute the majority of part-timers. In 1996 the government proposed the removal of all employment rights in companies employing twenty or less, on the grounds that statutory rights undermine enterprise and employment in small companies. However, it is probable that any such legislation would have been challenged in the courts as discriminatory under EU law.
4. Thus in the Bullock Committee's recommendations (Committee of Inquiry on Industrial Democracy 1977): 'if we look beyond our immediate problems it appears to us certain that the criterion of efficiency in the world of tomorrow, even more than in that of today, will be the capacity of industry to adapt to an increasing rate of economic and social change' (p. 161).
5. Taylor notes the apparent paradox that Britain achieved greater success in putting its economy on a total war footing than Germany, without using

draconian powers (1993: 19). Here he cites Albert Speer, Hitler's Minister of Armaments. Speer also included the USA in his judgement: 'It remains one of the oddities of this war that Hitler demanded far less from his people than Churchill and Roosevelt did from their respective nations' (Speer 1970: 256).

6. See Emmerson's graphic evidence on the prosecutions of the Kent miners for taking illegal strike action in December 1941—a critical time in the war (Royal Commission on Trade Unions and Employers' Associations 1965–68, 340–1, appendix 6). For general accounts of strikes during the war see Knowles (1952).

7. e.g. in 1945 the government sent teams of managers and trade unionists to the USA to study, and report upon, explanations for the productivity gap between the two countries. Similar teams, but without trade unionists, now travel to Japan under the sponsorship of the British government (see Ch. 5).

8. For an account of the origins of British wage policy in the 1939–45 war see Roberts (1958: ch. 2).

9. This was the first, of several occasions, when the TUC agreed to cooperate with a Labour government to control wage inflation. The last was under the Wilson/Callaghan governments' Social Contract. The main lesson to be drawn from this lengthy experience still seems not to repeat it.

10. This was perhaps the first attempt, by a British government, to make collective agreements legally binding. Other similar proposals have failed to make progress into legislation, with the major exception of the 1971 Industrial Relations Act. This is discussed later in the chapter.

11. For an informed, highly readable account of a senior, influential academic centrally involved in Donovan and subsequent debates see McCarthy (1992).

12. For an excellent, detailed historical account of the relationship between government and trade unions in Britain since 1945, and drawn upon in this volume, see Taylor (1993).

13. Trade unions also have an ambivalent political role in capitalist society. They are potentially an independent source of opposition to the state and its policies but depend upon the state's benevolence for their existence.

14. Full employment as an objective of policy to be achieved through Keynesian demand management was abandoned by the Thatcher government in the early 1980s. It was replaced by low (even zero) inflation targets through monetary controls.

15. i.e. according to the neoclassical economics model, by 'pricing workers out of jobs'.

16. Examples of temporarily influential leaders in the 1950s and 1970s, respectively, were Jack Dash of the London dockers and Derek Robinson in the car industry at British Leyland (later Rover). Communist stewards' influence was greater than their numbers but remained limited (McIlroy 1995: 104–5). Overall, academic research reveals the limited ideological perspectives, pragmatism, and non-radicalism of shop stewards. See especially Batstone *et al.* (1977).

17. For an interesting account of British journalists and their influence see Taylor (1993: 116–18). The most comprehensive and detailed US academic study of the British economy remains that of Richard Caves and his colleagues

for the Brookings Institution which included a chapter by Lloyd Ulman (1968) on collective bargaining and industrial efficiency, which was mainly concerned with policies to improve productivity performance, including addressing the negative effects of the dichotomy between national and plant bargaining, a view which paralleled the central feature of the Donovan Commission's analysis and recommendations (Royal Commission on Trade Unions and Employers' Associations 1968).

18. As e.g. following the publication of the widely read and influential pamphlet of Conservative Party lawyers, *A Giant's Strength* (Inns of Court Conservative and Unionist Society 1958).

19. *Rookes* v. *Barnard* (1964) ranks perhaps with *NLRB* v. *Mackay* (1938) as a legal judgement which seriously frustrated the intentions of the legislators. Both removed important protections guaranteeing the right to strike. In Britain, since 1964, the immunities of the 1906 Trade Disputes Act have had a chequered history under different governments. They presently remain but have been significantly narrowed under legislation since 1980. In the USA, the Mackay judgement remains to seriously weaken the right to strike. See Ch. 2. For an interesting discussion of the contrast between Britain and other European countries on the law's treatment of the right to strike see Wedderburn (1995). In Britain the employee, when on strike, is in breach of his or her contract of employment. In Germany, Sweden, Italy, Spain, and France the contract is suspended.

20. The Donovan Commission included the union and employer interests as well as the prominent labour and economic journalists Eric Wigham and Andrew Shonfield. The membership, in its composition, was likely to favour broadly 'voluntarist' recommendations. The TUC's General Secretary, George Woodcock in particular favoured this approach. The part played by academics was, however, a major feature of the Commission's work, conclusions, and recommendations. Hugh Clegg and Otto Kahn-Freund, from within the Commission, and Allan Flanders as a witness were a decisive influence. Additionally, William McCarthy (now a Labour life peer in the House of Lords) directed the Commission's substantial research programme. Eleven important research papers were the outcome, with McCarthy himself directly involved, as full or part author, in the writing of five. All four academics shared similar positions on the case for reform but within a voluntarist framework.

The Commission's terms of reference were 'to consider relations between managements and employees and the role of trade unions and employers' associations in promoting the interests of their members and in accelerating the social and economic advance of the nation, with particular reference to the Law affecting the activities of these bodies; and to report' (p. 1). The socioeconomic contexts of the terms of reference reflect the conditions which gave rise to the Commission's appointment. Donovan was the fifth Royal Commission concerned with labour relations. Three of these were appointed in the 19th century: 1867, 1874, and 1891. All of these led to significant legislation. The 1903 Royal Commission was followed by the 1906 Trade Disputes Act. Though not a Royal Commission, the Committee on Relations between Employers and Employed produced five reports in 1917 and 1918.

This was chaired by J. H. Whitley (of 'Whitleyism' fame), an MP. The reports were a significant factor in the establishment and development of collective bargaining, minimum wage legislation, and arbitration (Royal Commission on Trade Unions and Employers' Associations 1965–68: 2–3).

21. The Commission's own research confirmed earlier findings that managers, where they had a choice, preferred to deal with shop stewards. The stewards themselves also found their local managers to be reasonable and, for the most part, stewards were seen as 'supporters of order exercising a restraining influence on their members in conditions which promote disorder' (Royal Commission on Trade Unions and Employers' Associations 1965–68: 29).

It should also not be supposed that shop stewards were commonly at odds with the full-time officials of the union. For example, the biggest and arguably most powerful British trade union, at that time, the TGWU under its General Secretary Jack Jones, deliberately devolved influence and authority to its shop stewards as the 'greatest instruments for democracy' (Taylor 1993: 149).

22. Lord Donovan, himself, provided an 'addendum' on the legal enforceability of collective agreements. Four members signed 'supplementary notes' recording some dissent from the majority and Andrew Shonfield, in his 'note of reservation' provided a lengthy critique of trade union power and the case for legal controls.

23. Protection against unfair dismissal was later provided, via industrial tribunals, under the Industrial Relations Act of 1971. The tribunals were first set up under the Industrial Training Act in 1964 to adjudicate on employers' appeals against training board levies. Despite changes in the qualifying conditions before an unfair dismissal claim can be brought and tighter rules regulating access to a tribunal, the system has been retained intact despite major reservations by Conservative administrations since 1979. However there are now proposals to use ACAS arbitration procedures for unfair dismissal cases as an alternative to tribunals. See Conclusions: n. 5.

24. 'Trade unions' would also be redefined, to include a requirement to register with the Registrar of Trade Unions and Employers' Associations. This new register would supersede that of the existing Registrar of Friendly Societies which already listed most trade unions who would automatically transfer to the new list.

25. See Freedland (1992). In 1995 the DE lost its separate identity and its main functions on its merger with the Department for Education. The Department of Trade and Industry (DTI) became primarily responsible for industrial relations. ACAS's reporting relationship was also transferred from the defunct DE to the DTI.

26. Recent reviews of the legacy of Donovan are to be found in the *British Journal of Industrial Relations* (1993).

27. The Chairman of the Commission was George Woodcock who had recently retired as General Secretary of the TUC. A prominent member was Allan Flanders, the Warwick University academic who had been an important influence on the Donovan Commission's deliberations and recommendations.

28. There was also determined opposition to the proposals from within the Labour Party. In the Cabinet, Barbara Castle and the Prime Minister (Harold

Wilson) were isolated and effectively withdrew the legislation in its original form. For an entertaining account, see Jenkins (1970).

29. Another, and contradictory, perspective, which has also been prominent in debates on trade union reform, is that British trade unions are not too strong but too weak (Taylor 1993: 1–4; Weekes *et al.* 1975: 6).

30. The Act was a massive statute of 8 parts, 170 sections, and 9 schedules. Detailed accounts of the Act and its contexts as well as authoritative commentaries are to be found in Weekes *et al.* (1975) and Thomson and Engleman (1975). For the implications for management see Armstrong (1973). These sources have been heavily drawn upon in this summary of the Act.

31. The agency shop agreement provided three choices for the employee: to become a member of the union or one of the unions; not to join but pay the appropriate level of dues to the union; or to pay the same sum to charity if objecting to membership on grounds of conscience. Approved closed shops required an order of the NIRC on the recommendation of the CIR. Under the closed shop, 'conscience' was the only way of avoiding union membership. See Weekes *et al.* (1975: ch. 2) and Thomson and Engleman (1975: 93–6), for detailed discussion of the Act's union security provisions.

32. See n. 24.

33. Employers and their organizations favoured legal sanctions against trade unions imposed by the government but were reluctant to take action themselves which, in the main, the Act required. Employers also objected, like the unions, to legally binding collective agreements which were universally avoided. Over 200 employers' associations voluntarily registered under the Act but few saw any advantage in registration and some found the Registrar's advice unhelpful (Weekes *et al.* 1975: 64). By 1974 the main employers' association, the Confederation of British Industry (CBI), supported repeal.

34. Campbell Adamson, Director-General of the CBI, cited in Taylor (1993: 216).

35. Brian Walden, a Labour MP, cited in Thomson and Engleman (1975: 27–8).

36. An interesting comparative discussion written at the time is in Thomson and Engleman (1975: 33–7). An Appeal Court judge (Lord Justice Stephenson), in the case of limiting the organizing rights of unrecognized unions *vis-à-vis* those recognised, found 'it extraordinary that with that [American] example before them those who framed the English Act did not make clear whether they were or were not adopting the American limitation'. Cited in Weekes *et al.* (1975: 296).

37. James Prior, Mrs Thatcher's first Secretary of State for Employment, is credited with the 'step by step' approach of the government's industrial relations policy. But the first Employment Act was his only piece of legislation (he then became Minister for Northern Ireland) and he seemingly intended the 1980 Act to be the last, favouring traditional rapprochement with the unions (McCarthy 1992: 48–9).

38. Many expert commentators, beyond the mid-1980s, were predicting a 'bottoming-out' of the decline in trade union density. See e.g. Bain (1987).

39. A joint, agreed, statement between the Labour Party and the TUC, in 1973 when Labour was in opposition, laid the foundations of the Social Contract. The TUC's commitment was confirmed in its policy statement, *Collective Bargaining and the Social Contract*, when Labour returned to power in 1974 (TUC 1974).

40. The government's 'guidelines' and 'limits' failed to control prices and incomes. By 1978–9 the 5% pay limit, as well as the policy itself, were being ignored by the trade unions, culminating in the wave of strikes in the 'winter of discontent' and the electoral defeat of the Labour government.

41. Hugh Clegg, probably the most influential member of the Donovan Commission, writing in 1972 on what should replace the 1971 Act, pointed out that simple repeal would expose the unions to 'the full rigours of the common law', since the 1971 Act itself repealed all previous legislation which protected the unions. This is analogous to what would be the impact of simple repeal of the US labour legislation, which some advocate from within the US labour movement. For Britain, Clegg recommended keeping some of the 1971 Act's provisions in new legislation, in particular statutory procedures for unfair dismissal and a strengthened recognition procedure under a retained Commission on Industrial Relations (Clegg 1972: 8–9). Statutory unfair dismissal protection was retained but not the CIR.

42. Under the 1971 Act, the basic qualifying period for bringing an unfair dismissal case to tribunal was two years' service. It was reduced to one year under the 1974 Act and then to six months by the Employment Protection Act, 1975. The Conservatives increased it to one year in October 1979 and two years in 1980. Longer qualifying periods have applied to part-time employees and employees in small firms. For thorough analysis and discussion of the origins and development of unfair dismissal protection see, especially, Weekes *et al.* (1975: ch. Two); Dickens (1985); and Hepple (1992).

43. A compulsory arbitration award is unusual in British contexts. Arbitrators from the early days at the Ministry of Labour and continuing through to ACAS at the present day make awards which the parties agree to accept at the outset of an arbitration hearing but which are not legally binding. The case for 'binding' arbitration in public sector disputes again became an issue in British politics at the end of 1996 in the run-up to the approaching General Election. See Conclusions: n. 26.

44. For a comparison of the statutory recognition procedures under the CIR and ACAS see Beaumont and Towers (1992). Townley (1987) has also provided a comparison between the NLRB and British recognition procedures.

45. These resolutions required and require only a simple House of Commons majority. Their purpose was to ensure, though without the full force of law, that workers on public sector contracts would not be paid less than their counterparts in their trade, or industry, as a whole. The last resolution was passed under Labour in 1946 and it and all previous resolutions were overturned by the Conservative House of Commons in 1982. The intention of the resolutions, although not fully statutory in form, was analogous to that of the US Davis–Bacon Act of 1931 which regulates workers' pay on building contracts with the federal government.

The other British approach to minimum wage regulation was through the Wages Councils, dating back in their first form (as Wages Boards) to 1909, which set minimum pay levels in low pay industries. These were also tripartite in membership. Their coverage and powers were progressively restricted by the post-1979 legislation until final abolition in 1993. It had been the intention of the Labour governments of the 1970s to develop collective bargaining in the wages council industries.

46. For an overview of anti-discrimination legislation and its impact, see Dickens (1992).
47. These opportunities were only available to independent, recognized trade unions. Independence requires a certificate from the Certification Officer. Recognition, since 1980, is solely within the managerial prerogative. This, and the decline of membership, has inevitably made it more difficult to maintain statutory health and safety protection and has contributed to the decline in trade union influence in the workplace. See Millward *et al.* (1992: 354).
48. Alan Bullock was, and is, an eminent Oxford historian and author of cele- brated studies of Hitler and Stalin. Two prominent and influential general secretaries were members: Jack Jones of the Transport and General Workers' Union and Clive Jenkins of the white collar union ASTMS, later MSF fol- lowing a merger. The employers included two chairmen of large companies. The academic representation was George Bain of Warwick University and the labour lawyer Bill (later Lord) Wedderburn of the LSE. The Committee's terms of reference were:

    Accepting the need for a radical extension of industrial democracy in the control of companies by means of representation on boards of directors, and accepting the essen- tial role of trade union organisations in this process, to consider how such an exten- sion can best be achieved, taking into account in particular the proposals of the Trades Union Congress report on industrial democracy as well as experience in Britain, the EEC and other countries. Having regard to the interests of the national economy, employees, investors and consumers, to analyse the implications of such representa- tion for the efficient management of companies and for company law. (Committee of Inquiry on Industrial Democracy 1977: p. v)

49. There were also two prominent, and well-researched, public sector schemes in the Post Office and the British Steel Corporation. These were generally considered to have fallen well short of expectations (Brannen 1983).
50. Jack Jones, in addition to democratizing his own union by giving greater authority to the shop stewards, was also an important influence behind the formation of the statutorily independent ACAS and served on its council.
51. Two good overviews of the 1984–5 strike are Beynon (1985) and Adeney and Lloyd (1986). See also Towers (1985).

7

Change and Reform in the American Workplace

In the United States, the large majority of working people have no means to participate in the making of most of the critical rules under which they work. Politically, their situation is closely analogous to that of the common people under the authoritarian regimes of pre-democratic eighteenth-century Europe.

(Adams 1995: 174)

In a comparative sense the American employment relationship is ripe for regulation.

(Gould 1994: 65)

The regulation of the employment relationship has significantly changed in the USA over the past forty years. This has taken two main forms. First, as we saw in Chapter 3, the role of trade unions and collective bargaining in the private sector (though not in the public) has been reduced, in extent and influence, to near marginality, although in the particular case of wrongful discharge the traditional regulatory role of collective bargaining in the workplace has been partly met by the growth in favourable litigation outcomes and some state legislation.[1] Secondly, there has been an increase in the federal statutory regulation of workplaces to render them less discriminatory in the treatment of employees as well as safer places in which to work.

The USA is of course not alone in the growth of statutory regulation, although in European countries, for example, regulation has generally been more extensive in scope, especially in the area of job security rights[2] and at European Union (EU) level, there has been some success in extending these rights through the Social Dimension, especially since 1989. Nor has EU legal regulation been confined solely to extending the rights of *individual* employees. A notable recent advance in *collective* rights is the European Works Council under a Directive covering fourteen out of fifteen EU members (as well as three members of the European Economic Association: Norway, Iceland, and Liechtenstein) and has been, in practice, voluntarily extended to the UK despite that country's 'opt-out' of the Social Charter in 1989 and the Social Chapter in 1992.[3]

But the differences between the USA and the EU and its members go much beyond the extent of statutory regulation, leading to major differences in the totality of individual and collective rights within the employment relationship. In EU countries, the extension of regulation through the law has complemented that of collective bargaining which has not significantly declined in extent and influence[4] and is legitimized and embedded in the institutions of most EU members and the EU itself.[5] In the USA, the long-term decline in trade union membership and influence and the associated contraction of collective bargaining have increasingly exposed employees to the managerial prerogative—without a compensating growth in protection through the law.[6] Furthermore, in the Congressional elections of 1994, the political contexts sharply deteriorated and it would have required a major transformation in 1996 to favour trade union recovery, collective bargaining, and supportive legislation.

In these developments, the USA is therefore out of line with EU countries, except for the UK, as well as with the general pattern of developments in OECD countries. In relation to the weakening of effective employee representation through trade unions and collective bargaining, there have been two consequences. First, employers have been more easily able to advance their own interests by seeking improvements in productivity through technological investment, smaller and more flexible workforces, and radical changes in working practices without serious challenge. Secondly, real income from employment (as well as family income) is at a level no higher, and for blue collar workers lower, than twenty years ago; whilst benefits, notably for health care and pensions, are frequently not available for those in the contingent labour force, whilst for full-time employees, employers' contributions are on a downwards trend.[7]

In the longer term, the decline of trade unions and collective bargaining may also have negative consequences for corporate and national economic performance. As we saw in Chapter 5, though the evidence supports the proposition that trade union membership is generally associated with superior pay and benefits, good, and recent, empirical research also suggests that unionized companies are often high performers with a capacity to introduce organizational change and job innovation.

The implications for the employment relationship of the serious decline in trade union representation in the workplace, combined with the growing inability of the New Deal labour laws and agencies to relate to the far-reaching social and economic changes of the past sixty years, have attracted the attention of policy reformers—notably under the presidencies of Carter and Clinton. There has also been a vigorous academic debate on the case for, and shape of, reform, especially over the last twenty years. Public interest has, however, been minimal and, until recently, commonly hostile to trade unions and their leaders although not to trade unionism (Heckscher 1988: 53).

Attempts to restore or reform the regulation of the employment relationship have of course taken place in the special contexts of US industrial relations. Aside from the recurring concern of policy-makers over the relative performance of the economy and its supposed relationship to the industrial relations system, the special contexts, discussed in earlier chapters, may be identified as four. First, exceptionally low levels of unionization and collective bargaining coverage which, even at their highest point in the 1950s, did not exceed one-third of those in employment. Secondly, the existence of public policy and legal contexts generally unfavourable to trade unions as institutions. Thirdly (and this feature interacts, to a high degree with the second), powerful organized employer hostility to trade unions which has changed in form and tactics, but not declined in strength, since the nineteenth century. Fourthly, a highly decentralized system of collective bargaining which partly arises from employer preference but was also institutionalized by the labour legislation of the New Deal.

These powerful inhibitors to reform have also existed alongside disagreements in the labour movement, and among academics, on the direction reform should take.[8] Here there are two main views. The conservative view, which is the theme of this chapter, is that the New Deal framework remains essential, only needing appropriate amendments to roll back employer abuses, allow for certain changes in employment contexts, and encourage non-adversarial attitudes. The more radical approach, which will be discussed in Chapter 8, maintains that the Wagner Act has largely outlived its usefulness and new forms of employee representation are required to complement or replace it.

The conservative view has informed all the reform efforts from Carter's 1978 Labour Law Reform Bill up to, and including, Clinton's Workplace Fairness Bill of 1993 and the work of the Dunlop Commission. These efforts also failed although they were, of course, confined to the private sector. Democratic presidents, since Kennedy, using their executive powers, have made substantial progress in the encouragement and regulation of collective bargaining among federal employees, notwithstanding the efforts of Reagan and Bush to at least halt this progress, if not reverse it. Certainly the reform of the private sector has proved especially intractable even under the most favourable political circumstances, such as those of Carter and Clinton's first two years. These attempts at legislative reform are briefly discussed in this chapter followed by an extended discussion of the Dunlop Commission's terms of reference and recommendations. The chapter will, however, begin with an analysis of the New Deal system which, although it provided the platform for the growth of collective bargaining, many see it as the root of some of the present difficulties and problems in US industrial relations.

THE NEW DEAL SYSTEM

The New Deal system, which developed over the 1930s and 1940s and is still essentially intact, in form though not in extent, is much more than the legislative framework of the Wagner and Taft–Hartley Acts. Strauss's (1995: 335–6) analysis of the system describes it in three, though related, parts. First, the rights and procedures of the legislation itself of which the most important include 'majority unionism, representation elections, NLRB determination of bargaining units, the duty to bargain, protection against employer interference in organizational efforts, and bans on company unions, closed shops and secondary boycotts' (Strauss 1995: 335). Secondly, the rights and obligations added by the courts, notably the Supreme Court. None of these are in the legislation and include:

the rights of employers to replace economic strikers, the distinction between mandatory and permissive bargaining subjects (with mandatory subjects including fringe benefits but not basic investment decisions), the duty of fair representation, written contracts, and implied arbitration and no-strike clauses. (Strauss ibid.)

Thirdly, a web of industrial relations practices (Brody's 'workplace contractualism') which though lawful are not required by the legislation and have been widely adopted in the public as well as the private sector where collective bargaining exists. These include 'a heavy emphasis on seniority, detailed job descriptions, narrow jobs, elaborate, legalistic, multistage grievance procedures, employer-funded fringe benefits' (Strauss 1995). A further, and highly significant practice, is the distinction between workers and their supervisors and managers, although this is written into the legislation.

Strauss also traces the development of the management–labour 'accord' in the 1950s in unionized workplaces in which each side granted legitimacy to their respective roles: the unions as the legitimate representatives of employees negotiating regular increases in pay and benefits; and, in return, the unions recognized the 'right to manage' and agreed to maintain labour peace by controlling wildcat strikes. Wages were also largely taken out of competition in many industries under the practice of pattern bargaining.

The outcome was a fairly widespread and workable system. However it only worked under three assumptions which, according to Strauss, began to break down in the 1970s, that is, the prevalence of large companies in mass-production industry; permanent employment (except for periodic lay-offs) of most employees under a single employer in narrowly defined, easily supervised jobs; and limited foreign competition which guaranteed the other two conditions. A further, implicit assumption of the system, which goes back to the Wagner Act, was that collective bargaining would gradually be extended to cover most private sector employees. In the event this has proved to be far from the case so that only a very small minority of employees are currently covered by the New Deal system with about 90 per cent of employees in the private sector now lying outside its remit. Furthermore, as permanent jobs with a single employer continue to contract, both 'workplace contrac-tualism' and the labour–management 'accord' in unionized enterprises are breaking down (Strauss 1995: 336).

The New Deal system can be seen as contributing to union decline in encouraging adversarial industrial relations. Others argue that the Wagner Act itself provided the seeds of decline in its belief that even-handed laws can effectively regulate the permanent imbalance in bar-gaining power between employers and employees. Thus rights were given to employees but without any real means of enforcing them in the face of well-resourced, determined employer opposition (Heckscher 1988: 40–3; Weiler 1990: ch. 3). This has led to some advocacy for the repeal of the Wagner Act (including that of Layne Kirkland, former AFL-CIO President), although even in rejecting repeal, the case can still be made out for substantial reform (Gould 1994: 151).

The outline of a reform agenda to create the conditions for some recov-ery in the unions' power to organize and promote collective bargaining is clear enough, and is essentially covered in the Dunlop Commission's recommendations, discussed later. Yet even far-reaching changes in the law—such as to remove its bias against craft and occupational unions organizing and acting on an industry-wide basis[9] by abolishing the ban on secondary boycotts (Cobble 1994; Strauss 1995) or to address contingent employment growth by allowing temporary workers to vote in NLRB certification elections (Strauss 1995)—would not necessarily increase the positive appeal of unions to a much-changed labour force, including the large and growing numbers of semi-professionals and professionals. The essential truth is that any reform of the New Deal system—which would allow unions more freedom to, at least, consolidate their position—would be welcomed by them. However labour law reform, in itself, would not sufficiently address the primary origins of trade union decline and the contraction of collective bargaining.

LABOUR LAW REFORM: CARTER AND CLINTON

Attempts to reform US industrial relations through legislation did not begin with the New Deal. The detailed regulation of a strategic industry (later extended to air carriers) under the inter-state commerce powers was pioneered in the Railway Labour Act of 1926 which, unlike Wagner, also established statutory mediation and arbitration procedures.[10] Nor has legislation been confined to the private sector. In particular, the Civil Service Reform Act of 1978 codified the executive orders of three presidents (Kennedy, Nixon, and Ford) regulating unionization and collective bargaining rights in all federal agencies except the US Postal

Service. This was converted to an independent agency under the 1970 Postal Reorganization Act which also brought the service within the regulatory scope, for industrial relations purposes, of the Taft–Hartley Act.

Federal regulation has also been advocated as the 'model' for extending representation rights in the private sector: in the AFL-CIO's evidence to the Dunlop Commission, discussed later. Additionally, legislative initiatives have not been confined to Democrats or only been introduced under Democratic majorities.[11] However, the failure of the Carter and Clinton Bills illustrates the difficulties of even Democratic presidents, with Congressional majorities, to secure the passage of legislative proposals, of only modest ambition, that is, seeking only to restore the intentions and early application of the Wagner Act.

The Labor Law Reform Bill

The Labor Law Reform Bill, though a very limited and substantially amended measure, significantly attracted major opposition, coordinated by the employers. The eventual Bill brought to the House excluded the original intention of the AFL-CIO to seek to repeal Taft–Hartley's Section 14(b) covering the right-to-work legislation available to the states.[12] Its principal aims were merely to tighten up the procedures against employer unfair labour practices in representation campaigns and elections. Its failure, despite its modest aims, was partly explained by the deteriorating contexts and prospects for labour compared to 1935 and the continuing strength of employer opposition. There was also a new development: a shift in population and voting patterns affecting the House. These favoured representatives from the Southern states and, given that region's anti-labour tradition even extending to Democrats, contributed to the Bill's defeat (Clark 1989: 206–9).

The defeat of the 1978 Bill, though a shock to the unions, was also consistent with a series of Supreme Court decisions through the 1970s, weakening union and employee representation. At the same time, the old alliances between labour and other liberal groups were loosening. Unions defending jobs and seniority rights increasingly found themselves at odds with women and minority organizations pressing for their rights under the new equality legislation. Environmental regulation activists were also seen, by many union members, as threatening their jobs and the AFL-CIO's foreign policy positions often offended their old liberal supporters (Heckscher 1988: 71–2). This cold climate became even colder in the 1980s. With the Democrats out of the White House the employers took the opportunity to renew and strengthen their anti-union offensive. President Reagan was also setting the example with federal employees as those with liberal ideas were pushed increasingly on the defensive under sustained attack from the conservative right.

Yet alongside the growing crisis in private sector unionism, the public sector retained much of its membership and potential for growth, even in the 1980s. This is partly explained by the interaction between the much less aggressive tactics of public sector employers and the more successful organizing record of public sector unions. It is also difficult, constitutionally, for even the most anti-union (or pro-union) federal administration to encroach upon the separate, and varying, jurisdictions of fifty states relating to public sector employment and unionization.[13] The executive powers of the presidency can also be used to support the influence of unions and growth of collective bargaining and this remained policy, under both Democratic and Republican presidencies,[14] until the hiatus of the 1980s. It then resumed once more under Clinton, although with more difficulty given the Republican majorities in Congress.

Clinton and Reform

President Clinton attempted to redress trade union difficulties in three ways: the first through legislation in the Workplace Fairness Bill, 1993; the second through his executive powers in Executive Order 12954 of 1995. Both of these addressed the growing and effective use of permanent replacement of economic strikers by employers. This had not been a significant issue in the late 1970s and the aborted Labor Relations Bill omitted measures to ban the replacement of economic strikers given its primary concern with more effective, fairer, and expeditious certification procedures. It was only in the 1980s that permanent replacement became an established feature of private sector employers' anti-strike actions, following especially President Reagan's breaking of PATCO in the federal sector. President Clinton's third way of redressing trade union difficulties, the Dunlop Commission, sought a wider, more considered base for a legislative reform package for the private sector.

The second Workplace Fairness Bill was introduced by the Democrats (the first was in 1991 under Bush) and was the latest in many attempts by Congress to reverse the 1938 Mackay judgement allowing employers to carry on their businesses by the permanent replacing of economic strikers (Gould 1994: 194) who at that time enjoyed *de jure* (if not *de facto*) protection for the right to strike under the Wagner Act. The 1993 Bill prohibited permanent replacements but allowed employers to hire temporary replacements for the duration of the strike, however long it lasted. At the end of the strike, the strikers would have the right to return but would be required to accept the employer's terms and conditions. The employer would also be able to maintain, post-strike, that the running of the business did not require rehiring of all the strikers.[15]

Despite the manifest flaws in the legislation in relation to the post-strike powers of the employers, the AFL-CIO strongly supported its passage with both heavy expenditure of money and determined lobbying; but it was countered by the traditionally effective lobbying tactics by the employers in Congress. Nor did the President provide full support and the Bill, as in 1979, narrowly failed to muster enough votes to overturn a Senate filibuster,[16] despite having majorities in both chambers.

The failure of the legislation still left open the executive order route. The Order, introduced in 1995, prohibited the federal government from concluding contracts with companies which hire permanent replacements for economic strikers. However the Order excluded contracts for less than $10,000 and was not retrospective.[17] The Republicans attempted to overthrow the Order in the Senate[18] but were blocked by a Democratic filibuster. However the legality of the Order was challenged, by the employers, in two court actions in 1995 and 1996. The first was dismissed but the second, before the Court of Appeals in the District of Columbia, was successful and the Order was overturned. The administration, in May 1996, was considering an appeal to the US Supreme Court.

An additional labour law reform proposal under the Clinton administration, but initiated by the Republicans with the intention of weakening the unions, was the Teamwork for Employers and Managers (TEAM) Bill. It was introduced twice (as was the Workplace Fairness Bill) both before and after the 1994 elections but by the Republicans. It sought to amend the important provision in the Wagner Act, Section 8(a)(2), to allow employers to either establish or assist worker–management teams concerned with 'but not limited to, issues of quality, productivity, efficiency and safety and health'[19] The AFL-CIO saw such teams as rivals to independent labour organizations, recalling the 'company unions' which employers developed in the 1930s to resist unionization in the workplace.[20] The second Bill was also introduced not long after the final report of the Dunlop Commission whose terms of reference and recommendations were centrally concerned with measures to improve productivity through worker–management cooperation but without undermining the Wagner Act's support for independent trade unions.[21]

In the event, the TEAM Bill ran into early difficulties. President Clinton undertook to veto the measure if it emerged from Congress requiring his signature; and the votes against it in the House, towards the end of 1995, were easily sufficient to sustain the promised veto. The AFL-CIO claimed that the large vote against was strongly influenced by their 'stand up' campaign against the Bill.[22] Another influence was the argument, used by Democrats in the House, that labour–management cooperation was already widespread and therefore possible without removing the statutory defences for independent trade unions and collective bargaining. This was also the view of the NLRB, in the two 'landmark' cases in which it was a litigant—as we shall see later. However the Dunlop Commission supported a change in the law to favour labour–management cooperation schemes whilst reiterating the importance of strengthening collective bargaining. This we shall also discuss later.

Although the President vetoed the Bill in July 1996, the Congressional problems it faced raise a wider issue. Labour legislation with majority support, under both administrations, has now failed to pass hostile opposition. Indeed, US commentators are pointing out that significant legislation, of any kind, has not been enacted for over ten years, suggesting a political process providing 'checks but without balances'. This is in sharp contrast to the legislative and executive authority available to British governments with working majorities in Parliament, a constitutional context which made it possible for Conservative governments to enact, with ease, a substantial volume of labour law between 1980 and 1993.[23] These powers are of course also available to Labour governments.

THE DUNLOP COMMISSION

The possibility of a wide-ranging legislative reform agenda was still very much alive in March 1993 with the setting up of the Commission on the Future of Worker-Management Relations with a membership dominated by pro-reform academics and chaired by the high profile, former Secretary of Labor and prominent academic, John Dunlop.[24] The political contexts also remained favourable with Democrats still in control of Congress and the White House and pro-labour secretaries in the Departments of Labor and Commerce. The Commission published its *Fact-Finding Report* in May 1994 but its final *Report and Recommendations* were overtaken by political events in the form of the elections of October 1994 which gave the political control of Congress to the Republicans. The final Report was formally published in December 1994.[25]

The electoral outcome removed the possibility of any of the recommendations being put into effect, much less the recommendations *in toto*.[26] Even if the Democrats had retained political control any legislation would have experienced even more difficulties than the Workplace Fairness Bill: *both* the AFL-CIO and the employers were hostile to the recommendations, albeit for different reasons. The recommendations do, however, provide the basis for informing a debate on the form of future legislative reform. Furthermore, whatever the political contexts, the rebuilding and regulation of a viable employment relationship remains a policy issue of some importance: political priorities perhaps only exceptionally express actual needs.

Terms of Reference The Commission's terms of reference or 'mission statement' were narrowly specific and in the form of three questions:

1. What (if any) new methods or institutions should be encouraged, or required, to enhance workplace productivity through labor-management cooperation and employee participation?
2. What (if any) changes should be made in the present legal framework and practices of collective bargaining to enhance cooperative behavior, improve productivity, and reduce conflict and delay?
3. What (if anything) should be done to increase the extent to which workplace problems are directly resolved by the parties themselves, rather than through recourse to state and federal courts and government regulatory bodies? (Commission on the Future of Worker-Management Relations, December 1994, p. x)

A reading of the terms of reference makes it clear that the Commission was appointed to focus its attention on the economic, or efficiency, aspects of workplace reform rather than the representative, or democratic, outcomes. More specifically, it examined schemes of participation and cooperation with a view to improving productivity in the workplace, and two of the questions say precisely that. The rationale for this preoccupation with productivity was the view that the US economy's rate of growth of productivity had been in a long-term decline and this put limits on 'the feasible increases in wages and benefits that firms can pay and their international competitiveness at any given rate of exchange of the dollar' (Commission on the Future of Worker-Management Relations, May 1994: 2).

The terms of reference and the *Fact-Finding Report* therefore made it clear that adversarialism, and its assumed companions, conflict and litigiousness (the subject of the third part of the Commission's mission statement) are damaging to economic performance in the workplace with negative consequences for pay, living standards, and competitiveness. Hence the Commission was primarily required to recommend the appropriate participative institutions and changes in the law regulating collective bargaining, and its practices, which would lead to improved productivity and, by extension, to the economy as a whole. This restricted scope prevented the Commission from directly exploring the breakdown of effective employee representation in the workplace, that is, collective bargaining; a breakdown which, paradoxically to many, may have contributed to the economy's unsatisfactory productivity record.[27] The Commission did, in its fact-finding report, provide a review of the changing nature of the employment relationship and an assessment of the unsatisfactory relationship between labour law and collective bargaining. It was also eloquent, in its preamble to the recommendations concerning collective bargaining, on the importance of trade unions in society, listed their current problems in using the law, and stressed 'the need to improve the process by which workers decide whether or not to be represented at the workplace and engage in collective bargaining'

(Commission on the Future of Worker-Management Relations, December 1994: 15–18). Yet its actual recommendations only suggested minor changes in the law to increase employees' protection of their right to unionize and for those unions to have an effective right to be recognized and bargain on their behalf.

Key Recommendations The fifteen recommendations were in three groups following the terms of reference, except that the second group, headed 'Worker Representation and Collective Bargaining' (pp. 15–24), did not attempt to make a case for a link between strengthening collective bargaining and improvements in cooperative behaviour and productivity other than a brief statement that 'freedom of choice about whether to have independent union representation for purposes of collective bargaining remains one of the cornerstones of a flexible system of worker-management cooperation in our democratic society' (Commission on the Future of Worker-Management Relations, December 1994: 24).

The 'Representation and Collective Bargaining' section made four recommendations: earlier certification elections; easier availability of NLRB injunctions against employers; the use of third party intervention in first contract disputes; and easier public access for employees to union organizers on representation issues. Taken together, these recommendations were attempting to deal with the general inadequacy of the law and the remedies available to the NLRB to counter the use and abuse of resources and power by employers. Certification elections, following the Commission's recommendation, would be held no later than two weeks after a petition is filed (the average is seven) by postponing the delaying NLRB inquiries and hearings until after the election. The NLRB would be able to obtain injunctions against employers with the same facility and speed as unions. The vexed question of certification not always leading to a first contract (only one in three does, according to the available evidence to the Commission) would be addressed by mediation and, if necessary, arbitration through a tripartite, First Contract Advisory Board. Employers' easier access to employees would, as a first step, be redressed by Congress legislating to reverse the Lechmere decision (1992) so that privately owned areas (such as employers' parking lots) and privately owned, public access areas (e.g. shopping malls) would be available for union organizers to meet and address employees.

These recommendations together would make some inroads into the power of employers resisting representation and first contract negotiation. But they avoid recommending legislation to replace certification through an NLRB election by the counting of authorization cards ('card recognition'), a practice still available if employers acquiesce and also the procedure in most Canadian provinces. In fact William Gould (a member of the Commission until he became NLRB Chairman) favours such a reform (Gould 1994: 163–5). The recommendations are also silent, as are the observations, on the issue which most preoccupies the unions, that of the tactic of permanently replacing strikers. The Commission did in fact cite the Freeman and Rogers survey evidence that large numbers of non-union employees are afraid of dismissal should they seek representation (1994: 19). They are also of course afraid of being permanently replaced whilst on strike, a powerful weapon in the hands of employers, as the strike of the UAW at Bridgestone-Firestone in Decatur, Illinois graphically illustrates. It can of course be argued that the permanent replacement issue was, at the time, the subject of a bill in Congress, but this perhaps did not preclude at least some observations on its importance. These four recommendations were nevertheless seen by the Commission as a sufficient package of concessions to the unions for them to accept the main recommendation encouraging employee involvement.[28] But even then the Commission was specific in its recommendation that the ban on company unions be retained. Hence: 'the Commission supports some clarification of Section 8(a)(2) so that employee involvement programs . . . are legal as long as they do not allow for a rebirth of the company unions the section was designed to outlaw' (Commission on the Future of Worker-Management Relations, December 1994: 7).

The policy issue over what to do about 8(a)(2) is at least equal in significance with that over the permanent replacement of strikers. Even within the Commission it required a compromise to reach a majority recommendation[29] and Douglas Fraser, whilst he welcomed the fact that 8(a)(2) would still remain, was unable to accept the majority view that 'Congress clarify Section 8(a)(2) and that the NLRB interpret it in such a way that . . . non-union employee participation programs should not be unlawful simply because they involve discussion of terms and conditions of work or compensation where such discussion is incidental to the broad purposes of these programs' (ibid. 8). As a corollary to the recommendation, the Report pointed to survey research that employee involvement systems occurred more frequently in unionized than non-union settings (Freeman and Rogers 1994). However, to prevent abuse of the recommendation encouraging employee participation in non-union companies, the Commission reaffirmed 'the basic principle that employer-sponsored programs should not substitute for independent unions' (Commission on the Future of Worker-Management Relations, December 1994: 8).

The majority view was therefore that a distinction had been made between employee involvement programmes and collective bargaining. The former would deal primarily with issues such as 'production, quality, safety and health, training or voluntary dispute resolution' (ibid. 7); the latter with the negotiation of terms and conditions of work or compensation by employers and independent unions. Additionally, from survey evidence, it was believed the two processes would 'mutually reinforce one another' (ibid. 9).

The Commission was, however, aware of the heavy legacy of history and it is of interest that Douglas Fraser's dissent referred to 'employer-dominated employee representation plans'.[30] The substance of Fraser's dissent was, however, that whilst employee participation and labor–management cooperation should be encouraged, it required 'a truly equal partnership based upon workers having an independent voice'. Given the traditional propensities of US employers and in the context of a weak labour movement, it is difficult to envisage how the Commission's lawyer-like attempt to maintain two separate but mutually reinforcing processes could survive: Fraser's dissent, based on real experience, confirmed this.

The reaction of the labour movement to the 8(a)(2) recommendation and the report as a whole was uniformly hostile. Management also objected to the recommendation to speed up the NLRB election process by holding elections prior to legal hearings on, especially, the scope of the bargaining unit, whilst some former NLRB members argued that 8(a)(2) should be left alone since judicial decisions suggested that management was free to develop employee involvement programmes under the present law—provided they avoided discussing terms and conditions of employment and did not 'dominate' the committees set up under the programmes (*Inside Labor Relations* 1995: 5).[31]

The Recommendations and the Reform Process   The degree to which the Commission could have initiated and influenced a politically viable reform process was obviously limited. When the political contexts were favourable, before October 1994, the Workplace Fairness Bill had failed to pass and nor was it certain that the Commission's recommendations would have made any progress even if a Congress controlled by the Democrats had survived. The Workplace Fairness Bill had not become law despite the political debt which the President and his party owed to the labour movement for their contribution to his electoral success and the lobbying efforts of the AFL-CIO. Nor were the recommendations welcomed by the political insiders as an attempt to craft a package which lay within the limits of political realities (*Inside Labor Relations* 1995: 3). Additionally, Fraser's dissent on the 8(a)(2) recommendation, though generally constructed on grounds of principle (i.e. workplace democracy), also argued, on instrumental grounds, that 'fully effective worker management cooperation programs . . . "required" . . . . workers having an independent voice' (Commission on the Future of Worker-Management Relations, December 1994: 13).

Fraser's suggestion of impracticality may have reflected the dominance of academic influence in the Commission's membership and

recommendations. All of them, in their writings, had over the years suggested similar policy reforms. Gould, 'Banquo's ghost', at the Commission table was especially enthusiastic in welcoming the recommendations
as 'bold and balanced, pragmatic and constructive in their approach to
the employment relationship and the development of labor policy during the coming years' (*Inside Labor Relations* 1995: 4). Kochan also took
the long view of the Report's outcome, as a starting-point towards the
eventual construction of a legislative reform programme backed by a
'broad-based coalition', but he did not think such a scenario was likely
(Kochan 1995: 365). Yet however negative the contexts in which the Commission worked, it is hard to escape the conclusion that it lost a unique
opportunity to establish a comprehensive agenda for change which would
have offered more than Kochan's 'starting-point'. Indeed, the political
irrelevance of the Commission paradoxically gave it unusual licence to
explore bolder, more fundamental proposals for reform.

CONCLUSIONS

The prospects for reform and regulation of the US employment relationship remain as bleak as they are necessary. The continuing decline in
trade unions and collective bargaining, with only limited redress through
judicial decisions and the threat of some rolling back of legislative protection, has increasingly exposed US employees to a managerial prerogative
which is fully exercised, up to, and often beyond, the limits of the law.
Nor is the New Deal labour law framework consonant with the far-
reaching changes which have taken place, over the past forty years, in the
economy and employment as foreign competition has undermined US
global dominance. Hence the assumption that collective bargaining would
gradually extend throughout the private sector has long since gone;
and the supposedly even-handed legislative framework now generally
operates to the benefit of employers adept at exploiting it. The New
Deal framework, as it was designed, is also most appropriate to single
employer, stable enterprises offering permanent, well-defined jobs. The
growing rarity of such enterprises, and the limitations of the New Deal
machinery available to unions seeking to organize them in the face of
determined employer opposition, point to the poor prospects for trade
unions. The labour law framework is also only operable in decentralized
collective bargaining contexts which reinforces the fragmentation of a
trade union movement already seriously ghettoized in a handful of Eastern and Midwestern states. The decline of trade unions and collective
bargaining may also have consequences for the economy through a
negative influence on productivity, as we saw in Chapter 5.

However collective bargaining in the USA remains a proven, generally appropriate, form of representing workers' interests (Kochan and
Osterman 1994: 199); but its decline leaves an employment relationship
which is in urgent need of regulation. Yet it is proving increasingly
difficult for reform to be achieved. The Wagner Act's progress through
Congress was difficult and the threat of constitutional challenge significant, even given the exceptional economic, social, and political crises
of the time. Nor did the Act survive in its original form for longer than
twelve years and, within three, the Supreme Court had, in law, effectively undermined Wagner's right to strike through giving employers
the freedom to replace strikers on a permanent basis. Since then, three
reform bills (including one under the Republicans) have significantly
failed and only the limited executive power has remained available to
presidents intent on reform.

The seeming incapacity of the political system to deliver even modest labour law reform has not inhibited academic analysts from making
recommendations.[32] Kochan takes the long view of the Dunlop recommendations. However, more immediately, he has proposed acceptance
of the case for amendments to Section 8(a)(2) of the Wagner Act to allow
for employer experimentation with employee participation but in return
for revisions of the Act directly helpful to the unions. He even sees the
8(a)(2) changes as a 'challenge' to the unions which would allow them
to become 'full service agents', that is, to combine their traditional collective bargaining role with full involvement in employee participation as
well as offering a range of advisory, representational, and informational
services for employees who do not want exclusive collective representation or to whom it is not available (Kochan 1995: 4–5).

Aside from tampering with 8(a)(2), the concept, if not the label, of 'full
service agent' is neither unacceptable nor a surprise to the AFL-CIO and
the unions (AFL-CIO 1985). American unions are also required, under
the exclusive representation principle, to represent all employees in the
appropriate bargaining unit even if some are not members of the union.
But the vast majority of US employees do not have any form of representation available to them. These include 'minority workers', that is
those who would wish to have union representation within an appropriate bargaining unit but cannot find enough support to achieve it, or
even to begin the election process.[33]

Minority workers in the private sector have recently attracted AFL-
CIO proposals, drawing upon recognition and representation procedures
for federal employees.[34] The proposals would allow workers with less
than majority support to form an organization and select representatives with escalating rights at three levels: informal representation with
the organization being able to present its views at the lowest level of
membership; formal recognition with the right to 'meet and confer' once

organization membership passed 10 per cent; and exclusive recognition with the right to bargain once a majority had been reached.

Here there is the danger of a number of poorly represented organizations emerging in bargaining units which could be used by employers to avoid majority, exclusive representation. They might also involve employers in excessive, time-consuming consultations, as the AFL-CIO conceded. A similar set of 'threshold' proposals (with similar potential problems) was also developed by the TUC between 1989 and 1991 suggesting a 10 per cent level for union representatives' rights to time off for union duties and training, with a 20 per cent threshold attracting consultation rights on specified issues. The recognition threshold within the TUC was, at that time, a stumbling block and a majority provision was eventually dropped in favour of 'substantial membership support'. The fear was that a precise statutory figure might attract skilful employer counter-attacks as well as provide a derecognition target. The TUC also drew upon the US certification experience and the use of representation thresholds, but took little comfort from the example (Beaumont and Towers 1992). In the event, the later, comprehensive proposals from the TUC, involving stages towards full recognition and representation rights under statute, modified the percentage thresholds to the right to a 'collective voice' at 10 per cent and 'automatic' rights to collective bargaining once 'majority membership' had been reached—under procedures supervised by a statutory public agency (TUC 1995*b*). The TUC and its affiliates were not, however, encouraged by the experience of the statutory procedure in Britain from 1975 to 1980 nor by that of the USA under the NLRB. Clearly both countries' unions need to tread warily in constructing proposals which provide a workable procedural framework but which retain some flexibility as well as minimizing the opportunities for employers to undermine the purpose of such a framework; that is, to provide a fair, practicable, and reasonably speedy means for employees who wish it, to achieve satisfactory representation and bargaining rights.[35] But what are the wishes of employees?

For the USA, some recent evidence is interesting. Coinciding with the publication of the Dunlop Commission's report was a Worker Representation and Participation Survey co-authored by a Commission member and a colleague (Freeman and Rogers 1994).[36] The survey identified 'major gaps' between what US workers would like and what their employers gave them, that is, trust,[37] participation, representation, and legal protection. The main findings were:

The Trust Gap. Employees' loyalty to their companies (53%) was greatly in excess of the employers' loyalty to them (38%). A majority preferred to act as a group when dealing with management rather than individually.

The Participation Gap. A large majority (63%) would like more involvement in company decisions affecting the workplace and this would be more likely to be achieved through joint employee–management committees rather than through unions or more laws.

The Representation Gap (Employer Opposition). Sixty-six per cent of employees who had experienced union organization campaigns report strong management opposition, including threats and harassment. In non-union companies, the same proportion believed that management would oppose a union drive and again would be prepared to use threats and harassment tactics.

The Representation Gap (Union Preference). A substantial minority (40%) would, if offered the opportunity, vote for union representation, that is, some three times the current rate of unionization.[38] However a large majority of employees believed that unions could not achieve their purposes without management acceptance and cooperation.

The Legal Protection Gap. A majority of managers (53%) are relatively confident that legal protection for employees is not necessary but less than half of non-managerial employees (44%) agree with them.

The Freeman and Rogers survey suggests an unsatisfied demand for union representation *and* participation in management decision-making. Employers, however, in meeting this demand, are considered to be the problem but also the key to the solution. They often do not return the loyalty of their employees and given their common and vigorous opposition to union representation, employees, from experience, expect that employers will resort to unfair tactics to keep unions out. On the other hand, perhaps because of their power and authority, employer cooperation is seen as essential to the success of unions and participation programmes—although employees would prefer joint management–employee committees, ahead of unions, in satisfying their wish for more involvement in company decision-making.

Whilst there is some contradiction in the finding that joint management–employee committees are favoured alongside a sizeable minority for independent trade union representation, contradictions are not necessarily a problem in the practice of industrial relations. What is clear is that the Dunlop Commission's emphasis on promoting participation and involvement whilst removing some of the constraints on the growth of union representation was not misplaced; however the weakening of union defences in the interests of advancing participation probably was, and employees in the survey revealed a widespread mistrust of employers from their own experience. It also seems probable that the recommendations to control employers' excessive opposition to union representation were too modest and were not a compensation for the proposed changes in 8(a)(2).

Perhaps, most significantly, the survey offers further evidence that employees are not losing interest in being represented by trade unions whatever the unions' problems, or because of dissatisfaction with their services.[39] Many more want to be represented by unions than the current figures indicate. The principal reason is employer power. It can then be inferred that if employers were less oppositional, then union decline might be reversed and that is what, it seems, 40 per cent of employees wish. It is interesting that such a figure is not much above the highest density achieved by US unions in the days before employer power and influence in the private sector was further enhanced by public policy and the law. The implication is that future workplace reforms intending to re-regulate and restore equity to the employment relationship[40] would primarily seek to redress employer power. If, at the same time, important economic benefits are to be found in encouraging a major expansion of participative programmes, the evidence suggests that this can be best achieved in unionized settings. Strong, independent unions are more likely to support such an expansion which can be stimulated by public policy and its agencies even without legislative intervention. The case for trade unions remains compelling on grounds of democracy and efficiency: the problem is how to advance the case in US conditions.

A determined, powerful, pro-labour administration and supportive Congress would be required to promote the appropriate policies and pass any necessary legislation. This combination of political conditions has not been seen for sixty years and even then it required the presence of a deep, socio-economic crisis and a resurgent unionism to help to ensure the passage of the Wagner Act and its endorsement by the Supreme Court. It was also a close-run thing. On a more modest scale, the recommendations of the Dunlop Commission might have done something for the unions if they had been put into effect. But Dunlop has been ignored politically and even if the Commission's mild tinkering with the New Deal system were to be introduced, that system is essentially out of alignment with an economy now much different from the mass-production, permanent employment model on which it was built. In present conditions there may be no alternative to the employment relationship's reconstruction and regulation by federal and state intervention under what has been termed the 'LBJ System' (Strauss 1995: 346–7), thus marginalizing the unions still further.

It is of course possible that the unions may have declined too far for their fortunes to be revived by public policy, especially given the constitutional and political constraints inhibiting even a modest reform process. But what of the unions' own efforts? The positive experience of some unions suggests that the fate of the movement as a whole may lie more in its own hands than it currently believes. Different, non-traditional types of campaign can substantially increase membership and morale and viable strategies may also be possible which take 'account of the changes in social and economic organization that have undermined their strength' (Rogers 1995: 367).

NOTES

1. See e.g. the general discussion in Gould (1994: 55–61) as well as the specific issue of wrongful dismissal (Ch. 3). William Gould is of course the present Chair of the NLRB to which he was appointed when a member of the Dunlop Commission.

2. In EU countries legal remedies, in courts and tribunals, exist for the redress of 'unfair' dismissal of individual employees and there are legal procedures for the regulation of, and financial compensation for, collective dismissals. These remedies and procedures are also, and increasingly in recent years, the subject of harmonization and extension at EU level. Additionally, employees' 'acquired rights' are the subject of an EU directive which protects collective agreements, pay, and benefits of employees affected by takeovers and mergers (transfers of undertakings), including public sector organizations privatized by government. For a comprehensive analysis of protection for job rights and other aspects of the EU's social dimension, see Gold (1993).

3. The European Works Council (EWC) directive became effective, in its compulsory form (voluntary negotiation was allowable until then), on 22 September 1996. Although it only provides for information and consultation rights (i.e. excluding co-determination) in European transnationals, it is seen as a significant development and for that reason was opposed by many European employers and their representative associations. A large number of British companies with European operations (and vice versa) have, however, already set up EWCs on a voluntary basis, and at an accelerating rate up to the voluntary deadline. American companies with EU operations have also been doing so. See Cressey (1993*a*) and Gold and Hall (1994) for overviews of the EWC's development. A recent detailed account of the extent of EWCs across the EU is to be found in Hall *et al.* (1995). See also Ch. 2 for the Conservative government's response to European Court of Justice (ECJ) rulings on the rights of employees to information and consultation under other directives.

4. The principal exceptions are the Netherlands and Great Britain although in the former their trade unions are achieving some organizing successes. Great Britain's collective bargaining coverage rate has fallen more than 20 percentage points since 1979. The United States, Japan and Australia have also declined over the same period, but not at the same rate. However, the New Zealand coverage is reported to have fallen by about half in the 1990s (*Employment Outlook* 1994: 184–8).

5. That is through the concept of the 'social partners' to collective bargaining. Under the Single European Act (SEA) of 1980, the concept was extended through the Social Dialogue between employer associations and trade union federations at EU and sectoral levels. The Social Dialogue is the procedure

under which the Commission sought to establish European Works Councils by voluntary means (Gold and Hall 1994).

6. Aside from the courts' developing limitations on the ability to dismiss employees. See the Conclusions.

7. Comparative evidence of the long-term erosion of the relative advantages of US employees is to be found in Freeman (1994*a*) and Mishel and Bernstein (1994: ch. 8). The most recent edition of the *State of Working America* (Mishel and Bernstein 1996) ascribes the stagnation of workers' real incomes and growing wage inequality primarily to the decline in trade unions and collective bargaining.

8. Heckscher (1988) provides a comprehensive, and readable, overview and analysis of the reform positions, especially in ch. 4. For a more recent contribution see Friedman *et al.* (1994).

9. Clark goes back to the debates in the 1935 Congress to suggest a design-fault of which some were aware at the time: 'From representation elections to the ratification and even the negotiation of contracts, the presumption of federal labor legislation is that these labor-management relations belong at the local level' (1989: 241).

10. The Wagner Act was in fact very limited in terms of its regulatory provisions. It sought, in the voluntarist tradition, to keep the government's role to an absolute minimum, only establishing a framework for the parties to establish their own relationship. This simplicity helped its passage through Congress although even then it failed to pass on its first introduction in 1934 and required Democratic gains in the elections and Roosevelt's positive support to become law. Some, seemingly, even voted for it in the belief that the Supreme Court would render it unconstitutional (Heckscher 1988: 40–3).

11. The Teamwork for Employees and Managers (TEAM) Bill was first introduced into the House by Republicans in 1992, under Democratic majorities in both House and Senate. It was reintroduced in 1995 under Republican majorities. The TEAM Bill's progress is discussed later.

12. The provision to certify a union when it had secured a majority of signed authorization cards (the practice in most of Canada) was also dropped. Nor was automatic reinstatement for economic strikers included. What remained was the granting of limited access to an employer's property for a union to address employees during an election campaign; a requirement for elections to be held within fifteen to twenty-five days; the penalizing of employers for consistent violation of labour law by debarment from federal contracts; and an increase in NLRB membership from five to seven. The Bill was even further watered down in the Senate when faced with the filibuster. Thus access was further restricted to after business hours; election deadlines were extended to thirty-five days; and employers could secure contracts after remedying unfair labour practices (Townley 1986: 123–6; Clark 1989: 204–6).

13. According to Ballot *et al.* (1996) two-thirds of the states have some form of statutory right to collective bargaining for their employees, although with wide variations in scope (p. 433).

14. The historic presidential initiative was President Kennedy's Executive Order 10988 of 1962 which allowed collective bargaining for federal employees, although with only a right to consultation on pay and benefits and, signi-

ficantly, without the right to strike—the source of PATCO's decertification in 1981. Later the Civil Service Reform Act of 1978 gave federal employees the Federal Labor Relations Authority, similar to the NLRB, and with powers to investigate and take action against unfair labour practice allegations. Postwar Republican presidents, with the exception of President Reagan's actions against PATCO and much more limited ones by Bush, have not tried to reverse presidential support for unionization of federal employees.

15. These provisions, available to the employer, were perhaps inevitable given the difficulty of challenging the right of the employer to run his or her business and the difficulty of regulating, by legislation, the numbers employed.

   Other problems arising from the banning of permanent replacements produced a proposed amendment (Packwood–Metzenbaum) to the earlier (1991–2) Bill which provided for voluntary mediation and fact-finding on the content of a new contract. Rejection of the recommendations by the union would allow the employer to respond to a strike with permanent replacements; rejection by the employer would disallow permanent replacements (Gould 1994: 194–5).

   An alternative proposal, not considered within either bill and drawing on the labour laws of Ontario, would provide a six-month period from the onset of the strike during which neither temporary nor permanent replacements could be hired. See Weiler (1990: 216–73) and Jain and Muthuchindambaram (1995) for detailed discussion.

16. Of the seven Senatorial votes short of the sixty required to overturn the filibuster five were Democrats: from Arkansas (two), Tennessee, South Carolina, and Oklahoma. This, as in 1979, reflects the anti-labour positions in the South, even among Democrats from Clinton's home state.

17. However the Order could have led to future contract sanctions against the Japanese-owned Bridgestone-Firestone Corporation, the world's largest manufacturer of tyres. From July 1994 to May 1995 the company faced a strike at its Decatur, Illinois plant over a new contract involving cuts in wages and benefits and changes in shift patterns. During the dispute the company's Japanese President refused an invitation to the White House and four Democratic Senators sought to mediate with the Japanese Prime Minister. Seventy per cent of the workforce were permanently replaced. In Japan, the permanent replacement of striking workers is unlawful. The NLRB has in total filed forty unfair labour practice charges against the company.

   Decatur was also simultaneously the setting for two other, long-running disputes. A. E. Staley, a subsidiary of the British multinational Tate and Lyle, used lockout and temporary replacement tactics against its workers who rejected contracts in 1992 and July 1995. In December 1995 the workers voted to accept a new contract which cut jobs, introduced twelve-hour shifts and compulsory overtime. Caterpillar, which has been in dispute with its workers across a number of its US plants since 1992, faced a one-and-a-half-year strike in Decatur involving 1,800 workers. The strike was called off without a contract in January 1996. One of the disputed issues was pattern bargaining which Caterpillar has been seeking to end at its US operations.

   At their peak, the three disputes at Decatur, which revealed the acute problems of the US labour movement in dispute with powerful multinationals, involved 7 per cent of the town's workforce of whom a substantial majority have not been rehired. For accounts of the Decatur disputes and their implications, see Kilborn (1995); Towers (1996); Parks (1996).

18. There was also an attempt by the Republicans in Congress to seek to block the appropriations bill to pay for the Executive Order.

19. Section 8(a)(2) of the National Labor Relations Act makes it unlawful for an employer to 'dominate or interfere with the formation or administration of any labor organization or contribute financial or other support to it'. This wording is comprehensive and clear in its intentions. It is also clear that this was the intention of the New Deal legislators, not least Senator Wagner, who saw the prohibition of company-dominated unions as critical to the development of free collective bargaining, i.e. the primary goal of the NLRA (Moberly 1994: 148–52). The text of the TEAM Bill which emerged from the House Subcommittee on Employer-Employee Relations in March 1995 included three purposes:

(1) to protect legitimate Employee Involvement programs against governmental interference;

(2) to preserve existing protections against deceptive, coercive employer practices; and

(3) to allow legitimate Employee Involvement programs, in which workers may discuss issues involving terms and conditions of employment, to continue to evolve and proliferate.

Section 8(a)(2) of the National Labor Relations Act was to be amended by inserting:

it shall not constitute or be evidence of an unfair labor practice under this paragraph for an employer to establish, assist, maintain, or participate in any organization or entity of any kind, in which employers participate, to address matters of mutual interest, including, but not limited to, issues of quality, productivity, efficiency, and safety and health, and which does not have, claim, or seek authority to be the exclusive bargaining representative of the employees or to negotiate or enter into collective bargaining agreements with the employer or to amend existing collective bargaining agreements between the employer and any labor organization. (House of Representatives, Washington DC, 7 March)

First, it is clear from the text that the Bill, in its third purpose, would allow employee involvement committees to discuss terms and conditions of employment. Secondly, in amending 8(a)(2), employers would be free to 'establish, assist, maintain, or participate in any organization or entity of any kind'. Thirdly, and confirming the third purpose of the Bill, 'matters of mutual interest' to employers and employees would not be 'limited to, issues of quality, productivity, efficiency and safety and health'.

Allowing (and encouraging) the employee involvement committees to discuss terms and conditions of employment would clearly challenge the formerly exclusive preserves of collective bargaining. Furthermore, allowing employers to establish and be fully involved in the committees would provide opportunities to 'dominate or interfere' (Section 8(a)(2)). Terms and conditions and employer domination were the key issues in the NLRB's rulings in two 'landmark' cases in 1992 and 1993 under the NLRA (see n. 31).

20. Not all of these 'employee representation plans' were dubious and a small number survived the NLRA ban. It was, however, clear that most employers initiated them as a union-avoidance tactic (Jacoby 1983; 1985) and this historical experience has strongly influenced the attitudes of trade union leaders to any attempt to remove, or amend, Section 8(a)(2).

21. The Commission, as we shall see later, was also concerned that its recommendations should be implemented as a whole, that is, any amendment or clarification of 8(a)(2) should be in a wider context of support for trade unions and collective bargaining.

22. The vote for the Bill was 221 with 202 against. The 202 included 22 Republicans of whom 13 (according to the AFL-CIO) had been directly influenced by labour campaigning against the Bill in their Congressional Districts. The numbers in favour of the Bill fell well short of that required to reverse a veto, that is, 290, representing two-thirds of a House membership of 435 (AFL-CIO 1995: 1; 3).

23. Extra-parliamentary opposition can, however, be significant in nullifying legislation, or preventing it. The 1971 Industrial Relations Act was rapidly rendered inoperable by the determined non-cooperation of the TUC and almost all its affiliates as well as much employer opposition. In the late 1970s, under Labour, TUC and employer opposition pre-empted any possibility of legislation to implement the Bullock Committee's recommendations, even though the government did in any case have substantial doubts of its own. Throughout the 1970s, of course, British unions were strong and influential. By the 1980s their capacity to resist legislation had largely evaporated.

24. The initial membership was Paul A. Allaire (Chairman and CEO, Xerox Corporation); John T. Dunlop; Douglas A. Fraser (former President, UAW and Professor of Labor Studies, Wayne State University); Richard B. Freeman (Professor of Economics, Harvard University); William B. Gould (Professor of Law, Stanford University); F. Ray Marshall (former Secretary of Labor and Chair in Economics and Public Affairs, University of Texas at Austin); Thomas A. Kochan (Professor of Management, MIT); Juanita M. Kreps (former Secretary of Commerce and Professor of Economics, Duke University); W. J. Usery (former Secretary of Labor and President, Bill Usery Associates, Inc.); Paula B. Voos (Professor of Economics and Industrial Relations, University of Wisconsin); Paul C. Weiler (Professor of Law, Harvard University and Counsel to the Commission); and June M. Robinson (Designated Federal Official for the Commission, US Department of Labor).

    William Gould resigned on 12 March 1994 on his nomination as member and Chair of the NLRB. He was replaced by Kathryn C. Turner (Chairperson and CEO, Standard Technology Inc.). Only Douglas Fraser came from a union background, albeit a significant one. However the two employer representatives were from unionized companies. William Gould, given his background and published views on reform, was a major loss to the Commission, although he gave a presentation as NLRB Chairman.

25. Political considerations (i.e. the outcome of the 1994 elections) probably influenced the timing of the final report's publication which did not reach the public until January 1995.

26. The Commission stressed that its recommendations 'constitute a highly interdependent whole' (Commission on the Future of Worker-Management Relations, December 1994, p. xi). Thomas Kochan, in reiterating this view of the Commission, recognized the risk in that one of its recommendations would be enacted out of context (Kochan 1995). The TEAM Bill, although it went beyond Dunlop's 8(a)(2) recommendations, could be interpreted in this way although in its first form it was introduced into Congress *before* the 1994 elections and the publication of the Commission's recommendations.

27. As we saw in Chapter 5. Note, too, that one of the academic members of the Commission, Paula Voos, has been active in research in this area. See Mishel and Voos (1992).

28. Another member of the Commission (Richard B. Freeman) did in fact recommend such a deal in 1993 (Freeman and Rogers 1993: 64).

29. Also, some of the members wished to abolish 8(a)(2) altogether (from a private conversation of the author with a Commission member).

30. There were two versions of the 'dissent'. The first, a loose-leaf one from which this quotation is taken. The second, a slightly shorter version, was bound into the report (Commission on the Future of Worker-Management Relations, December 1994: 13) and headed 'Statement of Douglas Fraser'. This did not contain the paragraph from which Fraser's quotation is taken. Employee representation plans were the name given to the 'company unions' of the 1920s and 1930s which the Wagner Act prohibited. See n. 20 earlier.

31. The Commission's fact-finding report, reviewing research on the extent of employee participation reported that 'between one fifth and one third of the workforce is covered by some form of employee participation' (Commission on the Future of Worker-Management Relations, May 1994: 36). Most of these forms were also concerned with direct employee involvement in work-related issues in contrast to the *representation* schemes of the inter-war period (ibid. 48). A further survey also found that there was no significant difference in the incidence of current involvement plans between union and non-union workplaces (Osterman 1994).

Some schemes can, however, run into legal difficulties. The Commission itself cited the case of the Polaroid Corporation which, in 1992, disbanded an elected employee committee, dating back to 1949, after an NLRB complaint that it carried out functions reserved for independent labour organizations. The Commission agreed with this decision (Commission on the Future of Worker-Management Relations, December 1994: 8).

The key ('landmark') cases in this disputed area are Electromation (1992) and Du Pont (1993). Electromation, an electronics manufacturer, in 1988 (when non-union) established 'action committees'. The company was held by the NLRB to be in violation of 8(a)(2) in that the committees, in discussing pay progression and attendance bonuses (*inter alia*), were 'labour organizations' within the meaning of the Act and were also dominated by management who sat on the committees and controlled membership structure and agendas.

Du Pont's large New Jersey chemical plant, unionized for about fifty years, introduced committees under its cooperative programmes in 1984. The company was also considered to be in violation given that management were on the committees, controlled membership, and could veto decisions or even abolish the committees; and the committees' remit included incentive bonuses. In both cases, however, the NLRB made it clear that cooperative programme committees—which restricted themselves to legitimate activities (productivity, efficiency, quality, safety, etc.), remained outside collective bargaining, and were not dominated by management—were not in violation.

For a detailed discussion of these and other relevant cases see Gould (1994: 136–49); and Moberly (1994).

32. As e.g. the protracted debate on the case for and against introducing works councils into US industrial relations, discussed in Ch. 8.
33. The NLRB requires authorization cards, before proceeding to a certification election, signed by 30% of employees in the bargaining unit.
34. These proposals were given in evidence to the Dunlop Commission on behalf of the AFL-CIO, on 10 August 1994, by David Silberman, President of the AFL-CIO's Task Force on Labor Law (AFL-CIO 1994*a*). Federal employees' unions were granted the right to bargain with federal agencies for the first time by President Kennedy in 1962 (Executive Order 10988). These rights were gradually extended in the executive orders of later presidents and codified in the Civil Service Reform Act of 1978. Collective bargaining does not, however, include the right to bargain over pay. Nor is there a right to strike.
35. The development of the TUC's thinking on consultation, employee representation, and trade union recognition are discussed in more detail in Ch. 8.
36. The survey used a statistically weighted representative sample of adult employees, i.e. excluding upper management, business owners, and their families, aged 18 years and over, employed in private companies or non-profit organizations employing twenty-five or over. The total sample was 2,408 who were interviewed by telephone from 15 September to 13 October 1994. Geographical and occupational focus groups were used in designing the questionnaire. This survey is part of a larger study of employee attitudes towards representation and participation also conducted by Freeman and Rogers. The survey, the authors stress, was independent of the Dunlop Commission.
37. A recent British survey broadly replicated that of Freeman and Rogers with similar responses. For example, only 26% of the sample had a high level of trust that their company would keep its promises (Baillie 1996: 17). See also Kessler and Undy (1996).
38. The Freeman and Rogers survey also found that 32% of non-union employees would vote for a union 'if an election were held today to decide whether employees like [them] should be represented by a union'. This finding, they report, is 'consistent with a large number of other polls' (Freeman and Rogers 1994: 12). A 1996 British survey reveals a similar level of demand for unionization. See Conclusions: n. 9.
39. This was also a finding of another study (Farber and Krueger 1993).
40. There is also the increasingly urgent problem of the growing part-time, temporary, and low paid labour force without adequate employment rights or benefits. The Dunlop Commission recognized this problem but did not recommend progress towards pro rata extension of rights and benefits.

8

Bridging the Representation Gap

[T]he U.S. is a leader in deunionization and it lacks any structure of worker representation, inside or outside the firm, to compensate for declining union coverage . . . Our major claim is that the decline of private-sector unionism in the U.S. and lack of an alternative formal mechanism for collective voice has created a representation gap inside firms that is harmful to the nation's economic progress and social well-being.

(Freeman and Rogers 1993: 13)

The aspirations of large groups of workers are . . . not being addressed. The call for social dialogue is an implicit recognition of this problem. For unions, the contradiction is between the maintenance of a cooperative stance in the face of continuing erosion of membership and confidence, and the opportunity to channel and articulate collective dissent.

(Waddington and Whitston 1995: 196)

As the New Deal protections are becoming less effective they are also affecting fewer and fewer employees so that American analysts increasingly talk of the 'representation gap' (Freeman and Rogers 1993: 14; Kochan and Osterman 1994: 17). Six out of seven US employees currently do not have access to the independent representation of their interests in the setting of pay and the defences provided by equitable grievance and disciplinary procedures. At the same time, as unions and collective bargaining have retreated, employees have become more vulnerable to the loss of full-time, secure employment and the gradual elimination of traditional benefits such as automatic cost-of-living adjustments to pay (COLA) and the cutting back of full access to others, especially the medical treatment benefits in labour contracts. For British employees, medical treatment benefits, on a universal basis, are still essentially state-provided despite the internal market reforms of the NHS in the 1980s and 1990s. Hence in this important respect British employees are not as exposed as the American to the consequences of the reduced coverage and influence of collective bargaining. However, although the consequences and size of the British representation gap are not as significant as in the USA, the gap has grown more rapidly in the last seventeen years. At present, two out of three British employees are not directly represented by trade unions. Furthermore, voluntarism, still surviving in some strength, means that legally based representation rights are less extensive than in other EU countries. These limited legal rights have been reduced further since 1980, including the removal of any legal protection against management's ability to derecognize trade unions, as well as extending management's scope to discriminate against trade union members.

The representation gap, in both countries, has been partly bridged by statutory and public agency intervention. This has been extensive in coverage in the USA. It is estimated to have increased four-fold over the past twenty years so that the US workplace is currently affected by more than 150 laws and regulations. Its effectiveness has not, however, followed its extent. This is partly because of the inflexibility of the law as a form of control—in contrast to collective bargaining—and the difficulty of enforcement (Kochan and Osterman 1994: 15–16). In Britain, statutory regulation of the workplace has also grown strongly, particularly since the 1970s, partly under the growing influence of the European Union (EU). But again, as in the USA, inflexibility and problems of enforcement limit legal protection. Both governments have also, from the 1980s, sought to deregulate the workplace, although British membership of the EU has increasingly limited government autonomy in this respect.

The legal regulation of the workplace can therefore be seen as a less than adequate substitute for the flexibility and enforcement potential of collective bargaining. The law may also negate some of the functions of trade unions and therefore reduce their attractiveness to their members and potential members. The best role for the law, as many have argued, may therefore be in providing both a protective and effective framework for collective bargaining and a floor of rights for individual employees—including, especially, those in non-union workplaces.

Discussion of the representation gap and the limitations of the law is also reflected in the extensive debate on the case for the statutory encouragement of representation for non-union employees, primarily through some variant of the much-studied, German works council. This debate has been particularly in evidence among American academics who, though commonly favouring collective bargaining as the best form of employee representation, nevertheless seek, as collective bargaining declines to near-marginality, an effective alternative. A similar imperative has also begun to influence policy discussions in British unions and the TUC. Unequivocal support for the 'single channel' form of employee representation, which significantly influenced the opposition of the TUC and the bigger unions to the Bullock Committee's 1977 proposals, was openly questioned in the TUC's debates in the early 1990s around the establishment of a statutory right to employee representation in the absence of trade unions. The eventual TUC proposals included some consideration of the viability of German-style works councils in British conditions.

The works council as an alternative, or a complement, to collective bargaining also informed the deliberations of the Dunlop Commission, several of whose members have written in support of introducing works councils into American industrial relations.[1] The US advocates, though strongly influenced by the experience of the German works council, have preferred a form without co-determination powers, a variant also favoured by the TUC delegation in the preparation for its first interim report on employee representation (TUC 1994b). These debates and proposals remain important since they could yet influence the nature of future industrial relations reform, that is, provided that trade union member-ship and collective bargaining continue to contract and governments come to recognize, and act upon, the case for restoring a viable system of employee representation; the second proviso is of course much more remote in US than British conditions, although in Britain much crucially depends upon some commitment from the Labour government and any supportive EU initiatives.

Works councils may also be seen, alongside collective bargaining, as one of a range of forms of 'corporate governance'. Others would include those forms which do not recognize trade unions but have in place extensive systems of employee involvement; schemes of worker, or trade union, representation on unitary or two-tier company boards; and those arrange-ments which share power, to a greater or lesser degree, between union and management: what has been termed 'joint governance' (Verma and Cutcher-Gershenfeld 1993).

High employee involvement without the presence of trade unions (or 'soft' HRM) can be seen in US contexts as an alternative to collective bargaining (Kochan et al. 1986). More recent US evidence is however now suggesting that this form of HRM can at least coexist with trade unions (Beaumont 1995: 86–8) rather than eliminate them or claim to replace their representational functions by more effective alternative arrangements. In this respect, the US situation may perhaps be moving closer to the British. There must however be a good deal of doubt as to the long-term capacity of HRM and collective bargaining to live together. Unions, in such situations, are likely to be relatively weak and their rela-tionship with management unstable and largely conditional upon their continuing cooperation and a positive contribution to management's corporate goals (Lucio and Weston 1992; Beaumont 1995).

Joint governance, that is labour–management partnerships which share decision-making on one or a range of issues, can be seen as both an extension of, and departure from, 'traditional' (adversarial) collective bargaining (Verma and Cutcher-Gershenfeld 1993: 198). In the USA, labour–management partnerships have been established by voluntary agreement, despite potential legal hurdles and without legislative sup-port, in a limited number of high-profile companies. This experience may yet be useful as a working blueprint for extending partnerships through enabling laws (Verma and Cutcher-Gershenfeld 1993: 231–2). In Britain there have also been some experiments with partnerships which bear some comparison, in form and ambitions, with those in the USA.

These, too, have been without legislative encouragement although this might have emerged in the 1970s through mandatory unitary board representation on the lines of the Bullock Committee's recommendations.

Of the range of alternatives, or complements, to collective bargaining, this chapter will therefore discuss the two which are, arguably, the most significant in British and US contexts: works councils and labour–management partnerships.[2] Although in the USA partnerships have developed without legislation, in the case of works councils they could not progress without changes in the law. In Britain, the growth of a works council form of employee representation does not require legislation but, should it be introduced by law, it would probably be difficult to attract trade union support without parallel, adequate legal protection for and encouragement of, collective bargaining. In that sense, the British context is not dissimilar to that of the USA.

WORKS COUNCILS

The German Model

Works councils have attracted substantial academic interest in both Britain and the USA, not least because of their widespread incidence in EU countries: nine members of the EU have statutory works councils composed of employee representatives only, or jointly with management, with functions extending from access to information, to rights to consultation and co-determination (Gold and Hall 1990; Ferner and Hyman 1992; Hyman and Ferner 1994; Bridgford and Stirling 1994; Rogers and Streeck 1995). Britain is the most prominent member of the EU without statutory works councils, although it has an array of voluntary institutions[3] and, under British law, employers have a statutory duty to provide information for collective bargaining purposes to recognized trade unions.[4]

Within Europe, it is the German form of works council which has attracted most attention. Its longevity – its origins were in the nineteenth century although it did not emerge in its modern form until 1920 under the Weimar Republic—has provided an enduring model to influence other countries. It has also undoubtedly influenced the development of the Brussels blueprint for the European Works Council, although the EU version does not have a co-determination dimension. German works councils are also more, or even only, viable as a part of a 'dual system' of industrial relations in which, although collective bargaining and employee representation are legally separate, in practice the two functions, and those involved, interlock in mutual interdependence. Furthermore, the system has proved itself to be adaptable, without major stresses, over several periods of rapid transformation and change. It has even been argued that the long-term success of the German economy is associated, in part, with the flexibility of the industrial relations system, perhaps especially in the car industry in the 1970s and 1980s (Streeck 1992: 177).

However, since the late 1980s, the German economy has faltered and it has also had to face the acute strains of reunification. Its relatively high labour costs and advanced systems of employment protection and employee benefits have also begun to be seen as major negative influences upon German competitiveness and employment as productivity performance has weakened. Yet the capacity of the German economy and its institutions to respond flexibly to economic crisis has been proven in the past. There are also those who see the signs of a return on the West's 'investment' in East Germany which may yet experience its own economic miracle, even leading a 'reunification boom' benefiting Germany as a whole (Jacobi *et al.* 1992; Goodhart 1994).

The adaptability of the works council has been demonstrated by its generally successful transfer to the East, although the legacy of the former command economy culture and the continuing, acute socio-economic problems are leading to works councils in the East participating directly in enterprise management (Müller-Jentsch 1995: 76). In the West, some companies are also beginning to opt out of multi-employer, sectoral bargaining, posing a second threat to the dual system. Employers are also seeking to bypass the works councils with new participative structures which could lead to the replacement of a 'dual' by a 'triple' system: sectoral collective bargaining, enterprise negotiations through works councils, and the direct participation of work groups with elected team leaders (Jacobi *et al.* 1992).

These important economic and corporate developments are clearly seriously testing the adaptability of the German industrial relations system, especially its works councils in their present form. But wider lessons may still be drawn from the German experience. These may be summarized[5] as follows.

(i) Works councils, established by law as institutions of employee representation in the workplace, should normally be seen as inimical to trade union organization. However, works council membership, in appropriate conditions, can be colonized by trade union members thus providing a second, complementary channel for trade union influence in the workplace. The outcome for German works councils between 1965 and 1990 is illustrated in Table 8.1.

(ii) A necessary condition for this outcome is the presence of a strong cohesive trade union movement which seeks to secure maximum representation on the works councils. Supportive legislation and favourable political contexts are important, though not necessary, conditions for trade union member domination of works councils.[6]

TABLE 8.1. *Union representation on works councils in West Germany, 1965–1990*

Year	Establishments with Councils	Elected Council Members	Union* Members %	Non-Union Members %
1965	23,813	142,672	87.0	13.1
1975	34,059	191,015	81.0	18.8
1990	33,012	183,680	79.4	20.6

Note: * Data exclude establishments where DGB (German Trade Union Federation) unions are not present, hence overstating council members' union affiliation.

Source: DGB cited in Müller-Jentsch (1995: tables 3.1, 3.2).

(iii) Majority representation of trade union members on works councils does not necessarily eliminate an uneasy relationship between works councillors and trade union representatives at the place of work, given the potential conflict between cooperative and adversarial ideologies.

(iv) Works councils, despite their apparent 'rigidity', can effectively cooperate with employers in the introduction of new technology and the reorganization of work whilst defending the interests of employees. However, some employers are seeking to bypass the works councils in introducing these changes.

(v) Works council influence in the workplace is not uniform across all enterprises. This is likely to be explained by variations in trade union density and the prohibition of industrial action.

(vi) A strong, established system of collective bargaining external to the workplace alongside legally established works councils provides mutual benefits and strengthens the system as a whole.

The German experience, that it is possible to combine viable collective bargaining with an effective, but complementary system of workplace *employee* representation, is superficially attractive to countries, such as Britain and the USA, where trade unions and collective bargaining are in serious decline—or at least to those who wish to see this decline halted, or even reversed. There is also some interest from policy-makers who see possible benefits from such a system, in terms of improved economic performance at enterprise level. The possibility of the introduction of such reforms into either system does, however, remain limited. This is particularly the case for the USA where an interesting, scholarly debate on the introduction of a form of works council, by law, has been rendered 'academic' by political change. However, as Weiler (1990) reminds us, such developments are no reason to throw in the academic towel.[7] It may also be that the Commission, and its recommendations, will, in the long term, serve as the basis for a reform package, as Kochan (1995) has suggested. That 'package' could include a works council option. For

Britain, the eventual introduction of measures under the Labour government to encourage greater employee representation cannot be ruled out. Such measures would undoubtedly be influenced by TUC thinking.

Employee Representation and the TUC

In March 1994, the TUC began a process of study, report, and wide consultation through a high level task group to 'campaign for a legal right to representation and recognition for workers, to win wide support for that objective and to explore the best ways of implementing such an objective' (TUC 1994b: 5) and, significantly, the work of the task group included a study visit to Germany to assess the lessons 'for the British system of industrial relations from the German model' (ibid. 13). The learning process also included the USA through analysis of 'the Dunlop Commission's report on employee representation' (ibid. 24).

The consultative process has been extensive. The task group, which began work in March 1994, reported, on an interim basis, to the TUC in the autumn (TUC 1994b). The task group published a second, consultative, report in January 1995 (TUC 1995a) which was approved by the General Council and formed the basis for a March consultative conference of TUC affiliates. This was followed by a third report (TUC 1995b) which was approved as policy by Congress in the autumn of 1995.

This exhaustive, consultative process led to some dilution of the earlier proposals through 1994 and 1995. The initial emphasis suggested that the TUC was prepared to abandon its insistence on 'single channel' workplace representation, through trade unions, to allow for statutory representation rights for employees even in cases where trade unions were recognized. This 'twin track' approach was clearly influenced by the continuing weakness of British trade unions and the lessons to be drawn from German works councils which, though formally independent of workplace trade union organization, in general complement rather than compete with it, with a large majority of works councillors combining their role with trade union membership. The reference to the Dunlop Commission reflects a mutual learning process between the British and American labour movements (which began to be particularly important in the early 1980s) as well as the TUC's special interest in the remit of the Commission to improve productivity and reduce conflict through reforms which promote cooperative and participative behaviour.

Not all the members of the task group were, however, impressed by German works councils. By the first 1995 report, the old fear that collective bargaining could be challenged by alternative forms of employee representation was much in evidence,[8] even though the proposed 'employee representative committees' would be without co-determination rights, on the German model, exercising information and consultation functions only. The intention of the TUC was to exclude the committees from collective bargaining which 'would remain the exclusive preserve of recognized unions' (TUC 1994*a*: 20).

The outcome, in the third report approved by the Congress in autumn 1995, was a comprehensive set of policy proposals establishing minimum rights to representation, consultation, and negotiation (TUC 1995*b*). The emphasis of the proposals was, however, still strongly influenced by the single channel approach. All workers, in their contracts of employment, would have rights to union representation and it would be unlawful for employers to discriminate against union members or their representatives. The union, subject to achieving majority support of *employees* voting in a ballot or survey, would be granted recognition. It would then have a right to negotiate on pay, conditions, and procedural matters and the collective agreement would apply to all in the bargaining unit. Where the union could show that of the employees in the bargaining unit over 50 per cent were *union members*, recognition would be automatic.

Union members, as a group, would also be given consultation rights where their membership, in the bargaining unit, reached 10 per cent. The employer would then have a duty to consult 'with a view to reaching agreement' (as under EU law). In the special case of the 1994 ECJ ruling concerning redundancies and business transfers (see n. 4 and Ch. 2), the TUC proposed that, where a union had not reached the 10 per cent membership level, its members could seek an agreement on consultation and, where this was not possible, there would be a requirement to consult with representatives elected by all employees ('fall-back' elections). In these elections unions would be able to nominate and seek support from other employees. This protection of union situations was seen by the TUC as an 'opportunity to encourage union membership, gain influence and work towards obtaining negotiating rights' (TUC 1995*b*: 24). Additionally, unions would have a formal right to recruit new members at the workplace.

Recognition, representation, and consultation rights would be enforceable through a new, statutory Representation Agency, with both trade union and employer membership, although those appointed would serve in their individual, rather than their representative, capacities. The agency would make awards across the full range of rights, including the 10 per cent consultation threshold, and with powers to order and regulate 'fall-back' elections through a code of practice. The agency would also be able to use ACAS to conciliate as appropriate, with enforcement through the Central Arbitration Committee.[9]

On the key issue of claims for representation, the TUC gave much space in its third report. It proposed a wide range of adjudicatory powers for the Representation Agency covering the definition of the bargaining unit; the level of support for the claimant union or unions; and whether or not the employer is bargaining in good faith. Claims would be restricted to 'independent' trade unions.[10] The level of support would be assessed by actual numbers through a ballot or survey leading either to automatic recognition at 50 per cent or it could also be determined by the 'level of support for collective bargaining by the union, rather than actual membership figures. Evidence suggests that after recognition has been agreed and employees appreciate the union has negotiating rights, membership increases' (TUC 1995b: 32). Finally, in cases of derecognition the union would be able to apply to the agency for a 'fast track' ballot; and, where it had a majority, derecognition would not be permitted.[11]

Works Councils in the USA

Proposals to introduce a suitably modified form of the works council into US industrial relations continue to attract interest (though mainly among academics), including in the form of detailed policy proposals. Yet it is clear that any attempt to introduce employee representation of this kind, or indeed any kind other than through independent trade unions, faces intractable legislative problems as well as those arising from history and employer attitudes. These problems were brought into sharper focus by the Dunlop Commission and the independent work of some prominent academic members of the Commission who have argued for the introduction of works councils.

The terms of reference of the Commission did not include consideration of employee representation in the form of the works council. It did examine the experience of works councils in Europe but only in the *Fact-Finding Report* and then only briefly. The Commission also distinguished between *indirect* (i.e. representative) participation and *direct* (i.e. employee involvement in new working methods) in order to direct its attention to the latter. This was not surprising since the central thrust of its remit was economic, that is, to establish a close relationship between participative and cooperative innovations and improvements in productivity in the workplace. The logic was then to see how far employee participation schemes which sought to increase productivity could be extended—without major changes in the law and without unduly pressing down on union sensitivities or resurrecting unhelpful labour memories of employee representation experiments between the wars. The outcome was the Commission's recommendation to legalize employee participation programmes which only marginally overlap with collective bargaining over terms and conditions. Yet in its emphasis 'that employer-sponsored programs should not substitute for independent unions' (Commission on the Future of Worker-Management Relations, May 1994: 8) it did not satisfy Douglas Fraser's dissent on the grounds that such programmes would 'deny the workers the right to a voice through the independent representatives of their choosing' (ibid. 13).

The Commission's view that it was possible to legislate to encourage employee participation schemes without threatening collective bargaining also had to deal with the claimed lessons of history as well as Douglas Fraser. The 'employee representation plans' or 'company unions' of the 1920s or 1930s may not always have deserved a bad name in trade union circles, and some even survived the Wagner Act's prohibition. But they were, in the main, an employer tactic to avoid independent union organization. Nor is there any evidence that US employers, in the 1990s, have softened their attitudes towards labour unions.

The debate over amending 8(a)(2) of the Wagner Act to encourage different forms of employee involvement and participation could also have negatively influenced the already doubtful case for works councils in US conditions. Gould, for example, argues that, although the lack of employee representation in the non-union sector is an important problem, and requires attention, the works council route would provide employers with another instrument for union avoidance (1994: 7–8). The strong views of Gould (now NLRB chair and former Dunlop Commissioner) on works councils are not however shared, from their writings, by at least two other Commissioners—Weiler and Freeman.

Weiler's carefully drawn blueprint for an employee participation committee (Weiler 1990: 284–98; 1993: 97–103) draws specifically on the German works council adapted to US conditions, but with the significant omission of its powers of co-determination. Despite this omission, Weiler's employee participation committee (EPC) model adopts many of the features of the German works council with membership available to all employees except senior management; extensive consultative and information rights; expectation of the development of cooperation and coordination between trade unions and EPCs in the workplace and beyond; and sanctions available to use against recalcitrant employers, although Weiler favours a right to strike for US councils in clear contrast to the German 'peace clause'. He also favours, in unionized workplaces, two EPCs for union and non-union employees.

A right to strike for the EPC would give it some authority in the absence of co-determination rights. However, the strike is a blunt weapon under US law against the power deployed by employers; and it is co-determination on personnel matters which gives authority to German works councillors. In practice, the availability of binding arbitration can be a more effective sanction for the union than the strike—assuming roughly equal win/lose outcomes—and has minimal risks for employees. Weiler's ultimate fall-back sanction of the right to join a national union or seek certification does not currently cause US employers to pause and many employees do not wish to join trade unions, either from conviction or fear. Furthermore, the existence of two EPCs in union-ized workplaces might provide organizational opportunities for trade unions; but they are more likely to provide institutional bridgeheads for management to exploit.

The wider contexts for Weiler's model are also unfavourable. Amer-ican private sector unions are fragmented, weak, and weakening and US employers have the readily available option of retreat into non-unionism, including relocation into the numerous, favourable non-union territories which are not restricted to the right-to-work states. In contrast, German unions retain a membership base which is more than twice that of the USA. They also have a widespread presence throughout the economy and a legitimacy conferred upon them by law as well as by employers who accept the situation, and some of whom even welcome it.[12] Weiler's proposals, given these important contrasts, must seek to allay the very reasonable fears that the EPC could be yet another Trojan horse inside labour's walls. But in having to weaken the EPC's role and authority, he also removes its potential for building the union's strength through colonization of its membership—the secret of the German works council's acceptability to the unions. In effect, though institutionally separate and independent, the unions and works councils complement each other in representing the interests of employees.[13]

Freeman's prescription (with Rogers) follows that of Weiler, even to the proposed name of the US councils, except that, in each unionized setting, the functions and powers of a single council would be assumed by union representatives—in contrast to Weiler's separate EPC for the unionized and non-unionized. Interestingly, Freeman and Rogers also recommend trading changes in Section 8(a)(2) for the strengthening of union organizing rights (Freeman and Rogers 1993: 64)—the central fea-ture of the Dunlop Commission's recommendations.

Exporting the German Model

The degree to which German works councils have succeeded in repres-enting and defending employee interests in the workplace, but without undermining, and even strengthening, trade union influence, continues to be seen as having lessons for other industrial relations systems. These lessons should not, however, be drawn *in vacuo*: representation in the German workplace works within a sectoral, collective bargaining system, in which trade unions have substantial influence. Nor is the 'dual system' static. As scholars are pointing out, the strains of unification, crisis levels of unemployment, falling productivity, rising labour costs, and the perceived need of employers to transform working practices are putting strains on the dual system which may even transform it (Jacobi *et al.* 1992: 267).

That the German works councils function within an industrial relations system and wider socio-economic and political contexts—all of
which are subject to change and even transformation—is a self-evident
observation. The system and its contexts are also very different from
those in Britain and the USA, although the greater residual strength of
trade unions and collective bargaining in Britain provides a context more
favourable to the successful introduction of a form of alternative employee representation which strengthens, rather than weakens, the trade
unions. In that respect, Britain is closer to Germany and both are very
different from the USA where the size of the non-union sector and the
continuing threat to union representation in the unionized sector are major
obstacles to works council style reforms. Such reforms are, in contrast,
politically viable in Britain should the Labour government favour them.
Even without political support, EU laws are already advancing consultation and information rights for employees, in both national and
transnational contexts. For the USA, Democratic political control cannot
guarantee even marginal improvements in employee representation.

Yet perhaps the biggest obstacle to introducing works councils into
Britain and the USA lies in the need for an historic shift in trade unions'
perspectives. This seems to be at least beginning in Britain but not at
all in the USA. The British trade unions' deliberations since 1994 have
not endorsed works councils, as such, but have partly accepted the case
for consultation rights for employees where trade union membership is
low as an opportunity for unions to gain members, influence, and negotiating rights. This is far removed from the 'single channel' of representation demanded when the unions were strong in the 1970s. In the USA,
the statutory support for collective bargaining through labour organizations independent of employers has existed for over sixty years, and is
historically rooted in trade union fears that employee representation
bodies are devices for employers to undermine trade unions. Hence
any reform in the USA, to be acceptable to the unions, must at least
guarantee—and if possible strengthen—their actual and potential
influence in the workplace. In American contexts, progress towards a
workable guarantee of this kind presents intractable problems.

American unions, in current policy debates, also have to justify themselves in terms of productivity and efficiency. The terms of reference of
the Dunlop Commission were specific on the assumption that greater
cooperation between management and unions could deliver an economy which is more productive and, in consequence, more competitive.
This has perhaps always been the case. Even in the New Deal and early
postwar era, unions were seen instrumentally, not altruistically, by
employers as contributing to a high wage, but also high productivity
economy. When they were later condemned as barriers to efficiency and
change, most academics challenging anti-unionism only did so through

empirical research into the impact of trade unions on company performance and the economy, and often disregarding their representative
and democratic functions. Of course, this kind of debate has also taken
place in Britain and Germany. The Thatcher administration saw trade
unions as neoclassical 'imperfections' limiting the operation of the free
market in its pursuit of macro and micro efficiency; in Germany, too,
the problem of the supposed 'rigidity' and high labour costs generated
by the industrial relations system has become an increasing preoccupation
of employers and policy-makers. But in Britain and Germany the debate
has never been conducted primarily within the narrow confines of economic outcomes. This is again largely because the trade unions in both
countries have greater strength and influence, as well as because of political perspectives which, although mainly moderate and gradualist, go
beyond the business unionism which has such a pronounced hold in the
USA. In Germany, for example, at a critical time in 1972, the German
Social Democrats passed the Works Constitution Act which cemented
the influence of trade unions on the works councils and in the workplace. Furthermore, the ruling Christian Democrats both saw, and see,
no reason for substantial change in the industrial relations system. In
Britain, too, the Labour Party remains, despite recent changes, the ally
(though increasingly reluctant) of the trade unions and could be in power
for perhaps ten years or more. The TUC also seems confident, given
the diminished but still reasonably intact strength of workplace trade
unionism, that it could use the extension of consultative rights to all
employees as a route to a revival in union membership and influence—
with actual German experience as the example.

Germany, though, has a legal (and therefore labour law) system greatly
different from the British and, in fact, closer to the American. Yet the
American approach to labour law-making also exists alongside a weak,
and fragmented, trade union movement which falls far short of the
influence and authority of the German trade unions. Hence US employers are more able (and more ready) to use the law against the trade
unions given that the unions can offer only relatively limited resistance.
These contrasts in the contexts of the relationship between the law and
bargaining power, as Thelen (1991: 214–24) argues, explain why German
trade unions and works councils are generally more ready to cooperate
in the negotiation of changes in the organization of work than their US
counterparts. The different structure of the German system may also be
a facilitating factor in that collective bargaining over pay and conditions
(i.e. adversarial) largely takes place outside the workplace. The latter
can then be the focus for cooperation and the implementation of joint
employee–employer gains (Wever 1994: 479).

However Britain, since 1980 especially, although the process goes back
to the 1960s, has moved closer to the USA in the increased juridification

of its industrial relations system and the tighter controls imposed upon strikes, collective bargaining, and trade unions. Its collective bargaining has also become more decentralized and fragmented and in that respect also closer to the American. This weakening, but not total elimination, of the national and sectoral levels in Britain drives the locus of collective bargaining into the workplace where trade unions are more vulnerable; and it is of some note that it is in the workplace that the TUC seeks to strengthen trade unions via a reformed, agency-led, trade union recognition procedure and extended employee consultation. The key to the success of such reforms is, on the German model, that trade unions control the employee representation committees rather than have to compete with them. That is also the key to any US reform in this area. History should not be allowed to repeat itself, as it has a habit of doing if not carefully watched. As Jacoby so aptly puts it: 'public policy should encourage new forms of representation. But to prevent a recurrence of the events of the 1920s and 1930s, policy must be designed so that any new forms become complementary to, rather than substitutes for, national unions. The goal is to expand the realm of representation, not merely to change its composition' (1989: 40).

LABOUR–MANAGEMENT PARTNERSHIPS

The US Supreme Court held in 1981 that it was not the intention of the 1935 Congress that labour should be an 'equal partner' with management. Indeed, a statute promoting collective bargaining and believing in its adversarial nature, could do no other. The potential legal problems do, therefore, constrain experiments in partnership unless they include the main features of adversarialism: the right to strike and lockout and grievance–arbitration machinery which is sufficiently adversarial (Gould 1994: 127–8; 172–3). This effectively means that US partnerships, to remain within the law, are required to include a full, unequivocal role for collective bargaining.

A strict definition of partnership, on this model, takes it much beyond joint consultation and participation. Verma and Cutcher-Gershenfeld's 'joint governance' maintains the centrality of *joint decision-making responsibility* (even if only involving a single issue) but also of equal representation for labour on decision-making institutions. This definition covers the Saturn case but not labour representation on boards of directors where this is less than equal. Comparatively, the definition would include the parity representation on boards under the 1951 German Co-determination Act for the coal, iron, and steel industry but would have excluded the 2x + y proposals of the British Bullock Committee in 1977, which did not offer parity but were still seen, by some, as threatening the managerial prerogative as well as collective bargaining.

The AFL-CIO's recent statement of the concept of partnership also stresses the 'principle of equality' which in practice 'means that unions and management must have an equal role in the development and implementation of new work systems, including equal representation and control over any bodies created as part of the work reorganisation' (AFL-CIO 1994*b*: 11–12). The TUC's position is similar, although within the context of the 'social partnership' experience of EU countries (TUC 1994*a*). Both, too, emphasize that partnerships must be based on the maintenance of collective bargaining although that emphasis is much stronger in the AFL-CIO document, as is the defence of the legitimacy of adversarialism, whilst conceding that employers and workers have 'common' as well as 'conflicting' interests.[14]

The 'principle of equality' and the view that collective bargaining reflects a mix of common and conflicting interests can make partnerships attractive alternatives to wholly adversarial collective bargaining, especially to senior trade union leaders in contexts of declining membership and influence. But their attractions are not always apparent to local union activists and members in the workplace, and managerial careers in the USA, if not in Britain, may be at risk following such innovations (Pfeffer 1994: 167–9; Verma and Cutcher-Gershenfeld 1993: 230). The outcome, despite some differences in contexts, is that they remain rare in both countries although this does not reflect their potential as a means of transforming 'traditional' collective bargaining (Verma and Cutcher-Gershenfeld 1993: 231).

In Britain, the TUC's support for partnership has been partly influenced by the EU as well as the need to respond to the serious and still growing problems of the trade unions. Some prominent employers have also come together with senior trade union leaders in support for the industrial partnership proposals of the Involvement and Participation Association (IPA).[15]

The IPA's 1992 publication was strongly influenced by British trade union ideas (GMB and UCW 1990), and those of the US Department of Labor (Department of Labor 1991) and its proposed 'joint aims', to be agreed by management and unions in industrial partnerships, were echoed in 1994 by the TUC.[16] The IPA then suggests how these aims could be applied to six 'key areas' requiring fresh thinking from management and trade unions. From management, the areas would be improved security of employment, the sharing of financial success, and enhanced rights to information, consultation, and representation. The unions, in return, would be required to cooperate in maximizing job flexibility, to accept new methods of employee involvement, and to concede the case for representation of employees within a legally guaranteed 'works council system' operating alongside trade unions.

The close similarity between the detail of the British and US proposals supporting union–management partnerships clearly reflects some mutual learning as well as the practical need to recognize conflicting as well as cooperative interests adjusted through collective bargaining processes. Furthermore, aspects of the IPA's 'key areas' are already developing. Workplace changes in both countries are increasing job flexibility and employee involvement; financial participation and gain-sharing are widespread; and in Britain, under EU influence, rights to information and consultation are slowly being extended. However, security of employment is rare, even in exchange for growing job flexibility within organizations, and support for any form of right to representation has not been a characteristic of employer and government policies, in both countries, since the late 1970s.

The IPA's 'works council' proposal does, however, point to an important contrast between Britain and the USA. The TUC, and some of its potential affiliates, have already begun to rethink their traditional insistence on single channel representation in the face of still declining membership—as we saw earlier in this chapter and in Chapter 6. The AFL-CIO and the US unions, on the evidence of their reaction to the Dunlop Commission's proposal to 'clarify' Section 8(a)(2) of the Wagner Act, are a long way from even considering such an item on a labour–management partnership agenda. It would also require a change in the law even to legitimate its inclusion.

Case Studies in Partnership

Labour–management 'parity' partnerships in the USA, given the legal constraints and the limited extent of trade union organization, are rare and mainly confined to auto, steel, chemicals, telecommunications, and electronics.[17] Of these, the partnership between GM's Saturn Corporation and the UAW is the most significant and may yet remain unique.[18] In Britain, partnerships which approximate closely to the general US model, let alone Saturn, are even more of a rarity. Rover's 'New Deal', though fully involving the trade unions, is essentially an innovative collective agreement rather than a 'partnership' and compares more readily with GM's NUMMI operation, as we saw in Chapter 5.

The British water industry, which was privatized in 1989, offers a number of examples of innovative arrangements described as partnerships.[19] Of these, the case of Welsh Water is an interesting example to place alongside Saturn. The Welsh case also appears to reveal the inherent threat to independent trade unions and collective bargaining when adversarialism is replaced by cooperation, an issue which remains very much alive in US conditions.

Saturn

The Saturn experiment arose out of several attempts, over a decade, by General Motors (GM) and senior UAW officials to move away from their long history of often bitter, occasionally violent, confrontation. The industry was also under an increasingly severe challenge, in its domestic markets, from Japanese competition, with jobs and even GM's future at stake. The outcome was the 'Committee of 99' representing the union and management with the aim of designing both an organizational and a labour–management system to build a small car which was capable of competing effectively with Japanese imports. Union leaders also took the view that the achieving of both employment and income security for its members was not possible without the union's full commitment to helping to maximize GM's economic performance. It was no longer considered viable for the union to rely upon collective bargaining alone, leaving all strategic decisions to management (Kochan and Osterman 1994: 151–2).

The UAW representatives in the company which emerged from the initial planning meetings were fully involved across all functions from design,[20] through manfacturing to sales. Decisions are also joint at all levels through the Strategic Action Council, the Manufacturing Action Council, Business Unit Groups (assembly, powertrain, etc.), and the Work Unit Teams on the shop-floor. Furthermore, whatever the actual number of management and union representatives, decisions are made on the basis of consensus, thus meeting Verma and Cutcher-Gershenfeld's essential criterion for joint governance of the equal sharing of the power to make decisions. In this main respect, the Saturn agreement, through the 'full partner' principle, significantly departs from GM's current national agreement with the UAW, that is, in Saturn's rejection of the traditional management prerogative. It is also a 'living agreement', that is, without a termination date and allowing for a modification procedure at any time. However, a 'no strike clause' limits union and employer action until after the procedures to reach consensus have been exhausted, an approach similar to that of Japanese companies in Britain (Gould 1994: 130–1).

For the workers the tangible benefits of the Saturn agreement are good pay and, unusually for US industry, a reasonable degree of job security. In the agreement, 'permanent job security eligibility' is limited to those 80 per cent of employees with the longest service but not in the case of 'situations which the SAC [Strategic Action Council] determines are due to unforeseen or catastrophic events or severe economic conditions'.[21] 'Severe economic conditions', which are of course far from unknown, would place the UAW representatives on the SAC under powerful, conflicting pressures. Inevitably, much depends upon the commercial success of the second generation car to consolidate the viability of the partnership approach against the older, but still significant, adversarialism. Certainly, it is noteworthy that neither the Saturn nor NUMMI 'models' have yet to inform a comprehensive UAW strategy across the auto industry.

Welsh Water

The labour–management partnerships in the British water industry companies were essentially an outcome of privatization in 1989, although some important conditions which gave rise to the innovations were in place in the early 1980s when the industry was still in public ownership.[22] Privatization of the water industry was, and is, unpopular with the public: 83 per cent of those polled in 1989 were against it. The employers too were far from enthusiastic. The Chair of the Welsh Water Authority openly argued against privatization in 1985 when the government announced its intentions. However, as we have noted, the employers moved against industry-wide bargaining before privatization and were implementing substantial labour force reductions long before 1989. Welsh Water, for example, employed 5,800 in 1979. This had fallen to 5,000 in 1985 and 4,200 in 1989 (Jones 1995: 6–8).

Welsh Water's experiments in partnership[23] originated in the appointment of a former trade union official as Personnel Director of the publicly owned Welsh Water Authority in 1985. His human resources strategy sought trade union cooperation but accepted legitimate conflicts of interest between unions and management. One union, the National Union of Public Employees (NUPE), was, however, derecognized on privatization as an 'exception to the mutual trust between management and local trade unions' (Jones 1995: 8).

There have been three, successive, two-year partnership agreements at Welsh Water since 1991, the third expiring in April 1996. All three agreements were initiated and developed by a Joint Officers' Group of five managers and five full-time union officials. Partnership I had three main aims, formulated by the Joint Officers' Group, which remained central features of the second and third agreements. First, the replacement of pay negotiations by an 'objective formula' reflecting changes in the Retail Price Index (RPI), the 'going rate' of pay settlements in Wales from a survey of seventy large organizations, and the company's profit performance. Secondly, the introduction of single status conditions, including a standard thirty-seven hour week for all employees. Thirdly, the bringing together of formerly separate negotiating and consultative arrangements within a single Representative Council on which the unions were required to develop common positions on the 'single table bargaining' model. The Council's membership include the Joint Officers' Group, *ex officio*. It could not of course bargain over pay although it could negotiate and consult over the detail of the partnership agreements following the proposals of the Joint Officers' Group. At local level, Divisional Forums were established for consultative purposes.

Partnership I required certain commitments from employees and their union representatives. They would be required to cooperate in improving workplace productivity through organizational and technological change, more flexible use of labour, and the necessary training and retraining requirements. Teamwork and team briefings were to be the key instrument of workplace change. The company, in return for these commitments, saw regular, 'objectively' determined pay increases, improvements in benefits and conditions, and employment security (no compulsory redundancies, but conditional upon cooperation in change) as important, tangible returns. The agreement was put to a ballot of union members and secured two to one acceptance.

Partnership II, which was agreed in 1993, consolidated or extended the features of the first partnership. The pay formula was retained but a unified pay structure (including a reduction in job classifications) was introduced. The link between employment security and cooperation in change was developed through team and individual performance reviews. The company could also hire temporary and agency labour, when necessary, to work alongside permanent employees. In the ballot, Partnership II was supported three to one by union members.

Prior to the discussions on Partnership III, the company held a series of local consultative meetings ('roadshows') to test employee opinion on the first two partnership agreements. Some trade unions also carried out their own consultations. The company and union consultations were supplemented by a postal opinion survey in 1994–5 (the third since 1990). The roadshows and the surveys revealed the importance of job security to Welsh Water's employees. A comfortable majority (62% in 1994) were satisfied with the company's commitment but this had declined from 70 per cent in 1992 and some were highly critical of the conditions attached to the job security guarantees. There was also some criticism of the pay formula and the use of temporary employees, although the company's other employment policies, including training, were generally well received and three out of four employees saw Welsh Water 'as a good company to work for' (Jones 1995: 19). However the employees' main criticism of the first two partnerships centred upon the participation, communications, and consultation arrangements, including local consultation through the Divisional Forums and the role of the Representative Council. The most trenchant criticism focused upon the team briefings and, by 1994, more than half considered them to be ineffective.

For Partnership III the company, sensitive to the main criticism of the earlier agreements, established a Communications and Consultation Group to review the working of the communications and consultation processes. Partnership III also undertook to name the comparator companies in the pay formula and to drop its performance-related pay proposals. The labour flexibility and temporary worker policies were, however, retained as well as the conditions attached to the employment security commitment.

Partnership III was, despite the serious criticisms, endorsed by an even larger majority than its predecessors (five to one) with 70 per cent of union members voting. Non-union members were also invited to send their views to their personnel managers.[24]

Assessing Partnerships

The increasing majorities of union members voting in favour of the Welsh Water partnerships are an important but not a sufficient measure of their success. The third of the original main aims of improving participation, consultation, and communications within the company through the Representative Council and the local forums has clearly not been achieved, despite five years of experience, and the team briefings are widely seen as ineffective. However the company has succeeded with its other aims: the introduction of single status pay and conditions and the replacement of collective pay negotiations by an 'objective formula' for settling pay levels. It is also possible that the problems of participation, consultation, and communication will ultimately respond to the company's and unions' attempts to redress them. From the company's perspective, the experiment in partnership must also be assessed in terms of how far it succeeds in improving the productivity and efficiency of the service with ultimate benefits for profits and dividends. Here the outcome is not yet clear and it is in any case difficult to separate the contribution of the partnership from other influences on productivity and efficiency, such as investment.

The success of the Saturn Corporation is also problematic. It may be significant that its innovations have not been implemented at other GM plants and, at Saturn as well as elsewhere, there remains much disquiet over the national officials' retreat from traditional adversarialism. Nor is the commercial success of the venture assured and much depends, as noted earlier, on the next generation car model.

The contexts and policy implications in respect of both Saturn and Welsh Water have, of course, been very different. General Motors was, and remains, a private sector company with an adversarial tradition, even though in the case of Saturn both management and the union were committed to moving away from 'armed truce' punctuated with 'open warfare'[25] aspects of their 'traditional' relationship as exemplified by the

Fremont plant before the NUMMI joint venture. Welsh Water, in contrast, formerly a publicly owned utility, after 1989 became a private sector company. One consequence was its partnership strategy which was
a departure, in its main elements, from the public sector traditions of
'good' industrial relations under 'Whitleyism'. The company signalled
its intentions early: it derecognized one of the unions involved and
removed pay from the collective bargaining agenda. A unilateral decision, by management, to withdraw recognition is not possible under US
labour law. Nor is it consistent, in practice, under British conditions with
an intention to develop a partnership. It suggests an unequal relationship
and the denial of mutual legitimacy (i.e. the 'principle of equality'),
although in the case of Welsh Water there would appear to be, as yet,
no intention to move towards derecognition of the other unions. Single
table bargaining may also be seen as a means of achieving some of the
benefits of the US sole bargaining agencies in the absence of a supportive
British legal framework.

The 'principle of equality' is an important feature of the Saturn partnership and a defining characteristic of Verma and Cutcher-Gershenfeld's
joint governance model. They also argue that equality is closely related
to a 'representative' form of participation. In both the Saturn and Welsh
Water cases it is unavoidable that collective bargaining should be that
form, although in Britain other forms of employee representation are
possible, especially in the context of the example of works councils in other
EU countries and the extension of the European Works Council. Welsh
Water, as we have seen, has indicated its support for these alternatives.
It also went much further, in seeking to minimize adversarialism, by
removing its principal focus—bargaining over pay. This poses a threat
to the credibility of collective bargaining[26] as well as making it difficult
to describe the company's employment innovations, whatever their
merits and outcomes, as a partnership with the trade unions. The unions
remain highly involved but that involvement falls short of a partnership.

The two case studies suggest that the ingredients of successful labour–
management partnerships may be more clearly understood in the USA,
especially the essential need for an equal partnership reinforced by
collective bargaining which accepts the legitimacy of conflict of interests
as well as encouraging and institutionalizing cooperation.[27] It also seems
essential that partnerships should be able to deliver tangible gains for
employees, especially employment security.[28] However it is likely, on the
partnership principle, that a company will only provide security guarantees in return for more efficient, productive workplaces. There is some
evidence that partnerships may have advantages in this respect.[29] Yet
more efficient workplaces may require fewer workers. This 'paradox'
pre-empts any direct association between employment security and efficiency gains, presenting 'an important challenge to public policy makers,

private decision makers, and individual employees alike' (Kochan and Osterman 1994: 102).

Although collective bargaining is not a relationship between equals— the balance of power normally favours employers other than in special circumstances and for limited periods[30]—it remains a tried, tested, and flexible means of setting the terms and conditions of employment as well as allowing employees, through their unions, to participate in the creation of a 'social order'[31] in the workplace, that is, the democratic function. At the same time, it is more than arguable that collective bargaining can contribute positively towards the economic performance of individual enterprises and the economy as a whole.[32]

Yet, despite its democratic and efficiency credentials, collective bargaining in the USA is now seriously threatened. In Britain, it still retains much of its presence and influence in the workplace but has been pushed to the broader margins of national life and policy formulation. British unions are also still losing members at an annual average rate of 3 per cent, although in 1996 the fall was only 0.8 per cent (Cully and Woodland 1997). This growing representation gap has been partly bridged by the law and public agencies, although this is normally through advancing individual, not collective, rights and both governments, for almost twenty years, have consistently pursued policies of deregulation. Legal regulation of the workplace in itself also lacks the flexibility and adaptability of collective bargaining and individual legal rights are commonly more effectively achieved through the agency of trade unions.[33]

In European countries, other than Britain, employee rights are commonly protected and extended through a combination of collective bargaining, the law, and representation at corporate and workplace levels. Workplace employee representation through statutory works councils is widespread in European Union countries, although it is the German form which has undoubtedly been the most successful and has attracted interest in both Britain and the USA. The experience of German Works Councils reveals that they complement, rather than conflict with, collective bargaining even though on their reconstitution in 1952 the trade unions saw them as a challenge to their claim to be the legitimate representatives of employees in the workplace. In the event, the German unions were sufficiently strong and influential to ensure that most works councillors were trade union members and that the unions have also retained their virtually exclusive involvement in collective bargaining.

The case for introducing works councils into US industrial relations is prejudiced by negative political contexts but also, more importantly, by the strength of employers and the corresponding weakness of the trade unions. However the unions also have substantial reservations concerning the compatibility of works councils and collective bargaining in US conditions. This reflects the still strong, anti-union position of most employers and the historical experience of the employee representation plans in the 1920s and 1930s, which, before they were outlawed by the Wagner Act, were generally employed as the means of avoiding, or undermining, employee representation through independent trade unions.

In Britain, the statutory encouragement of employee representation through a modified form of works council could yet reach the political agenda. The TUC has discussed representation rights for all employees alongside measures to protect the primacy of the trade unions' collective bargaining role, although the more recent emphasis is away from full 'employee' representation. Yet, unlike the US unions and closer to the German, British trade unions have perhaps sufficient strength and influence to turn works councils into institutions which could underpin, and even help to revive, trade union membership. British unions and collective bargaining also have the continuing advantage, relative to the USA, of employers who are still much less hostile and more likely to go with the grain of a public policy which supports the extension of employee representation whilst protecting the primacy of collective bargaining.

Labour–management partnerships in the USA and Britain have developed on a voluntary basis without legal encouragement, and in the USA each needs to be carefully devised to avoid legal challenges under the Wagner Act's prohibition of management incursions into trade union independence. This partly explains their rarity in the USA alongside the more general employer preference not to deal with trade unions in any circumstances. Certainly in their purest form, that is, involving unions on the basis of equal representation, they remain rare in the USA and British examples fall short of full partnership, although there is clear TUC and union support for the growth of genuine, equal partnership. The US cases provide for the integration of collective bargaining into the partnership process, thus providing a bridge towards union acceptance. This feature of partnerships is attractive to trade union leaders struggling with the problems of eroding legitimacy and membership loss. Yet the need for cooperation can attract criticism from lower-level union activists who see dangers, for the union, in undermining adversarialism and diluting what they see as the fundamental conflict of interest between employers and employed. Additionally, partnerships, despite some commonalities, need to be tailored to specific organizations and pose a threat, even if unintended, to independent unions seeking to be effective across individual workplaces and at levels beyond the local and parochial.[34] Single company or establishment experiments are also vulnerable to external shocks beyond their control such as, for example, deregulation in the case of AT&T (Heckscher and Schurman 1997).

Employers in British-style partnerships, on the evidence of Welsh Water, are reluctant to share power and control with trade unions or even to fully recognize trade union legitimacy. This reluctance is in line with the reaction of employers to the Bullock Committee's recommendations which would have allowed employer power-sharing with worker-directors but with the balance held by an independent group. British employers, it would seem, were happier with the known quantity of face-to-face collective bargaining rather than the unknown of workers, as colleagues, on the board. Most of the unions and the TUC were also opposed, guarding their traditional reliance on the 'single channel' of collective bargaining. Collective bargaining is, however, now even more in the gift of British employers as their power has steadily grown since 1979 and the legal recognition framework was removed in 1980. In the case of Welsh Water, this allowed management freedom to derecognize one of the unions, compel the others to bargain as a single unit, and remove pay from the bargaining agenda. Not surprisingly, this led some local union activists to be concerned over the consequences of a 'partnership' which weakens adversarialism and union independence. Nor do partnerships necessarily provide stronger guarantees of employment security than collective bargaining. The terms of the Saturn and Welsh Water guarantees have sufficient caveats to significantly reduce their value. Yet even these limited guarantees have to be bought with greater efficiency, which may lead to job losses and the further exposure of the guarantees.

Overall, it does appear that a significant closing of the representation gap is contingent upon the major support of public policy. This was the case in 1906 in Britain and 1935 in the USA, although at both times union membership and strength were growing through factors not easily connected with the efforts of, mostly, well-meaning legislators. Hence the prospects for the unions and employee representation may yet be, in some degree, within the powers of the unions themselves. Indeed, in the USA—short of an approaching political and ideological shift of landslide proportions, a wholesale change of heart by employers towards valuing trade unions, and the mass conversion of the judiciary to a collective philosophy—the unions must in any case realistically seek their salvation largely through their own efforts. There are, of course, signs that both labour movements are alive to these possibilities as we saw in Chapter 4, and we shall return to this in the next, and final, chapter.

NOTES

1. Perhaps, especially, Paul Weiler (1990). Note also, more recently: Freeman in Freeman and Rogers (1993) and Kochan in Kochan and Osterman (1994).

2. Others would include employee stock or shareholdings (ESOPs) in enterprises as well as employee buy-outs. ESOPs did of course originate in the USA following legislation in 1974 (Ballot *et al.* 1996: 546–8) where they are now estimated to involve about 10,000 firms, including large ones such as Avis. In Britain, their recent antecedents were the short-lived worker-cooperatives of the late 1970s. ESOPs first began to appear in the UK in 1987 and were given statutory, financial benefits in 1989. However they remain much less extensive than in the USA. Recently, the 1995 buy-out of a South Wales anthracite coal mine by its workers has attracted much attention, especially given its continuing commercial success and the involvement, as management, of the local union leadership of the National Union of Mineworkers. For a recent account of British ESOPs, including the colliery buy-out, see IRS (1995: 587).

3. The traditional approach outside collective bargaining is joint consultation between shop stewards and managers, although under different names such as joint works committees as well as those with 'consultative' in their titles. For a recent review of joint consultation, see Marchington (1994). Japanese companies in Britain have adopted a different form, often called a company council, with employee representatives normally nominated by management. The Company Council at Nissan, for example, although it negotiates an overall pay settlement, is without direct union involvement. See Bassett (1986); Wickens (1987); Garrahan and Stewart (1992); Oliver and Wilkinson (1992).

4. This of course means that employers, given their right to refuse recognition or withdraw it, can avoid the statutory duty. However the European Court of Justice (ECJ) in 1994 ruled that in the case of redundancies and business transfers, employers were required, under EU law, to consult with their employees, whether unionized or not. The ECJ ruling and the British government's response are also discussed in Ch. 2.

5. An early, seminal contribution to the English language journal literature on works councils was that of Adams and Rummel (1977). Recent contributions include Streeck (1992), Jacobi *et al.* (1992), Bridgford and Stirling (1994), Crouch (1994), and Terry (1994). Strong interest has also recently been shown in the American literature, drawing upon German experience in the context of reforming the US system. See e.g. Thelen (1991), Turner (1994), Wever (1994), and Rogers and Streeck (1995). Paul Weiler (1990), a member of the Dunlop Commission, has proposed a statutory package of reforms. These proposals are discussed later in the chapter.

6. e.g. the Works Constitution Act of 1952, initially strongly opposed by the trade unions, was turned, by their own efforts, to their advantage although they clearly benefited from the later favourable legislation, in 1972, under the Social Democrats (see Streeck 1992: 46–7).

7. 'it is not an argument against a scholarly work that its conclusions may be politically unpalatable' (p. 298).

8. Hence in *Representation at Work* (TUC 1995a):

As would be expected the views of the union participants on the merits of the German system varied. There was agreement, however, that the legislative model of co-determination was not a concept that could be simply . . . bolted on to the British system, but rather it must be introduced on a consensual basis with the full involvement of the unions. The divergence of views reflected the long-standing debate within British unions around different forms of worker participation and the impact they would have on traditional forms of collective bargaining. (p. 13)

9. The Central Arbitration Committee (CAC) was set up under the Employment Protection Act of 1975. It had compulsory arbitration powers but could also hear traditional voluntary cases. It lost its compulsory powers under the 1980 Employment Act.

10. i.e. those trade unions holding a certificate of independence from the Certification Officer, a public official. Applicants for a certificate must be able to demonstrate their independence from the employer on the criteria of their history, membership base, organization and structure, financial resources, the degree to which the employer provides facilities, and the collective bargaining record. Some 'staff associations' (i.e. organizations of employees with membership confined to one organization) have succeeded in their applications for certificates of independence.

11. These proposals suggest much learning from the defects of the US certification and decertification procedures. 'Automatic recognition' is also akin to recognition from authorization cards. This has often been advocated for the USA and is the system in most Canadian provinces. See also Ch. 2.

12. These employer attitudes do not, however, always travel well. German multinationals, in the USA, as well as the Japanese, are just as likely to be American-style union avoiders, if not union busters. Examples are Hoechst's chemicals plants in the Carolinas and the Mercedes Benz new auto plant in Alabama, both located in lowly unionized, right-to-work states. However Mercedes Benz, although hiring workers, is not planning to begin production until the winter of 1997. The UAW is already recruiting members and is likely to mount an organizing campaign in 1998.

13. This could have been otherwise. The German trade unions, as we noted earlier, saw the re-establishment of the works councils in 1952 as a defeat. They turned defeat into eventual victory, with some later support from public policy, by vigorous campaigns establishing shop steward committees and electing trade union members to the councils (Thelen 1991: ch. 3). A necessary condition for these successful campaigns was a trade union movement able to challenge employer power. This condition is not yet present in the USA.

14. The AFL-CIO 'general guidelines' as a basis for successful partnership are: mutual recognition and respect; a collective bargaining relationship; the principle of equality; and an intention to achieve agreed common goals such as 'more productive and more democratic and human workplaces'. However, the AFL-CIO stresses that such partnerships would not replace adversarialism by cooperation even though workers and employers have 'common' as well as 'conflicting' interests, although the latter did not imply 'antagonistic' relations (AFL-CIO 1994a: 11–12).

The TUC lists the 'common aims' of a joint commitment to the success of the enterprise, the building of trust, and a recognition of each party's legitimate role without either having to give up its independence. It also takes the same line as the AFL-CIO on conflict: 'In a true partnership those conflicts that do occur could be worked out in an atmosphere of mutual respect, trust and goodwill' (TUC 1994*a*: 24).

15. The IPA was founded in 1884. In 1992 its 'consultative document' on indus-trial partnership attracted twenty-seven supporting signatories, including eight general secretaries, and eleven senior employers from large organiza-tions (IPA 1992: 8).

16. The three joint aims of the IPA (1992) proposals, as those of the TUC, are a joint commitment to the success of the enterprise, a recognition of a joint effort to build trust, and a declaration recognizing the legitimacy of the role of each party (p. 2). See n. 14.

17. Verma and Cutcher-Gershenfeld (1993) analyse nine of the more prominent cases across the USA and Canada, within their strict definition of 'work-place governance'. For a recent British writer's review of the problems of reconciling job insecurity and 'jointism' in the 'big three' US auto companies, see James (1996).

18. Irving Bluestone, as UAW Vice-President in the 1980s, correctly claims to have helped create the conditions for Saturn. He sees it as 'Among the most penetrating modern-day experiments in joint action at almost every level of managerial decision-making, it represents the most far-reaching innovative development in all U.S. industry' (Bluestone and Bluestone 1992: 200–1).

   From a, perhaps, more objective position Kochan and Osterman also conclude that 'The co-management role played by UAW representatives at Saturn represents a fundamental break from U.S. labour-management law, custom and practice' (1994: 151).

19. A major restructuring of industrial relations has also taken place at Severn Trent Water but is not included here (IRS 1994: 571). For a detailed account, using case studies, of the privatization of the British water industry and its impact on employment relations, see O'Connell Davidson (1993).

20. Gould comments that joint decision-making in design seems to be unique to Saturn and an indicator of the innovative nature of the Saturn partner-ship (1994: 125).

21. Saturn Agreement, pp. 16–17, cited by Gould (1994: 126).

22. The 1983 Water Act ended the statutory obligation of the ten regional water authorities (established in 1974) to bargain with the trade unions, at national level, on pay and conditions. In 1988, in the context of declining trade union membership and influence, the authorities gave one year's notice of termina-tion of national bargaining. With privatization, single employer bargaining, and weaker unions, the conditions existed for major, employer-initiated changes in industrial relations, including the use of derecognition to achieve fewer unions at the bargaining table. See Ogden (1992; 1994).

23. This account of Welsh Water's partnership agreements is drawn from Jones (1995) which was kindly provided by Bryan Stevens, Director of the Involve-ment and Participation Association.

24. Here the company was responding to the increase in non-union employees and its commitment to take their views into account. It also declared its intention to extend information, consultation, and representation rights to

all employees, regardless of union membership, on the EU model (Jones 1995: 24).

25. These are the terms used by Larry Adams, a US consultant specializing in labour–management partnerships, who has worked in both countries. This experience includes working for the Department of Labor's Bureau of Labor-Management Relations and Cooperative Programs as well as for a period within ACAS from 1990 to 1992 (Adams 1993).

26. This was clearly recognized by the trade unions at Welsh Water and, implicitly, by management. 'For the trade unions, the most dramatic change was the proposed replacement of the annual wage claim and subsequent negotiations by the agreed pay formula. This removed what the great majority of trade union activists regarded as the most important function of trade unions' (Jones 1995: 10).

27. A recent analysis of five US cases studies identified 'six key ingredients to a successful partnership: mutual trust and respect; a joint vision of the future and the means to achieve it; continuous exchange of information; recognition of job security and its link to productivity; recognition of the central role of collective bargaining; and devolved decision making' (Rosow and Casner-Lotto 1994, cited in IRS (1995: 575, 3)).

28. Welsh Water are committed to *employment* but not *job* security and this is conditional upon accepting changes in job and geographical flexibility as well as organizational and technological change. Not surprisingly 'some employees have doubts about the importance of the employment guarantee' (Jones 1995: 22). However, although Saturn's job guarantee goes beyond that of Welsh Water, it is not applicable to all employees and could be abrogated by the flexible condition of 'severe economic conditions'.

29. This evidence is not for partnerships, strictly defined, but for union–management cooperation (Schuster 1983). Within the car industry, however, the collaborative approach 'coincided with significant improvements in both productivity and quality as well as a rising market share in the 1990s' (James 1996: 16).

30. For a recent, British, study of bargaining power, see Martin (1992).

31. This is the term of Allan Flanders (1970) who saw the unions' role in this respect as their 'most enduring social achievement'. He also argued that he was 'yet to be convinced that there is a better method than collective bargaining for making industry more democratic, providing its subjects and procedures are suitably extended' (ibid. 30).

32. As we saw in Ch. 5 (n. 50) the World Bank now seems to be a convert to this view.

33. A good example, in both the USA and Britain, is health and safety legislation in which workplace union representatives play a significant role in enforcement.

34. Enterprise-specific management strategies, such as human resource management, have a similar characteristic.

Conclusions: The Prospects for British and American Industrial Relations

[I]t probably is not possible to maintain a system based on the cooperation of the social partners when either partner thinks the system is not producing benefits for it; and it is unclear that such a system can be reimposed.

(Edwards 1995: 379)

Collective discontents will once again become a substantial source of uncertainty to employers . . . Both employers and law makers may thus need to rebuild institutional channels for the management of discontent.

(Brown and Rea 1995: 376)

I am not so daring as to predict a new spurt in employee organisations, but I am sufficiently impressed by the desire of American and British workers for a greater say in their working lives and by the EI movement among US firms to expect something quite different as we enter the twenty-first century.

(Freeman 1995*b*: 360)

If widespread, expanding, and meaningful collective bargaining—conducted by employers and independent organizations of employees within supportive public policy contexts—is the cornerstone of a stable and effective industrial relations system, then the US system is in obvious crisis with the British not far behind. The question then is: to what extent does collective bargaining in Britain and the USA have a future? Certainly the 'arithmetic' is daunting. Edwards estimates that the US unions would need to attract 1 million new members every year for twenty-five years to raise private sector membership density above 25 per cent (1995: 378–9); or, in actual numbers, above 400,000 per year simply to *maintain* current density levels.[1] For Britain, over the same period, an extra 250,000 members would be needed each year to take total membership back to the peak year of 1979 when membership is currently *falling* at about 300–400,000 per annum (Sweeney 1996: 51, table 1). Nor, perhaps even more ominously, is trade union membership an important part of most young workers' lives, as survey evidence is beginning to confirm.[2]

Weakening unions and declining membership imply a parallel shrinking in the coverage and influence of collective bargaining. This is especially serious in the USA and Britain, with systems which in spirit, and still partly in form, are driven by what used to be called 'free' collective bargaining but which also have always depended, and now do so to an increasing degree, upon the continuing support of a benevolent state. This support, though it is nominally available in the USA under the NLRA, is in practice limited, although there can be compensating support at state level. In Britain, official support has been progressively withdrawn since 1980, by policy and legislation, and for some public sector employees collective bargaining has been weakened and even dismantled. Collective bargaining, in both countries, has also become more regional, or 'ghettoized' in incidence and has, to a very large extent, been decentralized, by employers, to single enterprises or single locations.[3]

Yet these processes, initiated by employers, especially but not exclusively in the private sector, have allowed them to put downward pressure on pay and benefits and reduce job security. Some part of this employer response, but far from all, arises from intensifying international competition including that from inward investors in British and US domestic markets. Growing employer power has also made it possible to transform, to a significant extent, the organization of work and working practices, although often in unionized enterprises, and with the cooperation of the trade unions.

The weakening of employees' defences, the corresponding deterioration in pay and benefits, and the problems, for workers, associated with the transformation of work and workplaces, have also been associated with evidence of growing insecurity in employment. These developments are not necessarily universal but they are sufficiently widespread to justify speaking of increasing discontent in the workplace and its potential for providing a stimulus for a revival in trade union membership and action. The prospects for the unions, including an assessment of their current strategies to increase their membership, cannot however be separated from the reactions of employers and prospective developments in public policy. These are the themes of this concluding chapter.

DISCONTENT IN THE WORKPLACE

Comparative studies show that in the 1980s and early 1990s, among advanced industrialized countries, the USA and Britain experienced 'massive' increases in wage inequality whilst low paid US men actually suffered a *decrease* in their real wages. Furthermore, although the evidence that full-time, permanent jobs are disappearing fast is not yet conclusive, when such a job is lost it is more difficult to get another similar one and this is especially true for those who are without skills and education (TUC 1996a; Flanders 1996). This may explain the apparent 'paradox' that although job creation is at a relatively high level in the USA, and unemployment is falling in Britain (though unemployment is still at levels which are much higher even than in the 1970s when the upwards drift was well under way), people still feel insecure.

Work-related insecurity and discontent is also undoubtedly growing in Britain. The Citizens' Advice Bureaux (a voluntary organization) reported a doubling in work-related complaints between 1983 and 1993 from 469,000 to 882,257 (CAB 1993).[4] Kelly and Waddington (1995) maintain, reasonably, that such data reveal increasing employer power. There has also been a substantial growth in the number of potential and actual cases going to British industrial tribunals. ACAS data reveal that these cases, which require initial conciliation, averaged about 45,000 in the 1980s rising to over 91,000 in 1995, of which about half were complaints of unfair dismissal.[5] Yet at actual tribunal hearings, less than half of all claims succeed and compensation awards are small. In cases upheld, tribunals rarely award reinstatement or re-engagement (about one in eighty) and median compensation awards in 1995 were £3,289 ($5,000) with a current, normal upper limit of £11,300 ($17,000) (ACAS 1996: table 13; IPD 1996: 9–10; *Labour Market Trends*, July 1996*a*: tables 2 and 3). However, following an ECJ ruling in 1993, the government, in the same year, was required to remove the upper compensation limit in sex discrimination cases. Additionally, in 1994 the government supported a private member's bill into law which removed the limit for race discrimination.

A tribunal system on the British model does not of course exist in the USA, but *wrongful* dismissal[6] cases, in the courts, are numerous under the exceptions to the 'at-will' doctrine.[7] The total number of cases has been estimated, at any one time, at 20–25,000. Most workers also win their cases, with median awards, in one study, at about $177,000 (£118,000) (Edwards 1995: 382–3).

The incidence and growth of employee complaints against employers on the grounds of unfair dismissal is an important indicator of workplace discontent, perhaps the most important given the problems of finding 'good' jobs and the still high, though falling, levels of unemployment, the latter especially in Britain. Fears for job security when at work also have to be placed alongside the surveys, in both countries, reporting that employees have low levels of trust towards their managers (Rogers and Freeman 1994; Baillie 1995; Kessler and Undy 1996). In these circumstances, it is difficult to conclude that employees' 'demand' for union membership, as a defence against arbitrary treatment, is falling and that unions, to survive, must give their members what they 'want', that is, a package of 'services' much like the Automobile Association (AA) or the AAA in the USA.[8] A more plausible conclusion, and one supported by the Rogers and Freeman survey for the USA, is that employees are inhibited from joining unions for fear of the employer's negative reaction; and indeed that they see unionization as a non-starter without positive employer support and cooperation.[9]

The evidence that there is an untapped demand for the collective defence provided by unions against arbitrary management decisions is strong. British employers' practices to some extent confirm this when withdrawing recognition for collective bargaining from trade unions but retaining it for representation purposes under grievance and disciplinary procedures. Trade union organization in the workplace can also coexist alongside employer policies directed at the individual employee. On the ground, there is no conflict between collectivism and individualism in well-managed companies which recognize the right of their employees to independent representation.[10] Individualism is most commonly stressed as the guiding philosophy of human resource management (HRM). But British companies most closely identified with HRM also tend to be those which have no difficulty recognizing and bargaining with trade unions. This may be because HRM is no more than 'a series of practices which rose to prominence in management circles in the later 1980s . . . and given that most organizations operate without any clearly defined or consistent style, past experience suggests that as the prevailing climate changes, so too will the approach to managing labour' (Blyton and Turnbull 1992: 257–8). Nor is there any convincing evidence of a conversion to individualism in the attitudes of employees. The benevolence of 'soft' HRM is only the experience of a minority of employees. The widespread incidence and growth of workplace discontent reflects deteriorating pay, conditions, benefits, job security, and authoritarian management. Collectivism, in its trade union expression, originated and grew in these conditions. If it is not reflected in some recovery in trade union membership then this is partly, if not wholly, explained by the growth in employer power since the early 1980s.[11]

Whatever the prospects for attracting new members, existing members are showing some signs of reaction to the present discontents. In the USA, bitter, violent, and protracted strikes have always occurred such as that of the USWA copper miners in Arizona against the multinational Phelps Dodge which also used the permanent replacement tactic. The local union was finally decertified in February 1986 almost three years after the strike began.[12] Less than one year earlier the British coalminers of the NUM returned to work without an agreement after a strike lasting almost one year[13] and conducted with a bitterness equalling that at Phelps Dodge.

This kind of dispute has not necessarily disappeared, as in the three disputes in Decatur, Illinois in 1994–5.[14] At Decatur, the tactic of replacing strikers on a permanent or temporary basis provoked worker action as well as cuts in pay and benefits. Additionally, there was management insistence on changes in hours, shifts, and working patterns, reflecting

US corporate pressure for greater flexibility. Hours of work were also the issue in 1994 at General Motors' 'Buick City' plant in Michigan, where plans to increase overtime were resisted in a strike by the UAW. The union insisted that production should be increased by taking on more employees rather than extending overtime. The outcome was a partial reduction in planned overtime and an increase in hires, reflecting, perhaps, the increasing reaction of workers and the wider public against downsizing by the large US corporations.

In Britain, predictions of an 'upsurge in militancy' in September 1994 by the TUC's General Secretary at the annual congress proved to be accurate, albeit from a low base. Working days lost in the UK (in 1994 at 278,000, the lowest since 1891) totalled 415,000 in 1995 (*Labour Market Trends*, 1996*b*: table 4.2). At the end of 1995, national unofficial strikes were in progress at Ford and Vauxhall (a subsidiary of GM) over pay and hours, alongside a number of other smaller scale local disputes over pay and conditions, as well as that concerning the dismissal of unofficial, striking Liverpool dockers and others refusing to cross their picket lines.[15]

The British public sector, including those sectors recently privatized or subject to possible privatization, has also been a significant focus of recent strike activity given the still strong public sector unions and the issues involved. Members of the Fire Brigades' Union (FBU) have been involved in local disputes over job cuts followed by an unofficial walk-out by Royal Mail workers in the Communication Workers Union (CWU) in Scotland over pay, conditions, potential job cuts, and the introduction of teamworking. Teamworking remained the key issue in the series of one-day, national official strikes called by the CWU during 1996 although the prospect of privatization also stiffened union resistance.

The issues in the British public sector strikes do seem to suggest a rise in concern over job security and working conditions although pay remains a major issue as the Conservative government continued to limit public sector settlements and its Labour successor indicated similar intentions. Some unions, noted for their moderate tactics, are also adopting far more militant postures, for example, the nurses in the NHS who are in frequent confrontation with government and local hospital management over the impact of privatization on pay, job security, and the structure of collective bargaining.[16] The teachers' unions have also been involved in a series of disputes with government extending back to the late 1980s over the new national curriculum and management of schools. This new militancy of the British teachers' unions is paralleled by that of their US counterparts in the NEA and AFT.

Some significant features of the more important recent British disputes include their unofficial nature and the use of the one-day strike. This could suggest that the legislation regulating official disputes is too restrictive and does not allow for the expression of legitimate discontent.

Yet increasingly, the Conservative government had been using public sector disputes as evidence that further legislative restrictions covering workers in essential industries are required. This issue will be returned to later in the chapter.

The possibility of further Congressional or Presidential action against strikers can probably be ruled out in current US conditions: existing laws, judicial interpretation, and employer power are already sufficiently effective and strikes normally only have a local or regional impact in both the private and public sectors. There are, of course, important exceptions, such as, for example, strikes with national (i.e. inter-state) impact involving pilots, flight attendants, and baggage handlers on the airlines. There is also the example of the 1981 PATCO strike which evoked decisive executive action by President Reagan. A recent local strike with national effects was the 1996 UAW strike at GM's two brake plants in Dayton, Ohio. The strike lasted seventeen days and was the eighth at the company's plants since 1994. The 1996 dispute halted twenty-seven out of twenty-nine of GM's assembly plants in North America as well as some in Mexico. The main issue, was outsourcing (subcontracting) with GM eventually agreeing to bring in new work to restore the jobs lost. Outsourcing and job losses (with the lost jobs going to non-union workers) remain a major source of conflict in the auto industry and by the autumn of 1996 were dominating the 'Big Three' contract negotiations (Moody 1996*b*; Waters 1996).

The UAW's dispute at Dayton was distinguished by its capacity to halt all GM's operations. The main issue was again job protection and it was also important at Boeing in 1995 when 32,500 workers struck for ten weeks. The new, four-year, contract improved pay, but also limited outsourcing and lay-offs and postponed a switch from Boeing's comprehensive health care plan to a cheaper option (Moody 1996*a*). But perhaps it is the impact of the jobs issue on the Big Three in the auto industry which is the most significant for the longer term. The Ford 1996 contract with the UAW was agreed in two days and included two 'path-breaking' clauses: a job guarantee and a two-tier wage structure in the company's parts plants, with lower wages applying to new employees. These clauses allow Ford to control its labour costs and the UAW to protect jobs and union membership by limiting outsourcing (Waters 1996).

PUBLIC POLICY, UNIONS, AND EMPLOYERS

The recent successes of US trade unions in dispute with employers and the more limited gains for British unions may be the beginning of new offensives, built upon growing employee discontent and over-restrictive, unjust labour laws. However it is too early to detect any enduring patterns or trends and the clear balance of bargaining power still remains with employers in both countries, a power which has been growing without interruption for about twenty years. But employer power in explaining trade union decline, though highly significant, is not the whole story. The unions have been losing membership in the debilitating contexts of unemployment and structural economic changes influencing the nature of employment.

The shift in bargaining power towards employers has also taken place in political and policy-making contexts favouring employers and, especially in the British case, with government, since 1979, directly intervening in collective bargaining to weaken both the institution itself and the influence of trade unions within it. The hostile rhetoric, ideology, policies, and legislation of the eleven years of Margaret Thatcher's prime ministership have never been equalled in the USA. However anti-unionism in the USA is more durable and runs much deeper. The alliance between powerful, well-resourced and organized employers and their Republican (and some Democratic) allies in Congress to ensure that pro-labour legislation should be defeated at all costs, and that every opportunity to introduce anti-labour bills should be taken, poses great problems for US unions. The anti-union alliance is replicated at state level as, for example, in the substantial and vigorous campaigns to increase the number of right-to-work states, especially after the Republican victories in 1994. Faced with this resolute anti-unionism, organized labour has, however, had some recent lobbying and campaigning successes such as over the minimum wage and the TEAM Bill. However its weakening member-ship base and increasing 'ghettoization', combined with the dubious protections of the labour laws and the diminishing returns from its role in the Democratic alliance make the match much less than equal.

In Britain, this shifting triangular, power relationship between the trade unions, employers, and public policy has worked out differently. The links between the Conservative Party and business are important, not least in the Party's need for funds to win elections, but the Conservative Party and business are much less at one in their opposition to trade unions. Indeed, government policy, since 1979 towards trade unions, has been some distance away from the actual practice, if not the rhetoric, of employers, especially at the place of work where the old, voluntaristic practices have not disappeared and employers still largely value the role of collective bargaining in maintaining harmony and achieving change. Nor have British employers, in the main, shown much enthusiasm for using the new laws or taking advantage, in other cases, of the absence of law. For example, in the latter case, though recognition is still as difficult for unions to achieve as it was in the 1980s, and especially among inward investors, derecognition remains rare (ACAS 1996: 15). The employers have also been pragmatic in responding to the EU dimension of public policy, especially in their universal application of the European Works Council directive to their own employees, despite the Conservative government's opt-out of the Social Chapter.

PROSPECTS FOR PUBLIC POLICY

Predicting the future prospects for British and US industrial relations, as opposed to explaining the past or understanding the present, is a difficult task. Who could have foreseen the surging growth of the CIO unions from the depths of the Great Depression, and before the passage of the Wagner Act, as well as the long decline in density since 1955? Who could have predicted the startling reversal of British trade union membership growth after 1979 and its continuing decline towards the end of the 1990s? And, in the political context to industrial relations, in the years after 1992 who believed the opinion polls' prediction of a landslide victory for Labour in 1997?

Despite the difficulties, and the capacity of new, unexpected developments to make fools of us all, it seems reasonable to argue that continuing changes in economic structure and employment need not be a constraint on trade union membership growth. In Britain, these changes, notably the rise of the service sector and relative decline in manufacturing, were occurring as union membership was growing in the 1970s, including in the white collar and public sector unions. In the USA, the public sector, with large numbers of female and white collar workers, has proved a fertile ground for union membership growth. In the service sector itself, the SEIU has had major successes, whilst in both countries teachers are both highly unionized and no strangers to determined industrial action. In other EU countries, similar changes in employment have occurred, as they have in Britain, but without such dire consequences for trade union membership. Canada, too, has had a greatly different experience to the USA. The latter remains unique in the duration of decline—over forty years—and even the twenty years' spurt from the 1930s to the 1950s might even be seen as an aberration explained by a unique concurrence of circumstances: economic depression, supportive public policy, world war, and a truce in the long offensive of US capital against labour. It may also be that war, and economic depression on the scale of the 1930s, are long behind us. More significantly, US public policy is now only supportive in nominal terms and the employers' offensive against labour was seriously resumed twenty years ago as US union membership began to follow density downwards.

Employers and Public Policy

The combination of employer power facing trade unions with minimal benefit from labour law and mostly unhelpful judicial interpretation against a context of limited and ineffective public policy interventions, is a potent cocktail largely explaining the problems of US labour and the continuing contraction of collective bargaining. The political prospects for labour law reform, favouring trade unions and collective bargaining, bright but ultimately disappointing between 1992 and 1994, were also instantly buried as the Republicans captured both the House and Senate in 1994. For the future, though President Clinton was returned to office in 1996, the continued and unprecedented control of Congress by the the Republicans may be confirming enduring changes in old political allegiances and alliances.

In Britain, the cocktail has been mixed in different proportions but has been potent nevertheless. Employer power has clearly grown since 1979 and has been deployed to change the role and influence of trade unions, decentralize collective bargaining, transform working practices, cut labour costs, and limit, even remove, traditional job security guarantees. Yet only a small minority of British employers have sought to seriously weaken or destroy trade unions, unlike their American counterparts. In public policy terms British unions have of course fared much worse. The far-reaching industrial relations, employment, and trade union legislation from 1980 to 1993 was intended to emasculate the trade unions as an economic and political force in Britain. Whilst there have been exaggerated claims for the impact of this legislation, including from academics and from both ends of the political spectrum, there are three clear instances where it directly impacted upon member recruitment and thus on the principal source of trade union income and influence. First, in the post-1993 freedom for employers to discriminate against trade union members on pay and conditions; secondly, employers could also discriminate in the selective rehiring of workers involved in lawful strikes; and, thirdly, through the onerous restrictions, in the workplace, affecting the capacity of unions to collect and increase dues, with potentially adverse implications for membership and financial viability. For these legislative constraints and restrictions, as well as the wider legislation affecting matters such as the timing, conduct, and implementation of membership ballots for industrial action, the courts have generally provided supportive decisions. The hostility of government policies towards trade unions and collective bargaining has also been consistent, and effective, for both its own direct employees and those in the old (now privatized) public sector such as coalminers and, more recently, postal workers in an industry threatened with (or promised?) privatization. Nor has there been any respite, for eighteen years, from this almost wholly adverse political climate, given the concentration of power in the government and ruling party, under the British system, and the failure of the Labour Party (the other 'wing' of the old labour movement) to win office in four successive general elections.

Public Policy and the Labour Party

This adverse political climate changed dramatically in 1997. The new Government will, if pre-election manifestos are to be believed, repeal those parts of the Conservative legislation (cited above) which handicap the efforts of the unions to revive their membership and improve their financial base (Labour Party 1996: 5). The removal of potential employer discrimination against union members on pay and benefits[17] would take their position back to pre-1993. This would also be the case with the check-off restrictions, also introduced under the 1993 Trade Union Reform and Employment Rights Act. The ability of employers to dismiss even lawful strikers selectively (unofficial strikers have had no protection at all since 1990) has not been used extensively but the removal of this employer power would give the 'right to strike' more meaning. Severe restrictions still, however, remain, of which the most important is that lawful strikers, under British law, are in breach of their employment contracts and liable to dismissal. The development of a 'positive' right to strike may yet attract a Labour government, as it indicated in *Building Prosperity* (Labour Party 1996).[18]

The Labour Party was, however, clear in its commitment not to repeal the main substance of the 1980 to 1993 legislation. In particular, it would retain the balloting requirements for industrial action and in this it is clearly in line with most trade unions and their members who have found bargaining advantages in strike ballots to set against the onerous restrictions introduced by the legislation. It was, however, planning to introduce a right for individuals to be 'accompanied' (i.e. by a friend or colleague in the absence of a representative) during grievance and disciplinary procedures. This would benefit the many thousands of people without access to trade union representation. It is of course fairly widespread practice in Britain and is recommended by ACAS although it has never been an enforceable right (*Labour Research*, July 1996). It would also be appropriate to a new system using arbitration to process unfair dismissal claims, noted earlier.

A more problematic policy proposal concerns recognition. This issue has exercised the minds of many in the TUC, the unions, ACAS, and the universities since the repeal of the statutory procedure in 1980. The TUC has recommended 10 per cent union membership in the bargaining unit as the consultation rights threshold with full recognition following majority support from voting *employees*. In the case of a union showing it had 50 per cent of union *members* in the bargaining unit, it would be given 'automatic recognition'.[19] In the event, the Labour Party did not accept the case for a *legal* right to consultation but it did for recognition 'Where the majority of the relevant workforce vote to be represented by a trade union' (Labour Party 1996: 5). But it was silent on automatic recognition and its first legislative programme did not include any form of recognition. The enforcement of statutory rights would also require the involvement of an agency with the appropriate powers—as the TUC proposes. In the case of the agency, much would need to be learned from British experience under the Commission on Industrial Relations (CIR) and ACAS[20] when statutory procedures were in operation. There must also be much to learn, even avoid, from the NLRB and the unhappy certification, first contract, and decertification experience of many US unions.

Membership of the European Union has influenced Labour Party policy in a number of ways. First, it has for a long time been committed to ending Britain's opt-out from the Social Chapter.[21] This may not be a simple process since the Labour government could find it necessary to consult over, or even renegotiate, its provisions in the light of the growing influence of the case for greater labour flexibility in EU countries (notably among German employers) as well as in Britain. This has especially been reflected in the debate over the unemployment effects of the commitment to introduce a national minimum wage[22] as well as the implementation of the EU's Working Time Directive which, among other things, places universal, though in practice largely avoidable, limits on the length of the working week.

Secondly, and related to the ending of the opt-out, the Party has favoured adequate information and consultation for employees and, specifically, through the European Works Council (EWC) Directive. British and other EU multinationals have of course already included British employees in their EWCs despite the Conservative government's opt-out. This support for the EWC as well as improved information and consultation in companies is also replicated among the TUC and its affiliates and could influence possible legislation (though the Labour Party did not have a commitment on this possibility) to establish similar rights for employees in all British workplaces and not just those of multinationals affected by the EWC.

Thirdly, the Labour Party was committed to using legislation for a modest extension of individual employment rights. These would include a review of industrial tribunals' procedures leading to greater fairness and the reduction in delays;[23] rights for workers in small companies; the provision (in line with the current EU directive) of a right to three months' unpaid parental leave after the birth or adoption of a child; and a bill to outlaw age discrimination against older people. Here, of course, in relation to unpaid parental leave and age discrimination, there are echoes of possible US influence as well as European.

Fourthly, Party policy has endorsed the concept of social partnership, as does the TUC, in the running of successful companies as well as the latter's support for wider access to adequate information and consultation for employees and further advances and improvements in health and safety legislation. There is also a commitment to a statutory framework to improve training which would need to be implemented by joint involvement of employers and unions or other employee organizations.

The positive influence of the EU on the Labour Party (and the unions) is a relatively recent development. In the 1970s, strong British trade unions and a Labour Party still committed to a diluted form of 'socialist' planning in national contexts found little attraction in the Pan-European capitalism of the advocates of 'ever closer union'. The conversion was partly a pragmatic response to the need for support to counter the anti-collectivist, anti-union policies of the Conservative governments through the 1980s. But it was also genuinely inspired by the strong support for the 'social dimension' under the Commission presidency of Jacques Delors, the able and influential French socialist.[24] The pressure for extending and deepening social and employment protection in the context of the single European market is now much reduced as the opposing case for removing protection, and forcing down labour costs, to meet foreign competition gathers strength. The Labour Party itself also adopted this rhetoric in its manifesto.[25] More fundamentally, under its present leader-ship, the Party has begun to redefine its 'socialist' legacy and credentials and has declared its intention to continue to develop its 'evolving' relationship with the trade unions. This intention has led to major controversy within the Party and denunciations from the TUC and many unions. However, the leadership's intentions may not be sustainable unless it can secure alternative sources of funds to those provided by the trade unions. This, of course, may yet be possible in government under some recent proposals to fund all political parties from public expenditure.

Overall, despite some caveats, the public policy prospects for British trade unions and collective bargaining are looking much better than for a generation and certainly would have been bleak under the Conservatives.[26] Even though the new government will leave most of the 1980–93 legislation intact it is still likely to favour, perhaps even promote, cooperative ventures in the workplace. Furthermore, the scale of the Labour victory, and the political security it implies, perhaps over two terms, offers legislative scope for institutional experiments to encourage trade union recognition perhaps alongside the complementary development of forms of employee representation in workplaces where trade union influence is weak or non-existent. The latter, through extending works councils, is on the policy agenda of the EU Commission.

Public Policy and the Democrats

In the USA, although in 1992 the Democrats retained control of Congress and regained the presidency, almost all of the public policy interventions favouring labour unions and collective bargaining failed to pass; and NAFTA, which the AFL-CIO vehemently opposed in an expensive campaign, was enthusiastically supported by the Democratic President and endorsed by a Democratic Congress. There were, of course, some successes. In 1996 the TEAM Act, which would have significantly amended Section 8(a)(2) of the NLRA allowing employers to initiate and be involved in organizations rivalling independent labour unions in the workplace, was finally killed off by the Presidential veto. Effective union campaigning in the country prevented any additions to the number of right-to-work states. The minimum wage, after much political bargaining, was increased, although in two stages. Against these successes have to be set the failure of Executive Order 12954 to be implemented, although at the time of writing its fate is still subject to a possible appeal by the Administration to the Supreme Court. Should the present decision of the courts stand, it will, along with the failure of the Workplace Fairness Bill, confirm the inability of a Democratic President and, earlier, a Democrat-controlled Congress, to do anything about the use of the permanent replacement tactic.

Their inability to make any progress on permanent replacements has been a substantial setback for the unions, but perhaps the most significant long-term disappointment for labour during President Clinton's first term was that of the Dunlop Commission. Its recommendations were condemned by unions and employers. Its careful attempt to seek to amend 8(a)(2) to encourage employee involvement and participation schemes without threatening collective bargaining—as the TEAM Bill claimed to do but with less honourable intentions than the Commission —was criticized, even by one of its members. In any case the limited chances of turning its recommendations into law were overtaken by the political transformation, or 'revolution' of 1994 when the Republicans took control of both House and Senate for the first time since 1952. That revolution lost some of its revolutionary ardour in 1995–6, although the longer term shifts in voting patterns, especially in the South, which began to be reflected in Congress in 1994, could yet transform the Republicans into the 'national' party of government—at least in Congress if not, necessarily, in the presidency. It should also be observed that in 1978, when the Democrats also held Congress and the presidency and the labour unions were much stronger than in 1994, the modest, much-amended, Labor Law Reform Bill failed to pass, faced then, as now, with well-organized and well-resourced employer opposition.

The consistency and strength of the opposition of US employers to labour unions, even to their very existence, remains critical in any future attempts at labour law reform. The failure of public policy interventions to improve labour's prospects and strengthen collective bargaining in the private sector is largely explained by the capacity of employers, with their allies in Congress, to undermine legislation even when it has clear majority support. The AFL-CIO has, of course, its own expert lobbyists and has deployed substantial resources in Washington alongside ambitious campaigns in the States. However, despite some recent lobbying and campaigning successes, it is, in general, not able to match the resources or effectiveness of the employer-Republican alliance. The contrast with Britain is also clear: a reforming Labour government, with TUC and union support, can normally rely upon the cooperation, and not always reluctant cooperation, of the employers' organizations and employers themselves. British employers did strongly oppose the recommendations of the Bullock Committee but so did most of the unions, the TUC was ambivalent, and the Labour government had other urgent priorities to deal with—such as the deterioration in the economy. However, the earlier experience under Donovan was very different. The Commission's recommendations partly led to the creation of the influential agency, the Commission on Industrial Relations, and Donovan's support for comprehensive plant agreements, even without any public policy intervention, has been claimed to have influenced employer industrial relations policies (Dunn 1993).

These contrasts emphasize that a comprehensive public policy intervention leading to the reform of American industrial relations is therefore as unlikely as it is necessary. The failure of the Dunlop Commission was a major setback which may, given the way in which its recommendations were received, pre-empt a further exercise even under favourable political circumstances. It may, however, be seen as part of a longer term reform agenda and in that sense has been useful (Kochan and Weinstein 1994; Kochan 1995). Limited public policy interventions may however yet be possible. The significance of the President's executive order powers has been frequently demonstrated on several occasions in the last thirty years, especially President Kennedy's 1962 intervention, and this could yet be an instrument for extending the scope of collective bargaining, in the federal sector, to pay and conditions. This would of course be challenged in Congress and the courts especially since the Republican ascendancy has been confirmed (at least until the end of the decade) and, perhaps, even without it. Industrial relations, at state level, are of course subject to regulation under widely varying jurisdictions and political contexts. This can make available, to the states, the right-to-work provisions of the Taft–Hartley Act. The public sector unions are also vulnerable to the consequences of the privatization and deregulation of state-provided public services. Although the states can also provide alternative legislative possibilities, sanctioned by federal legislation, to assist trade unions and collective bargaining.[27] Yet even allowing for some rescue attempts at state level the New Deal system could still be in the first stages of disintegration, as Strauss (1995) suggests. The representation gap is now so wide that it covers a very large part of the employed population. A Democratic Congress and President may yet be able to enact some restorative legislation to remove the obvious legal handicaps to narrowing the gap, such as the strong anti-union bias in the certification and first contract processes and the judicial support for permanent replacement of strikers. They did, in fact, come close to enacting the Labour Representation Bill in 1978 and the Workplace Fairness Bill in 1995.[28] But these were limited measures which would not have seriously touched the entrenched power of the employers. Major reform measures attracting sufficient political support would require the articulation of substantial worker demand across the country for a change in the law. That would not be dissimilar to that which provided the context for the rise of the CIO unions in the 1930s; but its root causes would be more about the nature, conditions, and insecurity of employment rather than the incidence of unemployment.

PROSPECTS FOR THE UNIONS

In almost any conditions, other than the most desperate, seeking any change in US labour laws favouring unions and collective bargaining is always a difficult exercise. Unions do of course have a number of other strategies such as promoting collective bargaining through labour–management partnerships or increasing their bargaining power and financial viability through mergers. These may, however, have only a marginal effect, if any, on membership, which is the touchstone of economic and political influence.[29] Yet the conditions favourable to unions organizing strategies for membership growth may now exist.

US Unions: Organizing for Growth?

Labour unions, according to opinion polls have for a long time lost much of their unpopularity. They are also beginning to win some victories, as we saw earlier. The most prominent were the machinists' (IAM) success over Boeing at its Seattle plant in December 1995, followed in January by that of the autoworkers' (UAW) in its major dispute with GM in January 1996. Less dramatic, but perhaps having resonance among all workers, including the vast majority who are unorganized, was the increase in the minimum wage by a Republican Congress, in August 1996. This success has been largely ascribed to the AFL-CIO's national 'America Needs a Raise' campaign under its new leadership. The minimum wage success is also claimed to have drawn upon the widespread fears of white and blue collar workers of losing their jobs. In the autumn of 1996 it was even being maintained, within the Democratic Party, that the minimum wage success could help the Democrats regain control of Congress and that the President was beginning to take political advantage from the labour movement's growing influence and even to face up to the opposition of business (Mort 1996). The congressional election outcome was, of course, very different and the President, in such a context, is not likely to be able, or even willing, to take on business.

Yet, despite these very real political setbacks there is now some evidence, discussed earlier, of an unsatisfied demand for independent representation which could be encouraged by union successes, thus removing some of the fear of employer reaction to pressure for unionization. Furthermore, in the longer run, and importantly, the ongoing changes in the labour force and employment may now be beginning to favour, rather than handicap, labour union growth. Professional, semi-professional, technical, and managerial occupational groups are projected to grow in the next century in both absolute and relative terms. Even white collar, clerical occupations will grow in total employment although their relative shares will fall.[30] Heckscher (1988) points to semi-professional occupations such as paralegals, computer programmers, systems analysts, and medical assistants as among the fastest growing. He also argues that such groups, whose skills are important to the growth of the economy, but who do not have a share in its control, have historically been an important source of growth for the labour movement. He cites, for example, the machinists early in the century and the industrial workers of the mass-production era. Nor are the semi-professional occupations—vulnerable to corporate authority and further changes in the technology on which they have grown, and increasingly experiencing the new insecurities—necessarily immune to the collectivism of trade union organization although it may take different, newer forms such as what Heckscher terms 'associational unionism'. Clerical workers, an important target group for unions, are also through computer technology being increasingly organized into 'work-processing centres' providing classic, factory conditions favouring solidarity and unionization (Heckscher 1988: 62–70). Brody (1992) talks in similar terms of the potential for union growth in the new 'dynamic core' also suggesting parallels with the rise of the CIO unions in the 1930s. At the same time, the old blue collar, low-skilled, ageing labour force has lost jobs and income, joining the ranks of the growing numbers of the disaffected.[31] The low paid home health care and nursing home workers —an expanding occupational group—are also enjoying organizing successes on the Justice for Janitors model (see Chapter 4). The combination of perceived injustice, rising numbers, and unionization as forces for change may not yet have passed into history.

If the conditions for a revival in membership growth through the unions' own efforts are at least beginning to be in place, the unions may also now be beginning to take advantage of them. Recent changes and strategic decisions within the AFL-CIO certainly indicate some radical, new thinking about organizing. The two big service and public sector unions with good records of organizing achievement—the SEIU and AFSCME—provided two of the top leadership positions at the 1995

Convention.[32] They were also elected after a contest, the first in the AFL-CIO's history, on a commitment to a new style of aggressive leadership and a major reversal of the low-key, lobbying, consensual tactics of their predecessors. More significantly than a commitment, the new AFL-CIO President announced a progressive, fivefold increase in the organizing budget towards 30 per cent of available resources ($20 m.) by 1998. The first tranche of his new money was to be mainly used to fund a major organizing drive in 1996 ('Union Summer') to include the largely non-union states in the South as well as the relatively easier territory in the Northern and Midwestern states. Union Summer is also using students in large numbers[33] in an attempt to try to reverse the ageing profile of union members and activists.

The promise of Union Summer has yet to be tested. It is clearly more than an uphill task to reverse a decline in membership extending back over forty years but the new leadership of the AFL-CIO have much experience of successful organizing campaigns in their own unions.[34] There is also the example of the public sector to comfort struggling organizers. In 1991 and 1992, the overall win rate in public sector certification elections, nationwide, was 84.9 per cent compared to 48.0 per cent in the private sector. This can be mainly explained by the difference between public and private sector employers.[35] This contrast once again illustrates the significant impact of private sector employer opposition on US union membership as well as the unions' potential capacity for growth.

British Unions: 'Turning the Queen Mary'

British employers' ideologies and traditions do not of course present such a barrier to organizing as their US counterparts. However they do have the ability to refuse demands for recognition, or derecognize, without legal constraints even against the the wishes of even a majority of their employees. American employers, despite their legitimate and illegitimate recourse to labour law, can still be *compelled* to recognize the wishes of proven majorities. Here there is clearly a need for British legislation, to 'level the playing field', given the inadequacy and manifest injustice of the voluntary recognition system, and such a reform is now politically possible under the Labour government. However, a satisfactory, workable, procedure is not easy to devise. The obvious existing examples are the American and Canadian, offering examples of 'bad' and 'good' systems. Britain did have a statutory procedure for part of the 1970s and 1980s but these only offer negative lessons. The TUC has however developed its own proposals (including the appropriate role for a representation agency) and these could yet serve as the basis for a durable reform although reciprocal proposals were not included in the early agenda of the Labour Government.[36]

Yet even a satisfactory recognition procedure is only of value if suf-ficient numbers of new members have been recruited and organized. The evidence now is that British unions, like their US counterparts, are shifting the emphasis of their activities from servicing falling numbers of existing members to recruiting new ones. This is not before time. British trade union membership is now approaching half its 1979 level and, although it is still double that of the USA it is falling much faster. It is even falling in the public sector where, in the USA, membership is stable. The big five British unions between 1990 and 1995 lost more than 900,000 members, or 17.3 per cent; from 1995 to 1996 they lost a further 200,000, that is 4.7 per cent.[37] The scale of these losses also has serious financial implications, as we saw in Chapter 3, further underlining the need for giving the highest priority to reviving membership growth.

The 'big five' and the TUC have drawn upon the experience of organ-izing initiatives in Australia, the Netherlands, and, especially, the USA, including that of the AFL-CIO's Organizing Institute. In June 1996 the TUC held an 'Organising for Growth' conference in London, attended by representatives from the AFL-CIO, the Australian Council of Trade Unions (ACTU), and the Dutch Trade Union Confederation (FNV). At the TUC's General Council meeting, on the following day, John Sweeney was present and Richard Bensinger, Director of the AFL-CIO's Organ-izing Department, gave a presentation—emphasizing the influence of the AFL-CIO model on the TUC.

The practical outcomes of the conference were, however, limited. The TUC is reviewing the scope for using and training young organizers, as in the USA and Australia, and is setting up its own research programme, including a comparative study, largely concerned with how to recruit young people. The TUC will itself act as a 'clearing house' for the organ-izing initiatives of its affiliates and has established a task group to report on the potential for organizing with a budget from the Development Fund (TUC 1996*a*: 12). But the TUC will not play an active, leading role like the AFL-CIO, which has much greater financial resources than the TUC with its continuing, acute financial problems. The AFL-CIO also has more authority to lead and it is clear that the TUC will not be able to follow the example of the AFL-CIO's 'Union Summer' campaign. Much will therefore depend on the affiliates' own organizing efforts.

In both the British and US cases, academic research seems now to have established that people join unions primarily for representation and protection, with services far behind. For Britain, it is also clear that new members are more likely to be recruited either through their own efforts or through a shop steward: full-time union officers and leaflets are insignificant in recruiting new members.[38] The big five unions have all been strongly influenced by these findings. The emphasis of their cam-paigns has been on representation and protection with shop stewards, other local officials, and even members leading the membership drives. New full-time union jobs are also being created with recruitment respons- ibilities and all the unions are providing recruitment training. To iden- tify more closely with the characteristics of potential members the unions are also attempting to develop appropriate age, gender, and race profiles among their representatives.

These initiatives are intended to establish a recruitment or organizing 'culture' designed to halt the slide in membership and then restore growth. These are highly ambitious aims after seventeen years of rapid decline. As one senior union official put it: 'It's like turning the Queen Mary; it takes time' (IRS 1996: 605, 5). The big unions are also handi- capped by their decentralized structures. Senior regional or industrial officials commonly have substantial autonomy and authority and this has undermined previous campaigns. Decentralization may be the key factor determining the degree to which the British unions' new, well- conceived initiatives succeed, or fail. The early news from one union is not, however, promising. The TGWU increased its membership in four targeted areas by the end of 1995, but only by small numbers. Mem- bership as a whole still fell in 1995 but by less than in 1994 (IRS 1996: 605, 4; 7).

Although both labour movements have not yet begun to even replace their lost members, the US record and initiatives look more promising. Some unions are still growing; the public sector is holding its own; there are good models of highly successful, local campaigns for other unions to learn from; and the AFL-CIO, under its new leadership, is devoting much effort and resources to a high profile, national campaign. The 'relaunched' TUC is much less cumbersome and less policy-preoccupied than its predecessors and is offering fresh ideas and lively leadership under its General Secretary, John Monks. But it does not have the author- ity or resources to lead a major organizational drive from the front. Indeed, during the early acute stages of its continuing financial prob- lems, there was some speculation as to the bigger unions' need for a TUC. It may also be that the British unions are still largely locked into a culture in which recruitment has a low priority and they have yet to demonstrate that they can, through their own efforts, revive their num- bers. The alternative, or complementary strategy, dating back to 1906, which would restore some influence and maybe some members, is to work for the election of Labour governments.[39]

A Labour government has for long seemed to be the British trade unions' main lifeline. The less-politicized US labour movement, that is, in the party political sense, has had to learn to be much more self-reliant, keep- ing mainly to its business union traditions and expecting little from pub- lic policy. This may just enable it to organize itself out of continuing decline although it must continue to widen its appeal, as it is doing, at the grass roots, by associating itself with the causes of others in struggle such as minorities, the unemployed, and working poor, and in mainly local movements such as those concerned with rescuing declining neighbourhoods and protecting the environment, what Johnston (1994) calls 'social movement unionism'. The nascent Labor Party, with its close union links, might even have a future, at local level, in these kinds of alliances. It would be deeply ironic if the US unions should succeed in developing close links with their Labor Party just as the British Labour Party was moving in the opposite direction.

This possible divergence, at least from the British side, is now less likely. The strategy of the Labour Party leadership to weaken its union links in order to improve the Party's electability may yet re-emerge with major industrial conflict but, for the present, this strategy has been buried under decisive electoral success and the urgent and wider preoccupations of office. Furthermore, even the Government's modest industrial relations and employment policies would, when eventually implemented, allow a reasonable chance of at least a reduction in the pace of the downward slide in membership. The commitment to the current vogue for labour–management partnership (which the TUC and the biggest unions also support)[40] would also be strengthened through adherence to the Social Chapter and its 'social partner' ideology. This would once again legitimize collective bargaining after the sustained attacks on it after 1979.

THE ROLE FOR PUBLIC POLICY

Those who support the case for growing and effective trade unions and the extension of collective bargaining are always in danger of falling into excessive optimism. What is more realistic is that, for Britain and the USA, the prospects for these industrial relations institutions, and therefore the system which they largely determine, are still very uncertain. It is also possible that decline and contraction will continue and voluntary collective bargaining will be replaced, in part, by individual employment legislation but mainly by unenlightened forms of managerial control. So far, these processes have been gradual but their cumulative effect has been far-reaching. Furthermore, in Britain, in particular, the pace of trade union decline and the scale of the retreat of collective bargaining still shows no sign of slowing down. In the USA, the process is slower but this is partly explained by the degree to which the long attrition has already done its work. These processes have been much analysed and explained but few have expressed regret at the passing of institutions and systems which have developed over two centuries, accumulating valuable experience and practices which have also benefited the wider democratic society which encouraged them and allowed them to flourish. This lack of regret is surprising since the two systems, and their central focus of collective bargaining, were for a long time seen as so desirable that public policy actively took measures to encourage and extend their progress, and even sought to export them to other countries.

This encouragement has long since gone. In the USA, public policy rarely approaches even benign neglect and in Britain it took a decidedly hostile turn in 1979 with the prospect that collective bargaining may never recover full public policy support, even under Labour; and should the Conservatives resume government, even after a long interval, hostilities will likely resume.

What has always been clear is that the interests of large, even small, organizations can only be partly consonant with the interests of those many people who gain a modest living working for them. The employment relationship is also characterized by a major imbalance in power which can be partly redressed by effective systems of employee representation. These can take different forms although strong trade unions, for all their imperfections, have stood the tests of independence from employers and protection of their members' interests remarkably well. They have also contributed honourably to wider causes including the advocacy and development of 'good' societies concerned for the welfare of all their citizens. In the workplace, through collective bargaining, they also play a role in the maintenance of social and distributive justice. They are not of course the only means of advancing workplace justice and may sometimes do so, even more effectively, in association with other employee institutions or in contexts of constructive partnership with management. But these alternative experiments still remain limited in both Britain and the USA and it is likely that they can only be complementary to the tried and tested roles of trade unions and collective bargaining. Trade unions and collective bargaining also seem, in favourable circumstances, to contribute to economic efficiency, a valuable bonus, but no more than that: democracy, in the workplace as elsewhere, does not need to be justified on economic grounds.

Finally the role for public policy, in both countries, is clear enough. The closing of the representation gap ideally, but not necessarily exclusively, through a recovery of trade unions and collective bargaining, requires urgent and far-reaching intervention.[41] Unions, on their own, as in the USA, might be able to trigger a revival but that still seems unlikely given the formidable constraining power of the employers facing them. In Britain, employer power is much less effectively deployed but the unions also seem less able to shape their own destinies. Yet, although the case for supportive public policy intervention is evident, as is the form it could take, the problem is that the will to intervene is far from being in place in the USA and, even in Britain, the Labour government has other, earlier, priorities; but democracy is greatly diminished, as we will yet discover, if the representative institutions which are central to it are not even allowed into the workplace, let alone encouraged. It may also be that the decay of industrial democracy is symptomatic of a much wider process.

NOTES

1. Edwards's arithmetic compensates for the normal growth in the employed labour force, normal membership losses, and losses from decertification.
2. A 1996 Mori poll for the TUC reveals that 7% of workers aged between 16 and 24, belong to a union and only 36% said they would join a union if invited. Forty-two % said they knew 'nothing at all' about trade unions and 44% 'not very much'. Most would also go to a manager or supervisor if they had a problem at work, not a trade union representative (Taylor 1996*b*). See also Hudson *et al.* (1996).
3. Although decentralization does not mean disappearance. For example, John Monks, the TUC's General Secretary, has frequently pointed out that forty-seven of the fifty biggest UK companies recognize and bargain with trade unions.
4. Cited in Kelly and Waddington (1995: 422). A recent NOP poll commissioned by the TUC (TUC 1996*b*) also reveals that one in three 'are afraid to take time off work when sick and are pressurized into unpaid overtime' (p. 3).
5. In November 1994 the Conservative Government announced its intention to legislate to reform the industrial tribunal system. In particular it would introduce voluntary, independent, binding arbitration for unfair dismissal cases as an alternative to, but not a substitute for, the tribunal system. These cases would be under ACAS arrangements. ACAS welcomed the then government's intention (ACAS 1996: 24–5). A consultation paper and draft bill was published in July (Department of Trade and Industry 1996). Such legislation could form part of the Labour Government's legislative plans.
6. Wrongful dismissal litigation is also available in the British courts but is rare, largely because of the costs involved, although the remedy (damages) can be substantial. A non-legal alternative is private arbitration under ACAS. These settlements can be far more generous than at tribunals but access is limited for most employees, given the need for employers also to agree to go to arbitration. See also n. 5 and Lewis (1992: 191–3).
7. The 'at-will' doctrine dates back to a judgement in the Tennessee Supreme Court in 1884. It allows employers to discharge employees, at will, regardless of cause. The doctrine was accepted across all the states until the 1980s when the courts began to develop exceptions including protection against wrongful discharge (Edwards 1993: ch. 7; Edwards 1995: 382–3; Gould 1994: ch. 3).
8. This is part of the argument of Bassett and Cave (1993) which Kelly and Waddington (1995) have subjected to a rigorous critique. See also n. 11.
9. The Rogers and Freeman survey was discussed in detail in Ch. 7. For Britain, the NOP poll showed that 38% of non-union members would like unions

to negotiate on their behalf. This represents one-quarter of the working population and, from the survey, they are mainly young, female, and working for small companies in the private sector (TUC 1996c: 6).

10. For a recent British contribution to the individualism v. collectivism debate see Kessler and Purcell (1995).

11. Kelly and Waddington (1995), following Hofstede (1984) and Triandis (1989; 1993), argue that collectivism and individualism are 'cultural values' and hence subject to gradual change. Hence Bassett's and Cave's analysis would be unable to explain how the rapid growth in British trade union membership up to 1979 became an equally rapid decline thereafter.

12. For a recent, well-written account of the Phelps Dodge strike, see Rosenblum (1995).

13. This historic confrontation has stimulated a substantial literature although in the 1990s its emphasis moved towards the plight of the former mining communities. See e.g. Green (1990); Waddington *et al.* (1991).

14. These disputes are referred to in Ch. 7: n. 17.

15. For the Liverpool dockers' long-running dispute see Saundry and Turnbull (1996).

16. e.g. since its foundation in 1916 the Royal College of Nursing (see Ch. 3: n. 14) has included a commitment, in its rules, to avoid industrial action. In 1983, a proposal to change the rule was defeated by a large majority. In 1995, by an even larger majority, the rule was overturned.

17. There is also the more fundamental right for employees to be able to belong (or not to belong) to an independent trade union, or other organization, without the threat of dismissal, as at GCHQ. The Labour Government has now restored that right. See Ch. 2: n. 5.

18. 'The old approach of trade union immunities as the basis for legislation has gone' (p. 1).

19. See Ch. 8. p. 213.

20. For a recent, authoritative contribution see Kessler and Palmer (1996).

21. The Social Chapter of 1991 is that part of the Maastricht Treaty (Treaty on European Union) which implements the EU's social provisions, increasingly by qualified majority rather than unanimity. The provisions include information and consultation rights for workers but do not include pay, freedom of association, the right to strike or lockout, which are matters for member states.

22. This debate has brought pragmatism and principle into clear conflict. The Labour Party, since 1992, has abandoned its commitment to a formula, i.e. setting a minimum wage initially at half male median earnings rising progressively to two-thirds. Now the policy is to set the level after considering the recommendations of a Low Pay Commission (under its first chairman, Professor George Bain of the London Business School) which will include employers as well as trade unions and 'independents'. Hence it now seems that the minimum will be set much lower than the £4.26 per hour (i.e. half male, manual median earnings) widely advocated in some unions and among Labour Party and union activists and endorsed by a motion at the 1996 Blackpool Congress. For a recent detailed study advocating an initial national minimum of between £3.00 and £3.50, see Philpott (1996). Britain has never had a *national* minimum wage (see Ch. Six: n. 45) unlike the USA

which has increased the level even under Republican presidents. On 1 October 1996 it was raised, after much political bargaining, from $4.25 per hour to $4.75. On 1 September 1997 it will be increased to $5.15 per hour, which is £3.43 assuming a dollar/sterling exchange rate of 1.5. The European Union does not have any minimum wage legislation or even powers to propose it under the Treaties. Most EU members do, however, have provisions of their own establishing minimum pay.

23. However, the Party, in government, has not confirmed its long standing commitment to remove the two-year continuous employment qualifying period before employment rights can be defended at tribunals. The Labour government could, however, introduce a new system of arbitration for unfair dismissal claims (see n. 5 and 6 above). This seems likely given the existing backing of the proposals by the tripartite ACAS Council, which would oversee the new arrangements.

24. The high point was Delors's appearance at the 1988 Trades Union Congress in Bournemouth when his speech was given a standing ovation, a response still rarely accorded to visiting speakers at TUC gatherings. Another recently to receive the accolade was Richard Trumka, the AFL-CIO's Secretary-Treasurer, at the 1996 Congress.

25. 'we must avoid rigidity in labour market regulation and promote the flexibility we require, and . . . the best route to job security in the long term is a highly educated and skilled workforce, able to succeed in the labour market' (Labour Party 1996: 1).

26. Legislation, for example, to impose further controls on strikes, this time specifically aimed at the still highly unionized public sector, was possible should the Conservatives have remained in office. Public sector industrial action, in 'essential services', has of course often attracted the attention of British governments, including Labour. Following the rising trend in public sector strikes during 1995 and 1996 (especially one-day, continuing strikes) the Government began a review of alternative, legislative proposals. These eventually emerged, after protracted political debate in the media in the autumn of 1996, in the form of a consultative 'Green Paper' followed by draft legislation (Department of Trade and Industry 1996a; 1996b). There were four main proposals for legislation: the removal of trade union immunity in industrial action which has 'excessive or disproportionate effects' (p. 7); a doubling of the period of required notice of action from seven to fourteen days; to amend the majority required in an industrial action ballot from those actually voting to those entitled to vote; and to require ballots at least every three months in the case of long-running industrial action, including a succession of one-day strikes.

The Labour Party's contribution to the debate was not consistent but eventually it seemed to favour a voluntary arbitration procedure in public sector disputes but with legally binding awards. The TUC and the unions in the main strongly opposed the Labour Party's proposals and were vehemently against further government legislation, especially in the form proposed. It was also widely believed that defining the 'essential services' coverage of any legislation and the need, for the courts, to determine 'excessive or disproportionate effects' would create major problems.

27. In an interesting article Morand (1994) cites the example of Pennsylvania's own 'Baby Wagner Act', the Pennsylvania Labor Relations Act of 1937. Under the Act, the Pennsylvania Labor Relations Board conducts representation elections within twenty days (thirty for the NLRB) of the filing of petitions and (according to Morand) could authorize union certification by card check. It is also within the powers of the state's General Assembly to prohibit permanent replacement of strikers (ibid. 55–6).

    Generally, 'liberal' states (although Pennsylvania began to turn Republican in 1994 and 1996, including in its choice of Governor) can provide a more helpful executive and legislative climate for labour unions and collective bargaining. This emphasizes the importance of state and locality as well as Washington when analysing 'public policy' influences, in contrast to highly centralized systems such as that of Britain. See also Ch. 2.

28. It perhaps should also be added that the TEAM Act required a presidential veto to keep it off the statute book: i.e. under Republican-controlled Congresses, legislation further weakening collective bargaining remains possible.

29. Or as it was cogently put in a recent report: 'organized labor's clout follows its dwindling membership'. Attributed to the 'New Democrats' within the Democratic Party (Mort 1996).

30. See Ch. 1 for the projected employment data.

31. For a graphic account of the disappearance of blue collar jobs, see Rifkin (1995: especially ch. 9).

32. At the October 1995 Convention John Sweeney, the SEIU President, was elected President of the AFL-CIO with Linda Chavez-Thompson of AFSCME as Vice President (a new post). Richard Trumka of the Mineworkers (UMWA) was elected Secretary-Treasurer. The Executive Council was expanded from thirty-three to fifty-one to increase gender and minority representation.

33. The campaign was inspired by the 1964 'Freedom Summer' when thousands of young students mobilized in the South for civil rights. Union Summer was organized by Richard Bensinger who headed the AFL-CIO's Organizing Institute from its foundation in 1989 until becoming head of the new Organizing Department in 1996. The Institute, now part of the Organizing Department, recruits young people from universities to train as organizers. These work alongside the other rank-and-file union activists in the campaigns. Applications for the 1,000 places for the 1996 campaign were 3,000 of whom 90% were students (Davis 1996: 1; 12).

34. Especially the much written about SEIU's Justice for Janitors campaigns in the Los Angeles building maintenance industry. The SEIU is the union of the AFL-CIO President. For a recent account of a janitors' campaign in the Silicon Valley computer industry, see Cooper (1996).

35. Bronfenbrenner and Juravich (1995), in their analysis of state and local certification elections, conclude:

    In the private sector, the overwhelming majority of employers launch aggressive antiunion campaigns. These include a combination of legal and illegal actions, such as threats, intimidation, financial incentives, promises of improvements, discharges, and surveillance. In the public sector, however, nearly a quarter of the employers do not offer any opposition to union organizing campaigns, and most opposition that does occur is limited to a few legal actions of extremely low intensity. (p. 121)

36. At the time of going to press the much-delayed White Paper on the Government's proposed industrial relations reforms was delayed further, though promised for Spring 1998. The employers had also overwhelmingly declard their opposition to statutory recognition.

37. The big five are: UNISON (formed from a recent merger of three unions with substantial public sector membership); TGWU (Transport and General Workers' Union); AEEU (the product of a merger between the engineering (i.e. metalworking) workers' union and the electricians); GMB (the product of many mergers over its history); MSF (formed from a merger between two unions with members mainly among managers, supervisors, scientific workers, draughtsmen, and technicians). In 1996 their membership levels were: UNISON 1,300,000; TGWU 896,800; AEEU 764,700; GMB 718,000; MSF 452,000 (IRS 1996: 605: 4).

38. Large-scale survey research by British academics Waddington and Whitston found that 30.9% approached unions themselves with an additional 29.7% through shop stewards (cited in IRS 1996: 605, 4).

39. The TUC has however always been pragmatic about which party is in power. It sought to cooperate with postwar Conservative governments and has had famous rows with Labour governments over trade union reform and prices and incomes policies. The Conservative governments after 1979 were wholly different to their Conservative predecessors. They were almost uniformly hostile to the TUC and progressively dismantled the tripartite bodies on which it was customarily represented. Yet John Monks, in the 1990s, has had consultations with the Liberal Democrats and, for a brief period developed a good rapport with Sir David Hunt, the former Conservative Cabinet minister, during the latter's brief tenure at the Department of Employment. The TUC does of course need to allow for the Labour Party not being in government and the everyday business of the unions goes on whichever party is in power.

40. Notably the GMB and most recently the TGWU, through its General Secretary (Bill Morris), the union aiming 'to work hand-in-hand with employers to build a modern, productive, competitive economy in Britain' (Taylor 1996*a*).

41. For the USA, the appointment, hearings, and recommendations of the Dunlop Commission stimulated debate and, eventually, disappointment among those who saw the need for reform as an urgent and timely task. An early, comprehensive contribution to the reform debate saw a return to the spirit and 'promise' of Wagner as the route to follow, with a 'clear preference of the editors and of the vast preponderance of the authors . . . to find a means of strengthening the law so as to extend collective bargaining in the U.S. economy' (Friedman *et al.* 1994: 4).

For Britain, an equally comprehensive exercise was carried out in 1995–6 by a group of academics, labour lawyers, and trade unionists for a labour movement 'think tank', the Institute of Employment Rights. The outcome was published in 1996 (Ewing *et al.* 1996). It adopted a similar approach to the US study: 'A strong and vibrant trade union movement is a precondition of a free and democratic society. So too is a comprehensive framework of statutory rights promoting equality of opportunity, social justice and fairness at work' (p. xv).

APPENDIX 1

British Governments since 1945

Years	Prime Minister	Governing Party	House of Commons Majority When Elected
1945–50	Clement Attlee	Labour	146
1950–1	Clement Attlee	Labour	5
1951–5	Winston Churchill Anthony Eden (Apr. 1955)	Conservative	17
1955–9	Anthony Eden Harold Macmillan (Jan. 1957)	Conservative	60
1959–64	Harold Macmillan Alec Douglas-Home (Oct. 1963)	Conservative	100
1964–6	Harold Wilson	Labour	4
1966–70	Harold Wilson	Labour	96
1970–4	Edward Heath	Conservative	30
1974–9	Harold Wilson James Callaghan (Apr. 1976)	Labour	3*
1979–83	Margaret Thatcher	Conservative	43
1983–7	Margaret Thatcher	Conservative	144
1987–92	Margaret Thatcher John Major (Nov. 1990)	Conservative	100
1992–97	John Major	Conservative	21
1997–	Tony Blair	Labour	179

Note:* In the February 1974 General Election Labour was the largest party but fell short of an overall majority by 33 seats. In a second election of October 1974 the Labour Party's overall majority was 3.

Source: For 1945–50 to 1992–97 Kessler and Bayliss (1995: appendix 1 (slightly adapted)).

APPENDIX 2

American Governments Since 1945

Years	Congress	President	President's Party	Majority Parties in Congress	
				House	Senate
1945–7	79	Harry S. Truman	Democrat	Democrat (242–190)	Democrat (56–38)
1947–9	80	Harry S. Truman	Democrat	Republican (245–188)	Republican (51–45)
1949–51	81	Harry S. Truman	Democrat	Democrat (263–171)	Democrat 54–42)
1951–3	82	Harry S. Truman	Democrat	Democrat (234–199)	Democrat (49–47)
1953–5	83	Dwight D. Eisenhower	Republican	Republican (221–211)	Republican (48–47)
1955–7	84	Dwight D. Eisenhower	Republican	Democrat (232–203)	Democrat (48–47)
1957–9	85	Dwight D. Eisenhower	Republican	Democrat (233–200)	Democrat (49–47)
1959–61	86	Dwight D. Eisenhower	Republican	Democrat (283–153)	Democrat (64–34)
1961–3	87	John F. Kennedy	Democrat	Democrat (263–174)	Democrat (65–35)
1963–5	88	John F. Kennedy Lyndon B. Johnson (22 Nov. 1963)	Democrat	Democrat (258–177)	Democrat (67–33)
1965–7	89	Lyndon B. Johnson	Democrat	Democrat (295–140)	Democrat (68–32)
1967–9	90	Lyndon B. Johnson	Democrat	Democrat (247–187)	Democrat (64–36)
1969–71	91	Richard Nixon	Republican	Democrat (243–192)	Democrat (57–43)
1971–3	92	Richard Nixon	Republican	Democrat (254–180)	Democrat (54–44)
1973–5	93	Richard Nixon Gerald R. Ford (9 Aug. 1974)	Republican	Democrat (239–192)	Democrat (56–42)
1975–7	94	Gerald R. Ford	Republican	Democrat (291–144)	Democrat (60–37)
1977–9	95	Jimmy Carter	Democrat	Democrat (292–143)	Democrat (61–38)

Years	Congress	President	President's Party	Majority Parties in Congress	
				House	Senate
1979–81	96	Jimmy Carter	Democrat	Democrat (276–157)	Democrat (58–41)
1981–3	97	Ronald Reagan	Republican	Democrat (243–192)	Republican (53–46)
1983–5	98	Ronald Reagan	Republican	Democrat (269–165)	Republican (54–46)
1985–7	99	Ronald Reagan	Republican	Democrat (252–182)	Republican (53–47)
1987–9	100	Ronald Reagan	Republican	Democrat (258–177)	Democrat (55–45)
1989–91	101	George Bush	Republican	Democrat (259–174)	Democrat (55–45)
1991–3	102	George Bush	Republican	Democrat (267–167)	Democrat (56–44)
1993–5	103	Bill Clinton	Democrat	Democrat (258–176)	Democrat (57–43)
1995–7	104	Bill Clinton	Democrat	Republican (236–197)	Republican (53–46)
1997–9	105	Bill Clinton	Democrat	Republican (227–207)*	Republican (55–45)

Note: * 1 independent.

Source: *Congress A to Z* (1993: 468–72); *Congressional and Administrative News* (1996); US Information Service, London.

References

ACAS (1987), *Annual Report 1986*, London: Advisory Conciliation and Arbitration Service.

—— (1996), *Annual Report, 1995*, London: Advisory, Conciliation and Arbitration Service.

Adams, Larry (1993), *Time for a Change: Forging Labour-Management Partnerships*, Occasional Paper No. 52, London: Advisory, Conciliation and Arbitration Service.

Adams, Roy J. (1995), *Industrial Relations Under Liberal Democracy: North America in Comparative Perspective*, Columbia, SC: University of South Carolina Press.

—— and Rummel, C. H. (1977), 'Workers' Participation in Management in West Germany: Impact on the Worker, the Enterprise and the Trade Union', *Industrial Relations Journal*, 8/1: 4–11.

—— and Turner, Lowell (1994), 'The Social Dimension of Freer Trade', in Cook, Maria Lorena, and Katz, Harry C. (eds.), *Regional Integration and Industrial Relations in North America*, Ithaca, NY: Cornell University Press.

Addison, J. T., and Barnet, A. H. (1982), 'The Impact of Unions on Productivity', *British Journal of Industrial Relations*, 20/2: 145–62.

—— Kraft, Cornelius, and Wagner, J. (1993), 'German Works Councils and Firm Performance', in Kaufman, Bruce E., and Kleiner, Morris M. (eds.), *Employee Representation: Alternatives and Future Directions*, Madison: Industrial Relations Research Association.

—— and Siebert, W. Stanley (1994), 'Recent Developments in Social Policy in the New European Union', *Industrial and Labor Relations Review*, 48/1 (October), 5–27.

Adeney, Martin, and Lloyd, John (1986), *The Miners' Strike 1984–85: Loss Without Limit*, London: Routledge & Kegan Paul.

Adler, Paul (1994), 'Worker Responses to New Wave Manufacturing', in Storey, John (ed.), *New Wave Manufacturing Strategies*, London: Chapman.

AFL-CIO (1985), 'Committee on the Evolution of Work', *The Changing Situation of Workers and their Unions*, Washington DC: AFL-CIO.

—— (1994a), 'AFL-CIO Calls for Minority Form of Representation', *AFL-CIO News*, 39/18: 1–2.

—— (1994b), *The New American Workplace: A Labor Perspective*, A report by the AFL-CIO Committee on the Evolution of Work, Washington DC: AFL-CIO.

—— (1995), 'Campaign Cripples Company Union Bill', *AFL-CIO News*, 40/21: 1, 3.

Appelbaum, Eileen, and Batt, Rosemary (1994), *The New American Workplace: Transforming Work Systems in the United States*, Ithaca, NY: ILR Press.

Armstrong, Eric G. A. (1973), *Straitjacket or Framework? The Implications for Management of the Industrial Relations Act*, London: Business Books.

Aronowitz, S. (1973), *False Promises: The Shaping of American Working Class Consciousness*, New York: McGraw-Hill.

Aston, B., Morris, T., and Willman, P. (1990), 'Still Balancing the Books: The NUM and the 1984–85 Strike', *Industrial Relations Journal*, 21/3: 173–85.

Babson, Steve (ed.) (1995), *Lean Work: Empowerment and Exploitation in the Global Auto Industry*, Detroit: Wayne State University Press.

Baillie, John (1995), *Employment Attitudes in Britain: The 1995 IPD Employee Attitude Benchmark Survey*, London: Institute of Personnel and Development.

Bain, George Sayers, and Price, Robert (1983), 'Union Growth: Dimensions, Determinants and Destiny', in Bain, G. S. (ed.), *Industrial Relations in Britain*, Oxford: Blackwell.

—— (1987), 'End of Union Decline Foreseen', *Financial Times*, 2 October.

Ballot, Michael, Lichter-Heath, L., Kail, T., and Wang, R. (1996), *Labor-Management Relations in a Changing Environment*; 2nd edn., New York: Wiley.

Bamber, Greg J., and Lansbury, Russell D. (1993), *International and Comparative Industrial Relations: A study of Industrialised Market Economies*, 2nd edn., London: Routledge.

Barrett, Martin, and Heery, Edmund (1995), ' "It's good to talk"? The Reform of Joint Consultation in British Telecom', *Industrial Relations Journal*, 26/1: 57–64.

Barrie, Chris (1996), 'BMW Calms Fears over Rover Losses', The *Guardian*, 14 August, p. 18.

Bassett, Philip (1986), *Strike Free*, London: Macmillan.

—— (1995), 'Flexibility faces Jobs Test', London, *Financial Times*, 13 February, p. 42.

—— and Cave, A. (1993), *All for One: The Future of the Unions*, Fabian Pamphlet No. 559, London: The Fabian Society.

Batstone, Eric, Boraston, Ian, and Frenkel, Stephen (1977), *Shop Stewards in Action: The Organization of Workplace Conflict and Accommodation*, Oxford: Blackwell.

Bean, Ron (1994), *Comparative Industrial Relations: An Introduction to Cross-National Perspectives*, 2nd edn., London: Routledge.

Beatston, Mark (1995*a*), *Labour Market Flexibility*, Research Series, London, Department of Employment.

—— (1995*b*), 'Progress towards a Flexible Labour Market', *Employment Gazette*, 103/2 (February), 55–66, London: Department of Employment.

—— and Butcher, Shaun (1993), 'Union Density across the Employed Workforce', *Employment Gazette*, 101/1 (January), 673–89, London: Department of Employment.

Beaumont, P. B. (1992), *Public Sector Industrial Relations*, London and New York: Routledge.

—— (1995), *The Future of Employment Relations*, London: Sage.

—— and Harris, Richard (1990), 'Union Recruitment and Organising Attempts in Britain in the 1990s', *Industrial Relations Journal*, 21/4: 274–86.

—— —— (1995*a*), 'Union De-Recognition and Declining Union Density in Britain', *Industrial and Labor Relations Review*, 48/3: 389–402.

—— —— (1995*b*), 'Good Industrial Relations, Joint Problem Solving and HRM: Issues and Implications', paper presented at the International Industrial Relations Association, Washington DC.

—— and Towers, B. (1992), 'Approaches to Trade Union Recognition', in Towers, B. (ed.), *A Handbook of Industrial Relations Practice*, 123–36, London: Kogan Page.

Bélanger, Jacques, Edwards, P. K., and Haiven, Larry (eds.) (1994), *Workplace Industrial Relations and the Global Challenge*, Ithaca, NY: ILR Press.

Bellah, Robert N., Madsen, Richard, Sullivan, William M., Swidler, Ann, and Tipton, Steven M. (1985), *Habits of the Heart: Individualism and Commitment in American Life*, Berkeley and Los Angeles: University of California Press.

Belman, D. (1992), 'Unions, the Quality of Labor Relations and Firm Performance', in Mishel and Voos (1992).

Bennett, James T. (1991), 'Private Sector Unions: The Myth of Decline', *Journal of Labor Research*, 12/1: 1–12.

Benson, J. (1994), 'The Economic Effects of Unionism on Japanese Manufacturing Enterprises', *British Journal of Industrial Relations*, 32/1: 1–21.

Bercusson, Brian (1993), 'Employment Protection and Labor Relations: The Regulatory Model of Job Security in the United Kingdom', in Buechtemann (1993), 305–19.

Berggren, Christian (1992), *The Volvo Experience: Alternatives to Lean Production in the Swedish Auto Industry*, Basingstoke: Macmillan.

Beynon, Hugh (ed.) (1985), *Digging Deeper: Issues in the Miners' Strike*, London: Verso.

Bird, Derek (1994), 'International Comparisons of Labour Disputes in 1993', *Employment Gazette*, 10/12 (December), 433–9, London: Department of Employment.

—— and Corcoran, Louise (1994), 'Trade Union Membership and Density, 1992–93', *Employment Gazette*, 102/6 (June), 189–98, London: Department of Employment.

Blank, Rebecca (ed.) (1994), *Social Protection versus Economic Flexibility: Is There a Trade-Off?* Chicago and London: University of Chicago Press.

Blanchflower, D. G., and Freeman, R. B. (1990), *Going Different Ways: Unionism in the US and Other Advanced OECD Countries*, p. 9, Working Paper Series No. 3342, Washington DC: National Bureau of Economic Research. Cited in Gould (1994), 4.

Bluestone, Barry, and Bluestone, Irving (1992), *Negotiating the Future: A Labor Perspective on American Business*, New York: Basic Books.

—— and Harrison, Bennett (1982), *The Deindustrialization of America*, New York: Basic Books.

Blyton, Paul, and Morris, Jonathan (1992), 'HRM and the Limits of Flexibility', in Blyton, Paul, and Turnbull, Peter (eds.), *Reassessing Human Resource Management*, 116–30, London: Sage.

—— and Turnbull, Peter (eds.) (1992), *Reassessing Human Resource Management*, London: Sage.

Brannen, P. (1983), *Authority and Participation in Industry*, London: Batsford.

Bridgford, Jeff, and Stirling, John (1994), *Employee Relations in Europe*, Oxford: Blackwell.

British Journal of Industrial Relations (1993), Special Edition, Workplace Industrial Relations Survey 3, and Debate, 31/2: 169–283; 293–308.

Brody, David (1992), 'The Breakdown of Labor's Social Contract', in Mills, N. (ed.), 'Labor's Future?' *Dissent*, Winter, 32–41.

—— (1993), 'Workplace Contractualism in Comparative Perspective', in Lichtenstein, Nelson, and Harris, Howell John (eds.), *Industrial Democracy in America: The Ambiguous Promise*, Cambridge: Cambridge University Press.

Bronfenbrenner, Kate L. (1994), 'Employer Behaviour in Certification Elections and First Contract Campaigns: Implications for Labor Law Reform', in Friedman *et al.* (1994).

—— and Juravich, Tom (1995), *Union Organizing in the Public Sector: An Analysis of State and Local Elections*, Ithaca, NY and London: Cornell University Press.

Brown, William (1994), 'The Consequences of Dismantling British Collective Bargaining', *Review of Employment Topics*, 2: 1–11, Belfast: Labour Relations Agency.

—— and Rea, David (1995), 'The Changing Nature of the Employment Contract', *Scottish Journal of Political Economy*, 42/3: 363–77.

Buchanan, R. T. (1992), 'Measuring Mergers and Concentration in UK Trade Unions, 1910–1988', *Industrial Relations Journal*, 23/4: 304–14.

Buechtemann, Christoph F. (ed.) (1993), *Employment Security and Labour Market Behaviour: Interdisciplinary Approaches and International Evidence*, Ithaca, NY: ILR Press.

—— and Soloff, Dana (1994), 'Education, Training and the Economy', *Industrial Relations Journal*, 25/3: 234–46.

CAB (1993), *Job Insecurity: CAB Evidence on Employment Problems in the Recession*, London: National Association of Citizens' Advice Bureaux.

Cairncross, Alec (1985), *Years of Recovery: British Economic Policy 1945–51*, London and New York: Methuen.

Callus, R., Morehead, A., Cully, M., and Buchanan, J. (1991), *Industrial Relations at Work*, Canberra: AGPS.

Castells, M., and Aoyama, Y. (1993), *Paths towards the Informational Society: A Comparative Analysis of the Transformation of Employment Structure in the G7 Countries, 1920–2005* BRIE Working Paper No. 61, Berkeley Roundtable on the International Economy, Berkeley: University of California.

—— —— (1994), 'Paths towards the Informational Society: Employment Structure in G7 Countries, 1920–90', *International Labour Review*, 133/1: 5–33.

Caves, R. E. and Associates (1968), *Britain's Economic Performance*, Washington DC: Brookings Institution.

Certification Officer (1981–96), *Annual Reports 1980–95*, London, Certification Office for Trade Unions and Employers' Associations.

Chaison, Gary N., and Rose, Joseph B. (1991), 'The Macrodeterminants of Union Growth and Decline', in Strauss, George, Gallagher, Daniel G., and Fiorito, Jack (eds.), *The State of the Unions*, Madison: Industrial Relations Research Association.

Chang, C., and Sorrentino, C. (1991), *Monthly Labor Review*, 114/12 (December), Washington: Department of Labor.

Clark, Gordon L. (1989), *Unions and Communities Under Siege: American Communities and the Crisis of Organized Labour*, Cambridge: Cambridge University Press.

Clark, S., and Winchester, D. (1994), 'Management and Trade Unions', in Sisson (1994), 694–723.

Clegg, Hugh (1960), *A New Approach to Industrial Democracy*, Oxford: Blackwell.

—— (1972), 'Living with the Act', *Socialist Commentary* May, 6–9, London.

—— (1978), *Trade Unionism under Collective Bargaining: A Theory based on Comparisons of Six Countries*, Oxford: Blackwell.

—— Fox, Alan, and Thompson, A. F. (1964), *A History of British Trade Unions since 1889, Vol 1, 1889–1910*, Oxford: Oxford University Press.

Coates, David, and Hillard, John (eds.) (1986), *The Economic Decline of Modern Britain: The Debate between Left and Right*, Brighton: Wheatsheaf Press.

Coates, Ken, and Topham, Tony (1970), *Workers' Control*, London: Panther.

Cobble, Dorothy Sue (1994), 'Making Postindustrial Unionism Possible', in Friedman, *et al.* (1994).

Commission on the Future of Worker-Management Relations (May 1994), *Fact-Finding Report*, Washington DC: Departments of Labor and Commerce.

—— (December 1994), *Report and Recommendations*, Washington DC: Departments of Labor and Commerce.

Committee of Inquiry on Industrial Democracy (1977), *Report*, Department of Trade, London: HMSO, Cmnd. 6706.

Congress A to Z (1993) 2nd edn., Washington DC: Congress Quarterly Inc.

Congressional and Administrative News (1996), 104th Congress, First Session, St Paul, Minn.: West Publishing Co.

Conservative Political Centre (1968), *Fair Deal at Work*, London: Conservative Political Centre.

Cooper, Marc (1996), 'Class.War @ Silicon.Valley: Disposable Workers in the New Economy', *The Nation*, 27 May, 11–16.

Corcoran, Louise (1995), 'Trade Union Membership and Recognition: 1994 Labour Force Survey Data', *Employment Gazette*, 103/5 (May), 191–203, London: Department of Employment.

—— and Wareing, Andrew (1994), 'Trade Union Recognition Data from the 1993 Labour Force Survey', *Employment Gazette*, 102/12 (December), 441–51, London: Department of Employment.

Cressey, Peter (1993*a*), 'Employee Participation', in Gold (1993).

—— (1993*b*), 'Kalmar and Uddevalla: The demise of Volvo as a European Icon', *New Technology, Work and Employment*, 8/2: 88–90.

Crouch, Colin (1994), 'Beyond Corporatism: The Impact of Company Strategy', in Hyman and Ferner (1994), 196–222.

Cullen, Donald E. (1987), 'Recent Trends in Collective Bargaining in the United States', in Windmuller, John P. *et al.*, *Collective Bargaining in Industrialised Market Economies: A Reappraisal*, Geneva: International Labour Organisation.

Cully, Mark, and Woodland, Stephen (1996), 'Trade Union Membership and Recognition: An Analysis of Data from the 1995 Labour Force Survey', *Labour Market Trends*, 104/5 (May), 215–25.

—— (1997), 'Trade Union Membership and Recognition', Labour Market Trends, 105/6 (June), 231–240.

Curme, Michael A., Hirsch, Barry T., and Macpherson, David A. (1990), 'Union Membership and Contract Coverage in the United States', *Industrial and Labor Relations Review*, 44/1, 5–33.

Daniel, W. W. (1987), *Workplace Industrial Relations and Technical Change*, London: Frances Pinter and Policy Studies Institute.

Davies, P. (1980), 'How to Make the Unions feel Insecure', *New Society*, 7 August, 267–8.

Davis, Russ (1996), 'Union Summer Welcomes Students to Labor Activism', *Labor Notes*, 208: 1; 12.

Dean, Edwin R., and Sherwood, Mark K. (1994), 'Manufacturing Costs, Productivity and Competitiveness, 1979–93', *Monthly Labor Review* (October), 3–16, Washington DC: Department of Labor.

Deery, Stephen J., and Mitchell, Richard J. (1993), *Labour Law and Industrial Relations in Asia: Eight Country Studies*, Melbourne: Longman.

Delaney, John Thomas, and Masters, Marrick F. (1991), 'Unions and Political Action', in Strauss, G., Gallagher, Daniel G., and Fiorito, Jack (eds.), *The State of the Unions*, Madison: Industrial Relations Research Association.

Department of Employment (1988), *Employment for the 1990s*, Cm 540, London: HMSO.

Department of Employment and Productivity (1969), *In Place of Strife*, Cmnd. 3888, London: HMSO.

Department of Labor (1991), *Labor Management Commitment—A Compact for Change*, Washington DC: Department of Labor.

Department of Trade and Industry (1996a), *Industrial Action and Trade Unions*, Cm 3470, London: HMSO.

—— (1996b), *Resolving Employment Rights Disputes: Draft Legislation for Consultation*, London: Department of Trade and Industry.

Dickens, Linda (1985), *Dismissed: A Study of Unfair Dismissal and the Industrial Tribunal System*, Oxford: Blackwell.

—— (1992), 'Anti-discrimination Legislation: Exploring and Explaining the Impact on Women's Employment', in McCarthy, William (ed.), *Legal Intervention in Industrial Relations*, 103–46, Oxford: Basil Blackwell.

Dickson, M., and Tait, N. (1993), 'Optimistic State of the Unions', *Financial Times*, 15 February.

Disney, Richard (1990), 'Explanations of the Decline in Trade Union Density in Britain: An Appraisal', *British Journal of Industrial Relations*, 28/2: 165–76.

Doeringer, Peter B. *et al.* (1991), *Turbulence in the American Workplace*, New York: Oxford University Press.

Drago, Robert (1988), 'Quality Circle Survival: An Explanatory Analysis', *Industrial Relations*, 27/3: 336–51.

Dubofsky, Melvyn (1994), *The State and Labor in Modern America*, Chapel Hill, NC and London: University of North Carolina Press.

Dunlop, John T. (1993), *Industrial Relations Systems*, revised edn., Boston: Harvard University Press.

Dunn, Stephen (1993), 'From Donovan to . . . Wherever', *British Journal of Industrial Relations*, 31/2: 169–87.

Durcan, J. W., McCarthy, W. E. J., and Redman, G. P. (1983), *Strikes in Post-War Britain: A Study of Stoppages of Work due to Industrial Disputes, 1946–73*, London: Allen & Unwin.

Eaton, Adrienne E. (1994), 'Factors Contributing to the Survival of Employee Participation Programmes in Unionized Settings', *Industrial and Labor Relations Review*, 47/3: 371–89.

—— and Voos, Paula B. (1992), 'Unions and Contemporary Innovations in Work Organization, Compensation and Employee Participation', in Mishel and Voos (1992).

Economic Notes (1994), 62/9, New York: Labor Research Association.

Edwards, P. K. (1983), 'The Pattern of Collective Industrial Action', in Bain, G. S. (ed.), *Industrial Relations In Britain*, Oxford: Blackwell.

—— (ed.) (1995), *Industrial Relations: Theory and Practice in Britain*, Oxford: Blackwell.

Edwards, Richard (1993), *Rights at Work: Employment Relations in the Post-Union Era*, Washington DC: Brookings Institution.

—— (1995), 'New Prospects for American Labor: A Proposal', *Organization*, 2/3–4: 375–91.

EI Du Pont de Nemours Co. v. *Chemical Workers' Association* (1993), 311, NLRB Nos. 88, 143.

EIRR (1994), 'First European Committee in US-Based Multinational', *European Industrial Relations Review*, 248 (September), London: IRS.

Electromation Inc. v. *Teamsters Local 1049* (1992), 309, NLRB Nos. 163, 142.

Elgar, Jane, and Simpson, Bob (1993), 'Union Negotiators, Industrial Action and the Law', reported in *Industrial Relations Review and Report*, 547 (November), 3, London: IRS.

Employment Committee (1994*a*), *The Future of Trade Unions*, i, Third Report, Report and Proceedings of the Committee, House of Commons HC 676–1, 18 October, London: HMSO.

Employment Committee (1994*b*), *The Future of Trade Unions*, ii, Third Report, Minutes of Evidence, 18 October, HC 67611, London: HMSO.

Employment Committee (1994*c*), *The Future of Trade Unions*, iii, Third Report, Appendices to the Minutes of Evidence, House of Commons HC 676–111, 18 October, London: HMSO.

Employment Gazette (January 1983), 91/1, London: Department of Employment.

—— (July 1994), 102/7, London: Department of Employment.

—— (October 1994), Historical Supplement No. 4: Employment Statistics, 102/10, London: Government Statistical Service.

—— (November 1994), 102/11, London: Department of Employment.

—— (January 1995), 103/1, London: Government Statistical Service.

Employment Outlook (1994), Paris: OECD.

Employment Policy (1944), Cmnd. 6527, London: HMSO.

Evans, S. (1987), 'The Use of Injunctions in Industrial Disputes, May 1984–April 1987', *British Journal of Industrial Relations*, 25/3 (November), 419–35.

Ewing, K. D., Hendy, J., and Jones, C. (1996), 'Preface' in Ewing, Keith (ed.), *Working Life: A New Perspective on Labour Law*, London: Institute of Employment Rights, Lawrence and Wishart.

Farber, Henry S., and Krueger, Alan B. (1993), 'Union Membership in the United States: The Decline Continues', in Kaufman, Bruce E., and Kleiner, Morris M. (eds.), *Employee Representation: Alternatives and Future Directions*, Wisconsin: IRRA.

Fatchett, Derek (1987), *Trade Unions and Politics in the 1980s*, London: Croom Helm.

Ferner, A., and Hyman, R. (eds.) (1992), *Industrial Relations in the New Europe*, Oxford: Blackwell.

Fine, Sidney (1969), *Sit-Down: The General Motors Strike of 1936–1937*, Ann Arbor: University of Michigan Press.

Fisher, John (1995), 'The Trade Union Response to HRM in the UK: The Case of the TGWU', *Human Resource Management Journal*, 5/3: 7–23.

Flanders, A. (1970), *Management and Unions*, London: Faber and Faber. Cited in McCarthy, W. E. J. (ed.), *Trade Unions: Selected Readings*, Harmondsworth: Penguin.

Flanders, Stephanie (1996), 'Life, Jobs and the Safety Zone', *Financial Times*, 29 April, p. 19.

Forbath, William (1992), 'Law and the Shaping of Labor Politics', in Tomlins, Christopher L., and King, Andrew J. (eds.), *Labor Law in America: Historical and Critical Essays*, 201–30, Baltimore: Johns Hopkins University Press.

Fossum, John A. (1995), *Labor Relations: Development, Structure, Process*, Chicago: Irwin.

Foster, John, and Woolfson, Charles (1986), *The Politics of the UCS Work-In*, London: Lawrence and Wishart.

Fox, Alan (1985), *History and Heritage: The Social Origins of the British Industrial Relations System*, London: Allen & Unwin.

Franklin, James C. (1993), 'The American Work Force: 1992–2005: Industry output and employment', *Monthly Labor Review*, November, 41–57, Washington DC: Department of Labor.

Freedland, M. R. (1992), 'The Role of the Department of Employment—Twenty Years of Institutional Change', in McCarthy, William (ed.), *Legal Intervention in Industrial Relations: Gains and Losses*, Oxford: Blackwell.

Freeman, Richard B. (1989), 'The Changing State of Unionism Round the World: Some Emerging Patterns', in We-Chiao Huang (ed.), *Organized Labor at the Crossroads*, Kalamazoo: Upjohn Institute.

—— (ed.) (1994*a*), *Working Under Different Rules*, New York: Russell Sage.

—— (1994*b*), 'Lessons for the United States', in Freeman (1994*a*).

—— (1994*c*), 'How Labor Fares in Advanced Economies', in Freeman (1994*a*).

—— (1995*a*), 'The Future for Unions in Decentralized Collective Bargaining Systems: US and UK Unionism in an Era of Crisis', *British Journal of Industrial Relations*, 33/4: 519–36.

—— (1995*b*), 'Will the Union Phoenix Rise Again . . . in the UK or the US?' *Scottish Journal of Political Economy*, 42/3: 347–62.

—— and Medoff, James L. (1984), *What Do Unions Do?* New York: Basic Books.

—— and Pelletier, Jeffrey (1990), 'The Impact of Industrial Relations Legislation on Union Density', *British Journal of Industrial Relations*, 28/2: 141–64.

—— and Rogers, Joel (1993), 'Who Speaks for US? Employee Representation in a Non-union Labor Market', in Kaufman, Bruce E., and Kleiner, Morris, M. (eds.), *Employee Representation: Alternatives and Future Directions*, Madison: Industrial Relations Research Association.

—— —— (1994), *Worker Representation and Participation Survey: Report on the Findings*, Princeton: Princeton Survey Research Associates.

Friedman, Sheldon, Hurd, Richard W., Oswald, Rudolph A., and Seeber, Ronald L. (eds.) (1994), *Restoring the Promise of American Labor Law*, Ithaca, NY: ILR Press.

Fullerton, Howard N. Jr. (1993), 'The American Workforce 1992–2005. Another Look at the Labor Force', *Monthly Labor Review*, 116/11 (November), 31–40, Washington, Bureau of Labor Statistics.

Galenson, Walter (1986), 'The Historical Role of American Trade Unionism', in Lipset, Seymour Martin (ed.), *Unions in Transition: Entering the Second Century*, San Francisco: ICS Press.

Gall, Gregor, and McKay, Sonia (1994), 'Trade Union Derecognition in Britain, 1988–1994', *British Journal of Industrial Relations*, 32/3: 433–48.

Gamble, A. (1981), *Britain in Decline*, London: Macmillan.

Garrahan, Philip, and Stewart, Paul (1992), *The Nissan Enigma: Flexibility at Work in a Local Economy*, London: Mansell.

Geoghegan, T. (1991), *Which Side are you on? Trying to be for Labor when it's Flat on its Back*, New York: Farrar, Strauss and Giroux.

Gershenfeld, Walter, J. (1987), 'Employee Participation in Firm Decisions', in Kleiner *et al.* (eds.), *Human Resources and the Performance of the Firm*, Madison: Industrial Relations Research Association.

Ghilarducci, T. (1985), 'Freeman and Medoff, What Do Unions Do?' *Journal of Legislation*, 12/1: 119–21.

—— (1986), 'When Management Strikes: PATCO and the British Miners', *Industrial Relations Journal*, 17/2: 115–28.

Gifford, Courtney D. (1994), *Directory of U.S. Labor Organizations 1994–95*, Washington: Bureau of National Affairs.

Gill, Colin (1992), 'British Industrial Relations and the European Community', in Towers, B. (ed.), *A Handbook of Industrial Relations Practice*, London: Kogan Page.

Gilmour, Ian (1992), *Dancing with Dogma*, London: Simon and Schuster.

—— (1983), *Britain Can Work*, Oxford: Martin Robertson.

GMB and UCW (1990), *The New Agenda*, London: GMB/UCW.

Gold, Michael (ed.) (1993), *The Social Dimension: Employment Policy in the European Community*, Basingstoke: Macmillan.

—— and Hall, Mark (1990), *Legal Regulation and the Practice of Employee Participation in the European Community*, Dublin: European Foundation for the Improvement of Living and Working Conditions.

—— —— (1994), 'Statutory European Works Councils: The Final Countdown', *Industrial Relations Journal*, 25/3: 177–86.

Goldfield, Michael (1987), *The Decline of Organized Labor in the United States*, Chicago and London: University of Chicago Press.

Goodhart, David (1994), *The Reshaping of the German Social Market*, London: Institute for Public Policy Research.

Goodman, J. F. B., and Whittingham, T. G. (1973), *Shop Stewards*, London: Pan.

Gould, William B. IV (1994), *Agenda for Reform: The Future of Employment Relationships and the Law*, Cambridge, Mass.: MIT Press.

Green, Francis (1992), 'Recent Trends in British Trade Union Density: How Much of a Compositional Effect?' *British Journal of Industrial Relations*, 30/3: 445–58.

Green, Penny (1990), *The Enemy Without: Policing and Class Consciousness in the Miners' Strike*, Milton Keynes and Philadelphia: Open University Press.

Griffith, J. A. G. (1981), *The Politics of the Judiciary*, London: Fontana.

Griffiths, John (1996), 'Rover Output Surges after Export Drive', *Financial Times*, 26 January.

Guest, D. (1987), 'Human Resource Management and Industrial Relations', *Journal of Management Studies*, 24/5: 503–21.

Hakim, C. (1987), 'Trends in the Flexible Workforce', *Employment Gazette*, 95/11 (November), 549–60, London: Department of Employment.

Hall, Mark (1994), 'Industrial Relations and the Social Dimension of European Integration: Before and After Maastricht', in Hyman and Ferner (1994).

—— (1996), 'Beyond Recognition: Employee Representation and EU Law', *Industrial Law Journal*, 25/1: 15–27.

Hall, Mark, Carley, Mark, Gold, Michael, Marginson, Paul, and Sisson, Keith (1995), *European Works Councils: Planning for the Directive*, London: Industrial Relations Services.

Hashimoto, Masanori (1990), *The Japanese Labor Market in a Comparative Perspective with the United States: A Transaction-Cost Interpretation*, Kalamazoo: Upjohn Institute.

Heckscher, Charles C. (1988), *The New Unionism: Employee Involvement in the Changing Corporation*, New York: Basic Books.

—— and Schurman, Sue (forthcoming), 'The Limits of Intervention: Labor-Management Programs at a Crossroads', *Industrial Relations Journal* (1997), 28/4.

Hepple, B. A. (1992), 'The Fall and Rise of Unfair Dismissal', in McCarthy, William (ed.), *Legal Intervention in Industrial Relations*, 79–102, Oxford: Blackwell.

Hill, S. (1991), 'Why Quality Circles Failed but Total Quality Management might Succeed', *British Journal of Industrial Relations*, 29/4: 541–68.

Hirsch, Barry T. (1991), *Labor Unions and the Economic Performance of Firms*, Kalamazoo: Upjohn Institute.

—— and Macpherson, David A. (1994), *Union Membership and Earnings Data Book*, Washington: Bureau of National Affairs.

—— —— (1996), *Union Membership and Earnings Data Book*, 2nd edn., Washington: Bureau of National Affairs.

Hobsbawm, E. J. (1968), *Industry and Empire*, New York: Pantheon Books.

—— (1981), chapter 1 in Jacques, Martin, and Mulhern, Francis (eds.), *The Forward March of Labour Halted*, 1–19, London: Verso.

Hofstede, G. (1984), *Culture's Consequences*, London: Sage.

Hudson, Alan, Heyes, Dennis, and Andrew, Toby (1996), *Working Lives in the 1990s: The Provisional Findings of the Attitudes to Work Survey*, London: Global Futures.

Hughes, Amanda (1996), 'Employment in the Public and Private Sectors', *Labour Market Trends*, 104/8 (August), 337–80, London: Office for National Statistics.

Hughes, James J. (1984), *The Economics of Unemployment: A Comparative Analysis of Britain and the United States*, Brighton: Wheatsheaf.

Hyman, R., and Ferner, A. (eds.) (1994), *New Frontiers in European Industrial Relations*, Oxford: Blackwell.

IDS (1987), 'Public Sector Trade Unions', *IDS Public Sector Digest*, London: Incomes Data Services.

IIRA (1992), *Membership Directory*, Geneva: International Industrial Relations Association.

Industrial Relations Journal (1997) Special Issue, Jobs and Justice, 28/4.

Inns of Court and Conservative and Unionist Society (1958), *A Giant's Strength: Some Thoughts on the Constitutional and Legal Position of Trade Unions in England*, London: Inns of Court and Conservative and Unionist Society, and Christopher Johnson.

Inside Labor Relations (1995), Analysis and Perspective, 1/9: 1–5, Washington DC: Business Research Publications.

IPA (1992), *Towards Industrial Partnership: A New Approach to Management Union Relations, a Consultative Document*, London: Involvement and Participation Association.

IPD (1996), *Statement on Employment Relations*, London: Institute of Personnel and Development.

IRS (1992: 514), 'Lean Production—and Rover's "New Deal"', 12–15, IRS (1992: 519), 'Unions Respond to Membership Issues', 13–15; IRS (1993: 534), 'TGWU's Response to Lean Production at Rover', 5–7; IRS (1994: 566), 'ACAS and

Tavistock aim to Develop Teamwork in Manufacturing', 12–15; IRS (1994: 571), 'Partnership and Restructuring at Severn Trent Water', 7–12; IRS (1995: 577), 'Single-Table Bargaining: An Idea whose Time has Come?', 10–16; IRS (1995: 583), 'Lean Suppliers to Lean Producers 1: Changes in Working Practices', 3–9; IRS (1995: 584), 'Lean Suppliers to Lean Producers 2: Changes in Working Practices', 11–16; IRS (1995: 587), 'Employee Ownership: We're the bosses now', 4–9; IRS (1996: 605), 'Stopping the Rot: New Union Recruitment Initiatives', 3–10; IRS (1996: 611), 'TUC Launches Recruitment Drive', 4, *Employment Trends*, London: Industrial Relations Services.

Jackson, D., Turner, H. A., and Wilkinson, F. (1972), *Do Trade Unions Cause Inflation?* Cambridge: Cambridge University Press.

Jacobi, Otto, Keller, Berndt, and Müller-Jentsch, Walter (1992), 'Germany: Codetermining the Future' in Ferner and Hyman (1992).

Jacoby, Sanford M. (1983), 'Union Management Cooperation in the United States: Lessons from the 1920s', *Industrial and Labor Relations Review*, 37/1: 18–33.

—— (1985), *Employing Bureaucracy: Managers, Unions and the Transformation of Work in American Industry, 1900–1945*, New York: Columbia University Press.

—— (1989), 'Reckoning with Company Unions: The Case of Thompson Products, 1934–1964', *Industrial and Labor Relations Review*, 43/1: 19–40.

Jain, Harish C., and Muthuchindambaram, S. (1995), 'Strike Replacement Ban in Ontario and its Relevance to US Labor Law Reform', Working Paper No. 406, Hamilton, Ontario: McMaster University.

James, Phil (1996), 'Job Security and Jointism in the "Big Three" US Auto Companies', 604: 12–15, *Employment Trends*, London: Industrial Relations Services.

Jenkins, Peter (1970), *The Battle of Downing Street*, London: Charles Knight.

Johnson, George (1981), 'Changes over Time in the Union/Non Union Wage Differential in the United States', mimeo, University of Michigan, cited in Freeman and Medoff (1984).

Johnston, Paul (1994), *Success While Others Fail: Social Movement Unionism and the Public Workplace*, Ithaca, NY: ILR Press.

Jones, Ken (1995), *Welsh Water: Involvement and Change—Partnership Agreements, 1991–1995*, London: Involvement and Participation Association.

Katz, Harry C. (1993), 'The Decentralization of Collective Bargaining: A Literature Review and Comparative Analysis', *Industrial and Labor Relations Review*, 47/1: 3–22.

Keefe, Jeffrey, and Boroff, Karen (1994), 'Telecommunications Labor-Management Relations after Divestiture', in Voos, Paula B. (ed.), *Contemporary Collective Bargaining in the Private Sector*, Wisconsin: Industrial Relations Research Association.

Kelley, Maryellen R., and Harrison, Bennett (1992), 'Unions, Technology and Labor-Management Cooperation', in Mishel and Voos (1992).

Kelly, J. and Heery, E. (1989), 'Full-Time Officers and Trade Union Recruitment', *British Journal of Industrial Relations*, 27/2 (July), 196–213.

—— —— (1994), *Working for the Union: British Trade Union Officers*, Cambridge: Cambridge University Press.

—— and Waddington, Jeremy (1995), 'New Prospects for British Labour', *Organization*, 2/314: 415–26.

Kennedy, Paul (1987), *The Rise and Fall of the Great Powers*, New York: Random House.

Kenney, Martin, and Florida, Richard (1993), *Beyond Mass Production: The Japanese System and its Transfer to the US*, New York: Oxford University Press.

Kerr, C., Dunlop, J. T., Harbison, F. H., and Myers, C. A. (1960), *Industrialism and Industrial Man*, Cambridge, Mass.: Harvard University Press.

Kessler, Ian, and Purcell, John (1995), 'Individualism and Collectivism in Theory and Practice', in Edwards, Paul (1995), 337–67.

—— and Undy, Roger (1996), *The New Employment Relationship: Examining the Psychological Contract*, Issues in People Management No. 12, London: Institute of Personnel and Development.

Kessler, Sid, and Bayliss, Fred (1992), *Contemporary British Industrial Relations*, London: Macmillan.

—— —— (1995), *Contemporary British Industrial Relations*, 2nd edn., London: Macmillan.

—— and Palmer, Gill (1996), 'The Commission on Industrial Relations in Britain 1969–74: A Retrospective and Prospective Evaluation', *Employee Relations*, 18/4.

Kessler-Harris, Alice, and Silverman, Bertram (1992), 'Beyond Industrial Unionism', in Mills, Nicolaus (ed.), 'Labor's Future?' *Dissent*, Winter, 61–6.

Kilborn, Peter T. (1995), 'Illinois Town a "Testing Field" in Labor Relations', *New York Times*, 24 January, pp. A1, 10.

Kirkland, Layne (1986), 'It Has All Been Said Before', in Lipset, Seymour Martin, *Unions in Transition: Entering the Second Century*, San Francisco: ICS Press.

Kjellberg, Anders (1992), 'Sweden: Can the Model Survive?' in Ferner and Hyman (1992).

Kling, Jeffrey (1995), 'High Performance Work Systems and Firm Performance', *Monthly Labor Review*, 118/5 (May), 29–36.

Knowles, K. G. J. C. (1952), *Strikes*, Oxford: Oxford University Press.

Kochan, Thomas A. (1995), 'Using the Dunlop Report to Achieve Mutual Gains', *Industrial Relations*, 34/3: 350–66.

—— and Weinstein, Marc (1994), 'Recent Developments in US Industrial Relations', *British Journal of Industrial Relations*, 32/4: 483–504.

—— Katz, Harry C., and McKersie, Robert B. (1986), *The Transformation of American Industrial Relations*, New York: Basic Books.

—— and Osterman, Paul (1994), *The Mutual Gains Enterprise: Forging a Winning Partnership among Labor, Management and Government*, Boston: Harvard Business School Press.

Kumar, Pradeep (1993), *From Uniformity to Divergence: Industrial Relations in Canada and the United States*, Kingston: IFC Press.

Labor Party Advocates (1995), *Questions & Answers*, Highland Park: Labor Party Advocates.

Labor Trends (1995), 2/8, Washington DC: Business Research Publications.

Labour Market and Skill Trends, 1994/95, Nottingham Skills and Enterprise Network.

Labour Market Trends (1996a), 'Industrial Tribunal and Employment Appeal Tribunal Statistics, 1993–94 and 1994–95', 104/7 (July), 305–10.

—— (1996b), 'Labour Disputes, Stoppages of Work: Summary', 104/8: Table 4.2.

Labour Party (1996), *Building Prosperity* 'Flexibility, Efficiency, and Fairness at Work', Road to the Manifesto, London: The Labour Party.

Labour Research (September 1993), 'Shaping up for a Mega-Union', 82/9: 7–9.

—— (February 1994), 'Aims-Oriented Revamp for TUC', 83/2: 15–16.

—— (July 1994), 'Do Part Timers have Equal Rights?' 83/7.

—— (July 1996), 'Signing Up for a Good Deal', 85/7; 19–21.

—— (August 1996), 'Amber Light for Works Rights Plan', 85/8: 13–15.

Lane, Christel (1989), 'New Technology and Clerical Work', in Gallie, Duncan (ed.), *Employment in Britain*, 67–101, Oxford: Blackwell.

Lanning, Hugh, and Norton-Taylor, Richard (1991), *A Conflict of Loyalties: GCHQ 1984–1991*, Cheltenham: New Clarion Press.

Lawler, Edward E. III, and Mohrman, Susan (1987), 'Quality Circles after the Honeymoon', *Organizational Dynamics*, 15/1: 42–59.

Lechmere v. *NLRB* (1992), 112 S.Ct. 841.

Legge, K. (1989), 'HRM: A Critical Analysis', in Storey (1989).

Leopold, J. W. (1988), 'Moving the Status Quo: The Growth of Trade Union Political Funds', *Industrial Relations Journal*, 19/4: 286–95.

Levine, David I. (1995), *Reinventing the Workplace: How Business and Employees Can Both Win*, Washington DC: Brookings Institution.

Levitt, Martin Jay, with Conrow, Terry (1993), *Confessions of a Union Buster*, New York: Crown Publishers.

Lewis, Paul (1992), *Practical Employment Law*, Oxford: Blackwell.

Lewis, Roy (1983), 'Collective Labour Law', in Bain, G. S. (ed.), *Industrial Relations in Britain*, 361–92, Oxford: Blackwell.

—— (ed.) (1986), *Labour Law in Britain*, Oxford: Blackwell.

Lipset, Seymour Martin (1991), *Continental Divide: The Values and Institutions of the United States and Canada*, London: Routledge.

LRD (1995), *Human Resource Management: A Trade Unionists' Guide*, London: Labour Research Department, May.

Lucio, Miguel Martinez, and Weston, Syd (1992), 'Human Resource Management and Trade Union Responses: Bringing the Politics of the Workplace Back into the Debate', in Blyton and Turnbull (1992).

McCarthy, William (1992), 'The Rise and Fall of Collective Laissez Faire', in McCarthy, William (ed.), *Legal Intervention in Industrial Relations: Gains and Losses*, 1–78, Oxford: Blackwell.

McClure, L. (1995), 'AFL-CIO: A New Era?' *Labor Notes*, December, 18; 10–11.

MacDuffie, John Paul (1995), 'Human Resource Bundles and Manufacturing Performance: Organizational Logic and Flexible Production Systems in the World Auto Industry', *Industrial and Labor Relations Review*, 48/2: 197–221.

MacGregor, Ian (with Rodney Tyler) (1986), *The Enemies Within: The Story of the Miners' Strike 1984–85*, London: Collins.

McIlroy, John (1995), *Trade Unions in Britain Today*, Manchester and New York: Manchester University Press.

McInnes, J. (1987), *Thatcherism at Work*, Milton Keynes: Open University Press.

Marchington, M. (1994), 'The Dynamics of Joint Consultation', in Sisson, Keith (ed.), *Personnel Management: A Comprehensive Guide to Theory and Practice in Britain*, Oxford: Blackwell.

Marchington, M., Goodman, J, Wilkinson, A., and Ackers, P. (1992), *New Developments in Employee Involvement*, Research Series, Paper No. 2, London: Department of Employment.

Marginson, Paul, and Sisson, Keith (1994), 'The Structure of Transnational Capital in Europe: The Emerging Euro-Company and its Implications for Industrial Relations', in Hyman and Ferner (1994).

Marsh, David (1992), *The New Politics of British Trade Unionism*, Basingstoke: Macmillan.

Martin, Roderick (1989), 'Technological Change and Manual Work', in Gallie, Duncan (ed.), *Employment in Britain*, 102–27, Oxford: Blackwell.

—— (1992), *Bargaining Power*, Oxford: Oxford University Press.

Martin, Ross M. (1980), *TUC: The Growth of a Pressure Group*, Oxford: Oxford University Press.

Mason, Bob, and Bain, Peter (1993), 'The Determinants of Trade Union Membership in Britain: A Survey of the Literature', *Industrial and Labor Relations Review*, 46/2: 332–51.

Masters, Marick F., and Atkin, Robert S. (1993), 'Financial and Bargaining Implications of Free Riding in the Federal Sector', *Journal of Collective Negotiations in the Public Sector*, 22/4: 327–40.

Mayes, D., and Soteri, S. (1994), 'Does Manufacturing Matter?' in Buxton, T., Chapman, P., and Temple, P., *Britain's Economic Performance*, 373–96, London and New York: Routledge.

Mercury Communications Ltd. v. *Scott Garner and POEU*, (1984) ICR 74.

Metcalf, D. (1989), 'Can Unions Survive in the Private Sector?' Presented at an Employment Institute/TUC Seminar, Trade Unionism and the Economy in the 1990s. Cited in Disney (1990), 16.

—— (1993), 'Industrial Relations and Economic Performance', *British Journal of Industrial Relations*, 31/2: 255–83.

—— (1995), 'Workplace Governance and Performance', *Employee Relations*, 17/6: 5–24.

Miller, Kenneth, and Woolfson, Charles (1994), 'Timex: Industrial Relations and the Use of the Law in the 1990s', *Industrial Law Journal*, 23/3: 209–25.

Millward, Neil (1994), *The New Industrial Relations*, London: Policy Studies Institute.

—— and Stevens, Mark (1988), 'Union Density in the Regions', *Employment Gazette*, 96/5 (May), 286–95, London: Department of Employment.

—— —— Smart, David, and Hawes, W. R. (1992), *Workplace Industrial Relations in Transition*, Aldershot: Dartmouth.

Milne, Seamus (1994), *The Enemy Within*, London and New York: Verso.

Mishel, Lawrence, and Bernstein, Jared (1994), *The State of Working America*, Economic Policy Institute, New York and London: Sharpe.

—— —— (1996), *The State of Working America*, Economic Policy Institute, New York and London: Sharpe.

—— and Voos, Paula B. (eds.) (1992), *Unions and Economic Competitiveness*, New York and London: Sharpe.

Moberly, Robert B. (1994), 'Worker Participation after Electromation and Du Pont', in Friedman *et al.* (1994).

Moll, P. G. (1993), 'Black South African Unions: Relative Wage Effects in International Perspective', *Industrial and Labor Relations Review*, 46/2: 245–61.

Moody, Kim (1996a), 'Machinists Fix Boeing Contract', *Labor Notes*, 202: 1; 6.

—— (1996b) 'G. M. Goes Down, Sub-Contracting Goes On', *Labor Notes*, 206: 1; 14.

Morand, David A. (1994), 'The Changing Situation of U.S. Labor Law: Alternative Legislative Initiatives for Workers and Workplaces', *Labor Studies Journal*, 19/3: 40–58.

Mort, Jo-Ann (1996), 'Unions Flex Political Muscle in America', The *Guardian*, 26 August, p. 14.

Müller-Jentsch, Walter (1995), 'Germany: From Collective Voice to Co-Management', in Rogers and Streeck (1995).

Nau, Henry, R. (1992), *The Myth of America's Decline*, Oxford and New York: Oxford University Press.

Nicholls, T. (1986), *The British Worker Question: A New Approach to Workers and Productivity in Manufacturing*, London: Routledge & Kegan Paul.

NLRB v. *Health Care and Retirement Corporation of America* (1994), 128 lc 11,090.

NLRB v. *Mackay Radio & Telegraph Co.* (1938), cited in Gould (1994).

NLRB v. *Yeshiva University* (1980), cited in Gould (1994).

O'Connell Davidson, Julia (1993), *Privatisation and Employment Relations: The Case of the Water Industry*, London: Mansell.

Ogden, S. (1992), 'Decline and Fall: National Bargaining in Water', *Industrial Relations Journal*, 24/1: 44–58.

—— (1994), 'The Reconstruction of Industrial Relations in the Privatized Water Industry', *British Journal of Industrial Relations*, 33/1: 67–84.

Oliver, Nick, and Hunter, Gillian (1994), *The Financial Impact of Japanese Production Methods in UK Companies*, Judge Institute of Management Studies, Paper No. 24, Cambridge.

—— and Wilkinson, Barry (1992), *The Japanization of British Industry: New Developments in the 1990s*, Oxford: Blackwell.

Osterman, Paul (1988), *Employment Futures: Reorganization, Dislocation, and Public Policy*, New York and Oxford: Oxford University Press.

—— (1994), 'How Common is Workplace Transformation and Who Adopts It?' *Industrial and Labor Relations Review*, 47/2: 173–88.

Panagides, Alexis, and Patrinos, Harry Anthony (1994), *Union-Nonunion Wage Differentials in the Developing World: A Case Study of Mexico*, Policy Research Working Paper No. 1269, Washington DC: World Bank.

Parker, Mike (1993), 'Industrial Relations Myth and Shop-Floor Reality: The "Team Concept" in the Auto Industry', in Lichtenstein, Nelson, and Harris, Howell John (eds.), *Industrial Democracy in America: The Ambiguous Promise*, Cambridge: Cambridge University Press.

—— and Slaughter, Jane (1995), 'Unions and Management by Stress', in Babson, Steve (ed.), *Lean Work: Empowerment and Exploitation in the Global Auto Industry*, Detroit: Wayne State University Press.

Parks, James B. (1995), 'Decatur Strikers Praised and Fortified', *AFL-CIO News*, 40/5 (March), 7.

—— (1996), 'Bridgestone Faces Worldwide Worker Solidarity', *AFL-CIO News*, 41/6: 12.

Parks, Susan (1995), 'Improving Workplace Performance: Historical and Theoretical Contexts', *Monthly Labor Review*, 118/5 (May), 18–28.

Pavy, Gordon R. (1994), 'Winning NLRB Elections and Establishing Collective Bargaining Relationships', in Friedman *et al.* (eds.), *Restoring the Promise of American Labor Law*, Ithaca, NY: Cornell University Press.

Perline, Martin M., and Sexton, Edwin A. (1994), 'Managerial Perceptions of Labor-Management Cooperation', *Industrial Relations*, 33/3 (July), 377–85.

Pfeffer, Jeffrey (1994), *Competitive Advantage Through People: Unleashing the Power of the Work Force*, Boston: Harvard Business School Press.

Phelps Brown, Henry (1986), *The Origins of Trade Union Power*, Oxford: Oxford University Press.

Philpott, John (1996), *A National Minimum Wage: Economic Effects and Practical Considerations*, Issues in People Management No. 13, London: Institute of Personnel and Development.

Pimlott, Ben (1992), *Harold Wilson*, London: Harper Collins.

Piore, Michael J. (1993), 'Perspectives on Human Resource Management', *Review of Employment Topics*, 1/1: 7–16.

—— and Sabel, Charles F. (1984), *The Second Industrial Divide*, New York: Basic Books.

Pollert, Anna (ed.) (1991), *Farewell to Flexibility*, Oxford: Blackwell.

Poole, M. (1990), 'Editorial: HRM in an International Perspective', *International Journal of Human Resource Management*, 1/1: 1–15.

Price, Liz, and Price, Robert (1994), 'Change and Continuity in the Status Divide', in Sisson, Keith (ed.), *Personnel Management: A Comprehensive Guide to Theory and Practice in Britain*, Oxford: Blackwell.

Price, Robert, and Bain, George S. (1989), 'The Comparative Analysis of Union Growth', Proceedings of the International Industrial Relations Association Congress, Brussels, pp. 99–110. Cited in Chaison and Rose (1991), 32–6.

Purcell, John, and Ahlstrand, Bruce (1994), *Human Resource Management in the Multi-Divisional Company*, Oxford: Oxford University Press.

Rajan, A. (1993), 'Where the New Jobs Will Be', Centre for Research in Employment and Technology in Europe, cited in *Labour Market and Skill Trends, 1994/95*, Nottingham Skills and Enterprise Network.

Ramsay, H. (1991), 'Reinventing the Wheel? A Review of the Development and Performance of Employee Involvement', *Human Resource Management Journal*, 4/1: 1–22.

Reed, Christopher (1996), 'Americans try out Labour', The *Guardian*, 13 June.

Regini, Marino (ed.) (1992), *The Future of Labour Movements*, London: Sage.

Rifkin, Jeremy (1995), *The End of Work*, New York: Putnam.

Roberts, B. C. (1958), *National Wages Policy in War and Peace*, London: Allen and Unwin.

Rodgers, Gerry (ed.) (1994), *Workers, Institutions and Economic Growth in Asia*, Geneva: International Labour Organization.

Rogers, Joel (1992), 'In the Shadow of the Law: Institutional Aspects of Postwar US Decline', in Tomlins, Christopher, L., and King, Andrew J. (eds.), *Labor Law in America: Historical and Critical Essays*, 283–302, Baltimore: Johns Hopkins University Press.

—— (1995), 'A Strategy for Labor', *Industrial Relations*, 34/3: 367–81.

—— and Freeman, Richard B. (1994), *Worker Representation and Participation Survey: Report on the Findings*, Princeton: Princeton Survey Research Associates.

—— and Streeck, Wolfgang (eds.) (1995), *Works Councils: Consultation, Representation and Cooperation in Industrial Relations*, Chicago and London: University of Chicago Press.

Rookes v. *Barnard* (1964), AC 1129 (HL).

Rosenblum, Jonathan D. (1995), *Copper Crucible: How the Arizona Miners' Strike of 1983 Recast Labor-Management Relations in America*, Ithaca, NY: ILR Press.

Rosow, Jerome, and Casner-Lotto, Jill (1994), 'People, Partnership and Profits: The New Labor-Management Agenda', cited in IRS (1995: 575), London: Industrial Relations Services, 3.

Royal Commission on Trade Unions and Employers' Associations (1968), *Report*, Cmnd. 3623, London: HMSO.

Sabel, Charles F. (1981), 'The Internal Politics of Trade Unions', in Berger, Suzanne (ed.), *Organizing Interests in Western Europe*, Cambridge: Cambridge University Press.

—— (1982), *Work and Politics: The Division of Labor in Industry*, Cambridge: Cambridge University Press.

Salvatore, Nick (1984), 'Introduction' to Gompers, Samuel, *Seventy Years of Life and Labor*, New York: ILR Press.

—— (1992), 'The Decline of Labor', in Mills, Nicolaus (ed.), 'Labor's Future?' *Dissent*, Winter, 86–92.

Sandberg, Åke (1993), 'Volvo Human-Centred Work Organization—The End of the Road?' *New Technology, Work and Employment*, 8/2: 83–7.

Sapper, S. (1991), 'Do Members' Services Packages Influence Trade Union Recruitment?' *Industrial Relations Journal*, 22/4: 309–16.

Saundry Richard, and Turnbull, Peter (1996), 'Mêlée on the Mersey: Contracts, Competition and Labour Relations on the Docks', *Industrial Relations Journal*, 27/4: 275–88.

Scarbrough, Harry, and Terry, Mike (1996), *Industrial Relations and the Reorganisation of Production in the UK Motor Vehicle Industry: A Study of the Rover Group*, Warwick Papers in Industrial Relations, No. 58, Warwick University, Industrial Relations Research Unit.

Schonberger, Richard (1982), *Japanese Manufacturing Techniques*, New York: Free Press.

Schregle, Johannes (1981), 'Comparative Industrial Relations: pitfalls and potential', *International Labour Review*, 120/1: 15–30.

Schuster, M. (1983), 'The Impact of Union-Management Cooperation on Productivity and Employment', *Industrial and Labor Relations Review*, 37/3: 415–30.

Sengenberger, Werner, and Campbell, Duncan (eds.) (1994), *International Labour Standards and Economic Interdependence*, Geneva: International Labour Organization.

Shafer, Byron E. (ed.) (1991), *Is America Different? A New Look at American Exceptionalism*, Oxford: Oxford University Press.

Sheflin, Neil, and Troy, Leo (1983), 'Finances of American Unions in the 1970s', *Journal of Labor Research*, 4/2: 149–57.

Silvestri, George T. (1993), 'The American Workforce, 1992–2005. Occupational Employment: Wide Variations in Growth', *Monthly Labor Review*, 116/11: 58–86, Washington: Bureau of Labor Statistics.

Sisson, Keith (1994), 'Personnel Management: Paradigms, Practice and Prospects', in Sisson, Keith (ed.), *Personnel Management: A Comprehensive Guide to Theory and Practice in Britain*, 3–50, Oxford: Blackwell.

Slaughter, Jane (1996), 'Overflow Crowd Expected for Labor Party's Founding Convention', *Labor Notes*, 207 (June) 16.

Smith, C. T. B., Clifton, Richard, Makeham, Peter, Creigh, S. W., and Burn, R. V. (1978), *Strikes in Britain*, Department of Employment, Manpower Paper No. 15, London: HMSO.

Snape, Ed (1994), 'Reversing the decline? The TGWU's Link Up Campaign', *Industrial Relations Journal*, 25/3: 222–33.

Speer, Albert (1970), *Inside the Third Reich*, New York: Macmillan.

Standing, Guy (1992), 'Do Unions Impede or Accelerate Structural Adjustment? Industrial Versus Company Unions in an Industrialising Labour Market', *Cambridge Journal of Economics*, 16/3: 327–54.

Statement on Personal Incomes, Costs and Prices (1948), Cmnd. 7321, London: HMSO.

Stepina, Lee P., and Fiorito, Jack (1986), 'Towards a Comprehensive Theory of Union Growth and Decline', *Industrial and Labor Relations Review*, 25/3: 248–64.

Storey, J. (ed.) (1989), *New Perspectives on Human Resource Management*, London: Routledge.

—— (1994), 'New Wave Manufacturing Strategies: An Introduction', in Storey, John (ed.), *New Wave Manufacturing Strategies: Organizational and Human Resource Management Dimensions*, London: Chapman.

Strauss, George (1995), 'Is the New Deal System Collapsing? With What Might It Be Replaced?' *Industrial Relations*, 34/3: 329–49.

Streeck, Wolfgang (1992), *Social Institutions and Economic Performance*, London: Sage.

Sweeney, Kate (1996), 'Membership of Trade Unions in 1994: An Analysis based on Information from the Certification Officer', *Employment Trends*, 104/2 (February), 49–54.

Taylor, Robert (1993), *The Trade Union Question in British Politics: Government and Unions since 1945*, Oxford: Blackwell.

—— (1994), *The Future of the Trade Unions*, London: André Deutsch.

—— (1995), 'Children of the Thatcher Era Shun Trade Unions', *Financial Times*, 1 March, p. 9.

—— (1996a), 'TGWU to "work hand-in-hand with employers"', *Financial Times*, 22 May, p. 12.

—— (1996b), 'Young Workers know little about Trade Unions', *Financial Times*, 22 August, p. 8.

Teal, Francis (1994), *The Size and Sources of Economic Rents in a Developing Country Manufacturing Labour Market*, Oxford: St John's College.

Temple, Paul (1994), 'Overview: Understanding Britain's Economic Performance', in Buxton, P., Chapman, P., and Temple, P., *Britain's Economic Performance*, 31–56, London and New York: Routledge.

Terry, Michael (1983), 'Shop Steward Development and Managerial Strategies', in Bain, G. S. (ed.), *Industrial Relations in Britain*, 67–91, London: Basil Blackwell.

—— (1994), 'Workplace Unionism: Redefining Structures and Objectives', in Hyman and Ferner (1994), 223–49.

—— (1995), 'Trade Unions: Shop Stewards and the Workplace', in Edwards (1995).

The Economic Implications of Full Employment (1956), London: HMSO.

Thelen, Kathleen A. (1991), *Union of Parts: Labor Politics in Postwar Germany*, Ithaca, NY and London: Cornell University Press.

Thomson, A. W. J., and Engleman, S. R. (1975), *The Industrial Relations Act: A Review and Analysis*, London: Martin Robertson.

Tillsley, Christine (1994), 'Employee Involvement: Employees' Views', *Employment Gazette*, 102/6 (June), 211–16.

Towers, B. (1985), 'Posing Larger Questions: The British Miners' Strike of 1984–85', *Industrial Relations Journal*, 16/2: 8–25.

—— (1989), 'Running the Gauntlet: British Trade Unions Under Thatcher, 1979–1988', *Industrial and Labor Relations Review*, 42/2: 163–88.

—— (1992), 'Collective Bargaining Levels', in Towers, B. (ed.), *A Handbook of Industrial Relations Practice*, 167–84, London: Kogan Page.

—— (1994), 'Unemployment and Labour Market Policies and Programmes in Britain: Experience and Evaluation', *Journal of Industrial Relations*, 36/3: 370–93.

—— (1996), 'United States Trade Unions in Peril', *International Union Rights*, 3/1: 19–21.

—— Cox, Derek, and Chell, Elizabeth (1981), 'Do Worker-Directors Work?' *Employment Gazette* 89/9: 384–93.

Townley, Barbara (1986), *Labor Law Reform in US Industrial Relations*, Aldershot and Brookfield, Vt.: Gower.

—— (1987), 'Union Recognition: A Comparative Analysis of the Pros and Cons of a Legal Procedure', *British Journal of Industrial Relations*, 25/2: 177–99.

Triandis, H. (1989), 'The Self and Social Behaviour in Differing Cultural Contexts', *Psychological Review*, 96/3: 506–20.

—— (1993), *Culture and Social Behaviour*, New York: McGraw Hill.

Troy, Leo (1986), 'The Rise and Fall of American Trade Unions: The Labor Movement from FDR to RR', in Lipset, S. M. (ed.), *Unions in Transition: Entering the Second Century*, San Francisco: ICS Press.

—— (1992), 'Convergence in International Unionism, etc.: The Case of Canada and the USA', *British Journal of Industrial Relations*, 30/1: 1–43.

TUC (1974), *Collective Bargaining and the Social Contract*, London: Trades Union Congress.

—— (1994*a*), *Human Resource Management—A Trade Union Response: Report to the 1994 Congress*, London: Trades Union Congress.

—— (1994*b*), *Representation at Work: Interim Report to the 1994 Congress*, London: Trades Union Congress.

—— (1995*a*), *Representation at Work: A TUC Consultative Report*, London: Trades Union Congress.

—— (1995*b*), *Your voice at work: TUC proposals for Rights to Representation at Work*, London: Trades Union Congress.

—— (1995*c*), *General Council Report*, London: Trades Union Congress.

—— (1996*a*), *General Council Report*, London: Trades Union Congress.

—— (1996*b*), *Attitudes to Work, Trade Unions and Employment Rights*, London: Trades Union Congress.

—— (1996*c*), *A Five Million Strong Challenge*, London: Trades Union Congress.

Turner, Lowell (1991), *Democracy at Work: Changing World Markets and the Future of Labor Unions*, Ithaca, NY and London: Cornell.

—— (1992), 'Industrial Relations and the Reorganization of Work in West Germany: Lessons for the US', in Mishel and Voos (1992).

—— (1994), 'Social Partnership: An Organizing Concept for Industrial Relations Reform', *Workplace Topics*, 4/1: 83–93, Washington: AFL-CIO.

UAW (1994), *The UAW makes US Strong*, United Automobile Workers: Education Department.

Ulman, Lloyd (1968), 'Collective Bargaining and Industrial Efficiency', in Caves (1968), 324–80.

Undy, R., Ellis, V., McCarthy, W. E. J., and Halmos, A. M. (1981), *Change in Trade Unions: The Development of UK Unions since the 1960s*, London: Hutchinson.

Upham, Martin (1993), *Trade Unions and Employers' Organizations of the World*, Harlow: Longman.

Verma, Anil, and Cutcher-Gershenfeld, Noel (1993), 'Joint Governance in the Workplace: Beyond Union-Management Cooperation and Worker Participation', in Kaufman, Bruce E., and Kleiner, Morris M. (eds.), *Employee Representation: Alternatives and Future Directions*, Madison: Industrial Relations Research Association.

Visser (1988), 'Trade Unionism in Europe: Present Situation and Prospects', *Labour and Society*, 13/1: 125–82. Cited in Chaison and Rose (1991), 31.

Voos, Paula (1983), 'Union Organizing: Costs and Benefits', *Industrial and Labor Relations Review*, 36/2: 571–91.

—— (1994), 'An Economic Perspective on Contemporary Trends in Collective Bargaining', in Voos, P. B. (ed.), *Contemporary Collective Bargaining in the Private Sector*, Wisconsin, Industrial Relations Research Association.

Waddington, David, Wykes, Maggie, and Critcher, Chas, with Hebron, Sandra (1991), *Split at the Seams? Community, Continuity and Change after the 1984–85 Coal Dispute*, Milton Keynes and Philadelphia: Open University Press.

Waddington, Jeremy (1995a), *The Politics of Bargaining: The Merger Process and British Trade Union Structural Development, 1892–1987*, London: Mansell.

—— (1995b), 'UK Unions: Searching for a New Agenda', *Transfer: European Review of Labour and Research*, 1/1: 31–43.

—— and Whitston, Colin (1995), 'Trade Unions: Growth, Structure and Policy', in Edwards (1995).

Waters, Richard (1996), 'Ford Union Deal Challenges GM', *Financial Times*, p. 6.

Watson, Gary (1994), 'The Flexible Workforce and Patterns of Work in the UK', *Employment Gazette*, 102/7 (July), 239–47, London: Department of Employment.

Wedderburn, W. (1976), 'The Employment Protection Act 1975: Collective Aspects', *Modern Law Review*, 32: 168–83.

—— (1986), *The Worker and the Law*, Harmondsworth: Penguin.

—— (1992), 'Laws about Strikes', in McCarthy, William (ed.), *Legal Intervention in Industrial Relations: Gains and Losses*, Oxford: Blackwell.

—— (1995), *Labour Law and Freedom: Further Essays in Labour Law*, Chapter 4, 'Trade Union Liability', in 'Strikes in Britain and France', 164–79, London: Lawrence & Wishart.

Weekes, Brian, Mellish, Michael, Dickens, Linda, and Lloyd, John (1975), *Industrial Relations and the Limits of Law: The Industrial Relations Effects of the Industrial Relations Act 1971*, Oxford: Basil Blackwell.

Weiler, Paul C. (1990), *Governing the Workplace: The Future of Labor and Employment Law*, Cambridge, Mass.: Harvard University Press.

—— (1993), 'Governing the Workplace: Representation in the Eyes of the Law', in Kaufman, Bruce E., and Kleiner, Morris M. (eds.), *Employee Representation: Alternatives and Future Directions*, Madison: Industrial Relations Research Association.

Wever, Kirsten (1994), 'Learning from Works Councils: Five Unspectacular Cases from Germany', *Industrial Relations*, 33/4: 467–80.

Wheeler, Hoyt N., and McClendon, John A. (1991), 'The Individual Decision to Unionize', in Strauss, George, Gallagher, Daniel G., and Fiorito, Jack (eds.), *The State of the Unions*, 47–83, Wisconsin: Industrial Relations Research Association.

Whitfield, Keith, Marginson, Paul, and Brown, William (1994), 'Workplace Industrial Relations under Different Regulatory Systems', *British Journal of Industrial Relations*, 32/3: 319–38.

Whittingham, T. G., and Towers, B. (1972), 'Strikes and the Economy', in Butterworth, Eric, and Weir, David (eds.), *Social Problems of Modern Britain*, London: Fontana/Collins.

Wickens, Peter (1987), *The Road to Nissan: Flexibility, Quality, Teamwork*, Basingstoke: Macmillan.

Wiener, Martin J. (1981), *English Culture and the Decline of the Industrial Spirit*, Cambridge: Cambridge University Press.

Wighton, David (1996), 'Labour to call for "Social Clause" in Trade Deals', *Financial Times*, p. 16.

Wilkinson, Barry, and Oliver, Nick (1996), 'Human Resource Management in Japanese Manufacturing Companies in the UK and USA', in Towers, B. (ed.), *The Handbook of Human Resource Management*, 2nd edn. Oxford: Blackwell.

Williamson, Lisa (1995), 'Union Mergers: 1985–94 Update', *Monthly Labor Review*, 118/2 (February), 18–25.

Willman, Paul, and Cave, Alan (1994), 'The Union of the Future: Super-Unions or Joint Ventures?' *British Journal of Industrial Relations*, 32/3: 395–431.

—— Morris, T., and Aston, B. (1993), *Union Business: Trade Union Organisation and Financial Reform in the Thatcher Years*, Cambridge: Cambridge University Press.

Womack, James, Jones, Daniel, and Voos, Daniel (1990), *The Machine that Changed the World*, New York: Rawson Associates.

Wood, Lisa (1995), 'Nurses Abandon Strike Ban', *Financial Times*, 17 May, p. 7.

World Bank (1995), *Workers in an Integrating World*, World Development Report, Oxford: Oxford University Press.

Index